Henry Parkes

**Fifty Years in the Making of Australian History**

Volume 1

.

Henry Parkes

**Fifty Years in the Making of Australian History**
*Volume 1*

ISBN/EAN: 9783337313104

Printed in Europe, USA, Canada, Australia, Japan

Cover: Foto ©Andreas Hilbeck / pixelio.de

More available books at **www.hansebooks.com**

# FIFTY YEARS

IN THE MAKING OF

# AUSTRALIAN HISTORY

BY

SIR HENRY PARKES, G.C.M.G.

*IN TWO VOLUMES*

VOL. I.

WITH PORTRAIT

LONDON

LONGMANS, GREEN, AND CO.

AND NEW YORK: 15 EAST 16th STREET

1892

# PREFACE

This book is not a history nor yet an autobiography. It leaves my life still to be written, should it be deemed worth the writing. It leaves, in fact, the first thirty years after my birth almost a blank. My residence in New South Wales has extended over fifty-three years; I began, in association with others, to take an earnest interest in the affairs of the colony within two or three years after my arrival. My first acquaintances were Charles Harper, William Augustine Duncan, and Henry Halloran, the latter of whom, now a hale man of eighty-two years, is still my warm personal friend, whose high generous spirit and fine gifts of mind have contributed much to my enjoyment of life. Some years before the advent of Responsible Government I was drawn into the active politics of the country; and of all the men who laboured conspicuously in public in preparing the way for the new Era, I now stand alone.

My objects in publication may be thus stated. To exhibit the stream of Australian progress as it has come within my own knowledge and been subjected to

my individual influence; to make clear my opinions
on some questions of first importance; to vindicate my
aims and the motives by which I have been actuated
in the part I have taken in moulding the policy of the
country; to explain my views on some possibilities of
the future, and what I conceive to be the destiny of
the new Commonwealth. It is no part of my purpose
to discuss the conduct of others except in instances
where the actions of others have been inextricably
mixed up with my own, or in one or two other cases
where the conduct of others has in my judgment been
perilous to the public liberties. My exposition of
principles is chiefly confined to the thread of my own
life and my own endeavours so far as they have related
to the public life of the country. Matters of ephemeral
or merely local interest, although they may have given
rise to much controversy at the time of their occurrence,
are for the most part excluded from these pages.

In a work of this kind it has not been found possible, and it has not been desired, to suppress my
personality. But my wish has been that my public
actions should be placed in the full light of day, and
left naked and unscreened to public criticism. Whatever my work may amount to, it cannot be made more
by words from me or from too tolerant friends, and it
cannot be made less by the comments of adversaries.
It must stand or be swept away according to the nature
of its substance.

Still it seems to me that, looking beyond the span of my existence and the limits of my exertions, much may be gathered illustrative of the steps taken in untrodden fields and the materials brought together from opposite sources, in laying the foundations of Empire in the great English-speaking land under the Southern Crown. My broken record may be a help among many aids when the time comes for strong hands to write the History of Australia.

HENRY PARKES.

SYDNEY, *May*, 1892.

# CONTENTS

OF

## THE FIRST VOLUME

———

## CHAPTER XI

## CHAPTER XII

## CHAPTER XIII

# ILLUSTRATIONS

# FIFTY YEARS

IN THE MAKING OF

# AUSTRALIAN HISTORY

## CHAPTER I

### EARLY LIFE IN AUSTRALIA—1839 TO 1852—THE ANTI-TRANSPORTATION MOVEMENT

On July 25, 1839, a large full-rigged ship, one of the old build, with square stern, high poop, and bluff bows, worked her way up the harbour of Port Jackson and anchored off Neutral Bay. It was the good ship *Strathfieldsaye*, commanded by Captain Spence, 109 days from Plymouth, with immigrants. I was one among that floating crowd of adventurers; I had spent my twenty-fourth birthday on the voyage, and my young wife had given birth to a child a few days before our arrival. Of necessity we had to remain on board some days. In those wearisome days of vague hope, fitful despondency, and youthful impatience, many hours of the early morning I spent hanging over the ship's side, looking out upon the monotonous, sullen, and almost unbroken woods which then thickly clothed the north shore of the harbour, my thoughts busily employed in speculating on the fortunes which that unknown land concealed for me. I knew no single human creature in that strange new land; I had brought no letter of introduction to unlock any door to me; and in this state of absolute friendlessness I and my wife and child landed in Sydney, which great city I was thirteen years afterwards destined to represent in the Legislature. One of the last books I had bought in London was a cheap edition of Campbell's Poems, and I had committed to memory the 'Lines on the Departure of Emigrants for New South Wales'; and often then and in the sad succeeding years of struggle and suffering, when my heart sank within me, I drew fresh inspirations of strength and hope from passages of that, my favourite poem.

> The deep-drawn wish, when children crown our hearth,
> To hear the cherub chorus of their mirth,
> Undamped by dread that want may e'er unhouse,
> Or servile misery knit those smiling brows:
> The pride to rear an independent shed,
> And give the lips we love unborrowed bread;
> To see a world, from shadowy forests won,
> In youthful beauty wedded to the sun;
> To skirt our home with harvests widely sown,
> And call the blooming landscape all our own,
> Our children's heritage, in prospect long.

In the year 1839, and for years afterwards, all the territory of the colony of Victoria and all the territory of Queensland were included in the colony of New South Wales. In the whole of this vast tract of Australia, 1,068.341½ square miles, there were only 114,386 inhabitants. The price of land was 12s. per acre, and the sales in that year amounted to 152,962l. 16s. 4d. The area of land under crop was 95,312 acres. The wool exported was 7,213,584 lbs., valued at 442.504*l*. The vessels inwards at the port of Sydney were 563, giving a total of 135.474 tons; the vessels outwards 548, giving a total of 124.776 tons. Twelve small vessels were built in the colony, their total burden amounting to 773 tons. The number of vessels registered at Sydney was 79, giving a total of 10,862 tons. The following table will indicate the position of the infant commerce of the country :—

| — | Great Britain | New Zealand | Other countries | South Sea Islands | Fisheries | United States | Other foreign countries | Total |
|---|---|---|---|---|---|---|---|---|
| | £ | £ | £ | £ | £ | £ | £ | £ |
| Imports . | 1,251,960 | 71,709 | 501,828 | 3,863 | 186,212 | 23,093 | 194,697 | 2,236,371 |
| Exports . | 597,100 | 95,173 | 194,684 | 1,317 | 31,729 | 18,598 | 7,175 | 918,776 |

Three years afterwards, in 1842, the population consisted of

| | | | | |
|---|---|---|---|---|
| Male adults | . | . | . | . 75,474 |
| Female „ | . | . | . | . 33,546 |
| Male children | . | . | . | . 20,636 |
| Female „ | . | . | . | . 20,011 |

149,667 souls.

The average number of children attending school was 7,289, but the schools were of a very imperfect character. Four years after my landing, in 1843, the colony possessed 56,585 horses, 897,219 head of horned cattle, and 4,804,946 sheep. Such, then, was the country of my adoption, and for me 'life had ample room,' beyond what is in the power of most men to conceive. For many weary days following weary days I searched in vain for suitable employment in Sydney. A severe drought had just passed over the country; the price of bread rose as

high as 2s. 8d. for the 4 lb. loaf, and the other necessaries of life were correspondingly dear. The first
public gathering I attended was a meeting held in the
Market to raise subscriptions to establish a soup-kitchen
for the poor and destitute. For fully twelve months I
could not muster sufficient fortitude to write to my
friends in England of the prospect before me. Finding
nothing better, I accepted service as a farm-labourer at
30l. a year, and a ration and a half largely made up of
rice. Under this engagement I worked for six months
on the Regentville estate of Sir John Jamison, about
thirty-six miles from Sydney, assisting to wash sheep in
the Nepean, joining the reapers in the wheat-field, and
performing other manual labour on the property. At
the end of the half-year I applied to be released from
my agreement, being anxious to try my fortunes again
in Sydney, and the superintendent, a Mr. Gale, who at
all times treated me very kindly, acceded to my request.
Returning to Sydney, I obtained employment first in a
wholesale ironmongery store, then in an iron foundry,
and, shifting as best I could, I worked on among the
unknown crowd of strugglers for several years, during
which period I made the acquaintance of several young
men who afterwards achieved positions of fair distinction, including Angus Mackay, Minister of Education
in Victoria in later years, and Charles Harpur, one of
the earliest of Australian poets. For fully eight years
I never ventured to take part in public affairs. I
watched the course of events with a keen interest from
my obscure station; entered into fervent discussions on
the topics of the day with my few humble friends; and

occasionally wrote letters to the papers, always anony-
mously.

In 1843 a new Constitution for the colony came
into force, under which the principle of representation
was first introduced, though in a partial and very
restrictive form. The Legislative Council consisted
partly of members still nominated by the Crown, and
partly of elective members chosen by a suffrage based
upon high property qualifications. The first election,
however, sent into the hybrid Legislature the ablest men
in Australia—William Charles Wentworth and William
Bland for the city of Sydney; John Dunmore Lang,
Charles Nicholson, Thomas Walker among the members
for the district of Port Phillip (now Victoria); Charles
Cowper, Richard Windeyer, George Robert Nichols, and
other men favourably known for country electorates.

The new Council, in which the people of Australia
found their first imperfect representation, was opened
by the Governor, Sir George Gipps, on August 3, 1843.
The opening and the closing paragraphs of the speech
alone possess any interest for later times :—

Gentlemen of the Legislative Council,—The time is at
length arrived which has, for many years, been anxiously
looked forward to by us all; and I have this day the pleasure
to meet, for the first time, the Legislative Council of New South
Wales, enlarged as it has been under the statute recently
passed by the Imperial Parliament for the government of the
colony. I congratulate you very sincerely on the introduction
of popular representation into our Constitution, and I heartily
welcome to this Chamber the first representatives of the people.

The period, Gentlemen, at which you enter on your functions
is one of acknowledged difficulty, and it is therefore the more

grateful to me to have my own labours and responsibilities lightened by your co-operation and assistance.

I shall most readily concur with you in any measures which may be calculated to develop the resources of the colony by calling into action the energies of the people, taking care, however, that we proceed on sure principles, and not overlooking the great truths that the enterprise of individuals is ever most active when left as far as possible unshackled by legislative enactment, and that industry and economy are the only sure foundations of wealth. Great as, undoubtedly, are the embarrassments under which numbers even of the most respectable of our fellow-subjects in the colony are now labouring, it is consolatory to me to think that, grievous though they be to individuals, they are not of a nature permanently to injure us as a community; that, on the contrary, they may be looked on as forming one of those alternations in the progress of human events which occur in all countries, and perhaps most frequently in those whose general prosperity is the greatest.

.    .    .    .    .

The Council, Gentlemen, is composed of three elements, or of three different classes of persons—the Representatives of the People; the Official Servants of Her Majesty; and of Gentlemen of Independence, the Unofficial Nominees of the Crown.

Let it not be said or supposed that these three classes of persons have or ought to have separate interests to support— still less that they have opposing interests, or any interest whatever save that of the public good. Let there be no rivalry between them, save which shall in courtesy excel the other, and which of them devote itself most heartily to the service of their common country.

(Signed)    GEORGE GIPPS,
Governor.

Sydney, Aug. 3, 1845.

The elections had been attended by much excitement, and in one or two instances riotous proceedings had taken place, and strong animosities had been en-

gendered. But the leaders of the Representative
division of the new Council set themselves to deal,
according to their lights, with the disastrous state of
the colony. The first measure brought in was a Bill by
Mr. Wentworth to regulate the rates of interest; but
an amendment was moved that the Bill be read the
second time that day six months, and, for reasons which
appear to have been economically sound, the amendment
was carried by 21 to 12. This was the first important
division in the new House, and, in the popular con-
tentions which followed, it fairly represents the relative
numbers,—the nominee element, recruited by timid and
weak-kneed elective members, nearly always outweigh-
ing the little band of faithful representatives. Within
the first six weeks, the question of education was raised
by Dr. Lang; the land question was discussed on the
motion of Mr. T. A. Murray; a Bill for legalising advances of money on wool and on sheep and cattle was
brought in and passed by Mr. Wentworth; a committee
was appointed to revive and stimulate immigration;
and, on the motion of Mr. Windeyer, a committee was
appointed 'to consider the means of staying the further
evil consequences to be apprehended from the monetary
confusion lately and still prevalent in the colony.'

Mr. Windeyer's committee took the evidence of
several leading men connected with the commercial
and monetary affairs of the colony, and in due time the
chairman brought up his report. That report reads
strangely in the light of monetary science at the present
day. It recommended, chiefly on the evidence of Mr.
Thomas Holt, that the credit of the colony should be

pledged to a scheme of monetary relief analogous to
the Prussian Pfandbriefe system, thus described :—

A landed proprietor wishing to raise money upon his property applies to a Land Board, which values it, and agrees to
lend him the credit of the State for one-half of the valuation.
The landowner mortgages his property to the Board, which
then gives him a paper called a Pfandbriefe, or pledge certifi-
cate, which contains the name of the mortgagor of his estate,
the letter and number of the transaction in the books of the
Board, and two official signatures. The interest to be received
by the holder of the Pfandbriefe is made payable in two half-
yearly dividends on fly-leaves called coupons, calculated for two
years in advance, which are guaranteed by the Board. These
coupons are cut off and presented at the Treasury, where they
are paid, as they become due, or they may be cut off beforehand, and circulated till they become due.

Other suggestions were also derived from the law
of Prussia, such as the issue of notes of small amounts,
made a legal tender, and convertible into coin on demand at the Treasury. A Bill embodying the views of
the committee was introduced, and finally read the
third time on December 6 ; but the Governor withheld
from it the Royal assent.

Such were some of the proposals brought forward
in the first session of the first partly elective Council,
at a time of general depression and stagnation in the
colony, and they will serve to show the activity and
public spirit of that body. It might well have been
expected that mistakes would be committed ; and some
of its measures were seriously in disaccord with sound
principles ; but that early Council contained men of
statesmanlike conceptions and large ability, and its de-

liberations must ever hold a place in Australian history. The Legislature which had birth in 1843 held on its course, with notable constitutional modifications, until the year 1856; and its struggles for constitutional liberty give to that period of thirteen years a memorable character. The model of the constitutions now existing throughout Australia was cast, and the first University was founded, before its labours came to an honourable close.

I had now formed the acquaintance of two men of more than ordinary character and ability, Mr. Charles Harpur, one of the most genuine of Australian poets, and Mr. William Augustine Duncan, then proprietor and editor of the 'Weekly Register.' They were my chief advisers in matters of intellectual resource and enquiry, when the prospect before me was opening and widening, often with many cross lights and drifting clouds, but ever with deepening radiance. Even then we talked of the grand future and the wonderful changes which a few years would bring. Both men are gone to their great account; but I cherish their memories among the pleasant crowd of associations which have brightened my path since they passed away.

In the latter part of this eventful period I was first drawn into taking part in the public proceedings of the colony. I may say with truth that I was drawn into the turbulent stream of politics rather by the influence of events than by any voluntary step of my own. It was not until the year 1848, nine years after my arrival in Sydney, and when I was thirty-three years of age, that I first ventured to speak in public. From the years of boyhood in England I had looked on silently throughout the tremendous agitations for the first Reform Bill, and I was a solitary listener among the 250,000 persons who attended the great Newhall Hill meeting in Birmingham, my whole being stirred by the solemn strains of the Union hymn as they were pealed forth under the thousand waving flags of that gathered multitude. I became a member of the famous Political Union, and wore my badge openly till the Bill was carried into law by the Grey Ministry. I hung upon the voice of Daniel O'Connell with an unspeakable interest, on occasions when he spoke in Birmingham on his journeys from Ireland to London; and the tones of that marvellous voice, and some of the Liberator's images, have never left my memory. But I never dreamed of ever passing the barrier which shut me out from the wielders of impassioned speech. In those days, from the age of sixteen to twenty-four years, I heard frequently Thomas Attwood, who to me was an impressive speaker; I heard Lawless and Shiel, and I felt myself moulded like wax in the heat of the splendid declamation of George Thompson, the anti-slavery orator. I heard William Cobbett, and that thunderous preacher, John Angell James. I was among the listeners to the wild lectures of Charles Pemberton. These were my teachers, together with the living poets of the time, such as Byron, Moore, Shelley, and Leigh Hunt. I spent the winter of 1838–9 in London; but still in the solitude which a friendless man feels in the crowded streets of a great city. I passed those days almost exclusively in the company of my wife, and I have known but few happier days.

When the scene of my life was changed from England to Australia, as already stated, my loneliness and friendlessness were deepened and not soon relieved. But my mind found nurture in observing the public occurrences around me, analysing the characters of conspicuous men, and trying to forecast the developments of the future. Slowly I became acquainted with men in my sphere of life who thought much as I thought. While the hybrid Parliament was struggling against the repressive powers of Downing Street, and through clouds of error, to solve the problems of colonial freedom, I was growing into a keen critic of the legislative work going on. I and my little group of friends privately discussed every question that arose ; of course each of my friends communicated his opinion of me to a wider circle, and by degrees men in higher walks of life made my acquaintance. The time was just coming when I was to make my plunge into the public life of New South Wales.

In the meantime the question of the continuance of the transportation of British convicts to the colony was assuming an irresistible importance ; and it is curious to look back now on the effect which that question had in colouring the fortunes of public men of that day. Most of the leading members of the Legislative Council had been all their lives familiarised with the system of prison labour—of assigned service, as it was called, and some of the rougher and more impetuous resented the first murmurings of opposition to

which the immigrant classes gave voice, by loudly expressing their preference for convicts over free labourers.
Others again took the pseudo-philanthropic view that
the system was not only beneficial to the colony, but
beneficial to the convicts themselves.   Hence, then,
the anti-transportation cause fell largely into the hands
of the new men supported by the free immigrant working classes, and the movement was directed against the
popular leaders of the past, with Mr. Wentworth at
their head.   In 1848, Mr. Wentworth and Mr. William
Bland, the late members, were again candidates for the
representation of Sydney, and a meeting of electors
opposed to their re-election was held, at which Mr.
Robert Lowe, afterwards Viscount Sherbrooke, whose
death is announced as these pages are passing through
the press, was selected as the champion of the anti-
transportation and Liberal cause.   At this meeting I
was nominated on Mr. Lowe's committee, and appointed
one of the secretaries.   That was the beginning of my
political career.

In the election nearly all the men of known influence were ranged on the Wentworth side.   They carried
out a house-to-house canvass, while the new men had
to labour under the disadvantage of Mr. Lowe's personal
absence from all the meetings held in his support.
Before his own name was brought forward, he had committed himself to another candidate, and, therefore, he
declined to take any part beyond appearing on the
hustings at the nomination.   On the polling day, however, he was returned as the second member by a good
majority, defeating the old member, Mr. Bland.   I took

a very active part in the return of Mr. Lowe; the
address to the electors was written by me; and I
attended all the meetings as the organising secretary.
At one meeting I attempted to speak; it was my first attempt, and it was, I think, a sorry failure. Mr. Lowe's
election, under all the circumstances of the hour, was
regarded as an unprecedented popular triumph.

Under the Constitution Act which came into force
in 1843 (the 6 Vict. cap. 76) the elective franchise was
confined to householders of 20l. and freeholders of 200l.
The household suffrage in England at the same time
was 10l. One of my first public acts was to assist in
getting the qualification reduced. A Bill was before
the Imperial Parliament to confer a more liberal constitution upon the colony, and to provide for the creation
of the colony of Victoria. In the beginning of 1849
I and some of my friends got up a public meeting to
petition both Houses for a reduction of the suffrage
qualification in the new Bill. Our petitions arrived in
time, and proved successful. On the motion of Lord
Lyttelton in the House of Lords, accepted by the Secretary of State, the qualification was reduced to 10l.
household and 100l. freehold. I made my first political
speech at this meeting in seconding a resolution which
asserted the principle of universal suffrage. I was cordially received, but it must be admitted that my speech
was a very weak performance. It contains one sentence, however, which was a kind of prophecy and
which, improbable as it appeared then, was virtually ful-
filled within the next ten years. Alluding to universal
suffrage, I said: 'The time will come, more quickly

than some dark prophets could foresee, when it will be in possession of the Australian people.' I and my friend Mr. Angus Mackay had personally waited upon some gentlemen and written to others, inviting them to take part in the meeting, and the answers we received, warning us of the dangerous ground we were treading upon, were no doubt in my mind when speaking. Our petition to the Commons was presented by Mr. William Scholefield; that to the Peers by Lord Monteagle, both of whom in letters to myself expressed the pleasure it afforded them to be of service to the colony.

The question of the revival of transportation had been raised by an address from the Legislative Council, 'expressing the willingness of that body to concur in the introduction into the colony of convicts holding tickets of leave or conditional pardons' on condition that an equal number of free immigrants should be sent out at the expense of the Imperial Government. The English Minister did not wait long before acting upon this official communication from the Legislature in Sydney, and though he was not prepared to send the immigrants as asked for, he supplied the convicts in advance. It was long known beforehand that ships were on their way to the colony with English prisoners, and the feeling of opposition discovered itself in murmurous uneasiness and resentment among all classes, the defenders and apologists of the Secretary of State and his policy being confined to individuals and small sections. Little else was talked about for days before the arrival of the first ship. On June 8, 1849, the convict ship *Hashemy* entered Port Jackson, and anchored off the

city of Sydney. On the same day, and the following
day, several ships with immigrants arrived under the
old regulations, the emigrants having left England, it
was presumed, in the belief that transportation to New
South Wales had ceased. On June 8 the ship *Emigrant*,
with 320 immigrants on board, and the ship *John Bright*,
with 236 on board, arrived in port. On the 9th the
*Emma Eugenia*, with 181 immigrants, the *Diana*, with
229, and the *James Gibb*, with 284, also arrived. Thus, to
furnish material for the anti-transportation orators, the
detested convict ship lay upon the waters of Port Jackson, surrounded by ships full of free immigrants whose
total number had reached within the two days 1,250.
Immediately an open-air meeting was called to protest
against the landing of the convicts: the place chosen was
at the Circular Quay, almost in sight of the ships. The
day of meeting opened very unpropitiously, heavy rain
falling all the morning; but, regardless of the weather,
most of the places of business in the city were closed,
and the people assembled, to the number of 7,000 to
8,000, in the pouring rain. This meeting was of a
character which for its self-reliant spirit and enthusiastic resolve was hitherto unprecedented in Australia, and
it was long known as the Great Protest Meeting. The
following is a copy of the Protest adopted :—

We, the free and loyal subjects of Her Most Gracious
Majesty, inhabitants of the city of Sydney and its immediate
neighbourhood, in public meeting assembled, do hereby enter
our most deliberate and solemn protest against the transportation of British criminals to the colony of New South Wales.

*Firstly.*—Because it is in violation of the will of the

majority of the colonists, as is clearly evidenced by their expressed opinions on the question at all times.

*Secondly.*—Because numbers among us have emigrated on the faith of the British Government that transportation to this colony had ceased for ever.

*Thirdly.*—Because it is incompatible with our existence as a free colony, desiring self-government, to be made the receptacle of another country's felons.

*Fourthly.*—Because it is in the highest degree unjust to sacrifice the great social and political interests of the colony at large to the pecuniary profit of a fraction of its inhabitants.

*Fifthly.*—Because, being firmly and devoutly attached to the British Crown, we greatly fear that the perpetration of so stupendous an act of injustice by Her Majesty's Government will go far towards alienating the affections of the people of this colony from the mother-country.

For these and for many kindred reasons—in the exercise of our duty to our country, for the love of our families, in the strength of our loyalty to Great Britain, and from the depth of our reverence for Almighty God—we protest against the landing again of British convicts on these shores.

The continued agitation against the renewal of transportation brought together a band of influential men, some of them appearing on the public platform for the first time, others representing old families which hitherto had been little identified with public affairs. Amongst the former were Mr. E. C. Weekes, Mr. W. R. Piddington (both of whom at a later period filled the office of Colonial Treasurer), Mr. T. S. Mort, and Mr. Daniel Henry Deniehy; and among the latter may be mentioned Mr. Robert Campbell (afterwards Colonial Treasurer), Commander John Lamb, and Mr. James Norton. Other men of remarkable ability gave weight and character to the agitation, including Mr. Robert Lowe (Viscount

Sherbrooke), and Sir Archibald Michie. The proceedings of this new combination of men surprised, and produced something like consternation in the minds of, the old colonial magnates, who hitherto had ruled with a peculiar order of absolutism representing the artificial feeling of domination on the one hand and of submission on the other which characterised old Virginian society. Mr. James Norton, long regarded as the leading solicitor of the colony, was a stately old gentleman of patrician appearance and peremptory manner, who lived on a fine estate a few miles out of Sydney, which is now (1889) a populous suburb. He was unquestionably a person of much consequence in those days. I heard Mr. Norton, addressing a public meeting, describe the effect of the convict system upon the character and morals of the 'country gentlemen' of the period as similar to that produced by slavery on the slave-holding planters of the Southern States of America. It had enervated their character, depraved their manners, given them false notions of labour and capital, and in many instances had sown the seeds of their own ruin. At first the outspoken sentiments of Mr. Norton and others like him gave much offence to their own class; but a rapidly-forming public opinion had set in, which soon became too strong for any attempt at social ostracism. Nine out of ten of the immigrant classes had from the first joined the movement against the revival of transportation, and most of the merchants and shopkeepers, and the whole artisan body of the metropolis, gave breadth and force to the wave which in a short time swept all before it. On the one side were ranged the large country employers—the men who, having obtained free grants of land and free assignments of convict servants, appeared to cherish as the one great end of life the ambition to found families, and, combined with them, the great officials who held their appointments direct from Imperial authority in England, with a few aristocratic sympathisers about Sydney. On the other side were united all the independent elements of the population, and of these it might have been as truly said as of the Romans, that

> None were for a Party, and all were for the State.

I have in my possession now a document signed by nearly all the merchants and business men of Sydney, pledging themselves to close their establishments on the day of a great Anti-Transportation Meeting held in the old Barracks Square, that part of the metropolis now bounded by the busy thoroughfares of George, Barrack, York, and Jamison Streets, on September 16, 1850. Fully 10,000 persons attended this meeting. One of the resolutions, moved by Mr. Thomas Sutcliffe Mort, a wealthy and enterprising citizen, was in support of the formation of an association to 'unite every individual in the colony interested in preventing the revival of transportation,' and declaring that the association should not be dissolved until the question was finally determined. I began my career as a public speaker at the meetings of this stormy agitation; I seconded Mr. Mort's resolution; and I spoke at nearly all the meetings held from first to last. I not only spoke, but I did my best, privately and publicly, writing in the newspapers, and encouraging others, to assist in giving intensity and success to the movement. The association formed in September 1850 merged in the 'Australian Anti-Transportation League,' which united all the colonies as one in the work of resistance; and the triumph was not long delayed, for the hateful Orders in Council, which authorised the revival of transportation, were finally revoked in 1852. The fair land of Australia was now free for evermore.

It is impossible, in view of the marvellous progress of New South Wales during the last forty years, to overvalue the importance of that first popular movement in Australia. It formed truly a new epoch in Australian life. A people, emerging from the indistinct mists of scattered settlement in a wild country, appeared in tangible form, claiming to be ripe for freedom and representative institutions. A public spirit was awakened never more to be lulled to rest.

I may, I hope, be pardoned in giving one or two instances of my own share in this movement, as it was my first work in the cause of Australian progress. I originated a petition in favour of abolition, which was signed by 12,000 ladies, including Lady Stephen, the respected wife of the Chief Justice. I suggested and wrote the Protest which, on the motion of John Lamb, M.L.C., seconded by Lord Sherbrooke, was adopted unanimously at the Great Protest Meeting against the landing of the convicts by the ship *Hashemy*. The following are the concluding sentences of Lord Sherbrooke's speech in seconding the adoption of the Protest :—

They had taken their stand—they had felt that the people were with them, and thanks to the noble declaration which the people had made on this question, that stand had been maintained, and the perfidy and insult which had been endeavoured to be perpetrated had been met and repelled. But he looked not on this question by itself alone—he looked at it in connection with another question, in which the liberties of the people of this colony were almost equally concerned, a question on which, as on this, he hoped the colonists would make themselves heard. He viewed this attempt to inflict the worst and most degrading slavery on the colony only as a sequence of that oppressive tyranny which had confiscated the lands of the colony—for the benefit of a class. That class had felt their power—they were not content to get the lands alone. Without labour they were worthless, and therefore they must enrich them with slaves. He (Mr. Lowe) warned them not to be deluded by the simple aspect which the question had hitherto borne, when argued by those whose interests were involved in maintaining the system. He was for the liberty of all, and he protested not only against deluging the colony with crime, but the insidious attempt to introduce serfdom and slavery amongst them. This was not a question of the injury which the 250 felons on board the *Hashemy* could do the colony. They would perhaps cause but little evil; but it was a question—a question in which they had a right to be heard in protest—whether the inhabitants of this colony should be subjected to the contamination of trebly convicted felons, and whether they should submit to a measure which was necessary to fill up the confiscation of their lands. He therefore contended that those who branded the people of the colony with mere worldly selfishness in the part they had taken on this question did them injustice. It was not the mere fear of competition amongst operatives that now united them on this question; it was not a mere breeches-pocket question with the labouring classes, though it might be with the employers. It was a struggle for liberty—a struggle against a system which had in every country where it had prevailed been destructive of freedom. Let them not be deluded by this insidious attempt. Let it go home that the people of New South Wales reject, indignantly reject, the inheritance of wealthy shame which Great Britain holds out to her; that she spurns the gift, deceitfully gilded though it be; that she spurns the degradation, however eloquently it may be glozed over. Let them send across the Pacific their emphatic declaration that they would not be slaves—that they would be free. Let them exercise the right that every English subject had—to assert his freedom. He could see from that meeting the time was not far distant when they would assert their freedom not by words alone. As in America oppression was the parent of independence, so would it be in this colony. The tea which the Americans flung into the water rather than pay the tax upon it was not the cause of the revolt of the American States; it was the unrighteousness of the tax; it was the degradation of submission to an unrighteous demand. And so sure as the seed will grow into the plant, and the plant to the tree, in all times and in all nations, so will injustice and tyranny ripen into rebellion, and rebellion into independence.

As a sample of my early speeches I give the chief portion of a speech at a large meeting in Malcom's Circus, April 6, 1852, towards the close of the agitation :—

After all the pain and toil of the protracted agitation of this question—after an agitation, conducted with the fullest enquiry and the deepest earnestness, which had stirred the heart of the country to its very core—after these communities, having been polled almost to a man, had declared with one voice against receiving English criminals as an evil which all believed was in the highest degree disastrous to their moral and social interests —a canker eating into their very souls—after all this, they were forced back to its renewed agitation by the perverseness of one obstinate man who happened to hold a seat in the British Government. He agreed with previous speakers that the time for deliberation and argument was past. Why, they had

deliberated for years, they had exhausted all arguments. The
matter now resolved itself into a simple question of natural
right, and they had only to consider how best to vindicate
that right. No man or body of men could have a right to
force upon a community a thing from without which they
unanimously refused to receive; which they abhorred and
believed would be ruinous to them. Argument and discussion
had been of no service to them; their remonstrances and petitions had fallen upon deaf ears. They had done all in this way
which men could do, and they could pursue this course no
longer. It was a singular and striking feature of this agitation
that a very large amount of talent had been exhibited in it.
The last debate in the Legislative Council the year before last
was one so ably sustained that it would have done honour to
the British Parliament. Their petitions from all parts of the
country had been able and argumentative documents, and such
was their unanimity of sentiment, that when the question was
last under discussion in this colony the numbers were 36,000
against and only 500 in favour of the system. But in the face
of all this—notwithstanding their repeated protests and petitions
—notwithstanding the intelligence which they had brought to
bear in the discussion of the question, and the unanimity in the
decision which they had arrived at, the tyrannical Minister persisted in thrusting upon them the evil which they were determined not to receive. Well, then, what was to be done? As a
free people, as men, they could not retreat from their position;
they could no longer go through the farce of remonstrating
against an injustice which was persevered in with an utter disregard of their wishes and their interests; they must do something else. He was well pleased to hear their president, Mr.
Cowper, talk of fighting. Knowing the mild, affable, and
benignant character of that gentleman, he was at first half afraid
that he was hardly stern enough for the duties which he might
be called upon to perform in his mission to Van Diemen's Land.
They had been told that night of the serious consequences
which might ensue. Now, he had no desire to bring before
them rebellious examples, or he might most properly point to

the example of the American colonists; for in the progress
of events which led to the loss of those colonies there was a
remarkable analogy between some stages and their own case.
He would pass over this, because he believed the meeting did
not need to be reminded of the glorious and successful struggle
of men who were treated with contumely and oppressed in a
manner similar to themselves. There was, however, a suggestive passage in a speech of one of those early patriots which he
would with their permission repeat to the meeting. When
young Patrick Henry, in the General Assembly of Virginia,
was moving his resolutions in reference to the odious Stamp
Act, he exclaimed, 'Cæsar had his Brutus, Charles the First
his Cromwell, and George the Third——' 'Treason!' cried
the Speaker. The young patriot, standing up more proudly
than ever, and fixing his eyes on the alarmed Speaker, concluded the sentence—'George the Third may profit by their
example; if that be treason, make the most of it!' He would
point to the successful resistance of the American colonists, and
in the name of that meeting tell the British Government to
profit by that example. He had no treason to promulgate; on
the contrary, the man did not breathe whose heart beat with a
truer loyalty to the gracious and glorious lady who presides
over the destinies of the British Empire. But, as was said by
their chairman, there was a higher loyalty than that to any
earthly monarch—our loyalty to our own nature and to the all-
wise God, who has planted in us pure and holy sentiments, and
warmed our being with the love of justice and truth. To fall
away from this loyalty would be to debase ourselves before
our Creator—to deface the divine impress of humanity which
had been printed on our hearts. They must go right onward
in their course. There could be no mistake in the matter. If
Earl Grey had indeed been deceived and misled, the last elections throughout the colonies would surely undeceive him.
Even under a Constitution concocted by his own Government,
the people of Van Diemen's Land had in every instance elected
anti-transportationists to their representative seats. In that
unfortunate island—that very sinkhole of English iniquity,

where the prison population was so alarming in numbers, and where it could not be doubted many of that class possessed the elective franchise—no representative favourable to the continuance of transportation had been chosen. It was fair to assume that many of the emancipist class in that island had recorded their votes on the side of the anti-transportationists. How could it be otherwise? How could men wish to continue to their children the curse of their own lives? What was it, this desire to get rid of the infamy and degradation of which they had themselves been victims, but the triumph of all that was good and virtuous and lofty and aspiring in the human breast? They were about to send Mr. Cowper as a delegate to the conference of the League at Hobart Town. When he approached the shores of the island-home of these sturdy and stout-hearted patriots, it was to be hoped that the bracing influences of their climate would make him even bolder than he had been in his speech that evening; and that if the Tasmanian colonists should determine to resist the landing of any more convicts, he would solemnly assure them that the inhabitants of New South Wales were ready to assemble again in some place under heaven, where all the people could be gathered to ratify all the acts so done, and to share in all the consequences. The example of the Cape Colonists was before them. The time was come when their only course was to follow that example; and whenever a prison-ship should arrive in the Derwent, or in any other port, to resist at all hazards the landing of the prisoners thus tyrannically forced upon us.

The party brought together by the anti-transportation cause naturally grew in numbers and strength, and extended its operations into other provinces of public investigation and criticism and of urgent demands for reforms. Mr. William Charles Wentworth, then the senior member for Sydney in the old Legislative council, and beyond doubt the ablest man in the colony, had, from association with the advocates of transportation and other unpopular proceedings, be-

come the principal figure in support of the old order of
things, and no epithet of condemnation was too strong
for him and his friends to hurl at the heads of the men
who dared to question the wisdom of the colony remaining longer under what was scornfully designated
the reign of Nomineeism and Squatterdom.   Mr.
Wentworth exhausted his great powers of invective in
denouncing the new party of reformers as Socialists,
Communists, uprooters of law and order, and everything else for which a vile name could be found, though
it included many of the most respectable men in the
country.   I was myself at that early stage of my public
life denounced by him from his place in the Legislative
Council as the 'arch-anarchist.'   Before the storm
which had thus been created could have time to sub-
side, Mr. Wentworth produced another popular tempest
by his proposals in framing his new Constitution Bill.
The first draft of the Bill provided for the creation of
hereditary titles, an Upper Chamber on a very restrictive basis, the necessity for a two-thirds majority for
any subsequent modification of the Constitution, and a
very unpopular distribution of electoral power.   Public
feeling rose at once in strong opposition to these proposals.   But the Constitution struggles must be reserved
for a separate chapter.

Towards the end of 1849 I established 'The Empire'
newspaper, which continued as a daily journal a little
over seven years.   The next seven years of my life
were mainly devoted to this undertaking; but this part
of my public work must also be left for treatment at a
later stage.

# CHAPTER II

THE party brought into existence by the opposition to the pro-transportation policy of the English Government, even while the cause of that bitter agitation was dying away, found a fresh field for its activity in resisting the unpopular proposals of Mr. Wentworth and the men who had taken in hand the business of framing a new Constitution for the colony. Mr. Wentworth's name is the name most justly associated with the free Constitution which came into operation in 1856, and under which the colony is still governed. He had in past years, before the advent of the imperfect representative system of 1843, made himself popular by his sturdy condemnation of the arbitrary conduct of Governor Darling; by that and other services he had secured a place in the public regard superior to that occupied by any of his contemporaries. Endowed by nature with a powerful physical frame and large capacities of mind, Mr. Wentworth had been educated at Cambridge, and trained for the Bar. After a residence of some years in England, he returned to the colony and engaged in the practice of his profession, at the same time, in conjunction with an English friend, Dr.

Wardell, establishing a Liberal newspaper called 'The
Australasian.' Dr. Wardell, who is reputed to have been
a man of large ability, was shot by a party of bushrangers whom he surprised in the bush a few miles
from Sydney, and attempted to arrest; but Mr. Wentworth, with other friends, supported 'The Australasian'
for a considerable time as the strenuous organ of Liberal
thought and opinion. Steadily exposing the abuses of
Government and supporting Liberal principles, he naturally grew to be regarded as the leading patriot of those
early days. Soon after his election for Sydney in 1843,
he began to move in the cause of a fuller system of
self-government for the colony. He was saturated with
Lord Durham's report on the constitutional grievances
of Canada, and stimulated to activity by his intercourse
with liberal-minded men in England; and there is no
ground for doubting his sincerity in espousing the cause
of the people. But it may be, with just reason, doubted
whether the phrase so often idly used, 'The People,'
ever in his mind included the masses of his fellow-men.
Mr. Wentworth spoke of the people as the old conventional Whig gentlemen of England spoke of the people
a hundred years ago. When indignantly repelling the
charges, which were often made against him between
the years 1847 and 1854, of having abandoned his
former Radical principles, I once heard him myself
exclaim, in vindication of his political consistency, that
he was never a Radical, but always a Whig. Constitutional reform with him meant putting an end to government from Downing Street, and handing over the affairs
of the colony, including the public lands, to his own

class. During the last few years of his public life, before his departure for England in 1854, he became irritated and embittered by the opposition he met with, and by seeing his popularity of a former period departing from him; and he seemed to be carried away by the fear of some imaginary ascendency of mob-rule. It thus came about that almost insensibly he veered round from the opinions by which he first made himself known. His writings in 'The Australasian,' his violent and unsparing condemnation of Governor Darling, and, at a much later period, his assaults upon the character of Governor Sir George Gipps, were on record in marked contrast to his conduct from 1848 to 1854. As some proof that he had changed his opinions, on arriving in England in 1854 he became a member of the Conservative Club; and at one time he was spoken of subsequently as a candidate in the Conservative interest for Liverpool.

For some years after the first elections to the partly elective Council in 1843, Mr. Wentworth's proceedings on behalf of constitutional changes in the government of the colony attracted comparatively little notice from the bulk of the inhabitants. The population was widely scattered, the means of discussion were few and imperfect, even the newspapers in Sydney were weakly conducted and of limited circulation. But to Mr. Wentworth belongs the great merit of forcing public attention to the 'wrongs' of the colony, and with unwearied labours urging their 'redress.' In 1844 the Legislative Council, not long in existence, adopted a protest at his instance against the withholding of the rights of self-government from the colony. In every session afterwards he battered at the door of the Secretary of State with his burden of 'grievances.' In 1851, the English Minister, Earl Grey, sent out to Governor Sir Charles FitzRoy an 'Act for the better government of Her Majesty's Australian Colonies' [the Constitution Act 13 & 14 Vict. cap. 59], which provided, among other things, for the separation of the district of Port Phillip from New South Wales, and its erection into the colony of Victoria. It also contained provisions for the separation, on petition from the inhabitant householders, of certain parts of the territory lying northward, and their erection into a separate colony or colonies (now the colony of Queensland). In the first Council, the City of Melbourne was represented by one and the district of Port Phillip by five members. Before that first Council ceased to exist, Mr. Wentworth, on May 1, 1851, moved another Declaration and Remonstrance, which is so important as one of the foundation-stones of the fabric of our constitutional liberties, that I do not hesitate to copy it here from the Votes and Proceedings of the time :—

We, the Legislative Council of New South Wales, in Council assembled, feel it to be a duty which we owe to ourselves, to our constituents, and to posterity, before we give place to the New Legislature established by the 13 & 14 Vict., cap. 59, to record our deep disappointment and dissatisfaction at the Constitution conferred by that Act on this Colony. After the reiterated reports, resolutions, addresses, and petitions which have proceeded from us during the whole course of our legislative career, against the Schedules appended to the 5 & 6 Vict., cap. 76, and the appropriations of our Ordinary Revenue under the sole authority of Parliament—against the administration of our Waste Lands, and our Territorial Revenue thence arising—against the withholding of the Customs Department from our control—against the dispensation of the patronage of the Colony at the dictation of the Minister for the Colonies—and against the veto reserved and exercised by the same Minister, in the name of the Crown, in matters of Local Legislation—we feel that we had a right to expect that these undoubted grievances would have been redressed by the 13 & 14 Vict. cap. 59; or that power to redress them would have been conferred on the constituent bodies thereby created, with the avowed intention of establishing an authority more competent than Parliament itself to frame suitable Constitutions for the whole group of the Australian Colonies. These our reasonable expectations have been utterly frustrated. The Schedules, instead of being abolished, have been increased. The powers of altering the appropriations in these Schedules, conferred on the Colonial Legislature by this new Act, limited as these powers are, have been, in effect, nullified by the subsequent instructions of the Colonial Minister. The exploded fallacies of the Wakefield theory are still clung to; the pernicious Land Sales Act (5 & 6 Vict. cap. 36) is still enforced; and thousands of our fellow-subjects (in consequence of the undue price put by that mischievous and impolitic enactment upon our waste lands, in defiance of the precedents of the United States, of Canada, and the other North American Colonies, and even of the neighbouring Colony of the Cape of Good Hope), are annually diverted from our shores, and thus forced against their will to seek a home for themselves and their children in the backwoods of America. Nor is this all. Our Territorial Revenue, diminished as it is by this most mistaken policy, is in a great measure confined to the introduction among us of people unsuited to our wants, and in many instances, the outpourings of the poorhouses and unions of the United Kingdom, instead of being applied in directing to this Colony a stream of vigorous and efficient labour, calculated to elevate the character of our industrial population. The bestowal of office among us, with but

partial exception, is still exercised by or at the nomination of
the Colonial Minister, and without any reference to the just
claims of the Colonists, as if the Colony itself were but the fief
of that Minister. The salaries of the Officers of the Customs
and all other departments of Government, included in the
Schedules, are placed beyond our control ; and the only result
of this new enactment, introduced into Parliament by the Prime
Minister himself, with the declared intention of conferring upon
us enlarged powers of self-government and treating us, at last,
as an integral portion of the Empire—is, that all the material
powers exercised for centuries by the House of Commons are
still withheld from us ; that our loyalty and desire for the maintenance of order and good government are so far distrusted that
we are not permitted to vote our own Civil List, lest it might
prove inadequate to the requirements of the public service ; that
our Waste Lands, and our Territorial Revenue, for which Her
Majesty is but a trustee, instead of being spontaneously sur-
rendered as the equivalent for such Civil List, is still reserved,
to the great detriment of all classes of Her Majesty's subjects,
in order to swell the patronage and power of the Ministers of
the Crown ; that whilst, in defiance of the Declaratory Act (18
Geo. III. cap. 12, sec. 1), which has hitherto been considered
the Magna Charta of the representative rights of all the British
Plantations, a large amount of our Public Revenue is thus levied
and appropriated by the authority of Parliament, we have not
even the consolation of seeing that portion of it which is applied
to the payment of the Salaries of our Public Officers distributed
as it ought to be, among the settled inhabitants ; and that, as
a fit climax to this system of misrule, we are not allowed to
exercise the most ordinary legislation which is not subject to
the veto of the Colonial Minister.

Thus circumstanced, we feel that, on the eve of the dissolution of this Council, and as the closing act of our legislative
existence, no other course is open to us but to enter on our
Journals our declaration, protest, and remonstrance, as well
against the Act of Parliament itself (13 & 14 Vict. cap. 59)
as against the instructions of the Minister by which the small

power of retrenchment that Act confers on the Colonial Legislature has been thus overridden; and to bequeath the redress of the grievances, which we have been unable to effect by constitutional means, to the Legislative Council by which we are about to be succeeded.

We, the Legislative Council of New South Wales, do accordingly hereby solemnly protest, insist, and declare as follows :—

1st.—That the Imperial Parliament has not, nor of right ought to have, any power to tax the people of this Colony, or to appropriate any of the monies levied by authority of the Colonial Legislature ;—that this power can only be lawfully exercised by the Colonial Legislature ;—and that the Imperial Parliament has solemnly disclaimed this power by the 18 Geo. III. cap. 12. sec. 1, which Act remains unrepealed.

2nd.—That the Revenue arising from the Public Lands, derived as it is ' *mainly* ' from the value imparted to them by the labour and capital of the people of this Colony, is as much their property as the ordinary Revenue, and ought therefore to be subject only to the like control and appropriation.

3rd.—That the Customs and all other Departments should be subject to the direct supervision and control of the Colonial Legislature ; which should have the appropriation of the gross Revenues of the Colony, from whatever source arising ; and as a necessary incident to this authority, the regulation of the salaries of all Colonial Officers.

4th.—That offices of trust and emolument should be conferred only on the settled inhabitants, the office of Governor alone excepted ; that this Officer should be appointed and paid by the Crown ; and that the whole patronage of the Colony should be vested in him and the Executive Council, unfettered by instructions from the Minister for the Colonies.

5th.—That plenary powers of legislation should be conferred upon and exercised by the Colonial Legislature, for the time being ; and that no Bills should be reserved for the signification of Her Majesty's Pleasure, unless they affect the Prerogatives of the Crown, or the general interests of the Empire.

Solemnly protesting against these wrongs, and declaring

and insisting upon these our undoubted rights, we leave the redress of the one and the assertion of the other to the people whom we represent, and the Legislature which shall follow us.

W. C. WENTWORTH,
Chairman of Select Committee.

This Declaration and Remonstrance was adopted on division by eighteen ayes to eight noes, the noes consisting of all the office-holders and two nominee members, and the ayes of the elective members and two nominees.

The struggle for a Constitution similar in scope and outline to that of England had now fairly taken hold of the people; but the popular struggle had expanded beyond Mr. Wentworth's control, and it was soon to eventuate in equal electoral districts, a residential suffrage, and voting by ballot. The Legislative Council elected under the provisions of the new Imperial Act without loss of time renewed the constitutional struggle under Mr. Wentworth's leadership. In his despatches the Secretary of State, Earl Grey, combated the statements and arguments put forth in the Remonstrance of the old Council, and stoutly maintained the soundness of his own views on all points. But the public began to take a more earnest interest in the several questions raised by the Council's debates, and a surprising vitality was infused into the demands for a full measure of self-government by the complete victory which had been achieved by the Anti-Transportation League. In 1852 two events occurred—a change of Ministry in England and the gold discoveries in Australia—which

had much to do with hastening the introduction of
Responsible Government. The Russell Ministry fell by
the successful assault on their Militia Bill by Lord
Palmerston, and Lord Derby formed his first Ministry
with Sir John Pakington at the Colonial Office in the
place of Earl Grey. The effect of the gold discovery
in New South Wales was described by Mr. Wentworth
as precipitating the colony into a nation. It fell to the
lot of Sir John Pakington to take up the task of Earl
Grey in dealing with the Petitions and Remonstrances
from the mother colony, and he set about the work in a
way which must have disgusted his philosophical pre-
decessor. In a despatch dated December 15, 1852, the
new Secretary of State for the Colonies says that the
Ministers, after deliberating upon the Petition from the
Legislative Council,

have been fully impressed with a sense of the importance to
be attached to that Petition, not only as proceeding from a
great majority of the Legislature of the Province, but as reiter-
ating that statement of the causes of discontent felt by the
community which had been deliberately urged by their predecessors upon the attention of Her Majesty's then Government
—a statement, moreover, which was accompanied by your assurance that its sentiments were shared by the most loyal,
respectable, and influential members of the community.

The despatch proceeds :—

But they are influenced, in addition, by considerations
arising from those extraordinary discoveries of gold which have
lately taken place in some of the Australian Colonies, and which
may be said to have imparted new and unforeseen features to
their political and social condition. They are sensible that they
have now to consider the prayer of the Petition thus laid before

Her Majesty with reference to a state of affairs which has no parallel in history, and which must, in all human probability, stimulate the advance of population, wealth, and material prosperity with a rapidity alike unparalleled.

The general conclusions at which the new Minister had arrived were virtually to yield on all heads to the demands of the colony. Her Majesty's Government, the despatch continues, in reference to the revenue to be derived from the disposal of the public lands, 'are willing to rely in this, as in other respects, on the foresight and political judgment' of the Colonial Legislature; and the wish of the Government is definitely expressed that the Legislative Council, under the provisions of the existing Constitution Act, should proceed to frame a new Constitution in accordance with the outlines so repeatedly and persistently presented for the sovereign's sanction. The Derby Ministry had a short lease of power, and the Duke of Newcastle succeeded Sir John Pakington at the Colonial Office. In a despatch of January 18, 1853, to Governor FitzRoy, the Duke says, 'My colleagues and myself cordially adopt the conclusions of Her Majesty's late Government respecting the future administration of the Waste Lands of the Crown,' and inferentially the other important matters embraced in the Petitions and Remonstrances. He then adds :—

I am ignorant of the shape which the project under the consideration of the Committee of the Council may eventually assume. The Legislative Council, indeed, in the Petition before adverted to, favoured a Constitution similar in its outline to that of Canada. It would be premature for me, without materials for forming a judgment, to pass an opinion upon the

policy of totally reconstructing the frame of Government recently established ; but I may state that I have always thought
it probable that the experience and wisdom of the Council
would dictate better provisions than Parliament for securing
good government in New South Wales, and promoting harmony
in the connection subsisting between Great Britain and this
important Province of the Empire.

Thus within two years after the Constitution Act,
13 & 14 Vict. cap. 59, came into operation, the colony
was on the eve of gaining a free Constitution, framed
by its own great 'son of the soil,' transferring all the
revenues and patronage of the Crown to the local
Legislature. In 1852 I began to take an active part
in the constitutional discussions outside the Legislature.
In 'The Empire' newspaper, and on the platform, I
strenuously opposed what were popularly regarded as
Mr. Wentworth's retrograde tendencies. The gentlemen
who took part with me in those agitations were certainly
not demagogues, or men wanting in social influence.
Among them were Mr. John Gilchrist, Mr. J. L. Montefiore, Mr. John Brown, Mr. T. S. Mort (whose statue
now stands in front of the Sydney Exchange), and other
of the leading merchants of the colony; the late Sir
John Darvall, K.C.M.G., Mr. Robert Johnson, and Mr.
George Kenyon Holden, two of the most influential
solicitors; the gifted Daniel Henry Denichy, and many
other important citizens. In 1852 Mr. Wentworth
obtained a Select Committee to consider the question
of a new Constitution. The committee reported, and
brought up a draft Bill, but the matter was not carried
further in the Council. In the early part of 1853 he
again moved for the appointment of a Select Committee

to prepare his great measure. I give the names of the committee as they were known in later years :—

Mr. W. C. WENTWORTH, Chairman.
Mr. JAMES MACARTHUR (of Camden).
Mr. JAMES MARTIN, afterwards Chief Justice.
Mr. CHARLES COWPER, K.C.M.G.
Mr. T. A. MURRAY, afterwards Speaker and President of the Legislative Council.
Mr. GEORGE MACLEAY, K.C.M.G.
Mr. E. DEAS THOMSON, K.C.M.G.
Mr. JOHN HUBERT PLUNKETT.
HENRY GRATTAN DOUGLASS, M.D.
Mr. WILLIAM THURLOW.

The committee thus constituted, after a ballot which changed three of the names, met on May 27, and fifteen meetings altogether were summoned. Strange as it may appear, considering the momentous task entrusted to them, many of the members very irregularly attended to their duties. In due time Mr. Wentworth brought up his report, which was the signal for an outburst of popular dissent from several features of his scheme. On August 9 he obtained leave to bring in his ' Bill to confer a Constitution on New South Wales, and to grant a Civil List to Her Majesty.' The Bill, having passed through its first stages, was, on the motion for the second reading, debated at great length, and with striking ability. The speeches of Mr. Wentworth himself, Mr. Plunkett (the Attorney-General), Mr. Martin (afterwards Sir James), and Mr. Darvall (afterwards Sir John), for their eloquence and power were deemed worthy of any legislative body. The second reading was carried by 33 votes against 8; but that

minority represented a party (many of them yet outside,
and waiting to enter the Parliament to be created by
this Bill) who were destined very soon to rule the
country. I give some extracts from Mr. Wentworth's
speech when opening the memorable debate on the
second reading of his Bill. Having expressed a strong
opinion that the absence of petitions against the measure
was a conclusive proof that the people were satisfied—
that the apathy to which I have alluded was really a
silent assent of approval—he proceeded to complain of
a public meeting in opposition that had been held on
the previous day, and to denounce members of the
Council who had attended it :—

I do not know whether it is worth my while to refer at all
to the proceedings out of doors yesterday in regard to this
question. But I cannot help expressing my deep regret that
so many members of this House should, by taking part in
these proceedings, have forgotten alike what was due to themselves and to the dignity of the Council. (Cheers.) I feel
that, by the part they have taken in this matter, they have
destroyed the freedom of the representatives of the country ;
they have degraded the position which the Legislature of the
country ought to occupy, and I lament much to see some hon.
members, my friends, and who have on most occasions acted
with me, consent to sink from the rank of representatives to
that of mere miserable delegates. (Loud applause, and 'No,
no,' from Mr. Darvall.) My honourable and learned friend
says 'No, no,' but I ask the House, Can any hon. members
who have identified themselves with the proceedings of yesterday act in this House as free agents? (Cheers.) Why, if the
arguments they have put forward were refuted to their own
absolute conviction—if the declamation and reasonings, if they
could be called such, used at that meeting could be utterly
demolished — blown into thin air — if it could be proved to

demonstration that the Constitution this Bill offered was calculated to secure on the most permanent basis the free institutions, and the moral, social, and the material interests of the colony, they could not now support it. They had become the delegates, the pledged delegates, of a noisy and intemperate faction, and they must continue in that degraded position to the end. (Cheers.)

This reads in strange contrast to the practice of the leading statesmen on both sides in the Imperial Parliament, both then and now taking vehement part out of doors in condemnation of measures to which they are opposed. The Mr. Darvall to whom Mr. Wentworth referred (afterwards Sir John Darvall) was a leading member of the colonial Bar, and enjoyed a position equal to that of Mr. Wentworth himself. The orator then plunged into a set denunciation of the merchants and the people of Sydney generally, in the following language :—

What interest does the population of Sydney represent? True there are hosts of people in the city calling themselves merchants, and I admit these give employment to a large number of others of lower degree. These merchants, however, are simply engaged in exchanging one commodity for another— the sending the produce of the colony home and getting out the goods of foreign countries instead. But they, as a class, with the exception of the shipowners, are productive of absolutely nothing to add to the real wealth of the colony. There is no urgent necessity for them—the colony could do without them ; all that this class of people have done for me, for instance, I could have done for myself. I could have sent abroad for the tea, the sugar, the tobacco, the silks, the wine and spirits, and other articles I might require, and have obtained them just as well without the instrumentality of the merchants, and what I could thus have done any other person might have done also.

Excited, and, as it were, infuriated by the indiscriminate cheers of his pliant majority, made up largely of those officials and nominees whom in former years he so bitterly denounced, Mr. Wentworth proceeded to foretell the ruin of the country by the flood of democracy that was setting in, and to defend some of his most unpopular proposals. The report of the speech goes on :—

What incentive is there now held out to those who, having made fortunes here, desire to see their sons occupied in higher pursuits than those of trade? Here are no poor, no middle class in the sense in which these words are used at home; all are rich; yet what do people aspire to here, who, having accumulated perhaps 50,000*l.* or 100,000*l.*, do not care to pursue the drudgery of money-making any longer? I will tell the Council; they aspire to a speedy migration to other lands, seeing it is better for themselves and families to build up homes where the democratic and levelling principles, so rapidly increasing here, are scouted, and where there are high and honourable pursuits and distinctions to which the children of the prudent may aspire. (Loud and prolonged cheers.) Who would stay here if he could avoid it? Who with ample means would ever return if once he left these shores, or even identify himself with the soil so long as selfishness, ignorance, and democracy hold sway? (Renewed cheers.) And yet what a glorious country would this be to live in if higher and nobler principles prevailed; blessed with the most bounteous gifts of Providence, it affords in its rich and illimitable tracts happy homes for the millions yet unborn. (Hear, hear.) With regard to the clauses in question, I know not the opinion of honourable members, but I can only say that if they be not adopted the colony will be virtually disfranchised. (Loud cries of 'hear' from all sides.) Why, I ask, if titles are open to all at home, should they be denied to the colonists? Why should such an institution as the House of Lords (which is an integral part of the British Constitution) be shut out from us? I cannot now 'pause for a reply,' but I, nevertheless, should like to hear my honourable and learned friend (Mr. Darvall) answer that interrogatory. (Hear, hear.) A great deal of ridicule has been cast on these hereditary clauses, but those who cast it knew very little of those who proposed them. (Hear, hear.) They had been twitted with attempting to create a mushroom, a Brummagem, a bunyip aristocracy; but I need scarcely observe that where argument fails ridicule is generally resorted to for aid. I seldom care to allude to personal attacks upon myself, and if I allude to some which have been recently made, it is but to express my utter contempt for the vagabonds who made them.

Although he passionately denounced American institutions, and held aloft his copy of the British Constitution, as he persisted in calling his Bill, in happy contrast, it is curious to observe how much he relied on American authorities, including, of all others, Mr. Calhoun. I do not notice the weak side—I had almost written the violent side — of Mr. Wentworth's public character with any desire to diminish the credit which is richly his due in fighting the battle of the Constitution. What I have said appears to be necessary to give a clear view of the party then forming to take up the constitutional cause on a wider basis, and the public opinion beginning to assert itself in a spirit of equality with England. The British subject who had emigrated to Australia began to cry aloud that he had lost none of his privileges by coming to the colony, and the native-born part of the population were not slow in making common cause with their fellows. The narrow class distinctions of earlier days were fast melting away, and a new order of things was developing itself on all sides.

As in most cases of popular contention, in the heated

opposition to the objectionable parts of Mr. Wentworth's scheme, not sufficient attention was given to its great merits, and positive injustice was done to his indomitable efforts year after year to uplift the colony from its politically lifeless condition. His unwise proposals to secure his handiwork from alterations by those who might come after him, and his hasty and intemperate epithets of ' democrat,' ' communist,' and ' mob-rule ' applied to his opponents, made him extremely unpopular with large numbers who had not watched his steady, unwearied, and enlightened labours in championing the main principles of constitutional government. His aversion to an unrestricted franchise, and his desire to tie the hands of the Legislature he was endeavouring to call into existence, were eagerly seized upon, and his noble contention throughout for the right of the country to dispose of its own lands, impose its own taxes, expend its own revenues, and appoint its own public servants, were lost sight of in the transient fury of opposition. I took part in nearly all the public meetings against the unpopular provisions of the Constitution Bill, and these did not cease till the Bill had been finally dealt with in the Imperial Parliament and returned to the colony. In the Session of 1853 Mr. Wentworth (whose intention to visit England was known) was appointed, in conjunction with Mr. Edward Deas Thomson (the Colonial Secretary of that day) to support the Bill in England in its passage through the Houses of Parliament, and in any other manner deemed expedient. In the following year Mr. Wentworth, on his departure from the colony, resigned his seat for the

city of Sydney, and Mr. Charles Kemp, the senior proprietor of the 'Sydney Morning Herald,' was brought
out as a candidate in the same interest for the vacant
seat.   I had become so well known by this time that a
few days before the nomination I was brought into the
field as an opposition candidate.   At that time Sydney
was one electorate, and returned three members to the
old Council; the election was by open voting, and the
lowest qualification for the franchise was a 10*l.* household.   On the day of polling, May 2, 1854, I was returned by the following record of votes :—

| | | | | |
|---|---|---|---|---|
| Parkes | . | . | . | . 1,427 |
| Kemp | . | . | . | . 779 |

By this election I took my seat in the old Council which
had passed the Constitution Bill, and as the successor
of its author, two years before the advent of Responsible
Government.   In this contest for the representation of
Sydney I was supported by several influential men, who
remained my staunch political supporters, through good
and evil report, until they passed away to their graves.
Mr. Jacob L. Montefiore and Mr Edward Flood were of
the number of these—my unchanging friends.

Mr. Wentworth had now disappeared from the scene,
but the agitation against the unpopular provisions of
his Bill went on with increasing strength and numbers.
Petitions were sent to the Imperial Parliament praying
both Houses not to assent to them, and powerful support to the views of the oppositionists was awakened in
England.   Among the men who rendered valuable service to our cause in England was Viscount Sherbrooke

(then Mr. Robert Lowe). After a few years of lucrative practice at the bar in Sydney, Mr. Lowe had left the colony, and had been returned for Kidderminster to the House of Commons. He soon was offered and accepted office. In reply to a letter from myself congratulating him upon his entrance into official life, Mr. Lowe wrote in April 1853 unhesitatingly expressing his views of the designs of the authors of the Constitution Bill as it reached England. Many other influential men—Mr. A. W. Young, M.P., for example—shared these views to the full. Though the field of contention was changed from Sydney to Westminster, the adversaries of the Wentworth proposals, which had been so generally condemned in the colony, were at their posts in England. The following is a copy of Mr. Lowe's letter:—

34 Lowndes Square, London,
April 6, 1853.

My Dear Sir.—I am very grateful to you for your kind congratulations, and hope my future career may justify them. Of one thing you may be sure, that I never have lost, and never will lose, my interest in Australia, and that I am happy to have been the means of serving her, if not prominently, at least effectually. I very much disapprove of the provision in the proposed Constitution which appoints an Upper Chamber for life out of the existing members of Council. Such a proposal lowers the colony very much in the opinion of people here. Your present public men are not as a body worthy of so marked a distinction, or rather so close a monopoly; and I am quite sure that, if they are appointed for life, in a few years you will be heartily ashamed of them, and find that you have anticipated your resources by putting worse men in a place which might have been occupied by better.

The scheme appears to me to be designed to retain power

in the hands of the present public men, and to exclude, or at any rate to render helpless for your good, the talent and respectability which every ship is carrying to you. A nation ought no more to squander its moral and intellectual than its physical resources. You are about to re-create in Australia the family compact which for so many years oppressed Canada. If you must have a nominated Council, at any rate throw it open to everyone, and limit the term of office to a few years, so that any evil you do may not be without remedy. But why have a nominated Council? Opinion in this country is in favour of two elective Councils, the upper one to be for a longer period, of more mature age, chosen from larger districts, and going out one-third at a time, so as to have a more permanent element in it. I trust that before you receive this letter the colony will have shown that, having shaken off the interference of the Colonial Office in its affairs, it is not going to load itself with fetters of its own forging. If you wish to be hampered with a nominated Council, it is no part of my duty as a Member of Parliament to contravene you; but I will not, if I can help it, allow the present generation to sacrifice the hopes of their children by fixing them with a Council *for life* chosen exclusively from your present public men.

If you think the making these views known would do good, you are quite at liberty to do so.

I ought to mention that, in giving me the office I now hold, Government intimated to me that it was partly in consideration of my public services in Australia, a fact which I trust will prove that an independent course is not always impolitic.

Believe me,

Very truly yours,

Henry Parkes, Esq.                                        R. LOWE.


In the colony I continued my course in association with the opponents of the Bill as it left the Legislative Council. After the triumphant second reading, I attended an open-air meeting of fully 5,000 citizens which was held near the Circular Quay, on September 5, 1853, and moved the following resolution :—

That this meeting records its surprise and indignation at the unconstitutional doctrines advanced in the Legislative Council during the discussion of the present measure, whereby the great maxim of just and enlightened government, that ' All power emanates from the People,' is sought to be denied ; and that, viewing the inherent defects of nomineeism and class interest in the existing Legislature, this meeting publicly records its total want of confidence in that body in reference to this measure, which is fraught with the most momentous consequences to the whole people.

In my speech I quoted Bentham against Mr. Martin's notions of the value of property qualifications in securing political fitness, and Lord Chatham against Mr. Wentworth's estimate of the importance of the merchants. I dealt with the personal attacks which at that early stage had been made upon myself, and I advocated the adoption of my resolution in a manner which secured its unanimous acceptance amidst the general applause of the meeting. The following are the principal parts of my speech on that occasion, and this must serve to represent the many speeches I made before the agitation came to an end. The newspaper report makes me say :—

It would be his duty, in the first place, to show that the doctrines which had been advanced in the Council were unconstitutional, and in the next, that they had just grounds to declare that they had lost all confidence in the Legislative Council with regard to this measure, from the inherent defects of nomineeism, and the prevalence of class interests in that body. He would then advert to the speeches that had been made in that House by the honourable member, Mr. Wentworth, and the honourable member for Cork and Westmoreland, Mr. Martin, and he should rely mainly on those two speeches, which had been received with so much applause, to prove his case. Mr. Wentworth in the course of his opening speech had informed them, doubtless much to their astonishment, that the mercantile and trading classes were altogether unnecessary and did not need representation. That gentleman could not see what there was to represent beyond the squatting interest. This was in strange taste as coming from the senior member for the city, to say nothing of its injustice and absurdity. The other honourable member, Mr. Martin, did not regard the 'lower classes' at all. If he understood Mr. Martin's speech aright, he contended that the great body of the people had no right to be considered at all in questions of government. He told us plainly that man had no inherent right to representation; that it was for the Legislature to determine to whom should be granted this right; that the franchise was a mere matter of convenience, to be fixed by those who had the power to fix it. The Solicitor-General (Mr. Manning), who, he was bound to say, had met the question in a more fair and liberal manner than any of the other supporters of the Bill, had also talked about the people 'as one of the estates of the realm.' The learned gentleman repeatedly made use of that expression. Now, he would like to know, if that estate were taken away, where all the other estates would be. According to all the constitutional authorities he had ever read, the people were regarded as the basis of the realm itself. It certainly seemed strange to him to hear the people set down by a law officer of the Government as 'one of the estates of the realm.' If that estate were taken away, he should imagine that the honourable gentleman's salary would soon follow. Mr. Martin, in his speech, went on to state 'that he did not recognise the right of any meeting or any body of men to sit in revision of the acts of that Council. The Council was elected for the purpose of legislation, and he (Mr. Martin) wanted to know what was the superior body that was to sit in review of their acts.' This, let it be remembered, was the legislative body which was condemned by the very Constitution Bill which Mr. Martin himself was endeavouring to pass. Old-fashioned people thought that there was such a thing as the right of petition, as the right of free discussion—to review in public meeting the conduct of the Government, and the conduct of the people's representatives. It would be found that there was an ulterior right when their legislators were acting treason against the liberties of the people—the right to punish, the right to send them back into the obscurity from which they had emerged. These were some of the unconstitutional doctrines against which he for one protested, and against which the resolution was aimed. And considering how loudly they had been cheered, how cordially they had been responded to in the Legislative Council, he thought the reception they had met with was sufficient to destroy all faith in the Council's intelligence and sense of justice. But having some consideration for the large array of authorities which these members had brought to bear upon the question, he would beg permission to place before the meeting the opinions of men not less distinguished, in order to fortify his own opinions, which were of very little value in themselves. He would assure them that his authorities were not perverted as others had been in the Legislative Council, but that the sentiments expressed in the extracts he was about to read were in accordance with the doctrines which these illustrious men had spent their lives in establishing. The first authority he would trouble them with was Jeremy Bentham, and he ventured to think that he was almost as great a philosopher as James Martin. Another of his authorities would be a statesman, who was now known in English history as the 'Great Commoner'; he meant the illustrious Earl of Chatham. He ventured to think that he might be considered nearly as great as William Charles Wentworth. Bentham, then, said, 'Property, it is continually said, is the only bond and pledge of attachment to country. Not it, indeed. Want of property is a much stronger one. He who has property can change the shape of it, and carry it away with him to another country whenever he pleases. He who has no property can do no such thing. In the eyes of those who live by the labour of others, the existence of those by whose labour they live is indeed of no value; not so in the eyes of the labourers themselves. Life is not worth more to yawners than to labourers; and their country is the only country in which they can so much as hope to live. Among a hundred of them, not ten exceptions to this will you find.'

I then quoted Dr. Channing on the spiritual inner life of the better portion of the labouring poor. 'You may shut him out of your houses, but God opens to him heavenly mansions. He makes no show indeed in the streets of a splendid city; but a clear thought, a pure affection, a resolute act of a virtuous will, have a dignity of quite another kind, and far higher than accumulations of brick and granite,' &c. Coming back to our denouncers in the Legislative Council, I said :—

They had been told by Mr. Martin that they were not able to form a serious opinion, or one of any value on important questions; but he would rather take the judgment of Dr. Channing. Let them now hear what Lord Chatham had said upon the subject, speaking in the House of Peers :—

· I myself am one of the people. I esteem that security and independence which is the original birthright of an Englishman, far beyond the privileges, however splendid, which are annexed to the Peerage.'

He hoped these authorities would be sufficient to prove that the people of this colony had been treated with a contumely and arrogant disregard which were foreign to the feelings of Englishmen of whatever rank, and that the course pursued in the recent debate did not entitle the Council to their confidence and respect. What was the doctrine that had been advanced in the Council but, in effect, that the people were unworthy of the free expression of opinion or the exercise of political influ-

ence? He would now address himself to the other part of the
resolution, which declared that, from the inherent defects of
nomineeism and the existence of class interests in the Council,
that body was not deserving of the confidence of the people.
And on this subject he must trouble them with one more quota-
tion. It was from a gentleman in the colony, one who was now
living an active life in their midst, one who was universally regarded as one of the most powerful intellects that this country
had produced. He was about to read the opinions of no less
a personage than Mr. Wentworth himself on the subject of
nomineeism.

I then quoted a passage from a letter published by
Mr. Wentworth some years before, in which he spoke of
the nominee members of the Council as 'a body of
official and unofficial members, the former of whom are
given to understand, notwithstanding their oaths, that
it is a condition of their tenure of office that they are
to support all measures of the Government, whether
good or bad ; and the latter of whom, for the most part,
seem only to have been selected from their utter incompetency to offer any effectual resistance to such
measures.' Of course Mr. Wentworth would have
answered that his nominee Upper House would be composed of far different men from those whom he had
here described. I contrasted his description of the
nominees now with his earlier picture of them, and
proceeded :—

No wonder those gentlemen, seeing his vivid powers of
description, were now delighted to get him on their side. This
was Mr. Wentworth's opinion in 1842 ; no doubt, if they could
penetrate the inmost recesses of that gentleman's heart, they
would find that he had the same opinion still of his new allies. But,
without any such supernatural scrutiny, they might arrive at

what was Mr. Wentworth's opinion now, or at least what it was
only a few months ago. He would give them an extract from
Mr. Wentworth's speech, on moving for a committee to draw up
this very Bill that they were now discussing :—

'In excluding from the list of the committee which he
proposed the name of any nominee, more especially any official
nominee, he was actuated by a consideration of delicacy towards
these gentlemen. To place them on such a committee as this
would be to place them in a false position—false to themselves
and the office they held—and a position in which they ought
not to be placed. This was the sole reason why, in the composition of the committee, he had confined it to the elective
members of that House, and to infuse any other element into
the constitution of the committee would be to prevent the
sense of the House from being properly arrived at. These were
his views in reference to the composition of the committee. He
trusted that if any opposition to such a course manifested itself,
the elective element in that House was strong enough to put it
down.'

This was an extract from Mr. Wentworth's speech in the
Legislative Council on June 16, 1852, and he thought it contained pretty strong language in condemnation of nominee
legislators. He would ask, if the nominees were unfit to deal
with the Constitution question twelve months ago, how much
better fitted were they on Friday night last, when Mr. Wentworth implored these very men to give him their votes ? There
remained one more point in the resolution, and that was the
assertion of the existence of a class ascendency in the House.
Since he had been on the hustings that afternoon, he had been
told by a member of the House that there were no less than
thirty-three members of that body closely connected with the
squatting interest. That was a very significant fact, especially
when they took it in connection with Mr. Wentworth's assertion
of the right of fifty or sixty families to erect themselves into an
aristocracy, and to form eventually, as he proposed, an Upper
House of Legislature. This right on the part of an arrogant
few was assumed in Mr. Wentworth's first speech, and in his

second speech we were told that he had devised his notable
scheme of hereditary titles with a view to the peculiar qualifications of the 'shepherd kings' of the country, who already possessed splendid acquisitions of land, and were on the high road
to fortunes which would maintain them in a state of nobility.
The squatters were, in fact, the only class in the country who
could support the dignity and splendour of a title.   If they duly
weighed all this, and then looked at the last clauses of the Bill,
they would see by the provisions Mr. Wentworth had made to
secure the possession of their lands in the hands of the squatting
interest that a deep design to exalt and aggrandise a class by
the spoliation of the people was at the bottom of the present
measure.   Unless two-thirds of the Legislature, a large proportion of whom they might clearly see would be connected with
the squatting interest, gave their assent to any alteration in the
Constitution, the lands would be theirs in perpetuity.   He
thought this was most conclusive evidence that there was this
class ascendency in that body which was denounced in the
resolution as dangerous to the liberties of the people.   If the
members of the Legislature were so daring, so deeply infected
with treason—he could use no milder term—towards the
liberties of the people, as to deny their right to meet and
express their opinions; and if they treated their petitions with
contumely and disregard, he must say that it was idle to petition that body any longer, and that it was indeed time to
express a public want of confidence in its deliberation and its
acts.   When they remembered that one-third of the members
of that House were there without the concurrence of the people
at all, and the majority of the elective members—elected, it was
true, but by a system which was a perfect mockery of representation—were opposed to the wishes and the interests of the
people, surely, in the name of everything that was just and
true, in the name of everything that was thoroughly British, it
was time to express our total want of confidence in that body.
He would now call their attention to the aspersion of the
mercantile interest that had been indulged in by Mr. Wentworth; and he thought he could not do better than contrast

his opinions with those of the great Earl of Chatham. Mr. Wentworth boldly declared that the merchants of Sydney were of no use, that the colony could do very well without them. The Earl of Chatham had said. in speaking of the same class : ' I hope, my lords, that nothing I have said will be understood to extend to the honest, industrious tradesman, who holds the middle rank, and has repeated proofs that he prefers law and liberty to gold. I love that class of men. Much less would I be thought to reflect upon the fair merchant whose liberal commerce is the prime source of national wealth. I esteem his occupation and respect his character.'

Though no arguments were required to expose the absurdity of Mr. Wentworth's notions, he could not help quoting the estimate formed of the value of the tradesman and the merchant by the great English Commoner. According to Mr. Wentworth, these great classes—whose intelligence and enterprise were of such immense importance to every civilised community, and who were themselves generally the most enlightened promoters of the well-being of the State—were perfectly useless, and disentitled to any consideration in the working of representative government. (Here the speaker was interrupted by much cheering and repeated cries of ' Bob Nichols.' ¹) Well, he had been frequently reminded of that honourable member, but he had not much to say about him. He would tell them what a witty friend of his had said respecting that gentleman a few days ago. On being told that Mr. Nichols had recanted and joined the nominees, he replied, ' Poor Robert! he has been canting all his life, and it is now high time he recanted.' It might be truly said that Mr. Nichols had been canting in more senses than one—canting like a ship without ballast, as well as dealing in all the discarded cant of political quackery. But with respect to Mr. Nichols. who was now so conservative in his ideas, they would all remember that that gentleman not

---

¹ The late George Robert Nichols, who, though carried away on the Constitution question by his admiration for his fellow-countryman, Mr. Wentworth, had been identified with most of the Liberal movements in the colony, and was the author of many useful measures.

long ago had talked very loudly about 100,000 American sympathisers coming over to enable the colony to obtain its independence. This was said at a public dinner in this city, presided over by Mr. Nichols; and who did they think was the person who on that occasion took exception to the anti-British language of Mr. Nichols? Why, it was Mr. Wentworth's arch-anarchist, the humble person now speaking, who in that room protested against the disloyal language of the honourable gentleman. And now with regard to the aspersions so freely cast upon himself. Mr. Wentworth had honoured him with the title of the 'arch-anarchist.' He supposed he was regarded as the leader of the imaginary 'ruffians' who were to go down to Vaucluse and pillage it.[1] He would tell that honourable gentleman that he had no such power, no such influence, as was attributed to him. The part he had taken in the present movement was a very humble one; he had done no more than any other member of this committee; and with regard to his being an anarchist, he most indignantly denied that he was in any respect a worse citizen than Mr. Wentworth himself. In the opposition he had felt it his duty to give to the measure now under discussion, he was actuated by the same singleness of purpose which he believed actuated all the gentlemen with whom he was associated. Mr. Wentworth had said that if certain persons—the 'arch-anarchist,' he supposed, among them—got the upper hand, they would trample on the country with an iron heel. But the truth was that they were seeking to rescue the country from the 'iron heel' of others. He had himself been charged with want of loyalty to his fatherland. It would be more pardonable in Mr. Wentworth than in him to be deficient in patriotic feeling and in loyalty. He, at all events, had right good reason to be proud of his fatherland, and there was no pulse of his life that beat with truer warmth than that which responded to the title of a loyal Englishman. He was born in the heart of Old England, within a few hours' walk of the spot where Shakespeare was born, where some of

[1] Language of the character indicated was frequently applied to the opponents of the Constitution Bill by Mr. Wentworth and his friends.

the noblest associations of English history were fresh in the hearts of even the rural population; and he had been reared in one of the greatest and most prosperous and public-spirited towns in Great Britain. He spurned the attempt to fix upon him any advocacy of republican government. He was sincerely attached to his native country and her institutions. It was his heartfelt desire that that flag (pointing to the British ensign over the hustings) might wave in peace and security over his grave, and over the graves of his children; and in ages to come might float the banner of a great and glorious people here, affiliated by all the bonds of affection and justice to that dear old land from which they were all descended. In his judgment, it would be a great and fatal mistake to attempt in Australia any mere imitation of the noble form of government under which the great American people had risen to such colossal power. Nor did he imagine that, with the progress of events, the character of any known nation would be slavishly reproduced here. He thought this country was destined to show the spectacle of a great nation perfectly free, profoundly prosperous, and glowing with distinctive national aspirations, and yet united in the bonds of affection and political interests to the mother-country. He did not want a ' Yankee Constitution ' any more than Mr. Wentworth. But by all that was sacred, by the God who had given them a great and fruitful country to dwell in, he for one would never consent to have a Norfolk Island Constitution. He objected —and the gentleman with whom he was proud to act on this occasion objected— to Mr. Wentworth's scheme, because it was a scheme in violation of the true principles of the British Constitution. He had thought it right thus publicly and explicitly to defend himself and those who were associated with him against the charges which had been so recklessly made; he flung back those charges with unutterable scorn; he desired nothing beyond that which he was entitled to ask as a loyal and patriotic subject of the Queen of England. Before he sat down he would briefly advert to some of the misrepresentations of matters of history which had been put forward in the Council. A gentleman for whose public character he had a high respect—he meant the Attorney-General (Mr. Plunkett)—had told them with an air of triumph that the great men who framed the American Constitution had sat for months and years in discussion on the measure with closed doors, and that when their plan was matured they promulgated it by authority. But the historical fact was that, in the eleventh year of the Confederation, it was found that the Articles of Confederation were so defective for affording adequate power for national purposes and this conviction had been forcing itself upon the minds of statesmen for several years—that it was determined to form a Convention for the revision of the form of government. Delegates for this purpose were appointed by twelve out of thirteen States, who met in Philadelphia on the 14th of May, 1787, to form a Constitution: and so far from sitting for years, he found that on the 17th of September in the same year they presented their report to Congress, which on the 28th of the same month remitted it to the several States for approval. To a certain extent it might be true that the delegates sat with closed doors, for as it was cold in America, they probably did not leave them open. But so far from the Constitution being promulgated by authority, he found that one State, Rhode Island, refused to accept it, and stood out from the Union for two years and eight months. Virginia, stirred up by the great eloquence of Patrick Henry, one of the most remarkable men of the Revolution, also opposed it and refused to accept it for many months. These were the facts of the case, and they showed the false basis of knowledge upon which gentlemen in the Council proceeded when they could listen to such distorted statements, and at the same time brand the people out of doors with ignorance and meddling with matters they did not understand. The Attorney-General had also told them that the Senate of the United States was elected by the Sovereign States, and therefore was appointed by a process analogous to the appointment of nominees by the Queen's representatives; this, at all events, was what he understood from the speech of that learned gentleman. But Mr. Plunkett must have been greatly misled; for it was known to

most of them that the Senators were elected by a majority of
the votes of the State Legislatures. He was somewhat at a
loss to understand why the Attorney-General had pronounced
such a high eulogium on the speech of Mr. Martin. He was
ready to admit that that speech in many respects was an able
one, but still he was surprised to hear the Attorney-General
speak of it in terms of rapture. But he found, on referring to
the conclusion of that speech, a very satisfactory reason for
Mr. Plunkett's admiration. Mr. Martin concluded with a very
patriotic avowal that he would pension off the officers of the
Crown at their full salaries, and doubtless such an idea of
constitutional government was very delightful to the worthy
Attorney-General. In conclusion, he urged them to consider
whether they had not just reason to assent to the resolution he
had read to them. After the contumely that had been heaped
on them and their petitions—after the unconstitutional doctrines which had been propounded by the Legislative Council—
he for one would never send another petition to that body on
this question. He denied the right of that House to force this
Constitution on the people of the colony; and it was the
bounden duty of all classes to appeal to a higher power—a
more impartial tribunal. He had no doubt as to what the
result of that appeal would be. Despite the overwhelming
majority in the Council, the reasonableness and justice of their
petitions would prevail, and the youthful energies of this fair
country would be freed from the infliction of this most detestable and un-British measure.

By the time when the Constitution was finally dealt
with in the Imperial Parliament, Lord John Russell had
become Secretary of State for the Colonies. By the
Imperial Act 18 & 19 Vict. cap. 54, enacting the Bill
from the colony in the form of a schedule thereto, and
enabling Her Majesty to assent to it, power was given
to the new Parliament which it created to repeal any
of the obnoxious clauses by a simple majority. In the

language of the Act, it was 'lawful for the Legislature of New South Wales to make laws altering or repealing all or any of the provisions of the said reserved Bill, in the same manner as any other laws for the good government of the said colony.' The Bill received the Royal assent on July 16, 1855, and the new Parliament was elected under its provisions in the middle of 1856. Not many months passed away before the two-thirds majority clause, the clause to exclude clergymen from election to the Assembly (notoriously aimed at Dr. Lang), and the other provisions which had called forth such strong opposition in the colony, were all repealed. This was the death-blow to the old party who had exercised all influence in former years, only checked by rancorous jealousies amongst themselves or the occasional stand of a spirited governor.

There were some political anachronisms, if not something worse, in framing the Constitution, which, so far as I know, have never been noticed. For instance, the 51st clause provided that pensions should be demandable by the judges of the Supreme Court to the amount of seven-tenths of their actual salaries after fifteen years' service as such judge in the colony; but while the Bill was in committee, an amendment was moved and carried, notoriously to meet the case of one of the existing judges who had held inferior offices before his appointment, in these words:—'So far as the present judges are concerned, every three years' service in any judicial office in this colony, other than the office of a judge of the Supreme Court, shall be equivalent to one year's service as such judge of the Supreme Court.' A Bill to confer a Constitution on the colony, which assuredly ought not to contain any provision to subserve a subordinate or collateral or an accidental object, is disfigured to favour the situation of one man, contrary to the studied text as it originally stood, and the blot remains embedded in the Constitution for all time. By the 18th clause provision was made for the Responsible Ministry of the future, but the offices designated as capable of being held by members of Parliament were copied from the offices held by the retiring officials sent out from Downing Street. They are fixed by the Constitution as under :

| The Colonial Secretary | The Attorney-General |
|---|---|
| „ „ Treasurer | „ Solicitor-General |
| „ Auditor-General | |

Thus the new Ministry would be two-fifths Law, two-fifths Finance and Accounts, and one-fifth for the Lands, Public Works, Military, Police, and general administration of affairs. In point of fact, the first administration was formed by holders of the above offices, the position of Auditor-General being given to a gentleman who was remarkable for his ignorance of accounts. It clearly is not unjust to say that Mr. Wentworth can never have thought of the ministerial arrangement by which his scheme of government was to be carried out. Not only were these anomalies found in the Constitution, but the first Premier appointed his Treasurer to the nominee Council—in other words, put his Chancellor of the Exchequer in his House of Lords.

A gentleman of great influence waited upon me to suggest that I should join in the formation of the first Ministry. He presented a list of the proposed names, which included mine, and exclaimed, 'Such a Ministry would last twenty years!' I was taken by surprise, but I think I must have smiled. The idea of the party he represented was to combine both sides of the new House; but, inexperienced as I then was, I felt that any such attempt would not succeed. It is due to myself to say that at that time I had no desire or thought about office, which derives proof, if proof were necessary, from the fact that I did not take office until ten years afterwards, though it was offered to me more than once. The Ministry which was actually formed lasted only eighty days. This was the beginning of our Parliamentary history, but the colony has no cause to be ashamed of the Parliamentary record since.

In the last session of the old Council, on October 16, 1855, the late Sir James Martin (then Mr. Martin) moved for a Select Committee to enquire into the powers and duties of the chief officers of the Executive Government, with a view to ascertain if any and what alterations will be necessary to carry out the principle of responsible administration contemplated by the Constitution Act of 1853, and to report thereon to the House. The Committee appointed by ballot consisted of Mr. Cowper, Mr. Donaldson, the Attorney-General, Mr. Parker, Mr. Parkes, Mr. Nichols, Mr. G. Macleay, Mr. Holroyd, and Mr. Darvall.

The Chairman submitted a draft report of great

length and ability, which, however, was not adopted by
the committee.   Mr. Martin's draft opened thus :—

There is no clause in the Constitution Act which directs
that any change shall take place in the tenure by which those
who may hereafter constitute the Executive Government of the
colony are to hold their appointments.  The Report of the
committee from which that Act emanated, the debates which
took place during its progress through the House, and the
recent Despatch of Lord John Russell, commenting on its
various provisions, show, however, that it is clearly contemplated, by all parties, both here and in England, that, on the
coming of that Act into operation, the Advisers or Ministers of
the Crown in this colony are to be subject to what, under the
British Constitution, is designated Ministerial Responsibility.
Besides, the Constitution Act itself, although it nowhere
directly alludes to such responsibility (as, perhaps, it could not
regularly do), in several places so evidently implies its introduction, that it must be taken for granted that, hereafter, our
Government is to be, in the fullest sense of the term, Responsible to the Legislature.

This document proceeded to discuss the question
whether the officials, whom it was proposed to pension
off, could accept office under the new Constitution,
taking up several other matters of cognate interest, and
then it boldly proposed a new distribution of ministerial authority.  The paragraphs proposing the new
arrangements are as valuable now as they were then,
though they have received but little attention, and I
cannot deny myself the satisfaction of including them
in this chapter :—

Your committee are of opinion that the number of Responsible Ministers, exclusive of those connected with the law,
ought not to be less than four.  Should that number be deter-

mined upon, your committee would then recommend that their
designation should be as follows :—

1. The Chief Secretary and Premier.
2. The Secretary for Finance.
3. The Secretary for the Interior.
4. The Secretary for Public Works.

To each of these Ministers your committee would recommend that the supervision and direction of several of the existing departments should be confided. The Premier might, with
great propriety, have placed under his immediate control the
Waste Lands of the Crown, and the Trade and Commerce, as
well as the Revenue and Expenditure of the Country, which
would include the management of Public Loans. For this
purpose it would be necessary to place under his direction the
offices of the Colonial Secretary, the Colonial Treasurer, and
the Surveyor-General, including that hitherto under the Chief
Commissioner of Crown Lands. Your committee have placed
the Waste Lands of the Crown in the foreground, because they
are of opinion that, beyond all other questions, it will make the
largest demands upon the ability and prudence of our statesmen, and that, upon the right adjustment of this question, the
prosperity, moral and material, of the colony will in a very
great degree depend.

The Secretary for Finance, like the Chancellor of the Exchequer in England, might look after the ways and means,
which would include the general taxation of the country. He
ought also to have under his control the regulation of the
currency, so far as it may from time to time be considered
desirable for Government to interfere with it. This would
involve the handing over to him the departments of the Auditor-
General, the Customs, and the Mint, as well as the public Bank
of Issue, should such an institution (as is very probable) be
called into existence.

The Secretary for the Interior, whose office would be similar
to that of Her Majesty's principal Secretary of State for Home
Affairs, ought to have the direction of Police and Gaols, of the

Post Office, and of the Administration of Justice, as well as the supervision of Educational and Municipal Institutions. He would then have under him, either for the purpose of control or inspection, the department of the Inspector-General of Police, the Sheriff, and all those officers and corporate bodies who might be connected in any way with the matters for the due management or regulation of which he would be responsible to the public.

The Secretary for Public Works would take the roads, railways, public buildings, docks, harbours, and fortifications under his care, and there should be subjected to his orders all departments engaged upon, or connected with, any of these matters.

Your committee think that the advantages of some such scheme as the foregoing are sufficiently obvious to render much argument in support of it unnecessary. By that plan of administration a fair division of ministerial labour would be made; and no one who considers the nature of the duties which the Ministers would be thus called upon to discharge can deny, that each of them would have amply sufficient to occupy his entire attention. By dividing the labour and responsibility of office in this way, public questions would receive an amount of attention which, under the present centralised system, is utterly impossible. The Governor would then occupy a position as nearly analogous as possible to that of the Sovereign whom he represents, and, instead of being called upon to decide all matters for himself, he would enjoy the great advantage of acting only in accordance with the views of his responsible advisers. Those multifarious duties which he now of necessity most imperfectly discharges would then devolve upon persons enjoying the fullest opportunity of carefully considering every question submitted to them, and nothing but want of ability would prevent our future Ministers from rising above the rank of mere officials into that of statesmen.

Mr. Martin, to secure independence and efficiency in his scheme of administration, proposed that the

Ministers should receive equal salaries, of not less than
2,500l. a year, with retiring pensions. The date of
these proposals is thirty-seven years ago, but no Minister
since, to my knowledge, has ever sought to increase his
moderate salary of 1,500l., though several have held
office at great loss in their private incomes. I have
now arrived at that epoch in Australian history since
which all the colonies, except Western Australia, have
been steadily learning the difficult but soul-elevating
lesson to manage their own affairs. Many of the actors,
like myself, were ill trained for this noble task; but
we look abroad, and fail to see any country where
more genuine good work has been done in the generation which has passed over free Australia. Some who
anxiously watched her cradle are still permitted to
guard the temple where Australian liberty is for ever
enthroned.

# CHAPTER III

As explained in the last chapter, I was elected to the Legislative Council in May 1854, just two years before the first election to the new Parliament. I had at this time been engaged for over four years as the conductor of 'The Empire' daily newspaper, and by the course taken by that journal, and by my speeches in public, I had made myself the object of much vituperation in some quarters, and of unfriendly, not to say hostile, criticism in others. One well-known gentleman of the old school used to think he had withered me up by denouncing me as a ' double-tongued slanderer.' But, on the whole, I received a very cordial greeting when I took my seat. Indeed, many of the leading men of the old party—among others I remember well Mr. Plunkett, the Attorney-General—had come to the polling booth and openly voted for me. Nearly all are now gone to their great account. Sir Charles Nicholson, Bart. (then Speaker), Sir Daniel Cooper, Bart. (Speaker of the first Assembly), Sir William M. Manning, and Mr. Augustus Morris still live (January 1890), but I cannot recollect another name.

I set about my new duties with a vigour and zeal

which, I am afraid, were not always guided by a sound
judgment. One of my first motions was in favour of a
more liberal system of immigration. Though identified,
if ever man was, with the working class, I was at the
outset of my career, and have ever remained, the advocate of the introduction of new population from without
as essential to the progress of a new country. My broad
contention has ever been that the more men of the
right class you have in a land ' where life has ample
room,' the better it must be for every man of every
class ; that where all is a wilderness before us, nothing
is so valuable as human labour. Years afterwards, in
my place in Parliament as Prime Minister, when speaking in support of a vote for immigration, I used this
language :—

I want men and women—free men and women—of our own
stock to assist us in laying the broad foundations of an Empire ;
and when the question is narrowed down to this inconceivable
contention between labour and capital, I would like to ask this
one pregnant question : Are not all, or nearly all, the employers
of labour in this country men who have sprung from the ranks
of labour ? If we could trace the immigrants who have arrived
here by the assistance of the State, we should find that they are
the very men who, by their perseverance, by their provident
habits, by their enterprise and their insight into industrial
affairs, have become the great employers in this country. They
do not come here to remain serfs, but to fight the battle of
free men where there is ample room for their exertions. I do
not feel surprised at the indignation of some of the first men in
the mother-country at the illiberal views of colonists in trying
to resist the influx of their brothers and sisters from the old
country. It is incomprehensible to men of enlightened minds
in England that such mean and detestable feelings can exist as

would prevent others from coming to our shores to share in the benefits of these new lands, which are just as much a portion of the Empire as any other.

But my motion was defeated by a large majority; not that the Council was opposed to immigration, but that it was opposed to the principles which I attempted to enforce.

I was placed on nearly all the more important committees; among others, to enquire into the construction of the Metropolitan sewers, in respect to which much abuse and wrongdoing were alleged to have taken place, and the enquiry into which proved to be a most laborious investigation; to consider and report upon the question of education; to consider the expediency of forming Volunteer corps; to enquire into the evils of intemperance; and to investigate and report upon other matters of pressing public interest. If regularity of attendance and zeal were merits, I was a most meritorious committeeman. I was always in my place, and I took my full share in the examination of witnesses. But I soon was engaged in several enquiries originated by myself.

In 1854, I moved for the appointment of a Select Committee to consider the expediency of establishing a Nautical School in the port of Sydney, which after some debate was carried. The committee sat and took a considerable amount of evidence, and in due time I, as chairman, brought up the report, which was in favour of the proposal. The report was adopted by the Council and sent by address, according to the usage of the time, to the Governor-General. His

F 2

Excellency informed the Council by message in reply :—

With reference to the address of the Council of the 5th instant, the Governor-General fully concurs in the opinion expressed as to the advantages which might result from the establishment of a Nautical School. Such a school, if properly conducted, would be productive of many benefits, not merely to the mercantile and shipping interests, but to society at large. It would, however, be more likely to succeed were it to form part of some general educational system, and were it not impressed with the character of a charitable institution—a character which would have the effect of closing it against the children of respectable parents.

The report, which is now before the Council relative to the working of the Asylum for Destitute Children, would not lead to the inference that an eleemosynary establishment of the kind would be likely to produce very satisfactory results.

In deference, however, to the expressed wish of the Council, the Governor-General will give directions for the insertion, upon the Estimates for 1856, of a sum of 2,000l., for the purchase and fitting up of a hulk, and of a further sum of 1,000l. for the current expenses of the Nautical School, on condition that an equal amount will be contributed from private sources.

I give the message in full because it supplies a fair example of the way in which the Legislature was treated in those days by the Governor, who was, in fact, the real executive of the country. It was difficult to see how the working of the Asylum for Destitute Children could affect the argument in favour of the Nautical School; but the Governor said it did, and there was no more to be done for the time. Years rolled away, the old Council died, the new Parliament took its place; and still there was nothing heard of the Nautical School.

Twelve years after the date of my report, I, as Colonial Secretary (then for the first time), bought the ship *Vernon*, on which the Nautical School was established. which is now admitted to be one of the most useful institutions in the colony. For nearly a quarter of a century the *Vernon* has been moored in sight of Sydney; hundreds of poor deserted boys have been gathered from the streets, carefully instructed, and trained to habits of industry and manly conduct on her decks, so that the name of a ' *Vernon* boy' is now received by good and kindly people everywhere with something like affectionate interest. During this period 2,090 boys have passed through the ship into various avenues of employment, and only 8 per cent. of the number have been reported as refractory or backsliding.

I obtained the appointment of another committee to enquire into the importation of Asiatic labourers. For some years past persons largely engaged in squatting pursuits had been casting about to discover an abundant supply of cheap labour. More especially in the far northern districts (now Queensland), South Sea Islanders had been tried; Indian coolies had been tried; other classes of Asiatics had been tried; and many disquieting reports prevailed of ill-usage and cruelty in the carrying on of this traffic. After taking evidence, the committee reported as their general conclusion that there was no necessity for any immediate legislation on the subject. Where this kind of labour had been tried on anything like a large scale, it had, from one cause or other, been found unsatisfactory, if not a total failure.

Another committee was appointed, on my motion, to enquire into the adulteration of food. It held six meetings and examined six witnesses. At this time a committee of the House of Commons was sitting on the same subject, and the report which I as chairman was authorised to bring up concluded thus :—

From the evidence of Mr. Stubbs, it is obvious that the trade in unwholesome articles of food has been subject to no adequate check in the present state of our laws; but, in the opinion of your committee, as already expressed, the whole question is surrounded by such complicated and peculiar difficulties, that it cannot be safely touched by the Legislature, until a complete enquiry has been carried out.

The Select Committee of the House of Commons, now sitting on the same subject, will, your committee respectfully submit, supply information of great value for the guidance of any future similar enquiry that may be conducted in this colony, as the evidence of the eminent scientific persons examined by that committee, and which is based on actual experiments, will apply to many articles of consumption in this colony with equal justice as to the same class of articles in England.

On July 3, 1855, I moved for the ' appointment of a Select Committee to enquire into the state of agriculture, with special reference to the raising of wheaten grain, and to the causes of hindrance or failure in that pursuit, whether arising from the habits of the people, the policy of the Government, or the physical character of the country.' To understand the interest that fairly attached to my motion, we must review, or rather glance at, the state of the colony. The colony still included the whole of Queensland, and embraced an area of 978,315 square miles. Men of leading positions, with seats in the Legislature, described it, for the most part, as incapable of tillage, and only fit for grazing sheep and cattle, and for 'nomadic tribes.' A population not numbering more than 277,579 souls imported largely its breadstuffs from South America and other foreign countries. It is now well known that in all divisions of the colony—north, south, or west—there are as rich wheat lands as in any part of the world; but then the mass of the population were densely ignorant of the true character of the country, and those who knew better were in too many instances personally interested in keeping them ignorant. The stories that were told of the fruitless endeavours of industrious men to obtain patches of land for a freehold home under the Orders in Council seem, to the present generation, like cruel bits of romance. A steady man in service might have saved sufficient money to start himself as a small farmer; he might apply for 40 to 100 acres to be put up for auction sale; months would elapse before his application would be granted; when the day of sale arrived his wealthy neighbour would attend by his agent, and buy the land over the poor man's head for the mere vicious purpose of hindering him from making his home and to protect his own sheep-run from intrusion. While suffering these delays and disappointments, the intending farmer's little money would melt away, and often, if of an irritable temperament, he would give way to drink and become a ruined man.

In moving my resolution I made a short speech, from which I copy the following passages :—

It must be admitted that whatever might be the circumstances of happiness in which we were placed individually, these circumstances would lose all their importance to us if it were not for the ministrations of the crowds round about us. However fertile and however beautiful the country might be, if it were barren of human life and activity, beauty itself would become only another name for desolation, and the very light of heaven would be fearful to our eyes. This extensive city, so cheerful in the sunshine to-day with its streets of palaces, its thousands of secure homes, its spacious marts and banks, would to-morrow, if population floated away from it, present the awful aspect of the tomb. Seeing, then, that our importance as individuals was in every respect just in proportion to the progress of the population as a whole, the Legislature and Government should pay every attention to supplying the people with that great staple of food, the extreme scarcity of which would be more severely felt in its consequences than the sword of an enemy. At a time when flour was being sold at from 55*l.* to 60*l.* per ton, when it was believed that there was a very inadequate supply of this article of food in the country, it seemed more than ever necessary that attention should be paid to the subject.

After alluding to the statements that the country was unfitted for agriculture, I said :—

If it were the case that the country was unsuited to the prosecution of those agricultural pursuits which in all really prosperous countries were of such magnitude and importance ; and that grain could not, under any possible circumstances, be produced in quantity adequate to the wants of the population, it would be best that whatever information could be collected should be brought together and published in a shape accessible to those persons whose energies were likely to be turned in that direction. Individual instances might be given of the failure of persons who had settled on the lands of the country for agricultural purposes, but such cases of failure might be accounted for by the spirit of neglect and suppression which had been manifested towards this interest in the public policy of the country.

The committee was granted, and the enquiry was rendered more than usually interesting by the evidence of one witness who was afterwards elected to the first free Parliament, and who became the popular land reformer of 1861. Mr. Robertson (now Sir John Robertson, K.C.M.G.) was well known as a vigorous writer in the newspapers, and a gentleman who held what were called 'strong Radical opinions'; he had for years resided in the country, and seldom came to Sydney. His knowledge of the operation of the Orders in Council, the abuses of the squatting system, and the hardships imposed upon the class of small settlers, and of the character of the soil in different districts, was that of a singularly quick observant mind, and it was derived from an extensive practical experience. In the light of his great moulding influence on the land question in later years, and his high public standing at the present time, Sir John Robertson's evidence, given more than a generation ago, possesses a curious and instructive interest for the student of land legislation. It is given here without abridgment :—

JOHN ROBERTSON, Esq., called in and examined :—

1. *By the Chairman*: You were invited to attend this committee some time since ?—I was.

2. You sent a letter, at that time, not expecting to be able to attend in Sydney ?—I did.

3. Is this the letter sent by you (*handing the same to the witness*) ?—It is. (*Vide Appendix.*)

4. Have you been long in the colony ?—Thirty-four years.

5. Have you been engaged in agricultural operations any great portion of that time ?—I have for twenty-two years—four

years as the superintendent of my father, and eighteen years on my own account.

6. In what part ?—On the Upper Hunter.

7. The whole of that time ?—I have cultivated lands within thirty or forty miles the whole of that time.

8. At the present time, to what extent are you engaged in agricultural operations ?—I have under crop about 250 acres.

9. Is that freehold ?—It is.

10. Do you think a great proportion of the land in that district is fitted for agriculture ?—There is a very great amount of land in the Upper Hunter fitted for agriculture.

11. Are you acquainted with any other district of the country ?—I am acquainted with the whole of the Hunter, and there are large quantities of available land upon the Hunter, and also in New England, and on the Namoi.

12. From your experience of the character of the country generally, should you think as large a proportion of the country is suitable for agricultural pursuits as is necessary for the progress of population, according to any reasonable calculation ?—There is sufficient for millions : there is not one acre in cultivation for every ten thousand that is fit for cultivation.

13. From your twenty-two years' experience, you would reject the idea that the country is unsuited to agriculture ?—Entirely.

14. *By Mr. Cowper:* Even the upper part of the Hunter ? —Even the upper part of the Hunter : my own experience bears me out there.

15. About Merton ?—Perhaps that is the worst part ; but, if you go higher, it is better : yet even about Merton and Jerry's Plains, and I apprehend that no part of the whole country bears a worse character than Jerry's Plains, I farmed during ten or eleven years, and never missed but one crop.

16. Was the country low or high ?—I cultivated the alluvial flats.

17. *By the Attorney-General:* In what year did your crop fail ?—My crops failed two years ; one at Jerry's Plains and

one at Scone. At Jerry's Plains the failure was twelve or thirteen years ago.

18. Was it in a season of drought?—Yes.

19. *By the Chairman:* You are also engaged in pastoral pursuits to some extent?—Yes.

20. Are you pretty well acquainted with the squatting system?—I have been acquainted with it ever since its first operation. I was one of the first that crossed the Liverpool Range.

21. Do you think there is much land occupied under pastoral leases that would be highly suitable for agriculture?—All the alluvial land in New England, under pastoral leases, is fit for agriculture, and a great portion of the land upon the Namoi, and the rivers in the district of Liverpool Plains.

22. *By the Inspector-General of Police:* Do you speak as regards climate as well as soil?—Yes. I believe the climate causes many difficulties, but it is not a drop in the bucket as compared with the difficulties which have arisen from the policy of the Government, which policy I have alluded to in the paper before the Committee.

23. *By the Chairman:* I should gather then that you have, for some years, paid particular attention to this?—I have, during many years, paid much attention to both agriculture and pasture.

24. Do you think the present squatting system imposes serious difficulties to the settlement of the country, having regard more particularly to small farmers?—I do. I have pointed out in the paper I have submitted, somewhat elaborately, the curious ways in which the squatting system has, in my opinion, checked agriculture.

25. *By the Attorney-General:* What remedy would you apply under the existing state of the law?—The remedy I would apply, in the existing state of the law, which I apprehend, by the way, is not a Minerva, is this:—I would submit large quantities of land for sale, in order that persons who wish to take up lands throughout the country could go at once to the Crown Lands Offices and obtain them, without the delay of applying

for them to be submitted to auction, besides the risk of their being then purchased by a neighbouring proprietor.

26. Are you aware that the principal delay now arises from the survey; they cannot be disposed of by auction, or by any other species of contract, until they have been measured?—I would remedy that in a most simple way, as it is done in America : the intending purchaser should sit down on the land, and pay for it when the quantity is ascertained. I would, however, insist upon his carrying out the provisions I have suggested on the subject, at the conclusion of the paper I have submitted to the committee.

27. Is that the American system?—It is part of the American system. In America, a squatter is very different from one who bears that name here; he, as the word implies, sits down on the land, and is allowed to hold not more than two hundred acres, and this he pays for at the minimum price when it is measured.

28. In those cases, is not the survey in advance, so that a person squatting upon land in America, previously knows the quantity contained in that particular piece?—Assuredly not, for in America he may hold the land for years before payment. The title ' squatter' is given from the fact of parties going on the ground, in advance of society, and sitting down in the meantime, until civilisation overtakes him, and the quantity of his land is ascertained by measurement. In the event of it not being possible, from legal difficulties, to adopt this plan here, I would suggest that, when a surveyor is called upon to measure off thirty or forty acres on any circle, for a particular applicant, he should be instructed to survey all the available land in the neighbourhood. The time of the surveyor would thus be saved, and there would be ample lands to submit to auction. I would, then, have the whole of these lands submitted at the same sale; and I assume that more might be offered than would be purchased, and this should afterwards be open to selection at the upset price.

29. *By the Inspector-General of Police*: That would amount to an evasion of the law, by allowing the lands to be taken at

the minimum price?—You asked me how I would do in the present state of the law.

30. Would not that throw more lands into the hands of the surveyors to be measured in places where there was not a demand, and prevent the survey of land in other places where it was applied for?—I am much acquainted with surveyors, and I know they are now put to much expense, inconvenience, and in many cases to absolute loss, from being required to go, as at present, twenty or thirty miles in one direction to survey a small farm of twenty acres, and then, as many miles in an opposite direction, to measure a small piece of land on some creek.

31. But, if the plan suggested by you were adopted, these applicants would have to wait until a large tract of country were measured before they could be attended to?—I think time would be saved in the end ; because, if a surveyor have not to move about to any distance, he can, in a few days, measure a quantity of land, which otherwise would occupy him for weeks. I have been with a surveyor measuring land, and I am aware that that can be done.

32. *By the Attorney-General* : You allude to licensed surveyors ?—Yes.

33. *By the Chairman* : Is it within your knowledge that many persons are applicants, in different parts of the country, for small portions of land, who cannot get them ?—Yes, many cannot get them.   I have pointed out in this paper the difficulties that are in the way of many small purchasers getting them. I could get them, and any one, who has, or requires, a large quantity, can get them.

34. Have you, in this paper, stated fully the difficulties and remedies of the system ?—Yes, I have stated fully my view of the difficulties ; but the question asked by the Attorney-General had not occurred to me.

35. Are you aware that there is a general impression, that persons will not accept offers of settling upon land as tenants ?— It is within my knowledge that a member of this House, who has property at Tenterfield, offered to let small portions of his

land, twenty, thirty, or forty acres, and to furnish the tenant with rations for a year, and seed grain; that he posted up a notice to this effect upon his barn door, and yet he could get no applicants; and this feeling of reluctance, on the part of persons who might be supposed to be anxious to enter upon agricultural pursuits, is alleged as an answer to those who object to the present system. There is another case which has been mentioned. In the year 1843, when so many persons were out of employment in Sydney, a deputation waited upon Sir George Gipps, to request that they might be employed on public works and buildings, and it was generally admitted that there was much distress. At that time a gentleman advertised farms, upon similar terms to those I have mentioned, and could get no applicants? Yes, and I could give another instance. I have a large quantity of agricultural land myself, and would be very willing to let it; but I have not been quite so unfortunate as the gentleman you have referred to, as I have been able to get several tenants. But they generally object, for two very obvious reasons. Very naturally, coming to a new country, they calculated that they should have a piece of land their own to sit down upon—and they live in hope yet to do so. Another reason is, that they cannot sit down upon lands held by any landed proprietor without making improvements thereon—improvements which they will feel to be the reason of the offer made by the proprietor; but, when a man, with ordinary caution and forethought, sees a fine flat covered with apple and gum trees, and is told, 'You may go and take that for seven years; you shall have it for four years for nothing, and the remainder of the term for a low rent,' I take it that the man may say, very naturally, 'By the time I clear this it will be yours, and the cost of my labour upon it will be greater than its original value.' This is a very different case from that of the farmer in England, where the owner of the property puts it into a workable condition. Here a man may spend his whole life in making improvements upon the property of others.

36. *By the Inspector-General of Police :* Might he not calculate that the rent which he would save would pay for the im-

provements ?—If a man sees that there are lands adjoining those he cultivates, the freehold of which is only worth from 1l. to 2l. an acre, he will feel that he is paying an exorbitant rent when it will cost him 4l. an acre for clearing, besides the expense of erecting a house; that, in fact, although nominally paying a low rent, he is really paying, annually, more than the entire value.

37. Thinly timbered land would not surely cost so much as 4l. an acre for clearing ?—It costs 4l. an acre to clear an apple-tree flat, which is the best for agriculture; and then it requires fencing, which cannot be done under 5s. a rod.

38. *By the Chairman:* Do you not think that the reluctance, in the mind of the working-classes, to enter upon agricultural pursuits, arises from the fact that agriculture has not a fair chance in comparison with the other industrial pursuits of the Colony ?—I have shown in this paper ample reasons why men should be reluctant to enter upon agricultural pursuits, in view of so many advantages in other occupations.

39. Have you paid much attention to the course of legislation and the policy of the Government of the country ?—Yes, I have watched the Government very closely during the last eighteen years, and the career also of a few gentlemen in the Council: I can almost give their votes upon most important public questions.

40. Has it appeared to you that there has been any unfair leaning towards pastoral pursuits, to the exclusion of the claims of other branches of industry ?—Yes. I am thoroughly convinced, from whatever motive or object, that there has been a tendency in the whole course of the legislation of this country—certainly since we have had a slight approach to representative institutions, since 1843—on the one hand, to depress the agriculturist, and to raise, at his expense, the pastoral interest. I have entered into this matter fully in this paper.

41. You say you are engaged in squatting as well as in agriculture—are you as largely interested in pastoral pursuits as in agricultural ? I have infinitely more capital invested in

pastoral pursuits than in agricultural, in my own hands: but my income from the two sources is about equal. I have, however, several agricultural farms under lease to tenants, which about equalises my property in each pursuit.

12. Do you think if Government exercised forethought, and displayed public spirit as to the survey of particular districts which are sought for for agriculture, and go to the expense of opening them by means of improved communication, by constructing roads, or if on a river, by removing impediments to its navigation, so as to make the metropolitan and other markets of easy access, the increased value of those lands would pay the expense of the necessary improvements?— I think it would, especially if coincident with this the laws were made equal, and the facilities afforded to the pastoral interest were also afforded to agricultural.

13. What facilities do you refer to?—I refer to the amended Impounding Act, which gives the grazier an unfair advantage over the agriculturist; I refer to the Lien on Wool Act, which gives the grazier facilities to raise money upon his produce which the agriculturist has not; to the Mortgage on Cattle Act; to a system by which the grazier can, without any time, trouble, or difficulty whatever, and at a mere nominal rent for 640 acres, occupy the Crown lands for pastoral purposes, while the agriculturist is subjected to innumerable difficulties, some of which I have set out in this paper, and is also compelled to buy the land, perhaps at 10l. an acre, as it was in our district the other day.

14. Is there any other information you have to give the committee not included in this paper?—Referring to the 21st question of the committee, I may add that I have grown wheat on the Namoi, in the pastoral district of Liverpool Plains; at ' Burrill '; and have seen it grown successfully, during several years, at ' Baa Au Baa,' the station of the late Sir John Jamison, also on that river. To questions 24 and 43:—that there is a regulation by which holders of land to the extent of 640 acres and upwards, in the settled districts, may, without competition, lease until it is required for sale, three times the

quantity of adjoining Crown land, at 10*s.* per annum for 640 acres; while no such advantage is extended to freeholders of smaller parcels of land than 640 in one block.

---

## *Appendix to the Foregoing Evidence.*

On entering upon the subject under enquiry by the committee, it is my purpose to assume that the state of agriculture in general, and of wheat culture in particular, in the colony is exceedingly unsatisfactory, and, if not absolutely declining instead of progressing, is at least so with reference to population. Because, on the one hand, I conceive that an elaborate exposition of facts, proving such to be the case, would be considered a work of supererogation : and, on the other hand, that should proof be required, it is to be found in the public statistics of the colony on the subject, and certainly can be obtained with greater accuracy and facility in the city than in a country district.

In considering the other branches of the matter, while promising not to be unnecessarily discursive, I hope I may be excused if I should require to travel out of the circle which the resolution of the Council, under which the Committee sits, may seem strictly to imply.

The causes of hindrance or failure of agriculture generally, and of the raising of wheat in particular, I take to be first and greatest, that for many years the policy of the Government of the colony, whatever may have been its object, has unquestionably tended not only to check the formation of new agricultural establishments but to depress existing ones.

While the agriculturist has been absolutely excluded from leasing any portion of the public land, and thwarted, harassed, and dispirited at every turn in his efforts to obtain the submittal of such lands to sale, and subjected to public competition at auction before suffered even then to purchase, the grazier has been allowed to use them under a system of leases, affording him the greatest possible facility of possession, and at the lowest imaginable rental, namely, at the rate of 10s. per annum for 640 acres, with the right, in an overwhelming majority of cases, to purchase choice spots therefrom, without the slightest delay or trouble, and at the lowest legal price, namely, 20s. per acre, and absolutely without competition.

Some of the difficulties above alluded to as attending the purchase of a farm from the Crown, by any other than the favoured pastoral class, may be stated thus:—The person seeking to do so must first make his selection—a matter not very easy of attainment—for persons holding land in a neighbourhood, instead of helping with information, almost invariably place every possible obstacle in the way of the new comer. The selection made, the next step to be taken is to apply by letter to the Surveyor-General to have it measured. Shortly thereafter that officer will reply and inform the writer that his application has been received and submitted to the District Surveyor for his report as to whether the land is fit for agriculture, &c., &c.,[1] and that when it is received the Surveyor-General will communicate the result, intimating at the same time that, should the District Surveyor consider the land suitable for agriculture, and should there be no other difficulty, such as its being held under a squatting lease, or any of several others, it will be submitted to sale by auction. The applicant may now expect to hear no more of the land for three or four months, when, if all goes on favourably, he will be informed that the District Surveyor, having reported satisfactorily, has received from the Surveyor-General instructions to measure it. Now another wearying delay of several months' duration will in all probability occur, before the expiration of which, if the applicant is not a person possessed of considerable determination of character, he will abandon, in despair, all hope of ever becoming an Australian farmer, and help to swell one or other of our overgrown towns, by accepting employment there. If, however, he possess sufficient perseverance, he may visit the District Surveyor, and probably learn from him that the land

---

[1] The grazier is subjected to no such delays; the Government leaves him to be the best judge whether the land is suitable for him or not.

cannot then be measured because the district under that officer is so very large that it would be highly inconvenient for him to move from one portion of it to another to measure a single farm; that when several are applied for in the same vicinity, he will proceed there; in the meantime he has several months' work where he is; or the District Surveyor may, after express-ing sympathy for the applicant's loss from delay, candidly assure him that, in consequence of the great delay in receiving pay for his public work, he is absolutely necessitated to accept private employment in order to obtain sufficient cash to keep himself and party of four men on until the Government make him his remittance, now three or four months due.

These and other preliminary difficulties the applicant must prepare to encounter; but, even when all are surmounted and the land measured, there will be two or three months' delay—in all probability eighteen months or two years from the date of the first application—before it is offered for sale. Then, at last, the applicant will obtain his land if he is fortunate enough to escape the determined opposition of some wealthy person in the neighbourhood, or has money enough and determination enough to purchase it, that opposition notwithstanding.

Calculated, on the one hand, to depress the agriculturist, and on the other to foster the grazier, as the particulars which I have mentioned connected with the administration of the public lands must be admitted to be, they are by no means the only disabilities which the farmer is by our laws placed under when compared with the latter.

That such a law as that at present in force for the regula-tion of the impounding of cattle could possibly be carried through the Legislative Council and assented to by the Governor of the colony, I take to be proof positive that the interests, and not only the interests but the absolute rights of the agricultural class, have been, by the policy of our Govern-ment, completely ignored.

I allude particularly to the amended Impounding Act which was passed for the purpose of providing an additional charge besides that for trespass, by making legal one for *driving cattle* that may have trespassed upon land held from the Crown under a pastoral lease—land which it would be illegal, under another law, to raise agricultural produce upon. Under that Act as much as 5s. and even 7s. 6d. per head *for driving* cattle to the pound, is frequently exacted throughout the colony by holders of pastoral leases.

No such provision is extended to the occupier of freehold land—the land upon which the country depends for agricultural produce. It matters not that he may have paid 10l., 20l., or even 30l. per acre to the Crown for the land he farms, or even a much higher price to a private individual, or that he is paying an exorbitant rent for it, he can make no corresponding charge upon the cattle of his Crown leaseholding neighbour, should they trespass upon his farm; and this entirely irrespective of the distance the different classes of land may be from the pound. It may be that the freehold land is situated many miles further from the pound than the land held under pastoral lease—still the rule applies.

The holder of a Crown pastoral lease may charge 5s., 7s., or more per head for driving the trespassing cattle of the freeholder to the pound, but the freeholder can make no such charge, under any circumstances, for driving the trespassing cattle of the Crown pastoral leaseholder to the pound.

I do not think it necessary to allude to more than one other proof that the acts of our Legislature and the policy of our Government have tended to depress agriculture. Laws have been enacted to facilitate the grazier through a simple and inexpensive instrument to obtain loans in anticipation of his coming produce, while no such aid has been extended to the agriculturist.

Like that of most other countries, the enterprise of the colony is mainly carried out with borrowed means by active and intelligent men of inconsiderable capital, and the effect of the 'Lien on Wool Act' and the 'Mortgage on Cattle Act' has been to allure such men into pastoral rather than into agricultural pursuits.

That such has been the case must be obvious, when it is

considered that the main difficulty to his success, which first strikes the mind of a farmer on entering upon agricultural pursuits in this colony, is not, how shall I get my land cultivated, and my crops in the ground?—for this may be done extensively, at comparatively inconsiderable expense—but how shall I find means to carry me through the reaping, housing, thrashing, and conveying of them to market?

He dare not invest all, or nearly all, his capital in the first operation, but must reserve at least two-thirds of it to enable him to *secure* his crops after they are grown.

The grazier with small capital need fear no such difficulty. He may not only invest all his available capital with safety in a pastoral establishment, but by the aid of the 'Mortgage on Stock Act' may make a purchase to the extent of double its amount—a course pursued at two-thirds of the stock sales in the colony. He may also, when his shearing is approaching, grant to any party who will lend him money to shear his sheep and bring their produce to market a preferable claim upon his wool to the extent of the money thus borrowed—a course pursued in hundreds of cases annually.

It may, and, doubtless, will be said, as a reason why a measure of the same character as the 'Lien on Wool Act' has not been extended to agricultural produce, that the agricultural pursuits of the country are, in consequence of the frequent occurrence of droughts, less sure of yielding their produce than pastoral pursuits, and that hence the security in the former case would not be so good as that in the latter. Without admitting the correctness of the allegations, I beg to submit that, even assuming such to be the case, it is a consideration which, however proper to be taken into account by the capitalist in calculating the rate of interest he ought to demand from the borrower, to cover his risk, &c., cannot possibly touch the principle raised in the question—Should a farmer, who has a crop of wheat ready to reap, and has not sufficient capital of his own, be allowed to borrow funds for the purpose, and to bring the wheat to market, and grant a *preferable lien* on the same, to secure the repayment of the advance?

If it is a fact that the agricultural interests of the country
are subjected to more climatic difficulties than are the pastoral
interests, I take it that that circumstance cannot, properly, be
brought forward as a reason why the agricultural interest should
not, under our laws, have a fair field and no favour, as compared
with the pastoral interest, in entering the market to borrow
money, in times of doubt and general want of confidence in
monetary matters.   If the agriculturist, in borrowing money to
secure his crop, has to encounter a higher rate of interest than
the grazier has to encounter, in consequence of the risk of
damage to his crops, from an unfavourable season, being greater
than the same in the case of the produce of the grazier, surely
that is no reason why he should be compelled to submit to a
still greater increase of interest, to compensate the capitalist for
the additional risk of the borrower's insolvency before the crops
are realised, especially when the grazier is, through the aid of
the 'Lien on Wool Act,' exempted from paying for such
risk.

An advocate of protection would find, in the increased difficulties which our climate is supposed to place in the way of the
agriculturist, a reason why he should have peculiar privileges
extended to him ; but I have no wish to ask for the cultivator of
the soil anything more than 'a fair field and no favour.'

It may not be out of place here to point out that, previous
to the passing of the ' Lien on Wool Act,' the pastoral interest
was all but defunct, certainly in a more advanced state of de-
cadence than the agricultural interest is at the present time,
and that it is admitted, on every hand, that the ' Lien on Wool
Act ' saved that interest.   I confess that I have never been able
to appreciate the strong objection which some persons have to
the principle of that Act.   It appears to me that if loans ought
to be accepted at all, the least objectionable system, that they can
be transacted under, is that which provides material pledges for
their repayment.

As to the policy of facilitating loans of the class contemplated, I take it that, let the produce to be saved thereby be of
what kind soever, it is an unmitigated benefit to the borrower,

to the lender, and to the country, that means should be furnished to secure it. The *registry* of the pledge is a complete guarantee against a dishonest and plausible man imposing upon several credulous persons by promising each his crop, and taking advances from all on the faith thereof. Besides, in practice, during the ten or eleven years that the ' Lien on Wool Act ' has been in force, it has much tended to develop the resources of the country, and has, at the same time, proved a preventative to the perpetration of the frauds I have described.

Showing the advantage such a measure would be to the farmer with small means, I will mention a case, among many that have lately come under my observation. A tenant farmer in this district, in order to raise money to pay for gathering and bringing his wheat to market, actually submitted to a loss of 50 per cent. for the accommodation of a cash advance, and that at a time when, if he could have granted a preferable lien to secure the same, he would readily have obtained the money at 8 or 10 per cent.

The absence of a law of the kind, and the necessity of quick returns, have, in many instances, prompted the cultivation of lucerne hay, which yields five or six cuts in a year, instead of wheat, which can only be made available at one season.

The precedent relied upon by the proposer of the ' Lien on Wool Act ' was a West Indian Act, to enable planters to borrow money to aid them in bringing forward their crops, and to grant preferable security on the same for its repayment. There can be no question that wheat or maize culture in this country bears greater analogy to sugar-cane culture in the West Indies than wool-growing in this country does to the same. At any rate, the principle of the measure is either good or it is bad ; if good, it ought to be extended to every class that requires it ; if bad, it should be abolished altogether.

The effects of the policy of the Government, which I have described, may be found, on the one hand, in the fact, that the number of persons who have been bred to agricultural pursuits, at present residing in the towns of the colony, is, beyond example, excessive, showing our social condition, in that regard, to be in a most unsatisfactory state; and, on the other hand, in the other fact, that the wholesale price of flour in the Colony is three times higher, per pound, than the wholesale price of animal food, of the very best description—a state of things not to be found in any other civilised country.

I am aware that the deficiency of agriculture, which is so remarkable in this country, is attributed to the aridity of the climate, by many gentlemen whose experience entitles their opinions to respect; but, as I have during the eighteen years last past annually cultivated and sown with wheat a large quantity of land, in various parts of the Upper Hunter District—a district generally considered to be unfavourable for the purpose —and have, in that long period, only failed twice in obtaining crops, and have reaped two self-sown, which, in a great measure, compensated for even their loss, I can come to no other conclusion than that, whatever may be the disadvantages of the climate, they are not sufficient to cause such neglect of agriculture as has occurred.

I think that if agriculturists would, where practicable, sow sufficient land with wheat to suffice their requirements, not only for grain but for hay, instead of sowing oats or lucerne for the latter, and would sow equal portions thereof in each year, on the 1st of April, the 1st May, the 1st June, and the 1st of July, or as near to those dates as there may be moisture in the land, instead of sowing all they intend to sow at once, as is usual, they would, by selecting for hay the least promising portion, seldom fail in housing a good average of grain, as well as a crop of hay.

Hot winds—the great enemy of the wheat-grower—are most injurious to a crop at the stage immediately preceding the bursting forth of the ear; therefore, as it is impossible to tell when they will come, it is only prudent to avoid risking on one chance all hope of grain for the year, by providing that all shall not be in that stage at the same time. For example; in 1849, my wheat sown on the 1st of April yielded upwards of forty bushels to the acre, that sown in May and June eighteen bushels, and that in July six bushels. The cause of the great difference was. that when the hot winds and dry weather came, the early wheat was out of danger. the two next lots were in ear, and, therefore, could only lose in quality and quantity by being 'pinched,' but the lot sown in July was caught when the ear was bursting from its wrapper, and was, consequently, all but destroyed; however, the average of the whole was a good one.

The season was different in 1851; the wheat sown in April yielded but five or six bushels to the acre, that sown in May and June twelve bushels to the acre, and that in July upwards of forty-two bushels to the acre—in all a fair yield. In that year the hot winds came in September, just as the early wheat was coming in ear, and destroyed it; the middle crops did not suffer so much, and the late crop scarcely suffered at all, and was brought to an abundant issue, by the timely rains which fell in November.

It will be observed, that one of the seasons I have mentioned was previous to the gold discovery, and the other before the increase in the consumption of hay, which followed that event, had become perceptible; therefore, at either period it would have been useless to make hay of the inferior portion of the crop. Now, the case is different; the demand for hay is so great, that, in a majority of cases, where wheat crops are thought to be unlikely to pay as grain, they can be profitably converted into hay.

Connected with the climate, another cause of hindrance of agriculture was recently mentioned in Council by Mr. James Macarthur. namely, the difficulty of preventing the ravages of weevil and fly, after the crop is housed. Without making the slightest pretension to scientific knowledge. I will communicate a simple and inexpensive means whereby I have, for many years. preserved my crops from injury from those insects. If, for a few nights before building a stack, precaution is taken to hurdle a flock of sheep on its intended site, or, that being inconvenient, if a few cartloads of sheep manure are laid there, and sprinkled with urine, there will be no danger of weevil or fly. The ammonia that will be generated in either case will keep both away. I may add, that my friend, Mr. Robert Meston, to whom

I communicated my plan for preserving wheat from weevil and fly, made some experiments, in Sydney, by which, I believe, he found that carbonate of ammonia may be used with advantage for the purpose. However, I merely state the fact that sheep manure is an effectual remedy, and leave the duty of further examination to those whose habit of thought is suitable for the enquiry.

On the whole, I am confident that the difficulties placed in the way of agriculture by the climate are as nothing compared with the overwhelming obstacles furnished by the policy of the Legislature and Government of the colony.

In urging upon the committee the expediency, as well as the justice, of extending to the operations of the agriculturist, wherever practicable, equal facilities to those enjoyed by the grazier. I hope my views may not be considered hostile to the pastoral interest. It appears to me that it can never be the real interest of the grazier to depress and drive out the farmer ; one interest should support the other, for complete prosperity can never reach either until both are in a satisfactory state ; certainly I can have no motive to foster their antagonism, as my property is invested in about equal proportions in each interest, and I have laboured, during many years—if not wisely or well, at least zealously—for the advancement of both interests.

Before concluding this communication, I cannot resist the opportunity it affords to place on record my opinion, that, even should all other means fail of providing the country with an ample supply of agricultural produce, a remedy may be found, by allowing any person to enter upon and occupy 80 acres of waste land, without competition or delay, and pay for it, at the upset price, four years thereafter ; provided that he clears and cultivates 10 acres the first year, and ten additional acres in each of the three succeeding years, and is at the end of the time residing on the spot.

John Robertson.

Yarrundi, August 6, 1855.

In 1855 that portion of Australia now constituting

the territory of Queensland was, as I have had occasion
to explain, part of New South Wales. The district of
Port Curtis, in consequence of its distance from the
seat of Government, was honoured by the appointment
of a Government Resident—a kind of deputy-governor
—and, as nearly always happens in such cases, all kinds
of complaints were made against the luckless functionary,
though he had through life borne an honourable
reputation. I was induced by representations made to
me of the petty abuses of authority of this officer to
move for a committee 'to enquire into, and report
upon, the establishment and working of the office.'
The committee held eight meetings and examined
fourteen witnesses, including the Government Resident
himself. I am afraid the result of the enquiry was not
worth our labours. The Report I was authorised to
bring up stated :—

A careful consideration of the evidence leads your committee
to the conclusions expressed in the following propositions :—

1. That the creation of the office of Government Resident at
   Port Curtis by Sir Charles FitzRoy was an error, which
   has already involved the colony in a loss of several
   thousand pounds, without any determinable public
   benefit.

2. That the gentleman appointed to the office was not
   peculiarly fitted for performing its duties, so as to
   promote the objects of the Settlement.

3. That the appointment of a Police Magistrate to the Town-
   ship of Gladstone would be a sufficient provision for
   securing the ends of justice, and the preservation of
   order at Port Curtis, under present circumstances.

4. That, supposing this change were immediately effected,

the capabilities of the District would have an equal chance of development, and the progress of the Port would be in no respect retarded.

Another enquiry by a Select Committee which I obtained in those early days was 'to enquire into all the circumstances connected with the unauthorised expenditure, by His Excellency the Governor, of the sum of 14,000l. and upwards, in the erection of that portion of the Semi-Circular Quay extending from the east side of the Tank Stream to Campbell's Wharf;—and the stability of the work; and to report thereon to the House.' Undoubtedly a serious expenditure had been met in a manner quite unauthorised, and there were good grounds for believing that the work was bad. The Report of the Committee concluded in the following terms :—

If this expenditure were to receive the sanction of a simple vote of your Honourable House, it would establish a precedent highly inimical to the powers of the future Legislative Assembly ; and, to guard against any such mischievous consequences, your committee are of opinion that the question ought not to be entertained, except on the introduction of a Bill of Indemnity by the Government.

Your committee are further of opinion, that the great and manifest injury sustained by the public in this instance, by bad work on the part of the contractor, may render it a question of grave consideration for the Government, whether this gentleman ought to be entrusted with the construction of any of the public works of the colony.

As the evidence of Mr. Rowntree and Mr. Russell leads to the conclusion that timber of the size and in the quantities required by the specification, and paid for, has not been used by the contractor, and that he has been overpaid, your committee are of opinion, that it is the duty of the Government immediately to institute a full enquiry into the facts of the case, and to direct the Attorney-General to take prompt measures for recovering any sums which may have been improperly overpaid, as well as compensation, by way of damages, for any work that may have been improperly performed.

Looking back upon my entrance upon the stage of Parliamentary life, I think it must be admitted that I was not idle. I at once entered into the work with an astonishing amount of zeal. Sitting up all night was a recreation to me. I did not know what weariness could mean. I would leave the Council when it adjourned and go to the 'Empire' Office, where I would remain until daylight. Day and night I was at work. Very often I was thirty-six and forty-eight hours without going to bed. I believe in those days I could have gone into the fire

> As blithely as the golden-girdled bee
> Sucks in the poppy's sleepy flame,

for the sake of my convictions. I must have been made of the stuff of martyrs. But the great gain to me in those two sessions of hard work in the old Council was that I was drilled into the methods of political thought, and brought into intercourse with men who, whatever might be their opinions, had the education and breeding of gentlemen. There were Admiral King, Mr. Alexander Berry, Mr. Icely, Mr. C. D. Riddell, Mr. S. A. Donaldson, Mr. Plunkett, Mr. James Macarthur, and the Speaker, Dr. Nicholson (as we familiarly called him before the baronetcy), who, though they held no opinion in common with me, were

always affable and kind. From Mr. James Martin
(then in the dawn of his manhood) I learnt much.
Not that I professed to learn or he to teach; but I had
already cultivated the habit (quite unsuspected, I
believe) of turning rebuke, ridicule, or condemnation to
good account; I do not think I ever shut out a wise
word because it came from an enemy. Mr. Martin was
not an enemy, but he was a very self-sufficient man,
with an absurd contempt for persons who did not agree
with him. He had fine generous qualities, in spite of
his efforts to imitate the rich and privileged, and, quite
unsuspected by himself, I carried off many a bit of
wisdom from his denunciatory conversations.

All this time my personal influence was spreading
and strengthening among the people. I had committed
no serious fault; I had the appearance of a young man,
though I was thirty-nine years of age; I spoke out
boldly what I thought, which people liked; and I did
not think my manner was offensive or pretentious. I
made friends rapidly, probably because I did not care
about making them.

As the old Council came to the day of its last meeting, I began to think that I could not go on attending
as I had done with such scrupulous zeal to the business
of legislation and to the management of a daily newspaper. From the first I had laid it down as a rule of
conduct not to accept any public position unless I was
prepared to discharge the duties belonging to it. I
have never been an alderman. I have always declined
to act on committees of public institutions to which I
have been elected as a compliment. Though my name

as Minister has been appended to the appointment of
thousands of magistrates, I have never consented to be
a magistrate myself. As a member of the Legislative
Council of 1854 and 1855, I made a point of being
always in my place when the Speaker took the chair,
and of remaining until the House adjourned. I voted
in every division of the House, and I regularly attended
the meetings of all committees. Without consulting
anyone and without any break in my activity, having
made up my mind to retire, I addressed the following
letter to the electors of Sydney :—

Gentlemen,—In the course of the ensuing week, the Legislature, to which you did me the honour of electing me by an
unprecedented majority of your votes, will virtually terminate
its existence, and its actual dissolution cannot be very long
delayed. It seems to me, therefore, that the time has arrived
when I ought to inform you of my intention not to present
myself again among the candidates for your suffrages.

During the two laborious sessions of my service as your
representative I have felt the conviction gaining strength in
despite, as I freely own, of some feeling of ambition, that
neither my time nor whatever humble ability I might possess
could be sufficiently subjected to my will to enable me to discharge the high and responsible trust reposed in me with that
uniform devotion to the public interest which is implied in its
acceptance. Though I have generally been in my place, I have
attended the sittings by wrenching myself, as it were, away
from other duties of an equally serious nature, which often left
me wholly unprepared for the business of the Council: and in
the part I have taken there I have never felt conscious of any
success to satisfy my sense of what is due from the Representative to his Constituents. While feeling all this, I have also felt
that the distinction conferred by your votes is the greatest within
the reach of the servants of the people, and should only be

enjoyed in association with the most efficient performance of public duty. Besides, the obligations of the trust are sacred, as covering momentous consequences to society, and neglect, as well as wilful violation of those obligations, must be positively sinful in proportion to the injury thereby inflicted upon our fellow-creatures. It is not, then, that I lightly value the post of your Representative, but because I am sensible of my inability to occupy it with advantage to the country, that I desire to give place to another, and, as I sincerely hope, a better man.

I am aware that, by taking this course now, I lay myself open to the taunt, in some quarters, of declining that which might never be offered; and I freely admit I have no reason to expect that I should be invited to stand a contest for your representation in the new Parliament. But I would rather incur this risk of ridicule than silently allow any trouble to be taken on my behalf by those from whom I have received such uniform kindness and so many marks of confidence.

The great change about to take place in our form of Government will, we all hope, be accompanied by vigour and enlightenment in the administration of affairs, diffusing the blessings of constitutional liberty through all classes and interests of the country. Outside the walls of the Legislative Assembly, it may yet be my privilege to assist in bringing about so desirable a consummation. In making up my mind to stay outside, I have had to conquer a strong feeling which my better judgment has told me ought not to be gratified; but the self-denial has been sweetened by the knowledge that I have before me another field, fairly won by my own efforts, for future usefulness. I leave the Legislature, as I entered it, from a sense of duty alone. You opened the door for me against singular obstacles. I cheerfully close it with my own hand.

If I am too poor to make the sacrifices incumbent on a Representative of the People, I am at least too proud to accept the honour and neglect the duties of that noble office.

I remain, Gentlemen,

Your very faithful Servant,

HENRY PARKES.

Sydney, December 8, 1855.

Like many other men under similar circumstances,
I did not adhere to my decision.   I met with no one
who approved of it;  and a month afterwards, on
January 7, at a public meeting of citizens convened for
the purpose of 'nominating four gentlemen as fit and
proper persons to represent the city in the new Parliament,' I was selected as one of the candidates, and a
week later, under pressure from all sides, I consented
to stand.   The result of the poll in that first election to
the new Parliament was as stated below :—

| | | | |
|---|---|---|---|
| Charles Cowper | . | . | . 3,075 ⎫ |
| Henry Parkes . | . | . | . 3,057 ⎪ Elected |
| Robert Campbell | . | . | . 3,041 ⎪ |
| J. R. Wilshire . | . | . | . 2,091 ⎭ |
| J. H. Plunkett | . | . | . 2,800 |

I am now the only man of the five who is still
living.

# CHAPTER IV

I SUPPOSE all men of average human capacity are more or less conscious of their own faults. I believe my cardinal fault through all the days of my physical strength has been precipitate zeal. If a thing of hazard had to be done, I was always ready to do it. It was this quality of my nature which impelled me to enter upon the career of a journalist. I had no practical experience in journalism; knew nothing of the printing business: and I was never reputed to be a man of good business capacity. But my personal reputation stood high, and my energies knew no limit. Though thirty-five years of age, I had never been sued in a court of law or involved in any serious dispute; and in all my personal relations I believe I stood well with my neighbours. My first appearance in the courts was as defendant in an action for libel, not long after my start as proprietor and editor of 'The Empire,' and all my personal troubles date from that, to me, unfortunate enterprise.

A public organ was wanted by our young party, and I came forward to supply the want; and while no one attempted to dissuade me from the undertaking, I

met with encouragement from nearly all my friends. I
was myself intoxicated with the hard and exciting
mission of a propagandist. It was assigned to me to
create and spread throughout the land a sound and
enlightened public opinion. So I regarded my task.
I looked steadily at the work to be accomplished, and I
never stopped to count the cost.

The first number of 'The Empire' was issued on
December 28, 1850, and the journal announced itself as
an advocate of a wide extension of the franchise, the
reconstruction of the representative system on a population basis, a more comprehensive system of education,
suited to the circumstances of the colony; and it declared against all taxation except such as was necessary
to meet the expenses of Government. The first four
numbers were published weekly, but on Monday, January 20, it appeared as a daily paper, for the first six
months only half the size of the weekly issue, afterwards the full size. At this time there was one daily
paper in Sydney, two or three weekly papers, and not
more than half a dozen papers in the country districts.
'The Empire' had an uphill struggle, but it pushed on;
and in the course of time it collected a staff of excellent
writers, among whom in its earlier years were James
Martin, Daniel Henry Deniehy, Sir Thomas Mitchell,
Edward Butler, Angus Mackay, and others. Very early
in the management I learnt some of the sound rules of
journalism—not to allow persons, under the guise of
contributed articles, to use the paper for their own
purposes; not to allow personal bias to colour the
reports of speeches, to insist upon facts as the basis of

criticism, and to respect the precincts of private life. On the whole, I was fortunate in the gentlemen who were associated with me, and I soon began to revel in the atmosphere of the editor's room.

Circumstances, to be spoken of with greater fulness at a later stage, opened fields for spirit and boldness in the conduct of the paper; and two events of special magnitude brought it into the broad light of day. These were the discovery of gold and the Crimean War. Steam communication with England was a thing talked of; the electric telegraph had no existence in the colony. It was quite a fierce competition—sometimes a work of ingenious strategy—to obtain English news from a sailing ship, which might make a long or a short passage, and whose arrival was a matter of calculation until she hove in sight. 'The Empire' had a whaleboat with a crew of four picked oarsmen, besides the reporter, which often went miles out to sea to meet an expected ship. By this kind of adventurous competition, and by other means, we were in the majority of cases the first to publish the news. There would be a crowd of many hundreds waiting in the street before the office for 'The Empire' 'extraordinaries.' There were occasions of much excitement all through the period of the war with Russia. At this time I had been elected to the Legislative Council. One of the nominee members was the late Mr. Broadhurst, a well-known barrister of the period, who was as eminent for his wit as for his law. I was on one occasion in the library watching the flagstaff from the window, expecting to see the signals hoisted for a ship from London. Mr. Broadhurst came in from the Chamber, where a heavy debate was going on. 'How is this,' said he, 'not listening to your colleague?' (the member speaking). I simply replied, 'I am watching for the ship signals.' 'Oh,' said he, 'I see your attention is flagging.

In respect to the gold discoveries, Mr. Edward Hammond Hargraves made his first revelations in our office, when they came, as it were, from a region of dimness and uncertainty, at the time when Mr. Wentworth foretold all kinds of ruin and disaster among the consequences. 'The Empire' was the first journal to send a 'special commissioner' to the goldfields, the person chosen being Mr. Angus Mackay, afterwards Minister for Mines in Victoria. Altogether the new elements of interest and excitement arising from these pregnant events gave a great impetus to 'The Empire.'

A serious economic difficulty in the management of 'The Empire' arose from the gold discoveries. The wild and sudden rushes to the goldfields were contagious among printers as well as among others, and wages rapidly increased until compositors could earn 10*l.* to 12*l.* a week. High wages nearly always have a vicious effect on the worst portion of those who are the recipients. Men of a reckless disposition and of irregular habits seem to take an inexplicable delight in embarrassing their employers, and in too many instances the better disposed weakly yield to their insidious influence. With money in their pockets and many demands for their services, they love to make their independence disagreeably felt. If they are urgently wanted at their post, for that very reason they will absent themselves. I hope I make it quite plain that I do not include the respectable portion—the large majority—of the artizan class in this description. In my case they combined in the following manner. One Saturday evening the compositors held a meeting among themselves, a 'Chapel,' as the trade term expresses it, and passed a resolution to the effect that my non-compliance with their demand for an increased price for one particular kind of work was equivalent to dismissal, and they accepted it as such. On this resolution being presented to me I sent for the men, who came into my office to the number of seventeen. I expostulated with them on the unreasonableness of their conduct, explained that I was acting under the advice of my overseer, who was a practical and an experienced member of their own craft, and that it was a rule in the office, both on the part of the employer and employed, to give a fortnight's notice in terminating their employment. I further reminded them that some of them were under a specific agreement for three months, and that their passages from another colony had been paid by me. Finally, I offered to withdraw from the paper altogether the particular work in dispute, which did not amount to more than 2s. to 3s. in each case, or, as an alternative, I offered to abide by the decision of a general meeting of the trade, and if it was against me, to pay the amounts which had been withheld. After all this the men came in for their wages, and, on paying them, I argued the case over again with each individually, but to no purpose. They persisted in refusing

to bring out the paper on Monday morning, which, in
the state of things then prevailing—the impossibility
of supplying their places—threatened absolute ruin to
me. I had, however, some means of averting the worst
consequences. Some of my reporters were compositors
by trade, I knew one or two gentlemen in other callings
who were compositors, and I had some smart lads as
apprentices. By the zealous help of this rather motley
group of emergency hands the paper duly appeared,
though reduced to half its usual size. On the Monday
I applied for warrants against the whole of the seventeen
men for conspiracy, which were issued; the men were
arrested, and committed to take their trial for the
offence. They were all admitted to bail, I myself
becoming bail for one of them. In due course they
were tried before the Chief Justice (Sir Alfred Stephen)
and Mr. Justice Therry, and convicted, all but four
receiving sentences of imprisonment varying from one
week to six weeks. The four others, in consideration
of their slight participation in the proceeding, and their
good conduct, were sentenced to a nominal imprisonment—namely, until one o'clock the next day.

This painful episode in my life as a journalist has
very often been brought forward in exaggerated
form to injure me in public estimation, but I do not
think I have ever suffered from such attacks. In less
than three months after the occurrence I became a
candidate for the representation of Sydney in the Legislature, and my infamous conduct in 'imprisoning the
printers' was posted everywhere on the walls of the
city; but I was elected by nearly two to one, and I

know that some of the men themselves gave me their
votes. In justice to myself I give one passage from my
evidence before the police magistrate (Mr. J. S. Dowling)
when the men were committed, omitting the names,
except that of my overseer, Mr. M·Kelly. I am thus
reported :—

I drew their particular attention to the fact that I did not
dispute the justice of their claims on my own judgment, but if
they could convince me that it was right I would pay it. They
then went away, and held another meeting. I waited until
they had done, and then they came up to be paid; I was there
till ten o'clock that Saturday night; they all came to be paid
with the exception of two. I spoke to them all individually as
I paid them; to ——, who came first, at some length; this is
one of the men engaged at Port Phillip, whose passage I had
paid from thence to Sydney; he had only been with me one
week, so I asked him if he was going to leave me in this
manner; he said he was under no agreement to stop, and he
should certainly leave. I then asked him if he thought he was
using me rightly by so doing; he shook his head, and said he
could not help it. I then asked him if he thought he was
justified in leaving without giving a fortnight's notice, as was
the usual custom in the trade. He said, ' Yes; on an occasion
like this he would do as the others did.' He then went away,
and has not since returned or offered to return to his work.
The next man was —— ; he said he was very sorry, he liked the
establishment very well, and also liked Mr. M·Kelly, the overseer.
I asked him if he was going to leave; he said he must do as
the others did. Mr. M·Kelly was present at this time. I made
similar enquiries of all as I paid them. ——, whose passage I
had paid from Port Phillip, said he wished to give me a fortnight's notice, as he thought of going to the ' Herald.' I said,
' Very well; will your three months be up then?' He replied,
' About it.' Knowing that his time had nearly expired, I took
his word as correct, and merely added that I was sorry he was

going, but could not expect anything more than a fortnight's notice; when, to my surprise, he said, 'But, as the others are going, I must also leave now.' I then said, 'What! Give me a fortnight's notice, and then leave instantly?' and he said, 'Yes, as the others are going, I will go with them.' I spoke to ——, for whom I felt some respect, and asked him if he was going. He said he was sorry, but he must do as the others did. I also spoke to ——, and I reminded him that a similar combination of the trade had prevented him from earning his bread in Melbourne, for he had informed me when I first engaged him that at Melbourne they would not allow him to work in any office, because he could not show his indentures. I engaged him in consequence of the earnest solicitations of his sister, who had been a fellow-passenger with me some years since. I reminded him of all these things and he said he could not help it, he must go. I spoke to ——, and Mr. M'Kelly reminded him of his distinct agreement to serve three months; he said he would not work unless the extra money was paid. I spoke to others, generally in the same way, who gave me similar answers, and several gave me to understand that they were satisfied with the office generally. They all left, none returned to their work, and I ascertained afterwards that they did not intend to come back.

The Attorney-General (Mr. J. H. Plunkett), who prosecuted, said, in opening the case :—

The public, he contended, was indebted to Mr. Parkes, the proprietor of 'The Empire,' for the stand which he had made against the attempt of the defendants, as nothing could be more detrimental to the interests of society than that such proceedings should be tolerated. It was the business of the Court and Jury in the present instance, by determining with an impartial mind between employer and employed, to establish a precedent which would be a guide for the future in similar cases. If a case had occurred wherein a number of employers had assembled together, and at once proceeded to dismiss those

in their employ, throwing them on society, and suddenly depriving them of the means of procuring bread for their families,
it would have been equally the business of the Public Prosecutor to institute rigorous proceedings.  On the other hand, it
was impossible that the business of the colony could be carried
on if the employed were allowed to meet together, as it appeared the defendants had done, and pass a resolution that
unless the conditions which they might choose to name were
complied with, they would leave off work at once.

And again he said :—

From what he had seen and heard of the case, he was of
opinion that the prosecutor had evinced all through a spirit of
the greatest liberality, and had shown himself even willing to
waive in a great degree his own rights in order to prevent the
course which the defendants had adopted.

In passing sentence, Mr. Justice Therry thus characterised the case :—

There were many modes in which the claim, if a just one,
might have been enforced ; and it is impossible to hear the
evidence of Mr. Parkes without acknowledging that the proposals he made for settling the matter were most reasonable
and just, and such as every honest man must have been satisfied
with.

And at a later stage in his summing up :—

If he had been a timid man, or one who regarded pecuniary profit in preference to the performance of a public duty,
it would have been Mr. Parkes's manifest interest to have
acquiesced in the demand, for the increase asked of him did
not exceed 1*l*. 15*s*. per cent. on the whole work ; but if he had
succumbed in this instance, in what instance could he afterwards have resisted a similar demand ?  If he had recognised
the right of the men to charge for any other description of
work whatever sum they thought proper, with what consistency

could he afterwards have attempted to shake off a tyranny to which he had once submitted, or resist their dictation to him at all future times, after he had once set up a precedent admitting their right to regulate and control his expenditure? He asked for a reason for this resolution. The defendants were silent, and refused to give any, and then forthwith proceeded—by substituting a menace to ruin him, for the reason the defendants refused to supply—to carry out their organised and preconcerted plan of going away if their wages were not raised.

The conduct of the compositors on 'The Empire' naturally compelled me to think of what might arise at any stage in the future. Not only had the men disregarded the usage of the trade which they would have expected me rigidly to observe, and all reasonable considerations between man and man, but some who were under specific engagements had deliberately broken them, while others, who admitted that they had nothing to complain of, nevertheless joined the plotters; and they had thus banded themselves together apparently to destroy me, without giving me an hour's notice. I at once determined to protect myself as I best could from a second inroad of this unreasoning selfishness. I was aware that in Madras there was a class of men known as Eurasians, the sons of European fathers and Asiatic mothers, many of whom had been brought up to the printing trade. I immediately sent an authority to Madras to engage twenty-five to thirty of these Eurasian compositors for 'The Empire.' I did not seek a reduction of wages, but only a certainty of the work required being done. The agreement authorised to be entered into on my behalf with the men was for a term of years at 4*l*. a week; and an eminent Judge of the Supreme Court of Madras, Sir William Burton, very considerately undertook to look after the interests of the men in their engagements. Not being sure that I could obtain compositors at Madras (there was no electric telegraph), I at the same time wrote to my London agents to engage ten English compositors. In due course the new hands arrived both from India and from England. My special object in sending to Madras was that, if the men could be obtained at all, they could be obtained in much shorter time.

I deem it necessary to explain these transactions as being among the consequences of the reckless strike of 'The Empire' printers. I was quite prepared for the odium which a class would seek to fix upon me, and for the use which my political opponents would make of my conduct in the matter; but I have never felt that my reputation suffered at any time from these attacks. The working-men of the colony could easily discriminate between my case and the wholesale importation of Indian coolies or South Sea Islanders at a nominal rate of wages, with the avowed object of escaping from the burden of free labour. No one can more sincerely regret than I do the origin of these unfortunate proceedings in connection with 'The Empire.'

It will hardly surprise the reader of these chapters that I often got into conflict with the law of libel, and looking back now, I am myself surprised that my afflictions in that way were so few. I held the opinion that timidity was one of the worst qualities in a public journal, and I cannot call to mind the occasion when any such charge was brought against 'The Empire.' The

gentlemen associated with me did not need much encouragement to write boldly, and there was no scarcity
of subjects for animadversion. Though I should be
sorry to defend everything that was written in 'The
Empire,' I still hold that in those times, when the country was passing from the Old to the New, a fearless
journal performed a public service which can scarcely
be over-estimated. From 1853 to 1857, all through
the throes of constitutional birth, 'The Empire' was a
powerful organ of Liberalism, and a well-arranged newspaper. Its reports were full and accurate; its news
columns generally had the attraction of life and fresh-
ness; and the medium through which it spoke its
opinions was seldom wanting in vigour.

During these days Mr. Edward Wilson presided
over 'The Argus' (Melbourne) and he and I became
friends. When he visited Sydney, he was often my
guest, and many an hour we spent in talking over the
prospects of the two papers and the fortunes of the
two colonies. I have before me now a bundle of Mr.
Wilson's letters which are full of interest in their
chatty and discursive comments on men and things
of the period. The colony of Victoria was in its very
infancy, three to five years of age, and the elder colony was passing rapidly through those changes which
gave it political enfranchisement and a vigorous public opinion. Both were still living under the hybrid
constitution of 1850, with the dawn of constitutional
liberty breaking over the new fields of their industrial
life. Edward Wilson was then a Radical of the Radicals, however he may have changed when he retired

from the active work of the colony with a fortune,
to spend his latter days in London clubs and amidst
the historic associations of Hayes, where he lived
his last years, and died. 'The Empire' introduced
me to other remarkable men outside the sphere of
journalism. Edward Smith Hall, in New South Wales,
John Pascoe Fawkner in Victoria, Charles Gavan Duffy,
and several men of much promise who are now nearly
forgotten. Smith Hall was a veteran in the service of
the colony. In the early times of oppression and cruelty,
when there was a severe censorship over the press, he
conducted a paper with marked ability, outspoken
honesty, and courage, for which he suffered more than
once the penalty of imprisonment. He battled bravely
against the high handed proceedings of Governor Darling and against every abuse of power. The name of
his paper, the 'Monitor,' remained with him, and to
the day of his death he was best known as 'Monitor
Hall.' I have had many chats with Mr. Fawkner on
the first settlement of Port Phillip, and, in my own office
in Sydney, on the political prospect before constitutional
government was achieved. He was a shrewd, clear-
sighted man, with fads and whims of his own, which
did not materially qualify the value of his opinion on
public questions. I shall have occasion to speak of Mr.
Charles Gavan Duffy in other chapters.

Nearly all the men who afterwards represented the
newly-formed Liberal Party in the early Ministries were
in the habit of frequenting 'The Empire' Office, and
with some of them I became intimately acquainted. It
is now more than a generation since my journalistic life

closed—closed in absolute ruin to my worldly prospects; and those seven years of continuous labour have remained a blank in my existence. In the midst of other unceasing work I have seldom recalled any circumstance of that period of my past, which, whatever may have been its influence on the progress of the colony, left me nothing but the gleanings of bitterness and regret. In my family and among my friends the name of 'The Empire' has been a forbidden word. Looking back to it now, and to the desperate efforts which had to be made throughout the agony of all industrial operations which followed the gold discovery, I recollect going home on the summer mornings when the sun was in the sky, and returning after three or four hours of sleep; and I recollect days and nights together without sleep at all.

But 'The Empire' did its work—on the whole an heroic work—for New South Wales and for Australia. Beyond doubt it created the first distinct party with a Liberal creed and the means of vigorous action. A strenuous public opinion, embodying the most advanced views of the leaders of thought in England, took root in the land, threw up a rapid growth and spread widely. Nearly all the generous actors in that first Liberal movement are now in their graves. Among the later writers in 'The Empire' were Charles Gavan Duffy, the Rev. B. Quaife, and T. L. Bright, and they sustained its power and influence to the last.

The enterprise of 'The Empire' awakened an appetite for newspaper reading among the people, and stirred into a new activity those already engaged in journalism. The only other daily paper in the colony put out fresh energies and recast its organisation; and under the direction of the Hon. John Fairfax, a gentleman of clear discernment and strong character, it went through a succession of literary and mechanical improvements which made it twenty years ago—what it continues to be to-day—the first journal in New South Wales, if not the first in Australia. While this effect was produced in the Metropolis, newspapers began to multiply in the interior, and soon nearly every country town had its organ of political opinion. The newspaper press at the present time is a powerful institution in Australia, and affords the truest safety to the infant liberties of the Australian people. Men succeed in obtaining election to the Legislative Assembly who, beyond a rude power of speech, have few qualities to sustain them and conduct them to right ends in the business of Parliament, and the principles of government suffer grievously sometimes from their rough workmanship. But it may be accepted as a rule that the persons in charge of any public journal of importance, such as the daily papers in the great Australian cities, will use their best endeavours to secure not only talent and education, but judgment and character in the expounders of their political opinions. It is indeed fortunate for Australia that the shortcomings of her public men—any attempt to deceive, however adroit, any backsliding or tergiversation, however carefully cloaked—are soon detected and laid bare by the vigilance of the press. When I started 'The Empire,' more than forty years ago, things were very different; and that journal's existence through the seven trying years from 1849 to 1857 had its share of influence in bringing about the gratifying condition of to-day.

The generation that witnessed the beginning and the ending is passed away. The electric telegraph, steam navigation, the higher and broader promise of Australian life, the inspiriting influences of Australian progress, have now given marvellous vitality and power to Australian journalism. The story of my efforts is hardly worth the telling, but as 'The Empire' absorbed seven of the strongest years of my life, it seems best that, once for all, it should be told.

# CHAPTER V

THE first idea of a Ministry was a Coalition—the short road chosen by short-sighted men to the solution of political difficulties. A gentleman of much influence, still living in England, waited upon me and sounded me as to my rendering assistance to the composition of the Government. But at that time the thought of accepting office had not passed through my mind, and my party sympathies were adverse to the gentleman who had been honoured by the Governor's commission. Mr., afterwards Sir Stuart Alexander Donaldson, was the person selected to form the first Responsible Ministry. He was a man of many fine qualities—of frank, open, mind, of fluent speech, and of reputed skill in finance. The men who had stood together unitedly in the abolition of transportation, and in opposition to the unpopular provisions of Mr. Wentworth's Constitution, found themselves divided into opposing sides in the new Parliament. A nebulous kind of weak Conservatism seized the minds of some who thought others were inclined to go too far, and the first Ministry was formed with a

visible endeavour to represent this nondescript feeling.
The effect was to throw into closer union the members
who joined in a common dissent from the steps taken
by the gentleman who formed the Government. Party
organisations of definite character could hardly be said
to exist, and men joined the Liberal Party, as the
Opposition called themselves, who had their own rather
than the country's purposes to serve.

Mr. Donaldson's Ministry was palpably before our
eyes—the tangible result of all our agitations ; the first
fruits of the precious tree we had been so many years
laboriously planting was in our mouths; and neither the
sight nor the taste was to our liking. Mr. Donaldson
brought in as his Treasurer Mr. Thomas Holt, a well-
meaning gentleman, who was held to be politically weak ;
as his Attorney-General, Sir W. M. Manning, who had
held the office of Solicitor-General under the old order
of things ; as his Solicitor-General, Mr. John Bayly
Darvall, a seceder from the Liberal camp ; and in
the office of Auditor-General, Mr. George Robert
Nichols, who notoriously had no knowledge of figures,
and who owed his popularity to his free-and-easy
character, and his flaunting advocacy of extreme Radical
opinion. This was the Ministry which was to satisfy
the Conservative craving, and at the same time pacify
the angered Liberals. It existed for two months and
twenty days. Yet I doubt if any other combination
would have met with a better fate. Indeed the next
Ministry, formed from the young Liberal party, with
the late Sir Charles Cowper at its head, was doomed to
a like brief existence. During these first few months

the men elected from the legal profession, or the ranks of trade, or fresh from the associations of the bush, had difficulty in finding their depths in the flood of political progress which had set in upon them. Nothing was done, and nothing could be done, by those brief-lived Ministries. The third Ministry, formed by the late Sir Henry Watson Parker, existed nearly a year, and from its advent commenced the conflicts of policy, from time to time assuming more distinct features, which divided the early Parliaments. At the same time legislation of a progressive character set in, and made steady advances. In the next three or four years the electoral system was reformed, State aid to religion was abolished, and John Robertson's sweeping Land Bill, the principles of which had horrified many worthy souls, was carried into law.

On the opening of the first Parliament the election of Speaker gave rise to a severe and animated contest. Mr. Henry Watson Parker had been Chairman of Committees in the old nominee Council, and he was proposed for the Chair in the new Conservative interest. On the part of the Liberals, Mr. Cooper (now Sir Daniel Cooper, Bart.) was put forward, and was elected by the narrowest majority. That contest had served very effectually to give cohesion and definite form to parties slowly gathering round selected leaders, and Charles Cowper became the chief of the Liberals. Mr. Cowper was a gentleman of good address and high personal character, the son of an Archdeacon of the Anglican Church; his Church principles were accepted as of the true pattern, but his Liberal political opinions had

to be cultivated. Step by step he forced himself, or
allowed himself to be forced, to a somewhat uncertain
level with his followers. He had a familiar acquaintance with the affairs of the colony, quick insight in
dealing with surrounding circumstances, and much
good humour and tact in dealing with individuals.
His political adroitness was such that it secured for
him the popular *sobriquet* of 'Slippery Charley.' But
Mr. Cowper was well suited to the demands of the time,
and supplied a valuable link in connecting the old with
the new. Apart from the Legislature, he was a good
administrator, and did excellent service in fitting the
state ship for her far-extending voyage. His second
Administration took office on September 7, 1857, and
lasted until October 26, 1859. It was a Ministry of
many changes in its composition; though there were
only seven offices, no fewer than thirteen persons were
sworn as holders of them at different times. In the
Treasury Richard Jones (a highly respected man, still
living) was followed by Robert Campbell, a man who
was loved by the people, long since dead, and he was
followed by Elias C. Weekes, who was Treasurer twice
afterwards. The late Sir John Robertson took office
for the first time in this Ministry as the successor to
Terence Aubrey Murray on January 13, 1858. John
Robertson at this time was regarded by many as a wild
visionary, who would abolish the Upper Chamber, and
do other extreme things, and I have heard one of the
Ministers say in company that the Premier, after having
made the offer of office to him, reported it to the Cabinet in the words, 'I have been and done it!' He was,

however, the only man who had made up his mind on the land question, in favour of 'men choosing homes for themselves,' and his views met with wide and enthusiastic acceptation and support. In a short time, if difficulties beset the Ministry, it was safe to appeal to the constituencies on the influence of John Robertson's name.

As was to be expected, the questions which were taken up most warmly in the new Legislature were the administration and disposal of the public lands and Electoral Reform. The first two Governments had too brief an existence even to pull themselves into working order. The third Ministry faced in earnest several questions of reform; and was wrecked on an attempt to change the Electoral law. It was composed of men who deserved well of the country, two of whom are still living, Sir John Hay and Sir William Manning (November, 1891). Among the earliest changes was an enactment repealing so much of the Constitution Act as rendered a two-thirds majority necessary to the amendment of the Constitution in other particulars; and a decision of the assembly bringing the Ministerial arrangement more in harmony with the operation of the new principles of Government. Mr. Martin, who had given much attention to this matter before the introduction of Responsible Government, proposed that there should be four Principal Secretaries, and that 'one of the Secretaries should occupy a position in reference to his colleagues similar to that occupied by the First Lord of the Treasury in England.' The motions actually carried were in substance that there should be four Departments: (1) The Principal Secretary; (2) The Treasury; (3) The Attorney-General; (4) Lands and Public Works. Acts were passed for the improvement of the administration of justice, and for the better management of the newly-discovered goldfields. It sounds strange to find the Governor, on closing the first Session, using the following words in reference to that part of the teritory which now forms the colony of Queensland: 'The reasonable demands of the northern district of the colony have been amply met by the establishment at Moreton Bay of a court possessing the most comprehensive jurisdiction, both civil and criminal.' Yet what was done in that first Session was a great improvement on the state of things previously existing. In the generation which has since passed away, Queensland has sprung into existence and has made her name known throughout the world. Another question had prominence in the Governor's closing speech which is now almost banished from Australian politics, that of the policy of introducing new population. The speech says: 'A liberal amount has been granted for the promotion of immigration; and as this question is one of very vital interest to the colony, it will, during the recess, engage the most anxious consideration of the Government'; and the hope is expressed that a system would be devised that would 'lead to the introduction of a steady and continuous supply of useful labour.' The Prorogation Speech also foreshadowed, as one of the blessings of the future, 'an enlightened and comprehensive system of education.'

The fourth Ministry, formed by the late Sir Charles

Cowper, took office on September 7, 1857, and before Christmas, having been defeated on December 17, on a Bill to increase the assessments and rents of the squatters, they dissolved Parliament. Three of the ex-Ministers, among the best men the colony has at any time possessed—Parker, Donaldson, and Hay—never again took office.

Sir John Hay still occupies an honourable place in the public life of New South Wales. After serving nearly five years as an independent member, he was elected, on October 14, 1862, to the Chair, being the third Speaker since May, 1856. A few years later, on July 8, 1873, on my recommendation, Sir John Hay was appointed by the Crown to the high office of President of the Legislative Council, which he still holds (November, 1891). A few years later still he received from Her Majesty the K.C.M.G. Sir John Hay is a man of peculiar graciousness in his personal bearing, which seems to have grown in the formation of his character from an innate love of truth and justice tempered by an unfailing kindliness of feeling. His political views are on the side of progress, giving much weight to the counsels of wisdom. Among Conservatives he would be held to be a Liberal; among extreme Democrats he would be regarded as a Conservative. In every walk of life he has been an exemplary citizen, and one of whom any country might be proud.

During these and the next few years I worked hard and without rest in advocating the principles which I thought essential in the growth of a free commonwealth. From the first I contended for the military defence of

the country by its own citizens, and warmly supported
the first enrolment of Volunteers. In those early days
I raised my voice and gave my vote in favour of immigration from the mother-country, at the same time
insisting upon care and discrimination in the selection
of suitable persons and precautionary steps against
exceeding the means of absorption in the industrial
pursuits of the colony. In my judgment, in no sense
modified by my life-long experiences, the unreasoning
opposition of a portion of the working classes to all
immigration is little short of a craze. My argument
has always been, and is still, that if there were four
times the people in the country, the men and women of
the right stamp, sober, industrious, and self-helping,
every one of the present population would be better off
from the economic effects produced by the larger
numbers. Nothing is so valuable or so much wanted
in a new country as labour. One of my first motions
after my election to the old Council in 1854 was in
favour of an improved system of immigration, and I
remember that among those who congratulated me on
that effort was Daniel Henry Denichy, one of the truest
Democrats that ever lived. A quarter of a century
afterwards, on March 10, 1881, I advocated the estimate for immigration which I submitted to the Legislative Assembly as Prime Minister, in the following
speech :

Sir HENRY PARKES : I am much surprised at the manner in
which this question has been discussed by the honourable
member for Newcastle.[1] Certainly the estimate is not brought

---

[1] The late James Fletcher, Esq., a strong opponent of immigration.

down with any such views as those he seems to entertain—I
mean with such views of the abstract question. The honourable member for Newcastle has considered the subject from first
to last as if it were a mere question of introducing labour to
depress the labour market. I have no such view as that, nor
do I think that any advocate of immigration to a new country
who understands what he is doing can entertain any such
object. I am not surprised that the honourable member should
oppose this vote, inasmuch as from what I gather from his
speech, he has never once looked at the question in the light in
which it is regarded by the Government. I have been an
advocate of immigration throughout the whole period of my
public life; but I never supported it on any such grounds as
have been set forth by the honourable member, and I may be
pardoned if, at the very commencement, I ask what I can have
to gain personally by advocating immigration? I am not identified with the class of large employers. Even my family will
all have to fight their own way in as hard a battle of life as any
other person; and I can promise one thing that they will never
get assistance from me as a Minister. I am identified with the
poorer classes of the people—people who must win their own
way; and it is because I believe I am identified with the great
classes of the people which lie at the foundation of society that
I am an advocate of immigration. But why? Because without the element of population we cannot build up a nation in
this new country. I want men and women—free men and
women—of our own stock to assist us in laying the broad foundations of an empire; and when the question is narrowed down
to this inconceivable contention between labour and capital, I
would like to ask this one pregnant question: Are not all, or
nearly all, the employers of labour in this country men who
have sprung from the ranks of labour? If we could trace the
immigrants who have arrived here by the assistance of the
State, we should find that they are the very men who, by their
perseverance, by their provident habits, by their enterprise and
their insight into industrial affairs, have become the great
employers in this country. They do not come here to remain

serfs; but to fight the battle of freemen where there is ample
room for their exertions.  I do not feel surprised at the indignation of some of the first men in the mother-country at the
illiberal views of colonists in trying to resist the influx of their
brothers and sisters from the old country.  It is incomprehensible to men of enlightened minds in England that such mean
and detestable feelings can exist as would prevent others from
coming to our shores to share in the benefits of these new
lands which are just as much a portion of the empire as any
other.

Mr. FLETCHER: We do not try to prevent them.

Sir HENRY PARKES: The honourable member does; and
those who for the sake of the colour of decency resist this trifling expenditure would resist the influx of immigrants altogether if they could.  What a specious attempt at argument it
is to say that the people of this country are taxed for the purpose of defraying the expense of immigration!  Do not these
broad domains belong to the people?  And do they not in
reality belong to the English people who may come here as
well as to those who are here?  And, if this is the case, why
should not a portion of the money derived from the sale of these
lands be expended to enable us to hold out the hand of fellow-
ship to our brothers and sisters in the old country?  I shall
return to this part of the subject by-and-bye, but I state at
once that I can neither entertain sympathy with the honourable
member's views nor comprehend his motives or his objects in
making the speech he has delivered.  I have to perform what
to me is a very unpleasant duty before I come fully to the
advocacy of immigration—before I come to the question as to
the object and the purposes of introducing new population.
The question is one surrounded with difficulties, and with many
painful differences of opinion.  Whilst the opponents of immigration by the aid of the State funds are against us, we find
that persons who are in favour of immigration are also opposed
to us on other grounds.  I, for instance, though extremely
anxious for the introduction of new population, and believing
that there can be no grander policy for a new country—for

instead of being a paltry question between capital and labour, it is a large question of national policy—one of the very grandest of all policies for a new country—I, nevertheless, whilst entertaining this view, confess that, in the introduction of new population, I am likely to come into conflict with people who entertain my own views on that question, and who have cheered me during the last few minutes. I am anxious to preserve the present elements of the population. I am, therefore, not of opinion with the honourable member for Boorowa, as I heard him express himself some weeks ago, that we ought to establish any system of immigration irrespective of the question whether it would be likely to change the character of the population of this country. I am as willing as I can be to assist in bringing Englishmen, Scotchmen, and Irishmen here; but I am not willing to bring the people of one country at the expense of the people of another kingdom. I would not, I say at once, give my support to any immigration which had a tendency to change the British character of the population as it now exists. I disclaim any hostility to the people of any of the three kingdoms; but I would lend no advocacy of mine—on the contrary, I would advance every opposition in my power— to the bringing here of a majority of people from Ireland. I hope I may be able to express this opinion boldly and without reserve, without being charged with bigotry or with a dislike to the Irish people. I say that I want to preserve a majority of Englishmen and the descendants of Englishmen in this country. I say, moreover, and, unpleasant and painful as it may be, it is a matter which ought not to be shirked, that I want to preserve the teaching and influence of the Protestant religion in the country, and I would lend no assistance whatever to any scheme which would have a tendency to depress the Protestant elements now in existence. For this reason I am an advocate for the immigration to this country being regulated by whatever the census returns will show to be the elements of the population of the three kingdoms now existing in the colony. I think that is quite fair and equitable, and that there ought to be no objection to it. I do not think that we ought to be charged with

illiberality because we object to a movement of the population
which would change the character of the country. I will
explain what are the changes in the regulations which the
Government propose to establish if this vote is passed. We
propose in the first place to ask the immigrants to pay one-half
the amount of their passage-money. That is a higher proportion than they have paid hitherto; but we have reason to think
that we can get as many immigrants as this vote would cover if
the amount to be paid were increased to that extent; hence,
under the new regulations, this 50,000*l.* will bring out as large
a number of immigrants as could be introduced if a sum of
100,000*l.* were voted without the regulation being in existence.
If it be a fact that we can get immigrants who would be prepared to pay half the cost of their own passage, there is in that
fact alone some evidence of provident habits; for it may be
roughly assumed that those of the working-classes who are able
to save money for purposes of this kind are in moral respects
superior to those who have not been able to save. We shall
have some evidence, therefore, under the new regulations of
obtaining a better, a more provident, steady, and sober class of
immigrants. That in itself would be a good thing, besides the
fact that the vote would extend over a much larger surface. In
the 3rd section of the regulations it is laid down with a little
more precision than in former regulations that the immigrants
shall be chosen in proportion to the elements of the population
of the three kingdoms, as shown by the census returns, to be
taken this year. The 4th section provides that instead of 20
per cent. of the immigrants being unmarried women, not more
than one-third may be unmarried women. Then we seek to
abolish the system of what I may call arbitrary nomination in
the colony. We continue the system of nomination in the
colony, but we subject these nominations to a system of inspection as to the fitness of the persons nominated in the mother-
country. The reason for this is that in the working of the
immigration regulations it has been found that notwithstanding
we say that the immigrants shall only come in a proportion
corresponding to the population of the three kingdoms, Ireland

has had one-half of the nominations. It has arisen in this way—nominations made in the colony by people from Ireland have been so far in excess of those made by the people from England and Scotland that they have absorbed nearly the whole of the money available by the regulation, and a considerable proportion more. The Agent-General had no means whatever of accepting emigrants from Ireland itself. I have laid on the table to-day a letter on the subject from the late Agent-General, and I will point out a passage in it inviting the attention of the Government to this anomaly in the working of the regulations. Writing on March 27, 1879, after describing what the immigration regulations are, the late Agent-General says: 'But I find that in the six nomination-lists in the colony, from July to December, 1878, 483 Irish statute adults have been approved out of a total of 838 adults, being $57\frac{1}{2}$ per cent. of Irish, or nearly double the census proportion.'

That is, instead of only one-third being emigrants from Ireland availing themselves of this system of nomination by friends in the colony, the emigrants from that country are nearly double that proportion, or $57\frac{1}{2}$ per cent. of the whole. The Agent-General goes on to say, 'It will be evident to you that if such infractions of the rule be permitted in the colony, it becomes most difficult, if not impossible, for me to regulate properly the numbers approved here in such a manner as to ensure the proper proportions in making up the aggregate totals of emigrants nominated in the colony and selected in the United Kingdom.'

To show that this is really the case, I take the report of the Agent for Immigration, which was laid on the table the other day, and I find if we take the religions which pretty fairly represent the three kingdoms, that 1,470 Roman Catholics came out as compared with 1,649 Protestants of all denominations, or that the Roman Catholics were within 179 of the Protestants of all persuasions. This shows how this system of nomination in the colony works to bring about these great anomalies—indeed breaches of the regulations. It must be admitted, and I admit it to the credit of the Irish people, that the Irish are more careful to send for their poor relations than people from the other two kingdoms. That is highly to their credit; but it does not follow that, because of the existence of this virtue so greatly to their honour, we should assist in bringing about a result like that which I speak of, and which would in a few years entirely change the elements of the population. In dealing with this difficult and rather painful subject, though I express my opinion freely and strongly, I hope I do so without giving personal offence to any gentleman who differs from me. However, these regulations are framed with a view of insisting upon the proportion of immigrants from each of the three kingdoms corresponding with the proportion of the population. Permission will still be given for the nomination of immigrants by persons in the colony, but all those so nominated must be treated in just the same way, under the responsibility of the Agent-General, as immigrants selected by his own officers. They must be of the right age, they must be of sound mental and bodily health, and they must not be in excess of the proportions defined by the regulations, or they will not be admitted. The only other matter in the regulations which is new, is the obligation thrown upon the Government to send home a report as to the state of the labour market every three months. The Agent-General will be required to be guided by this report so as not, when any trade is in a depressed state, to send out immigrants of that trade until he has received further advices. That, I think, will be a great assistance, and in many ways useful in promoting a sound and healthy system of immigration. I have before me the result of the working of the present system for the past four years, ending December 31, and I find by this return that nearly 6,000 immigrants were sent for by their friends. Now, whilst I object to the working of the present regulations in permitting the people of one kingdom to absorb the immigration grants so unfairly to the people of the other two kingdoms. I also admit, and have fully admitted, that there is great virtue in persons putting themselves to inconvenience, as they very frequently do, in raising money to send for their poor relations. I should like to ask whether, if the friends of these 6,000 who have come out during the last four years had felt that it was

impossible for them to get employment, they would have sent
for them? Would they have sent for them at their own
expense? Surely that is an answer to the assertion that we do
not want immigrants! Surely, if people in the colony belonging to the working-classes save up their shillings and sixpences
to assist their poor relatives to come here, it is because they
believe they are bringing them to a better country. I do not
see how that argument is to be met. Surely it shows that those
who understand the working-classes well, who understand their
conditions much better even than those honourable members
who profess to understand them, but who are withdrawn from
them, do not think the country is over-populated! I say that
if these people at their own expense, depriving themselves of
little luxuries and necessaries, provide the means of sending for
their own relatives, that is an unanswerable argument against
the statement that this is not the place for working-men. But
where have the immigrants gone? During the past four years
20,000 have arrived in the country, about 5,000 annually.
Where have they gone to? Do we hear much about dissatisfaction amongst them? It would be strange indeed if there were
not one or two bush lawyers amongst 20,000 people. In the
settling of a new country great hardships may be expected,
privation and hard work must be encountered. All these things
are incidental to the founding of a new country. They were
just as prevalent and far more trying to the Pilgrim Fathers
than they have been to the immigrants arriving in this country.
Making allowance for all that, there is every evidence that these
people have, in a natural process, mingled with the rest of the
population, and have advanced to their own satisfaction in their
various industrial callings. By reason of the office I hold, I
have not had the satisfaction of attending the meetings of the
committee presided over by the honourable member for The
Hunter. Time hardly ever permitted me to attend those
meetings, and having lost the run of the business, I thought it
better not to attend. I am told by the honourable member for
The Hunter, however, that the committee can find no evidence
to support the view that there are two or three men to be

obtained where one is wanted, and I declare that I have never seen that state of affairs in my life in this country. I have mixed with various classes, and I have shared the hard brunt of labour with people who toil for their daily bread. I do not want to boast of anything of that kind; but I am not ashamed of it. Why should I be? I have toiled for my bread with as much privation and hardship as any person. When I arrived in this country, bread was 2s. 8d. per loaf, and potatoes were 4d. per lb. For a long time I ate bread composed for the most part of rice meal, because I could not afford to buy wheaten bread. I have endured toil and hardship as much as any working-man can possibly do. I must confess that I never was confined to working only eight hours a day; if I had, I do not suppose I should have been here to-day. Why, then, should I not have sympathy with the working-classes? Who would be bold enough to say that I have no feeling for them? I declare that there is no sight from one end of society to another which is more gratifying to me, which gives me a higher sense of the character of my countrymen, than to see a well-regulated, well-filled home among the working-classes. More than this—I say that the happiest, the finest, the best regulated homes I think I have ever seen in my life have belonged to mechanics of the English labouring-classes. My sympathies are entirely with the industrial classes; and I say this without any personal object whatever. Nothing gratifies me more than to see any man steadily emerging from these classes by dint of his own perseverance and intelligence and habits of sober thought to a rank above that of the classes he has left. But I do not believe we can find any specific to convert all the working-classes into gentlemen. I do not believe that, and I never did. I believe there must always be a large class at the foundations of society who will live by manual labour.

Mr. MELVILLE: They are none the less gentlemen.

Sir HENRY PARKES: Perhaps I was not quite understood in my use of the term ' gentlemen'; I used it in a very conventional sense. I think I have admitted already that there must be a great number of gentlemen among the working-classes—

the truest of all gentlemen. But I was going to say that the real progress of the working-classes consists in their having leisure, means of education, and opportunities for the exercise of those faculties which will enable them to rise into some other class. In this country, on the right hand and on the left, wherever we tread, we find men of that character. The very centres of influence in this country are men who have risen by their own efforts from the great labouring-classes. I believe that applies to immigrants just as much as to any other class in the country. I have no doubt whatever that if the impossible were possible—if we could follow our immigrants and trace their daily life—we should find them steadily accumulating a wealth of comfort around them and acquiring the means, perhaps, of rising to positions of great influence in the country. Before I leave this return I should like to state the composition of the 20,000 persons who have arrived here in these four years. We find—of course this return applies only to male adults—that there were 4,725 farm labourers. These men, I venture to say, are scattered all over the country. Some few of them may have drifted away into the other colonies, but while they have done so a similar, and perhaps a larger, number have come from other colonies to us. Then there were 513 miners—that is, about 125 annually. They were miners of all kinds. There were 1,000 belonging to the building trades, and 598 belonging to the iron trades. I imagine that number would include black-smiths, who would go into the country towns. I presume it would not be confined to engineers who are employed in the large works in this city; I imagine that it would include any who work in any way upon iron. There were 233 belonging to the clothing trades, 128 belonging to the provision trades, and 162 belonging to other manufacturing trades. Then, of boys over twelve years of age and men engaged in general trades, there were 676. It would be difficult to get a fairer proportion of the industrial classes of the old country than this, or a pro-portion which on the face of it seems more suited to the indus-trial callings of the colony. Something was said just now by the honourable member for Newcastle as to the character of the immigrants.  I have not had many opportunities of forming a judgment of their character, but I have been on board one or two immigrant vessels on their arrival.  I have had special reason for visiting the vessels, and I declare that I have seldom seen a finer body of men and women than those immigrants. The Treasurer had occasion to pay more than one visit to the ship *Northampton*, which arrived the other day, and with regard to them he entertains the same opinion.  I do not think the Treasurer would form a mistaken judgment of the character of men and women—as to their physical appearance and their general suitableness for the colony.  This vote of 50,000*l*. will, under the new regulations, carry with it another 50,000*l*.. and that sum of 100,000*l*. will bring out 7,000 immigrants.  Will anyone say that the addition of 7,000 persons to the population will be anything but a blessing to the country?  I lay down this rule—of course it only expresses my opinion, and it is a thing which cannot be proved simply because one cannot prove what lies in the future—that if in this country instead of something like a million people—and I hope that number will be shown by the census to be taken next month—you had 4,000,000, and they were men and women of the right sort, every person who is in the country now would be better off for the increase.  To a colony like ours there is nothing so valuable as human muscle, skill, and intelligence.  It is impossible to pass through this country without observing in all directions property which is dilapidated and falling into decay for want of human effort.  You may tell me that there are persons here and there, or that there is a number in a particular district who cannot obtain employment.

Mr. MELVILLE : It is the case all over the country.

Sir HENRY PARKES : My answer to these statements is that you cannot find any city on the face of the earth where there are not some people out of employment.  It is inseparable from our system of civilisation.  Wherever civilisation exists, there will always be a large number of persons congregating in centres of population who, from one cause or another, often inexplicable, are out of employment.  Go through Sydney or the country on any festive occasion, or on any occasion which assumes the character of a holiday, and you will find more people well dressed, having an abundance of all the comforts of life, with leisure, with strong constitutions, and with every capability of enjoyment, than you will find in any other country in the world. You will not find such evidences of substantial prosperity in any other country. In most countries, not excepting the United States, shoals of people perish for want of the necessaries of life ; but do we ever hear of any case in this colony in which a person perishes from such a cause? It is impossible for such a state of things to exist ; and, beyond all doubt, the country is yet so new, so full of resources, so full of unopened avenues of labour, that any person who has the requisite *nous* may carve out for himself a means of employment by which he may go on progressing until he is in an independent position. But, in all directions and in all times there will be a certain number of unemployed. A district may be in a state of stagnation, and may make no progress for a number of years—six, ten, or more years, perhaps—until some enterprising man with his wits about him goes into that district and sees sources of wealth where no one else saw them. He may see chances for industrial enterprise where no one else saw them, and he becomes an agency for the employment of other people, bettering the whole district. The more men of self-reliant character, of enterprise and industrial skill, we introduce into this country—as long as we do not introduce them in such excessive numbers as to cause anything like a glut—by such a gradual process as is now proposed, the better will it be for every man, woman, and child in the country. Our prosperity consists, and must consist, in the number of human souls—or, to put it in a more material way, in the number of capable hands and of thinking minds, in the store of energy and intelligence we possess, to convert the rude country into a land of fruitfulness and plenty. Our prosperity must depend upon that, and the more people we can get the better for us. What is the grand criterion by which we distinguish between the more important and the less important of the colonies in this group? Every country of our stock

which has entered on the broad path of nationhood has made
every exertion in its power to bring population to its shores.
We are told that the United States do not pay for their immigrants. I say that they do. They alienate their lands in a
manner calculated to induce people to go there. Is not that
the same as paying for them from the proceeds of land sales?
Now, I for one would not favour the idea of introducing a
number of people here to settle all at once upon the public
lands, or all at once to follow any vocation in the country as
employers. I have invariably advised those who have been
introduced to me—and for years past a number of persons have
brought letters of introduction to me from the mother-country—
even where they had money, to make a point of obtaining employment at first, in order to learn the ways and usages of the
colony; to understand the population and the opportunities of
embarking in some pursuit on their own account. Even men
of good family, who have brought letters of credit for large
amounts, I have advised to obtain employment in the first
instance. I say that a system of immigration which brings
people here, and, in the first instance, distributes them into the
avenues of labour, is the best system. The better class of persons will soon find a way to emerge from these avenues of mere
manual labour. The doctrine of the Darwinian philosophy as
to the survival of the fittest applies here in an eminent degree.
The fittest will prosper most, and, of course, the unfit will have
to go on in the walks of manual labour. But this state of affairs
is in no way affected by a part of the passage-money being paid
by the State. Why do we propose to pay a part of the passage-
money? Because on account of the costliness of the journey
we stand no fair chance in competing with either Canada or the
United States for the redundant population of England, unless
we assist that population. Are we justified in this expenditure?
Is it a good thing to introduce new population? Of course I
have nothing to say to those gentlemen who would build up a
wall round the country and treat all outside as foreigners. I
have nothing to say to those who think that this country
belongs to them, and to them only. I say that it belongs to

every man and woman who acknowledges the empire of our
Queen, and that the territory of this country will be just as
much theirs when they come here as it is ours. If the country
wants new population, I say that new population which is
partly assisted by the State is just as valuable as new population
which is entirely paid for out of its own resources. I said, in
an early part of my speech, that some of those who are opposed
to paying away public money for the introduction of immigrants would be opposed to immigrants coming here altogether
if they had the opportunity.

Mr. MELVILLE : Who says so ?

Sir HENRY PARKES : I suppose the honourable member would
say so.

Mr. MELVILLE : Never.

Sir HENRY PARKES : Then I have the honourable member's
denial. He admits that it is a proper thing to have new
population.

Mr. MELVILLE : At their own expense.

Sir HENRY PARKES : He admits that it is a good thing for
population to come here ?

Mr. MELVILLE : If there is anything for them to do.

Sir HENRY PARKES : Does the honourable member mean that
this colony is not a place where they can find employment ?

Mr. MELVILLE : I say that at the present time there is no employment for the people you wish to bring here. There is a large
number of unemployed, and you want to overcrowd the market.

Sir HENRY PARKES : I want to ascertain the honourable
member's views upon this one point. Is he prepared to admit
that there is room for any persons if they come here at their
own expense ?

Mr. MELVILLE : At the present time there is not sufficient
employment for people who are inclined to work.

Sir HENRY PARKES : Then he says that we do not want any
more ?

Mr. MELVILLE : At the present time.

Sir HENRY PARKES : If we do not want them now we most
probably never shall want them, for we are in as great a state

of prosperity now as we were last year or are likely to be next
year. If there are many gentlemen holding the views of the
honourable member for Northumberland, their condition is simply
hopeless; they are irredeemable, they are beyond conversion.
They say that with a population of 900,000 upon a territory
which could support 9,000,000 we do not want a single soul
more. I have nothing to say to them. If the honourable gentleman admits that it is a good thing to have new population at
their own expense, then I say that, if it is good in that degree,
it is good in a greater degree. If the population is good when
brought at its own expense, it is equally good when brought
partly at the expense of the State. The honourable member for Newcastle (Mr. Fletcher) says we have no right to tax
the people to bring others here to compete with them in the
labour market. I say we are not taxing people to bring others
here. We are simply employing a portion of the proceeds from
the alienation of the territory to introduce people who by a
gradual process and natural course of events will settle on the
land so alienated. By no other means can you attempt to build
up a great nation. You cannot have a nation without people.

Mr. MELVILLE : We can have it by wise legislation.

Sir HENRY PARKES : I should like to know what wise legislation would be of any avail in the absence of people. If the
honourable member means that we are to rehabilitate the country
by protective laws, he is introducing an element which I decline
to discuss now. I contend, in the face of everyone, that in a
new country like ours it is a wise course of policy to introduce
as many persons as you can, provided they are of industrious
habits, and of sober and steady character, and that you do not
introduce them in such numbers as to paralyse the industrial
operations of the country. There is no fear of any dangerous
results from the proposals now made by the Government. They
will have a salutary effect in infusing new blood throughout the
ramifications of society, and the consequence from all reasoning
from probabilities would be to give more employment to those
who seek it, and to add to the prosperity of all classes of the
people. I hope that the example set by the honourable member

for Newcastle, and, I think, by myself, of trying to say the most we can from our points of view, will be followed, and that we shall not have this question, which is simply one of national policy, warped by an attempt at obstruction, or to bring about ridiculous reductions. Let us fight the battle out fairly; let opportunity be given to every man to vent his opinion; and let those who are elected here to represent the whole colony, arrive at a decision. That is all I ask; with these observations I submit this vote. I do not intend to address the committee again, unless to answer any inquiry which may be made, for I think I have already said as much as I need say.

I have given this speech because it fairly states the case for immigration from my point of examination, and because the interruptions by Mr. Melville supply a good illustration of the untenable position taken up by its opponents. Mr. Melville appeared as one of the members for a coal-mining constituency where the feeling against all new-comers was too earnest to be disguised. It would have cost him his seat if he had ventured to support immigration. But the debate which followed upon my proposal showed that other members were beginning to modify their opinions to meet the prejudices of those least capable of reasoning justly on the subject. In the end my estimate was reduced by 10,000l.; and since then little has been heard of assisted immigration. It is a disastrous mistake. The progress of the country for many years to come could be best assisted by new population. Nothing can arrest Australian progress, and as imaginary stages of an advance not actually before our eyes will never be taken into account, we shall have no means of comparing what might have been with what is; but the thoughtful will

need no argument to prove to them how much greater
Australia might have been to-day, if it had not been
for the narrow and selfish policy of those who seek to
deny to civilisation itself its principle of evangelising
brotherhood.   If there is a land under the sun which
ought to offer a home to all good men, it is Australia,
and if in any land good men are wanted to assist in
securing the fruits of freedom and civilisation, it is in
Australia. Yet there are to be found men blind enough
to resist in the noble work of making a nation the support of their fellow-countrymen.

On the question of military defence, I took up the
position that even if it were advisable to depend upon
imperial troops, the colony could not afford the cost of
the maintenance of a sufficient number of men, and that
compulsory inactivity in a colony must necessarily
prove prejudicial to efficient training and discipline,
and that such defence would always be liable, in times
of national danger, to be withdrawn to meet the exi-
gencies of the Empire.   I illustrated my arguments by
examples chiefly drawn from America; and while I
always combated the views of those who held that we
needed no defence at all, that 'nobody would ever
attack us,' I urged that we must depend upon ourselves
for our security.

Early in the third Parliament, on December 20,
1859, I moved the following resolutions :—

That this House, having had under its consideration the
subject of the defence of the colony, resolves as follows :

1. That having regard to the present complications of
foreign Governments, and the hold which the great maritime

powers have in the seas of this hemisphere, it is impolitic and
unsafe to neglect the means of preparation at our command for
protecting the colony in the event of its being attacked by an
enemy.

2. That the maintenance of regular troops in the colony for
its protection is unwise in policy, and cannot be effective without
becoming an excessive burden on the public revenue.

3. That the true principle of military defence, and the only
course which would ensure effective resistance in extreme circumstances, is to habituate the subjects of the Queen in this
colony to the use of arms, and to foster among all classes a loyal
and patriotic spirit of reliance on their own valour and military
organisation.

4. That any opinion herein expressed is not intended to
apply to the protection afforded by Her Majesty's ships of war in
the Australian waters.

At this time there was a widespread apprehension
in England as to the designs of Napoleon III. Lord
Lyndhurst had just made his stirring speech in the
House of Lords on the activity in the French dockyards
and the perfidious and aggressive character of the new
Empire. Tennyson was fanning the national uneasiness
by the bellicose lyrics:

Riflemen form!    Riflemen form!

I copy some extracts from my opening speech:—

It was scarcely possible to attach too much importance to
the necessary provision for protecting their national honour
as a British community. Nor was he amongst those who
thought that the time of hostility and warfare amongst the
nations of the civilised world had passed away. Looking to
the advance of arms in Europe, and to the unscrupulous
character of particular Governments, they might be fully prepared to anticipate any aggression that was practicable from

those powers; since the only considerations about such an
aggression would be the probability of its success, and whether
success would contribute to the end those powers had in view.
That this danger—the danger of a rupture between the parent
land and some one or more of the Great Powers of Europe—was
admitted by persons most competent to form an opinion on the
subject he should be prepared to show. But the most satisfactory way of proving this would be for him to lay before the
House the opinions of men entitled by their experience and
standing in the political world to be accepted as authorities.
He should not attempt to detain the House with any discussion
to prove the value of these authorities, but should confine himself to quoting from the speeches made in the House of Lords
by Lords Lyndhurst and Ellenborough. The powers from which
danger was to be apprehended were France, in the event of a
rupture with England, and Russia in connection with China,
although that was a more remote contingency in point of time;
but the danger of a rupture with France was imminent, and the
relations between the two countries were uncertain from one
day to another—whilst from intelligence received mail after
mail it seemed to be an almost universal opinion that war would
not be averted.

After quoting from Lord Lyndhurst at some length,
including the old statesman's noble words—' I will not
consent to live in dependence on the friendship or the
forbearance of any country. I rely solely on my own
vigour, my own exertion, my own intelligence '—words
containing eternal truths for the free life of nations, I
continued my speech as follows :—

Let them look at the situation of the colony. We had at
the present time an artillery corps, containing a trifle above a
hundred men, who were supplemented by the infantry at the
barracks, making the number altogether about 583 men. Now
he could not believe that in any attack that might be made

upon the colony this force would be of much avail to the community. He had every confidence that these men, before an
army of soldiers sixfold their number, or perhaps a greater
proportion, would do their duty; but he thought they would
lead a very forlorn hope, and the result would be their own
destruction without any protection to the country. The cost of
these men, comparatively speaking, was enormous; the sum
placed on the estimates for the payment of the 583 men was no
less than 16,308*l.*, and we were paying only the artillery in full,
giving an allowance to the infantry in barracks. So that for
this distant colony the cost of a very small and inefficient force
was 16,308*l.* It struck him very forcibly that a long residence
in a colony was not the best possible mode of discipline for
regular troops, and he should scarcely be inclined to expect the
same amount of efficiency in troops lying idle in the colony for
a number of years as in those under a more regular employment,
and who had more frequent opportunities of going into active
service. But be that as it might, these regular troops were not
formed of a different class, of a different nation, of a different
birth, of a different material from the common population of the
colony. They were recruited—as all persons acquainted with
recruiting operations in England would know—chiefly in the
English towns; and there was nothing in the circumstances or
condition or character of the men who formed the standing army
of England that could place them in a better position for effective
service than any body of our fellow-colonists who might be
enrolled and disciplined in the same manner here upon an
altogether different principle. If this system continued we
must have a sufficient number of these troops in the colony for
the effective resistance of such a force as would be sure to be
collected for an organised attack on the part of any of the great
maritime powers; and thus, by incurring an enormous expenditure, unnecessarily burden the resources of the colony. There
was no argument that he could discover why an Imperial force
should be more effective for the purposes of defence than a force
composed of residents in the colony. That we ought to raise
such a force he did not think required any argument. Even

the advocates of the Peace Society in England deemed that England ought to be placed in a state of effective preparation against attempted invasion. Both Mr. Bright and Mr. Cobden had within the last few months expressed their opinion that the country ought to be placed in an effective state of defence ; and this being admitted so generally, argument was not required to show its necessity here. The question he wished to raise was whether it was advisable to create a force of our own by enrolling the inhabitants of the colony, or to depend upon the armed forces that were eating out our vitals without contributing to our industrial powers or being of sufficient strength for our defence.

A lengthy debate took place upon my motion, and an amendment by the Premier was carried, substituting for the second section the following words : 'That the maintenance of regular troops in the colony ought to be supplemented by the formation of a national militia composed of citizens of the country.' In this amended form the resolutions were agreed to by 42 to 8 votes.

It may be fairly said that this decision of the Legislative Assembly implanted the patriotic principle of self-dependence in the system of military defence throughout Australia. The principle had to contend with disfavour and ridicule for some time, but the Volunteer movement through several changes grew steadily until the force in every colony may be regarded as a little 'citizen army.' Some ten years after my motion in the Assembly, Sir Charles Cowper (the Premier of New South Wales), proposed to the Imperial Government to retain in the colony four companies of infantry at an increased rate, on the condition that they should not be withdrawn in a time of war. This was

the last effort of the old spirit of former days clinging
to the Imperial arm. But the Secretary of State, Earl
Granville, sent the following depressing answer :—

> Although Her Majesty's Government readily acknowledge
> the reciprocal duty of defending every portion of the Empire,
> and that a colony which pays for the presence of troops during
> peace may fairly expect that they should not be removed during
> war except under the strongest necessity, yet the exigencies of
> a state of war are so unexpected, and the necessity for entire
> freedom of action so great. that it would not be possible for them
> to give a pledge to that effect.

A few years later still, another Secretary of State
(the Earl of Carnarvon) proposed to return to the
former system of defending the colonies by Imperial
troops. I will deal with this proposal when I come to
the proceedings of the first Ministry formed by myself,
and the state of affairs then and during the next few
years. At this time the proposal was warmly favoured
by the well-to-do classes. 'Let us pay for Imperial
troops and feel safe,' was the substance of the opinions
often expressed by those whose first consideration and
chief glory are in their worldly possessions—the men
who, I fear, are to be found all over the world, who
believe that money can purchase anything, from a
family pedigree to a 'reserved seat' in Heaven.

During my service in the early Parliaments, I paid
much attention to the means of ocean communication.
Looking to the geographical position of New South
Wales in relation to the other colonies, and to the
important islands of the Pacific, I was among the first to
advocate the Trans-Pacific route, the idea in those days

being to cross the American continent by the Isthmus
of Panama.    The gigantic trans-continental railway
systems which now pierce the United States and the
Canadian Dominion, connecting the Pacific with the
Atlantic Ocean, had not then assumed form in the
speculations of enthusiasts.    But the short land journey
from Panama to Aspinwall seemed ready made by the
hand of nature.    One or two steamships made experimental passages, and eventually two successive companies were formed in England to establish the service
between Sydney and Panama *viâ* New Zealand.    Years
before this was attempted I moved in the Legislative
Assembly, on August 6, 1858, the following resolutions :—

1. That the experience hitherto gained of steam communication between Australia and England *viâ* India has led to
general disappointment and dissatisfaction in this colony.

2. That any new arrangement for the performance of the
mail service by the India route, though it ensured postal regularity and speed, would confer no other considerable benefits on
New South Wales, while it must necessarily place this community, as the last point of intercourse in the Australian system,
at a permanent disadvantage in relation to the Southern
colonies.

3. That it is in the highest degree necessary that immediate steps should be taken to prevent the public inconvenience
and injury which would result from a total stoppage in the
mail service, with which the colonies are at present threatened,
and that the interests of New South Wales would be best promoted in this emergency by opening communication with
America and Europe, *viâ* the Isthmus of Panama.

4. That there are reasonable grounds for believing that a
line of steamers of the requisite power and capacity, running
between Sydney and Panama, in addition to the advantages of

regular postal communication, would induce a spontaneous and valuable passenger traffic to these shores from the large numbers of persons constantly arriving on the Isthmus from the United States, British North America, and the West Indies, as well as from the countries of Europe and from the communities of Anglo-American origin in the Pacific.

5. That in coming to a right determination on this subject the question of cost is not the first for consideration, but that the efficiency of the service to be performed should be secured beyond probability of failure, and that especial regard should be had to those social and commercial consequences which would tend most to the progress and prosperity of the colony of New South Wales.

I give some extracts from the speech by which I supported my motion. To be fairly considered, they must of course be read without reference to the progress of steam navigation across the Pacific since that period :—

Mr. PARKES, in moving the resolutions standing in his name, said he hoped that however inefficiently he might treat them, the importance of the subject would at least commend them to the attention of the House. He should endeavour to be as brief as he well could, and the decision to which the House was invited must have an effect one way or the other, for good or for evil, to determine not simply the relative prosperity of this colony, but its position as a country in the new empire now in course of being founded in this hemisphere. He submitted these resolutions not alone as involving the question of postal communication with England; they might be supported upon different and far higher grounds affecting the future character and comparative greatness of the country. It had always seemed to him that the question of obtaining regular means of communication with the Isthmus of Panama included the question of a supply of that element without which the progress of this country would be slow and unsatisfactory—the element of fresh streams of industrious, enterprising population. Although desponding views might be taken at a time of temporary distress like the present, though loud might be the cry among some classes against immigration, it was only by means of a large amount of population that the colony could rise to its true place and its people enjoy permanent prosperity. He was one who thought that immigration to the country would be healthy just in proportion as it embodies in its volume a due proportion of capital and labour to carry on the operations of civilised society; and for that reason he thought a great advance would be made on all former systems if it were entirely voluntary and of a spontaneous character. In that case, if they could offer sufficient attraction, and if other circumstances combined to direct the great movement of population to these shores, they would receive the most enterprising and the most self-reliant class of persons, those who have made provision to assist themselves; but so long as immigration continued to be promoted chiefly by the funds derived from this side it would consist of persons to a large extent the least provident, the least energetic, the least qualified, and therefore the least capable of assisting in the advancement of the colony.

This country had little in common with the inhabitants of the Asiatic countries. Beyond taking from them supplies of tea, sugar, and spices, they had scarcely any commerce with those countries; they had very little of social affinity with any of the populations of the East; their only connection with the Eastern world was one of Imperial policy. But these objections would not apply to the trans-Pacific route. It would be found that there were many reasons, which he would touch upon presently, why they should desire that the route he proposed should be opened. To a very large extent it appeared to him that the establishment of steam communication with India was an Imperial question. It was to the interest of the British Government to keep up rapid communication with India for political reasons, but those reasons did not affect this colony. It was most desirable that rapid and frequent communication

should exist between England and the East, and of course any
branch steam service that would tend in any degree to support
the lines of communication between London and India would
be of very great service to the mother-country; but he contended that the Australian colonies had scarcely any interest in
maintaining a line of steam communication *viâ* India, except so
far as it might be made an efficient and rapid means of postal
communication, and at the same time to some small extent a
convenience for the purposes of their Indian commerce. But a
great objection, in addition to those already stated, existed in
the case of this colony on account of its position rendering it
absolutely necessary that it should always be the last port of
arrival and the first of departure, and therefore placed at a
greater postal distance from Europe than the sister communities.

    .     .     .     .     .     .     .

He affirmed that it was to the interest of this country to
get such a means of communication established at the earliest
possible moment; and if it were to the interest of the country
to do this, the necessary cost was not the first thing they
should regard so long as there was no waste. Being determined by this means to maintain the colony in a leading position, they should secure this end without a niggardly regard
to price so long as they secured efficiency in the performance
of the contract, without which it would be comparatively useless. For his own part, he thought that if this could not be
obtained at less cost, it would be wise for the House to vote
half a million of money to have this communication established
without the possibility of interruption. He believed, so far as
the subsidy was concerned, it would be wise to give whatever
sum was necessary to have this communication in their own
hands; and, depending—as they might reasonably do—on receiving a contribution from New Zealand, and perhaps something from the Southern colonies, it would not be a very costly
undertaking for the Government of this country. But he felt
persuaded that the cost would be as nothing compared with
the benefits to be derived, not only from the improved means of

postal communication and the additions to our population, but from the new spirit which it would be the active cause of infusing into the commercial enterprise and social life of the colony. They had here a country richer than any other of the colonies, notwithstanding the rapid strides which Victoria had made in colonising enterprise. The natural resources of New South Wales were inexhaustible : its varieties of soil—its marvellous wealth of minerals—its many other advantages—made it second to none. And this highway across the Pacific seemed pointed out as by the hand of Providence to connect them with other countries—other countries, too, where the grand experiment of founding new empires, with a common origin and a common destiny, was going on. Those lands must be the teachers of this, for in no other part of the world were English liberty and English commerce transplanted to work out their ends on a new soil.

In my early parliamentary life I made it a rule in dealing with votes for the improvement of the interior —though I was one of the members for Sydney—that my support should be given to the proposed work, unless I was in possession of information which satisfied me that it was not a justifiable expenditure. Men of this generation in the colony can hardly conceive the state of the roads, and of the bridgeless creeks which dwellers in the country had to face in those days. Next to its public school system, the improved means of communication throughout the vast territory is the most creditable fruit of responsible government in New South Wales.

I gave my support to the Electoral Bill of the Cowper Government, voting with Ministers in nearly every division. This Bill passed into law, largely extending the franchise, more equally dividing the

colony into electoral districts, and establishing the
system of secret voting.   I also gave my general
support to the Robertson Land Bill, which passed
through a determined opposition, and became law
eventually, after the violent expedient of 'swamping
the Upper House,' which swamping, however, had no
practical or immediate effect, as the old members,
including the President, retired in a body when the
new members attempted to take their seats.   By the
constitution the first Council was appointed for five
years only,[1] and the term was near its expiration when
this historical incident occurred.   So nothing could be
done with the Bill, or anything else, until the next
Council was appointed, whose term was for life.   In
giving my general support to the Robertson Land Bill,
I took strong exception to the principle of 'deferred
payments' and to the provision for selling 'back lands'
at five shillings per acre.   I urged the view that it
would be unwise, and not free from danger, to place a
large class of citizens in the industrial walks of life
in the position of Crown debtors; that the Government
had already an embarrassing class of Crown tenants,
and that, if we added to that class a still larger class
of Crown debtors, who owed to the State the balances
on their purchases of land, it must tend to sap the
political independence of the population.   I went much
further, and argued that, if men took up small holdings

---

[1] Mr. Wentworth, in the debate on the Constitution Bill, stated distinctly that he limited the first appointment to five years, to enable the
people, if the nominee principle did not work satisfactorily, to introduce
the principle of election.

of forty, eighty, or 120 acres, and lived upon the
land, and turned the soil to the best account both
for themselves and society by systematic and productive cultivation, they were entitled to the freehold on
the first payment of five shillings; and that the sense
of absolute ownership would sweeten their labours, and
breed a feeling of mingled pride and contentment in
our peasant proprietors. At the same time I opposed
the proposal to sell the 'back lands' at five shillings
per acre, as that vague description would include much
of the finest soil of the territory, while so reckless
a mode of alienation would only facilitate the accumulation of large estates, and encourage mere land
speculation.

Mr. PARKES said: He denied the sound policy of a free trade
in the public lands of the colony. He drew a wide distinction
between the nature of those lands and the nature of personal
property. The Legislature, in dealing with the virgin lands of
the colony, was bound to consider what would be the effect
upon society in all time to come of the mode in which those
lands were now alienated. No doubt land ought to be open for
disposal to all who desired to purchase, but its disposal did not
stand on the same footing as other property created by human
labour and skill. The amendment he now submitted would give
the free selector, who should effect the required improvements,
the land in fee-simple without any further payment than the
first five shillings deposit. No stinted liberality ought to cha-
racterise the manner in which they approached the question of
the alienation of the public lands to that class of colonists who,
by their industry and discernment, would make them most productive for the whole. When they were satisfied that there was
a *bonâ fide* purpose to improve and cultivate, all further payment
should be remitted. It was doubted by many hon. members
whether payment would be made if the system of deferred pay-

ments were adopted—[Mr. ROBERTSON : Not by me]—at all events, there was provision made for such payments standing over for an indefinite period. He contended that no persons ought ever to be placed in individual and direct subordination to the State—in a relation different from that occupied by other classes. Under all the circumstances the justice of the case recommended the adoption of a wise liberality in dealing with this part of the subject.

During the debate one of the Ministers (Mr. Arnold) argued that the accumulation of the unpaid balances of the conditional purchasers ('deferred payments') would 'enable the State to raise by a sound system of borrowing the money required for public works.'

Mr. PARKES continued : The committee would not have failed to notice how the Government had changed their ground in reference to this Bill. Hitherto the principle was not to derive revenue from the sale of the lands, but the greater, though more remote, advantage of settling the people on the soil. Now, however, the Government based their arguments on the money value of the land. The committee must decide whether they were going to lend themselves to create an interminable class of Crown debtors in the country—upon whose indebtedness loans were to be contracted : for the Government contemplated paying for their railways out of the proceeds of those debts which were to remain for ever! [Mr. ARNOLD : At the option of the debtor.] The way to obtain railways was not by the miserably inadequate revenue to be derived from the land itself, but by increasing the population, and by the consequent natural increase of the revenue from the legitimate extension of taxation over as wide a surface as possible. The course pursued by the framer of the Bill could only be defended on the ground that these sales to free selectors were special and for special objects. Notwithstanding what had been said by the hon. Secretary for Public Works (Mr Arnold), he should think that a free selector would not fail to appreciate the difference between the semi-serf condition which it was proposed to create for him and the possession of the fee-simple of his land. Under the conditions proposed, would the persons who free-selected land know whether they were living under the blessings of the hon. gentleman's government or under the Czar of Russia, when they had to go year after year with their 9*d*. per acre to some Government official, while they called land their own which was in fact not their own? The advantage to be gained by the State from insisting upon this money balance from the free selectors would be trifling and embarrassing, and the provision would take away, to a great extent, the sweetness of possession, which it should be one of the objects of their legislation to encourage the free selector to desire.

In the light of our experience of the operation of the Land laws, I look back with some misgiving as to the wisdom of my opposition to the system of ' deferred payments.' Not that I entertain any doubt of the soundness of the principles I advocated, if we could have been sure of the *bonâ fides* of the men who free-selected land under that provision of the Act of 1861. But in a short time a system of ' dummying' grew up, by which men fraudulently got possession of large tracts of the choicest land with only a mock compliance with the conditions of the law, and in direct contravention of its spirit and intention.

The following are extracts from the speech in which I opposed the provision for selling ' back lands' by auction at an upset price of five shillings. The clause was negatived on division, the Minister himself voting against it :—

Mr. PARKES: He should give his vote so as to continue the upset price—if they were to continue to sell lands by auction—

at 1*l.* This might appear inconsistent with the course he took last night, when he moved an amendment to remit the balance of 15*s.* for land taken up under free selection, but on that occasion he acted on the special grounds that those who free-selected land would enter upon it under conditions enforcing them to its improvement. But here it was proposed to pass a provision which would open the door to mere trade in land—a thing entirely different from possession on condition of cultivation and improvement. It seemed to him that the class of persons they should encourage above all others by their legislation was that of small cultivators of the soil—men who by their industry would turn the land to the best possible account. If, however, they were to reduce the price in alienating the land to 5*s.* they would open the door to great abuse. The only argument in support of such reduction was that some of the land was not worth 5*s.* But that argument might lead to the adoption of an upset price of one penny, because he believed that there was land in this country not worth having at a gift on terms of compulsory occupation. Five shillings per acre would not reach the real minimum; it would only be an arbitrary price. What they had to fear under this provision was that some of the richest and most valuable tracts of land would be alienated as inferior land. The condition of this country was likely to facilitate such abuse. We had here a number of old and wealthy families with numerous connections—numbering, in some instances, as many as one hundred persons. In addition to these we had another class—the pastoral tenants—who, by reason of their pursuits, had also a practical acquaintance with the country. So that, although we were a small community, we had among us a comparatively large number of wealthy people, who had the colony, as it were, at their fingers' ends. And this clause, just as though it had been framed on purpose, would suit the purposes of those speculative persons.

.    .    .    .    .    .    .    .

He believed that this provision of the Bill, if carried, would not have the effect of alienating from the Crown land which was not worth more than 5*s.*, but it would be operative in alienating land in the highest degree valuable, but the valuable qualities of which would be known only to a few persons at the time of sale. It seemed to him very inconsistent to take such a course as that when they had extracted the 20*s.* per acre from the *bonâ fide* cultivators. Surely, in alienating the public land for the good of all, they ought to consider the use to which it was to be applied. They were not to obstruct the operation's of the capitalist in any way, but, at the same time, it was no part of their duty to smooth the way for his making a large fortune out of the public lands.

Sir John Robertson's Act did immense good. Its broad scope was to enable men to select land for themselves in blocks from 40 to 320 acres, at 1*l.* per acre, without waiting for any surveyor or other Government official, but subject to the conditions of a deposit of five shillings per acre, actual residence, and improvements to the value of one pound per acre in value. The balance of the purchase-money was to remain for a time, not limited by date, at 5 per cent. interest. It is no figure of speech to say that this law unlocked the lands to the industrious settler, and notwithstanding the abuses which too widely grew up, it was the means of bringing into existence hundreds of comfortable homes in all parts of the colony, where the name of its author is held in grateful remembrance. It will have been seen in a previous chapter what a network of difficulties surrounded the man of small means who tried to obtain a rural home in former years; and perhaps the highest tribute to the memory of Sir John Robertson is that, after all the amendments which have been carried, the chief principles of his Act are still embedded in the law of the country.

After the battle for unlocking the lands had been in reality fought and won, in the midst of the last act of the drama, I embarked for England, having lived in the colony upwards of twenty-two years.

# CHAPTER VI

IN 1861 I carried a resolution in the Legislative Assembly in favour of two persons with a good knowledge of the colony being sent to England to make known its advantages as a field for emigrants. The late Right Hon. William Bede Dalley (then a young man) came to me to urge me to accept one of these appointments, in which case, he said, he was prepared to accept the other. I assume that he had ascertained that we could be appointed if we chose to accept. After some consideration, and several consultations together, we decided to go to England on this errand, and we received commissions from the Government accordingly.

The following correspondence explains the nature and terms of the offer made to myself, and of its acceptance :

Department of Lands, May 11, 1861.

My dear Mr. Parkes,—It is the intention of the Government to appoint forthwith, at a salary of 1,000l. a year and allowances, two gentlemen, to proceed to the mother-country as Commissioners of Emigration; and my colleagues and myself are desirous of placing one of those appointments at your disposal. Will you, therefore, say whether or not you are willing to comply with our wishes? It is unnecessary for me to describe for you the nature of the duties of the office, as the proposal, sanctioned by Parliament, originated upon your own motion.

It may however be proper to mention that a similar communication to this has been made to Mr. W. B. Dalley.

I am, &c.

JOHN ROBERTSON.

*Mr. Henry Parkes to Secretary for Lands.*

Sydney, May 13, 1861.

My dear Mr. Robertson,—I beg to acknowledge the receipt of your letter of the 11th instant, offering me, on behalf of yourself and colleagues, the appointment of Commissioner of Emigration in England.

After mature consideration I have determined to accept the appointment, principally with the hope that I may be of material use in successfully carrying out the important undertaking sanctioned by Parliament. I beg the Government to accept my assurance that I shall enter on the duties of my office with an earnest and anxious purpose to disseminate a correct knowledge of this colony, to exhibit its real advantages as a field for the better class of emigrants, and to raise its reputation in the estimation of the British people.

I have this morning resigned my seat in the Legislative Assembly, and shall be prepared at once to receive the instructions of the Government, and to proceed to England by the first opportunity.

I have, &c.

HENRY PARKES.

We joined the steamship *Great Britain* at Melbourne, and arrived in Liverpool on August 4, after a very fair passage for those days. Mr. Dalley and I commenced our labours without loss of time. We took an office in London, and divided the field of our operations; Mr. Dalley selected the Home Counties and Ireland, and I took the West and North of England and Scotland. As no funds were placed at our disposal for the conveyance of emigrants to the colony, our duties were confined to diffusing information respecting the colony and answering enquiries. For these purposes I held meetings, about sixty altogether, in such large centres as Birmingham, Leicester, Nottingham, Derby, Leeds, Manchester, Glasgow, and Greenock, and in many small country towns in the agricultural districts; and everywhere I had crowded audiences. Among the chairmen at these meetings were Lord Lyttelton, Sir John Pakington, Sir Thomas Bazley, and many other influential persons of the time. If I could have given free passages, I might have sent out to the colony 10,000 emigrants. Mr. Dalley's meetings were, I believe, equally successful in point of numbers and unanimity, though I was never able to be present, being always in a different part of the kingdom. Though at this time the cotton famine was raging in the North of England through the blockade of the Southern States, and thousands of families were destitute, I found little sympathy for the cause of emigration among the class of large employers, or on the part of leading persons of the middle class generally. A few noblemen and philosophical reformers, and men connected with the colonies, were the principal promoters. The gentlemen forming Boards of Guardians and similar bodies were all for getting rid of the unthrifty and troublesome, and keeping the steady and industrious at home. The first letter I ever received from Mr. John Bright was in reply to an application which I had made to him to preside at one of my meetings, and it was as follows :—

Rochdale, September 7, 1861.

Dear Sir.—Before you return to your adopted country, I may have the pleasure of meeting you, should you be down in this neighbourhood or when I am in London during the Session of Parliament.

I cannot do anything in reference to your purpose of encouraging emigration from England. I have no doubt you will find persons willing to go away, but the argument for emigration is now much weaker than it was some years ago. There is now more demand for labour, and wages are generally much higher. In this country there has been great difficulty of late in keeping machinery at work owing to the scarcity of labour. Still it is wise for men to emigrate; but the case does not appear to me to require or to justify any special interest in it, or any effort to promote it on my part.

I am, truly yours.

JOHN BRIGHT.

Henry Parkes, Esq.

For fourteen months I worked hard in the mission I had undertaken, and though no visible stream of emigration flowed or could flow from the joint services of Mr. Dalley and myself, as each emigrant had to find his way out to the colony at his own expense, I have met many persons who brought character and skill and capital to New South Wales in consequence of our labours.

Some of the incidents at my meetings were curious

and sometimes comical, but everywhere an earnest attention was paid to what I had to say. The chairman usually enquired whether anyone in the audience desired to ask any questions. On one occasion I was asked, 'Is there any mosquitoes in that country?' At another time a gentleman, after a long pause, asked if I knew Tenterfield, 'because,' said he, 'I have got a son there.' At one meeting I had stated, in enumerating the live stock in the colony, that we possessed upwards of 2,000,000 of horned cattle, and in explaining the price of the necessaries of life, I had quoted the retail price of milk. A grave man in the audience asked me triumphantly how I could reconcile the two statements—2,000,000 of horned cattle and milk 8*d*. a quart? The work introduced me to many men of very interesting character; the late Mr. Charles Holt Bracebridge of Atherstone, Lord Hatherton of Teddesley, Mr. Podmore of Worcester, Sir John Pakington, and others, who made my stay at their hospitable houses very gratifying.

When I was leaving Melbourne, Charles Gavan Duffy gave me notes of introduction to three eminent men in London, one of whom was Thomas Carlyle, in whose estimation, as I discovered afterwards, the Young Ireland leader had a warm place. I sent my note to 5 Cheyne Row through the post. In two or three days I received the following :—

5 Cheyne Row, Chelsea, October 2, 1861.

Dear Sir,—We shall be happy to see you on your return to town. Tea is at 8 P.M.; in general my wife and I lean over it,

and nobody else. Have the goodness to name some evening
that will suit you—and then come, if *you* hear nothing to the
contrary.

In haste,

Yours sincerely,

T. CARLYLE.

On coming up to London some days afterwards, I
wrote to Mr. Carlyle, naming an early evening, and
'hearing nothing to the contrary,' I found my way to
Chelsea, and with a strange feeling of mingled curiosity
and reverence, I knocked at the famous door from which
celebrities were often turned away. My knock was
answered by a demure young person who at once
ushered me into the presence of the grim philosopher
and his gentle wife. The evening meal was of the most
frugal—thin cakes, I think of oatmeal, and a cup of
richly-made tea. After tea my host sat down on the
floor with his back straight up against the wall and his
legs stretched out at full length, and, charging and
lighting a long white clay pipe, he happily puffed away,
stopping at short intervals to talk on all manner of
things in the style of one of his later books. He spoke
unreservedly of great men whom he had known, and he
asked many curious questions about Australia, which
showed the original light in which he viewed some well-
threshed-out subjects of colonisation. For instance, he
contended that, if governing men could only free themselves from the trammels of custom and be truly wise,
they would remove the Sovereign and the Court and all
the machinery of Government to Australia, where the
field for national life was so wide, attractive, and unen-

cumbered, and so leave the contracted spaces and the
murky atmosphere of England behind them.    Of
modern statesmen he spoke most approvingly of Peel,
and in bitterest terms of Lord Melbourne.    Alluding to
the alleged compact between the Melbourne Ministry
and O'Connell, he said that a British statesman, inspired
by true patriotism, would have addressed the great
Irishman thus :—' What! I rule England with your
aid ? No, I'll hang you as a public enemy !'    He spoke
of America and of the Civil War then raging, which
subjects were renewed again and again in later conversations.    He said he had met Daniel Webster when in
England, and regarded him as a great man.    Something
brought up the name of Mr. Howe of Nova Scotia, who
was on a visit to England, and of whom he spoke very
favourably.

In this first visit to Cheyne Row, nothing could
excel the charming manner of Mrs. Carlyle, whose conversation sparkled with quaint humour and womanly
sympathy with noble effort.    Immediately after this
visit I went into Warwickshire, and among other places
I visited the birthplace of Shakespeare at Stratford-on-
Avon.    While there I wrote to Mrs. Carlyle, asking her
acceptance of a small volume of verse which I had
published some years before, and suggesting that, as a
break to his literary toil on ' Frederick the Great,' her
distinguished husband should spend a day or two with
me at Stratford.    I received the following letter in reply :

5 Cheyne Row, Chelsea, October 22.

My dear Sir,—Is it a compliment to my *judgment* or my
*mercy*, your sending the little book of poems to *me* rather than

to my husband, ' *on second thoughts* '?   Anyhow, I am decided
to take it as a compliment to *something*, which you think *I* have
*more* of, not *less* of, than my husband has! and so I thank you
heartily.   My husband, who is up to the roots of his hair in
work, has bade me thank you in his name for your kind invitation, which ' would be a fine thing to accept,' he says, ' if he
*were situated like other men*.'   And I was to explain to you how
it was ' impossible for him to take any holiday, or have any
peace or satisfaction, till this infernal——' &c. &c.

But Heaven forbid I should jest on so wide and woeful a
theme!

Also I was to tell you, that he found the Almanac a great
curiosity, and that you were ' not to suppose that he wished any
foul play to the wretched scoundrels of criminals, only he could
not approve of wild attempts to *wash* black men white—the
thing being hopeless!'

Please come back when you are again in London.

> Yours truly,
> JANE W. CARLYLE.

On the occasion of my next visit to Mr. Carlyle we
had some fresh conversation about Mr. Howe, which
awoke in me a desire to make his acquaintance.   Accordingly I wrote to Mr. Carlyle a few days after, asking if he could give me Mr. Howe's address.   I received
the following reply, which has a special bearing on what
I have already said of his views on colonisation :—

> Chelsea, December 31, 1861.

Dear Sir,—Mr. Howe's card seems to be irrecoverably lost,
and I am sorry therefore to answer that I do not know his
address.   He merely sent up his card ; was rejected (as many
have to be at this door) ; his name suggesting no notion or suspicion of who he was, not for two or three days after, when I
heard that the Nova Scotia Mr. Howe was in this country.   He
has not called again, nor did I yet find time to make a counter-

attempt on him. The card, I can remember, had 'St. James's ' on it—' Street,' 'Place,' or ' Square,' uncertain to me—and I have a dim persuasion that the number was ' 3.' This is all I can say. Of course, you will have no difficulty to make out the actual address when you return ; it is only enquiring of the postman in that locality, or at the utmost, investigating a little in the haunts of colonial people. I should be well pleased if you found him, and (among other more important matters) were so kind as explain to him the above mistake of mine on that head. In former visits of his, I found him an intelligent, energetic, sagacious man, very well worth talking to, of course especially if you had business in his department of activity.

I have no recollection what I said to you about colonisation that evening. The subject used to be of earnest, almost of painful, interest to me in old years ; it seemed to me there had no nation ever had such glorious opportunities of changing its nearly intolerable curses and choking *nightmares* into blessings and winged angels, as has Britain in our day, by *colonising* ; it was so scandalously throwing said opportunity away. I have since learned that Great Britain will go on with her parliamentary palaver—her &c. &c.—were the Day of Judgment close at hand, and turn a totally deaf ear to all considerations of that or the like kind ; and so I have dropped the speculation long ago, and it lies quite dead in me for years and decades past. And to tell you the truth, I am afraid my notions would be of little or no use to you, and indeed are not executable, except on the hypothesis that we had something of a *king* among us again, and that the reign of parliamentary jargon and penny-newspapering had a good deal terminated again, which is to say in other words that the current opinions of English and other men had (with the current *practices*) *immensely changed* for the better! Better to ' drop ' a subject of that kind, if one have practically any use to turn one's own poor span of life to! In a word, according to the *anarchic system* colonisation seems to me to be going on quite as well as one could expect, and anarchy (under fine names) being the established faith for the time being, there is nothing more to be said.

M 2

I was never in my life so busy; but if you came (about 8, some lucky evening) would try to give you an hour again.

Yours sincerely,

T. CARLYLE.

From this period, and throughout the first nine months of 1862, I often spent part of an evening with Mr. and Mrs. Carlyle, and, judging from letters addressed to me in Australia years afterwards, I had the good fortune to be more favourably regarded by them than I ever suspected at the time. These later letters will appear when I come to speak of the attack made upon the life of the Duke of Edinburgh at Sydney, and of the struggle for non-sectarian education. Sometimes I received quaint little notes asking me to come to Cheyne Row on particular evenings, or on a Sunday morning. I seldom did more than listen, as the 'Sage of Chelsea' resumed his place on the floor with his long clay pipe. Speaking of the war between the North and the South, he exclaimed, 'Let them blaze away—it is the dirtiest chimney that has been on fire for many a long day!' On one occasion I was rather incautiously led into speaking of the equality enjoyed in Australia, and used some such language as this: There every man can stand erect and look his fellow in the face. Mr. Carlyle looked at me with a half pitying, half-ironical gleam in his eyes: 'Did you see the Lord Mayor's Show?' he asked. I replied, 'Yes.' 'Well,' said he, 'there were a hundred men in that crowd who would stand erect, and look you in the face, and knock your hat over your eyes into the bargain!' On my next visit he said: 'I have been thinking over your praise of

your responsible governing machine out there which you
have set up in place of the Old Fogies of the Nominee
days; on the whole, I think it is better—if you must
have one or other—than the Old Fogies.' On another
occasion I said to Mr. Carlyle: 'I have sometimes
thought that it would be a good thing for a man like
me—imperfectly educated and with many things always
pressing upon his time, to put aside all books, save ten
or twelve authors, and thoroughly master them. In
such case, what authors would you suggest?' He
made some curt observation which I interpreted as unfavourable, and I felt half ashamed of what I had said.
When I called again he said, ' I have jotted down some
books for you, if you carry out your plan of studying
a few authors,' and he fetched me the list written in
pencil on a torn sheet of paper. A facsimile of it faces
this page.

I doubt if many persons would adopt this selection
of books, famous as was the selector, and excellent as
many of the works undoubtedly are. Another book
which Mr. Carlyle frequently urged upon my notice
was Collins's Peerage (I think the fourth edition), from
which, he said, he had learnt more of English history
than from all other books put together. He described
Collins as an old London bookseller, who devoted all
the spare hours of his life to the acquisition of knowledge, from original sources, about the governing
families of England ; and he thought much more of this
particular issue of his work than of the costly edition
by Sir Egerton Brydges.

On one of my visits (on a Sunday morning) I was

called upstairs by the voice of the philosopher, to a
room at the top of the house, where he was engaged
upon the proof sheets of 'Frederick the Great.' The
walls of the room bore portraits of his hero, and plans
of Frederick's battle-fields ; no other engravings or pictures of any kind. There were no books in the room
except a few relating to the subject of the great work
then going through the press.

One Sunday afternoon Mr. Carlyle had an engagement in Grosvenor Square, and he invited me to accompany him on the way. When some distance from
Chelsea I was accosted by a little begging girl. I gave
the child a sixpence, which called forth a rebuke from
my companion. 'The other day I was asked for alms
in one of these squares by a poor little weeping girl,'
said he : 'I had a profound conviction that no gift from
me could benefit her, but, nevertheless, I gave her some
loose pence. After walking a short distance, I turned
round to see what she did with herself, when I saw
another beggar girl taking the pence from her, and
beating her to make her cry for more. It is of no use
—it is worse ; it is supporting their tyrants to give to
these children.'

When the day came for my departure for Sydney,
I called on the Carlyles to say 'farewell.' We recalled much of our conversations during the year that
had passed since my first call ; again I sat down with
the grand old author of 'Sartor Resartus' and his
gracious wife at the simple tea-table. Mrs. Carlyle
unbent to a little innocent gossip of fashionable life.
A gentleman of rising reputation, who had lately re-

turned from the colonies, and had established himself
in London society, felt himself under an obligation
to entertain an old colonial acquaintance just arrived;
'but,' said he to Mrs. Carlyle, 'I don't know who to
ask to meet him—will you come?' As I was on the
point of leaving, never to see them again, Mrs. Carlyle
gave me a photograph of her husband, with his name
written underneath it; and that photograph is still
among the most precious things in my quiet home in
Sydney. The memory of those days will never leave
me; and I trust I have not altogether failed to profit
by the lessons I received from the great Professor of
heroic wisdom.

I became acquainted with Richard Cobden also
through an introduction from Sir C. Gavan Duffy. I
received an invitation to visit him at Dunford, his
country house near Midhurst. I arrived on a frosty
evening in the middle of November; Cobden met me at
the door, in a wide-brimmed straw hat and a morning
coat, and I received from him a warm homely greeting.
After dinner we chatted mostly about the colony; I
was aware that he had a brother at the diggings in
New South Wales, but the brother's name was never
mentioned by either of us. He spoke very kindly of
Duffy. When the hour for retirement arrived Mr.
Cobden lighted me to my bedroom; there was a glowing fire on the hearth, we sat down beside it, and it was
long after midnight before he bade me good-night. I
explained to him in our conversation the argument of
the Australian protectionist that the duty was necessary
to foster new industries in their infancy. His first words

were, 'There is no accounting for the vagaries and
perversities of the human mind.' He pointed out how
futile any attempt to give unnatural growth to any
industry must ultimately prove itself, and how the cost
of the experiment must always fall upon those whom it
is proposed to benefit. I listened to Mr. Cobden's quiet
wise words in that winter firelight, and, though I had
been bitten by the doctrine of fostering infant industries, I never afterwards wavered from the cause of
free trade. Dunford was blocked in by large landed
estates, and when I took the stage omnibus at Midhurst on my return (there was no railway) I had as my
travelling companions two tradesmen of the town.
There had lately been a skirmish between the game-
keepers and poachers on one of these estates, resulting in the capture of the poachers. My two fellow-
travellers were full of the story, and it struck me
strangely, fresh from Australia, that all their sympathies were with the aristocratic owner of the game,
and against the stealers of his pheasants. I had promised to send some Australian statistics to Mr. Cobden,
and in my letter I tried to describe the episode in the
omnibus. I received the following reply :—

Midhurst, November 21, 1861.

My dear Sir,—I am very much obliged by your kindness in
sending me the statistical and other tables upon your great and
growing country, which will be of interest and value to me.

I have been much amused by your graphic account of your
companions on the omnibus. They were genuine specimens of
traditional Englishmen, who cling to the habits of their an-
cestry with about as little enquiry as to their utility or suitable-

ness to our days as though they were inhabitants of Dahomy
clinging to the 'custom' of their forefathers.

I hope to have the pleasure of renewing our conversation in
London at no distant date, and remain,

Very truly yours,

R. COBDEN.

Henry Parkes, Esq.

I spent some hours with Mr. Cobden in London at
the house of his friend Mr. Paulton, in the spring of
1862, when our conversation on Australian protection
was renewed. His face appeared to me at this time as
one of mingled gravity and tenderness, his manner
unassuming and gentle, his conversation attractive
from its clear thoughtfulness, its point, and its occasional banter. Three years afterwards he died the
good man's death.

In the early part of this visit to England I formed
the acquaintance of the author of 'Tom Brown's
School Days.' Mr. Hughes had been described to me
in Sydney by a gentleman who knew him well as the
'manliest of men'; and I have often thought the words
had a rich application to his character. I saw much
of him at this time, frequently visited at his house in
Park Street, went with him to his occasional lectures,
accompanied him to the Vere Street Church to hear
Frederick Denison Maurice. Our acquaintance has
continued to the present time. To him I am much
indebted for many courtesies, and for many opportunities afforded me to meet important persons. I have
before me now a copy of the 'History of the United
States,' by J. M. Ludlow and Thomas Hughes, contain-

ing this odd inscription : ' *Thomas Hughes*—I meant to
have written Henry Parkes, but as he was persistently
talking to me all the time, went and wrote my own
name instead : but I hope he will accept this book as a
token of the good wishes of one of the authors. Lincoln's Inn, March 17, 1862.' Since then I have
received many interesting letters from Mr. Hughes on
public questions, especially on the legislation in the
cause of education in Australia and in England. The
last time I saw Mr. Hughes was in 1884, when I
dined with him at his house in Chester; but I never
met him or heard from him without feeling myself
a better man from the touch of his brave Christian
character.

When gold was discovered in Australia nearly forty
years ago, Mr. Thomas Woolner, the famous sculptor of
the present day, came to Sydney in the flood of adventurers. He executed medallions of many of the Australian celebrities of that time—Mr. Wentworth, Mr.
Martin, Admiral King, and others. I was then at the
head of a daily journal; Mr. Woolner and I soon began
to know each other. Indeed, I have heard him in later
years draw a picture at a distinguished dinner party in
London, with a good deal of graphic delineation, of the
manner in which we first met. Our acquaintance was
renewed on my arrival in London in 1861. I saw much
of Mr. Woolner during my stay in England, and received
from him many attentions which were of much value
to me ; and our friendly relations have grown warmer,
I trust, as time has worn away. When I first held
office, a few years afterwards, I had the privilege of

giving a commission to Mr. Woolner for the statue of
Captain Cook, which now occupies one of the finest
positions in Sydney, overlooking the waters of Port
Jackson. I have gazed upon many celebrated statues
in America, in England, and on the Continent ; but I
know of none more striking as the embodiment of the
sculptor's conceptive genius than Mr. Woolner's great
work in Sydney.

In the course of my journeys through England and
the arrangements for public meetings, I was brought
into communication with many men of the middle class,
sheriffs of counties, mayors, master manufacturers, and
other persons of local consideration ; and I was surprised by the sneering allusions to reform and reformers,
and the expressions of thinly-disguised sympathy with
the aristocracy which I heard at their social gatherings.
Mr. Cobden and Mr. Bright did not appear to me to be
idols with the new men of opulence whom their statesmanship had so conspicuously benefited ; and even the
masses seemed to be deadened by the want of sincerity
in high places. It was the period when the Palmerston
Ministry were playing with the question of Parliamentary
reform. I attended two or three political meetings,
but they were miserably tame in comparison with the
meetings in the agitations of the first Reform Bill ; nor
were they equal in spirit and enthusiasm to meetings in
Australia.

The American Civil War was dividing English
society into opposite camps, the majority of the higher
classes siding with the South, and the mass of the
working-men, with such leaders as John Bright, standing

steadily by the North.  In November, 1861, an event
occurred which shook the very soul of England.  The
English mail steamer *Trent* had left Havannah on the
7th with Messrs. Slidell and Mason on board as Confederate Commissioners to Europe ; on the 8th she was
stopped in the Bahama Channel by the United States
frigate *San Jacinto,* and the Commissioners were seized
under the British flag and carried away as prisoners.
The news was brought to England by the steamship
*Plata,* which should have brought Messrs. Slidell and
Mason, according to their arrangements at Havannah.
For some days war seemed imminent and hardly
avoidable.  After Cabinet consultations, and the assembling of the Privy Council, a Queen's messenger had
left on the evening of the third day with a special
despatch for the British Minister at Washington.  The
Southern sympathisers were for chastising the Yankees
at whatever cost.  The English side of the threatened
rupture was concisely expressed in four lines of contemporary poetry :—

> Dishonour hath no equipoise in gold,
>   No equipoise in blood, in loss, in pain :
> Till they whom force hath ta'en from 'neath the fold
>   Of her proud flag, stand 'neath its fold again.

There is no need now to discuss the questions which
then agitated the public mind.  Right was done and
the war-cloud passed away.  But the seizure on board
the *Trent* intensified the interest of Englishmen in the
tremendous conflict across the Atlantic which threatened
to split the great Republic asunder.  It is deserving of
record that, in all privileged circles, on all the higher

planes of English life, the rebels—the men who had been plotting and struggling through many years to extend and secure the domain of slavery—commanded sympathy and support. The recognition of the Confederates as a nation was loudly talked of, motions of a friendly character were made in Parliament, and in the great drawing-rooms few words of sympathy with the Federal cause were to be heard. I attended the Commemoration at Oxford, and the name most boisterously cheered by the undergraduates was that of Jefferson Davis. In the House of Commons I heard an attempt made to hoot down William Edward Forster, then comparatively new to Parliament, when speaking in support of the North.

On the morning of December 14, 1861, Prince Albert died. Whatever opinions we may have formed, and whatever may be our political leanings, to a right-minded man it is beautiful to see how the poor lose sight of their own privations and sufferings in the gloom of a mighty sorrow such as then fell upon the heart and home of Queen Victoria. It seemed as if death had entered every household in the land. Rich and poor, high and low, all alike joined in the national mourning. It could hardly be believed at first; it was so unexpected, so sudden, so entirely a thing never thought of. The tolling of the great bell of St. Paul's only set men wondering, until the cold, dark, unmitigable truth spread its shadow over the mighty city, and, far and wide, over the heart of the sorely stricken nation. At the time I wrote the following in a letter sent out to Sydney :—

The signs of mourning have continued everywhere until to-day, when the body of the Prince has been consigned to the grave. Never in English history has any death been so visibly felt by all ranks of the English people. The working classes, for the improvement of whose social condition Prince Albert laboured so earnestly, so wisely, so effectually, have assembled in thousands and sung together the Rev. Newman Hall's beautiful adaptation of the national anthem.

To-day I heard seven thousand people of all social degrees mingling their voices in this strain of national sorrow and supplication. In every city and town of England to-day the ordinary pursuits of life have been suspended. But it is not by closed shutters and doors, by habiliments of mourning, by the tolling of church bells, and by drooping flags wreathed with crape that the national sorrow is most touchingly expressed. You see it everywhere in the grief-burdened faces of the people. You see it in the utter absence of any expression or sign inconsistent with this sense of loss. Deeply and with a true love do the people mourn for the Consort of their beloved Queen.

And she, poor Royal Lady! how does her woman's heart bear up in this great and sudden trial? 'Many poor women have had to bear this trial' was the simple outburst of Victoria's grief and resignation. The people are told that their Queen is calm. Nothing more is known from the seclusion of her island-home.

In the cause of emigration I had the hearty assistance of several influential ladies, Mrs. Nassau Senior (sister of Thomas Hughes), Miss Florence Hill, and others. I held a meeting at Battersea (where a large number of navvies were working), at the instance of Mrs. Senior, and she and other ladies must have done all the work of getting up the meeting, which was very successful. Hundreds of letters used to reach the office every week, but in nearly all cases from persons who wanted free passages, and in many cases from persons who did not appear to care where they went if they could leave England without cost to themselves. Still, large numbers of excellent men and women were anxious to emigrate; but very few who possessed the means of conveying themselves and families to the Antipodes.

Mr. Dalley and I worked together very cordially on this mission; we had differences of opinion as to the most expedient course at times, but we always came to a satisfactory agreement. In after years we were drawn into hostile camps, and some bitter things were said; but for some time before his lamented death our friendly relations were renewed. He resigned his office as emigration commissioner, and returned to the colony some months before I did, and when on the eve of leaving England he wrote to me the following farewell letter:—

Liverpool, June 14, 1862.

My dear Parkes,—I write to you within a few moments of my embarkation to say that farewell which I found it difficult to speak last night. At the close of our relationship I am deeply sensible, my dear friend, of your uniform kindness during the whole period of our absence from home—the recollection of which at this moment almost reproaches me for leaving you. I shall religiously regard my undertaking to endeavour in any way which Heaven may suggest to me to bring about an improvement in your boy,[1] looking upon my success in the effort as the most gratifying proof I can give you of my sense of the value and sincerity of your friendship. God

[1] Robert Sidney Parkes, who died January 2, 1880.

bless you, my dear Parkes, and in the hope of soon welcoming
you home,

I am, your affectionate friend,

WILLIAM B. DALLEY.

My brother sends his love and heartiest wishes soon again
of seeing you.—W. B. D.


The success of men in the Australian colonies, who
have arrived from other countries without money and
without friends, is to be found on every side of us.
And the men born in the country of poor parents furnish as numerous examples of success. The richest
man in all Australia at the present time is a native-
born Australian, who began his career on his savings
as a farm labourer. One of the great men of the early
days, whose ambition was to found families, had an
assigned servant who acted as his coachman. A few
years afterwards, he found himself a ruined man, and
the coachman attended the sale of his effects, and
bought the carriage and horses, and this ' assigned servant' of the great man died a wealthy merchant. I
have myself seen a man standing by a door laid upon
trestles with a few locks, hinges, and nails upon it—all
his stock in trade—who soon established himself in a
regular hardware business, which grew into one of the
largest establishments in the colony. The man is still
living, the possessor of large wealth, a member of Parliament, and held in respect by all who know him. In
all substantial particulars there are many like him. In
a new state of society, when men are too busy to listen
to the explanations of others, or to make allowance for

their mistakes, there is one quality which, of itself, will always secure friends and lead to fortune. That is trustworthiness. I will select a case only distinguished by industry, temperance, thrift, and trustworthiness; it is the case of a personal friend.

In one instance out of very many which might be given, my friend's story shows how beneficial the change from England to Australia has proved a thousand times over to individuals. He was a compositor, and worked for small remuneration in England. He emigrated to Victoria during the early 'rush' caused by the gold discoveries. He dropped into employment at once at what must have appeared to him fabulously high wages, 10*l.* to 12*l.* a week. Fortunately, my friend was a young man of industrious and frugal habits, and instead of living at a rate corresponding to his high wages, he lived thriftily, and commenced saving his money. In a short time he had saved a sufficient sum to enable him to send to England for a 'general printing office,' namely, the necessary presses and types to establish himself in business as a printer. By the time that the printing office arrived, he had saved a further considerable sum of money, and at the same time had formed the acquaintance of a young woman whom he proposed to marry. The wedding took place without delay; the newly-married man purchased a light dray and a covered van, he put his printing office on the one and his wife into the other, and thus provided, he started off for the goldfields, to find a suitable locality for the establishment of a newspaper. He found a place for his purpose, a comparatively obscure 'dig-

gings' at that time, but a well-known goldfield of later
years; and the 'Bramblewood Advertiser' was started.
As he told me in his own house, with a blush of conscious pride, many years afterwards, he was himself
very often the editor, reporter, compositor, and press-
man. He and his wife folded the paper, and in part
delivered it at the diggers' tents.

It was more than thirty years since I parted from
my friend in London. Though I knew he was in Victoria,
I had never heard from him. He was too busy and practical a man to lose his time in useless letter-writing.
In 1870 I happened to be in Melbourne, and walking
down Collins Street, I was met by a well-dressed middle-
aged man, with the exclamation, 'This is a pleasure I
have been longing for through many years!' I explained that I could not recollect him. 'Not recollect
me!' he cried; 'do you recollect this walking cane?'
and held out the cane with which he was walking. I
took the cane, and recognised it at once as my own
handiwork when a lad—a gift from me to him when
we were both lads together. It was indeed my early
friend, whose story as a journalist at the goldfields I
will finish in his own words: 'By working hard and
keeping down expenses, we soon got on,' said he. 'The
paper grew in circulation and in the support of the
advertising public, so much so that a gentleman came
up to Bramblewood from Melbourne to establish an
opposition paper, and he brought with him a complete
newspaper plant, a young university man as editor, a
gentleman as overseer, and another as book-keeper.
We took the threatened opposition quite calmly. I

told my wife, who was my only overseer and book-keeper, not to be alarmed, we should soon want to extend our office, and it would be cheaper to buy out our new neighbours than to send to Melbourne for material. As I anticipated, the expenses soon broke down the opposition, and we bought the new office, stock, lock, and barrel, at very satisfactory prices. We went on gradually improving our paper, and all the time laying by money. I bought shares in promising gold companies and bits of land likely to rise in value. I have now come down to spend the rest of my days here, having transferred the paper to other hands, still retaining a large interest in it, and being secured in a good income from my other various little properties.'

I visited my friend in his new home. He had bought a block of land in a pleasant Melbourne suburb, which was bounded on three sides by streets growing every day more important. There were then two houses on this block of land; he lived in the smaller and let the larger. After warmly receiving me, and recounting some of the boyish experiences of our early days, my friend went to a room he called his study and returned with a bundle of mementoes of our divided past; scraps of rhyme written by me and printed by him on slips of paper when we were boys, little articles made by me and given to him as keepsakes in those far-gone days; newspaper portraits and personal descriptions of all which he had come across during his Australian life— all carefully treasured in evidence of that friendship which for so many years had found no voice, and which now broke upon me with such genuine beauty. A few years after this, I visited my friend again in his Melbourne home : his block of land was now occupied by rows of houses fronting the three streets ; he was himself a magistrate of the colony, a director of large charities, and a wealthy man. But the same features of neatness, economy, and homely comfort marked his unpretending home.

I have given this case because of my personal interest in the fortunes of the man, and also on account of the almost romantic incidents of the story. But on all hands successful men may be pointed out who began with nothing in the shape of worldly goods ; they had, however, what was of more value to them in their efforts—the homely qualities of industry, perseverance, and thrift. Idleness and extravagance will not lead to fortune in Australia any more than in other countries.

# CHAPTER VII

I REMAINED in England until late in October, 1862,
when I returned to Sydney by the ship *Spray of the
Ocean*, making the long sea passage in a little over eighty
days. Some few months after my return I was induced
to offer myself as a candidate for East Maitland in opposition to the re-election of Mr. J. B. Darvall, who had
joined the Cowper Ministry as Attorney-General. Mr.
Darvall had been strongly—it might be said bitterly—
opposed to that Ministry, and his acceptance of office
from Mr. Cowper was received with surprise and much
disapproval. Still I think I acted indiscreetly in entering into the contest, though I had a very warm and
influential support. I was nominated by Mr. J. N.
Brunker, afterwards Minister for Lands, and I polled
well, though I lost the election by a narrow majority.
Early in 1864 I was invited to become a candidate
for Braidwood, but declined to offer myself. In my
absence, however, I was nominated, but the candidate
on the spot, who had actively canvassed the district,
defeated me by ten or twelve votes. In the same

month, April 1864, I was elected to the Legislative
Assembly for Kiama, by a majority of two to one.   On
re-entering Parliament, I took my seat on the Opposition
side of the House.   Much had been done of which I
disapproved, and more had been omitted which in my
judgment ought to have been attempted to be done.
I was by no means in accord with the regular Opposition, and I found other members very much in my
frame of mind.   So things drifted on in vague distrust
and uncertainty during the Session.   Mr. Martin (afterwards Sir James), with Mr. William Forster and Mr.
Geoffrey Eagar, was in office at the head of his first
Ministry; and he certainly had managed affairs so as to
cause much dissatisfaction.   The Government had indulged in a recess of six months, and met Parliament
on October 18, when there was not sufficient time for
transacting the public business before the close of the
financial year.   An amendment on the Address, after a
debate of some days, was carried on November 2 by
thirty-six to twenty-nine votes.   As the immediate consequence of this motion, Parliament was dissolved on
the 10th.   The Elections proved very disastrous to the
Ministers.   The Premier and two of his colleagues were
defeated in Sydney by large majorities, and the discom-
fiture of the Martin party extended throughout the
colony.

When the new Parliament met, the Ministry was
defeated on the Address by forty-two to fourteen votes.
Efforts had been made by Mr. Martin to arrange a treaty
with the colony of Victoria for the non-collection of the
Customs duties on the borders of the two colonies; but

the negotiations had terminated unsuccessfully. Attempts to put the finances of the colony in a sounder
state had not proved more fortunate in results. And
in the interior the outrages of bushrangers had become
alarming.

Mr. Cowper was recalled to office, forming his fourth
Ministry, on February 3, 1865, which lasted till January 21 following. This Government was one with a
very uncertain hold on the feeling of the House and the
country, and during the eleven months and eighteen
days of its existence it had three different Treasurers,
three different holders of the office of Attorney-General,
as well as other changes in the occupants of office. It
was a Ministry of shifts and contrivances and had no
power to effect good. I received myself the doubtful
compliment of the offer of office from Mr. Cowper, while
he was looking out for means of gaining new support.
The head of the Post Office up to this period (the latter
part of 1865) had been a permanent appointment; it
was now proposed to make the Postmaster-General a
member of the Ministry. I waited upon Mr. Cowper
by invitation at the Colonial Secretary's office, when,
with the utmost cordiality, he informed me that he had
sent for me with the approval of all his colleagues to
offer me the office of Postmaster-General, with a seat in
the Cabinet, and with an undertaking that Parliament
should be invited to make the salary equal to the
salaries of the other Ministers (the salary at the time
was, I think, 950l.) I acknowledged the Premier's
courtesy and consideration, but told him briefly that I
must decline his offer; that I did not feel that I could

co-operate with the gentlemen with whom he was associated. In point of fact, I felt keenly that it was a
culpable neglect that no worthy endeavour had been
made to reconstruct the Legislative Council on an
elective basis during the five years allowed by Mr.
Wentworth for the trial of the nominee principle. I
felt also keenly dissatisfied that nothing had been done,
or worthily attempted, in the cause of popular education.
I disagreed with the Government in their financial
proposals as far as they had been foreshadowed.

On my refusal of Mr. Cowper's offer, Mr. James
Augustine Cunneen was appointed Postmaster-General
as ' a member of the Government without a seat in the
Cabinet.' But this condition of office only existed for
a short time, and has never been repeated.

At an earlier period of the year 1865, on August 10,
in a speech to my constituents, I had spoken of the
state of public affairs in the following terms :—

When the Treasurer came down with his budget he was in
a plight very much resembling that of a schoolboy, who has
got into a predicament, where he is forced to disclose something very bad of himself. As the words came out of his
lips the tears were all but coming down from his eyes, and he told
the House with fear and trembling that he did not know what
to do for money. There were many others in the same bad way it
was to be feared. Well, as the Government must have more
revenue, he voted for the plan they proposed for raising it by a
system of stamp duties. It was right that the electors should
know that in these money measures the Assembly must either
accept or reject the proposals of the Crown. Members could not
substitute financial notions of their own for those of the Minister,
and thus when the Minister told them that the public credit
was at stake in their measures, a great responsibility was cast

on the Legislature. He did not much approve of this system of stamp duties. He feared it would be found very vexatious in its working, and expressed himself to that effect at the time, but he voted for the Bill from the case of necessity put forth in its support, and he was there to take his full share of responsibility in assenting to it. There were some considerations too which induced him to assent to the Stamp Act on its merits. The public burdens hitherto had fallen very unequally on the different classes of society. The possessor of large properties and the man who only possessed a tobacco-pipe and pannikin paid the same rate of taxes, which was not just, and these stamp duties, objectionable as they were in many respects, would certainly fall principally on the classes identified with property. Still, upon mature consideration of the subject, he thought a system of stamp taxes was not suited to the circumstances of a new country, and the sooner a better system was substituted for it the better for all. But something else came after the Stamp Act. That wonderful financier, Mr. Smart, had a wonderful way of doing business. One morning when he thought the session was drawing to a close, he read in the newspapers that Mr. Smart was about to come down again upon us with a second budget. Two budgets in three months was enough to frighten us from our propriety. And sure enough Mr. Smart came down with two new Bills for imposing more burdens. He again pulled a long face and said he thought he had enough, but he found he had not. The first dip into the people's pockets was unsatisfactory, and he must dip again. We then had the famous Package Bill, which in its first inception imposed an equal duty on all packages of goods coming into the country, whether a case of gooseberries or onions from Tasmania, or a case of gold watches or silks from England or France. But the greengrocers rose up as one man, and the fruiterers moved in deputation upon the Treasury. It was represented that the gooseberries coming in one day would spoil before the Customs could be moved to permit their landing on the second, and the great gooseberry interest was too much for the Minister. The Government could not stand up against a cargo of rotten fruit and vegetables, and so gooseberries and other articles of colonial produce were exempted from the operation of the Bill. But the Package Act as it now stood levied the same amount of duty on a parcel worth 10s. as it did on a parcel worth 500l. Then there was another Bill for increasing the duty on all articles then dutiable. He had from first to last opposed both these Bills. He based his opposition on the ground that this bit-by-bit plan of submitting the financial measures of a Government was foreign to the parliamentary practice of England, and ought not to be tolerated. But if this objection had not existed he should have opposed these measures on their merits, as about the rudest and clumsiest ever devised by any Government. He should now with their permission say a few words on the present state of things, and the public questions presenting themselves for consideration in the future. The present condition of the colony demanded an earnest and honest investigation of the causes of the prevailing depression. And this was clearly the duty of the politician. Men who undertook the responsibility of interfering with the public interests beyond the province of the ordinary duties of the citizen were clearly bound to free themselves as much as possible from prejudice, to close their eyes to consequences affecting their own individual interest, and to endeavour to bring whatever ability they possessed to bear faithfully on all questions which they had power to influence. But at a season of popular discontent like the present, when it was felt on all hands that the affairs of the State were seriously disordered, and the forces which were available for giving us strength as a community were in a large measure misused or lost, it specially behoved public men to do their utmost, in justice to themselves and to the public, to discover why we are passing through this period of unnatural adversity, and then endeavour to supply the natural remedies. How was it that 400,000 people of British origin in free possession of a territory capable of sustaining a population of 40,000,000, and in a land abundantly blessed with all the natural elements of wealth, were nevertheless in a condition of commercial stagnation and suffering, in some respects positively worse than that super-

induced by the accumulated mismanagement and improvidence
of ages in older countries? This could not be the normal state
of things. The colony had suffered heavily of late years from
the visitations of Providence; but neither failing crops, nor
floods, nor droughts, were sufficient to account for the long
prevailing depression that spared no branch of industry and
seemed to afflict the most valuable classes with the greatest
severity. In this working-day world of ours the most valuable
thing—and viewed in its true light the most honourable thing
—was human labour; and in a new country this precious attribute of man, which dimly reflected Divinity itself in its creative
power, ought to find endless employment. One could not travel
through any district of this colony without seeing a thousand
things which required to be improved by human labour. No man
possessed houses or land which would not be rendered more
valuable if more labour were expended upon them. No man
occupied any position which subjected the forces of nature in
any degree to his control who would not be able to improve that
position if he had more labour to assist him in his operations.
And yet the fact could not be explained away that in this rich
and extensive country, occupied by a handful of population, and
where of all precious things labour was the most precious, and
of all the things wanted labour was most wanted, there were
men willing and able to work who had great difficulty in finding
employment. This was one of the strange and startling facts of
the present time. Could it be that there were too many industrious men in the country—that we had too much of what we
most wanted? No man not very ignorant nor absolutely insane
would say that such was the cause. The cause was to be found
in the defective nature of our industrial machinery and our
economical agencies. In every occupation of life our energies
were impelled by a too speculative spirit, and the idea of per-
manency had not sufficient hold of the mind. Our aims were
too extravagant and our efforts in consequence were to a great
extent spasmodic and self-exhaustive. A colonising population
had a natural tendency to waste its strength in this direction,
constantly striving to grasp too much and constantly missing

the true end of all exertion—that secure possession of a suffi-
ciency of earth's blessings which, tempered by repose and
enjoyment, constitutes happiness. Everywhere we might see
objects commemorative of this waste of life; houses built in
inaccessible situations, works begun to remain unfinished, traces
of enterprises that started to life on the wildest calculations and
failed. These ideas of extravagance and this misdirection of
energy infected the Government as well as the people, and the
consequence was that in proportion to these fruitless efforts the
productive power of the community was lost.

Amongst the measures of the Cowper Government
was a Bill for the suppression of bushranging, which
passed into law under the name of the Felons' Apprehension Act. This measure was unprecedented in the
severity of its provisions; it authorised the outlawry of
any bushranger, under certain conditions, by a special
warrant issued by a Judge of the Supreme Court, and
empowered any person, whether a constable or not, to
apprehend such outlaw, alive or dead, without being
accountable for using deadly weapons, and it gave a
reward of one hundred pounds for any such apprehension. It further provided that any person who harboured bushrangers or supplied them with firearms or
ammunition, or rendered them assistance, or gave false
information to the police concerning them, should forfeit
all his real and personal property, and be liable to imprisonment with hard labour for five years. Though I
supported the second reading of this Bill, I spoke and
voted against its severe provisions in committee. The
evil which had grown up was very great and alarming,
but the remedy appeared to many reasonable minds to
have that fatal flaw so often derived from times of ex-

treme excitement, of going too far and in too fierce a
spirit. What was wanted at the time was not so much
a severer law as more vigour and vigilance, and a
clearer and more penetrative judgment in carrying the
law into effect. Though the second reading of the
Felons' Apprehension Bill was carried by 37 to 4 votes,
the late Prime Minister and Attorney-General, and two
of his colleagues, voted in the small minority.

Mr. Cowper's financial proposals broke down completely, and, deluded by the soft phrases of his opponents, he adopted their policy, after having utterly failed
in his own. His Treasurer resigned after this failure ;
but Mr. Cowper faced the new difficulty and informed
the House on December 20, ' that in consequence of the
refusal of the committee to sanction all the proposals of
the late Colonial Treasurer for raising revenue, it was
necessary to have recourse to new methods.' He proposed to levy a duty on imports of 5 per cent. *ad valorem* as one part of his new scheme. I made a speech
against this proposal of which the following are the
opening sentences :—

That when the Honourable Chief Secretary submitted his resolution, amidst the rather noisy cheers of the House, he thought
the honourable gentleman must have felt rather uncomfortable.
At all events there were heard most distinctly amidst those loud
cheers two separate sets of voices. There were the cheers of
self-gratulation and rather pardonable exultation on the Opposition side of the House, amongst the late Ministry and their
friends, who had succeeded in imposing their protectionist views
on this Free-trade Government ; and there were the insolent
cheers of an unintelligent triumph on the other side—the
triumph of the successful double-dealing and manœuvre of

their slippery chief. But this kind of thing was only a
thing of the hour, and there would come a sober time of
reckoning even if they were successful to-night. If he could
have been induced by any considerations, in view of something less desirable that might be substituted, to have given
his vote for doubling the tea and sugar duties, he certainly
should have been prepared to have voted for doubling those
duties rather than for the proposition that had been made to-
night. But he certainly could never have been induced to do
that, because it did not follow that if this thing was intolerable,
we should accept something that was scarcely less tolerable.
He did not wish to misstate the arguments that had been urged
either for or against the proposition ; he did not wish to mislead
the sense of the committee. He was fully aware that the arguments, whatever they might be worth, against the proposition
submitted by Mr. Samuel, the honourable member for Wellington, were based upon what were conceived to be an inequality in
the incidence of taxation. But quite a different class of arguments rose up against such a proposition as this. Here we
have a proposition for increasing the burdens of the country in
a manner that, even if it should be successful in raising the
trifling sum estimated, would carry with it derangement and
injury to the infant commerce of the country in all its branches.
Any interference with that very tender and important branch of
the public interest—the intercolonial commerce—was to be de-
precated in the strongest possible terms. And all this was to
be done for the purpose of raising 130,000l. ! Because, after
listening with the greatest attention to the honourable member
for West Sydney (Mr. Joseph), he was much more inclined to take
that honourable gentleman's estimate of the probable revenue from
these new duties than that of the Collector of Customs. Large
deductions would have to be made for the free list, and for the
large amount of goods transhipped to other parts of Australia ;
and there would also be large deductions by reason of the system that now obtained of overvaluing the imports, which of
course would prevail no longer. He would call attention to
the remarkable speech by which this proposition was submitted.

A great deal was said to us about schemes of retrenchment, but these schemes were indicated in such dim phraseology, and were propounded in such a hypothetical way, that scarcely any honourable member could expect to see them carried out. Then there was something said about an income tax. But how was it that there was no promise of bringing in such a tax? All that was said was that it might be desirable to see whether the House would consider the propriety of giving their support to an income tax. But there was no mistake whatever as to what the honourable gentleman said about the *ad valorem* duties. They were submitted all ready to be crammed down the throats of the people because it was known that on the Opposition side of the House there were certain gentlemen who could not do other than vote for these duties. Did any honourable member believe for a moment that, if these *ad valorem* duties were passed, there would be any great pains taken to make reductions in the public service, or that any serious attempt would be made to introduce an income tax? But we were asked to swallow this nauseous dose of *ad valorem* duties, surrounded as it was by a coating of promises of the most vague and dim character. Were the committee prepared to accept these *ad valorem* duties? Let it never be forgotten that the whole of the members who sat on the Government side of the House who had seats in the late Parliament opposed the very same proposition as this when brought forward by the Martin Ministry.

Within the next few days the Cowper Ministry was a thing of the past, having been defeated on a direct vote by overwhelming numbers. The Opposition at the time consisted of two groups, one of which sided with me, while the other followed Mr. James Martin. We held some opinions in common, and were not in accord on other questions; but it was obvious enough that no efficient Government could be formed except by the union of the two parties.

# CHAPTER VIII

On January 21, 1866, I received a note from Mr. Martin[1] requesting me to call upon him at his chambers. On seeing me, he at once informed me that he had been sent for by Sir John Young to form a Ministry, and that he had accepted the commission. He explained some things which the Governor had said to him which had an interest for both him and me in relation to persons who might join us as colleagues, but which have no interest for the public at the present day. He said he wished me to take the office of Colonial Secretary, he himself holding the office of Attorney-General with the premiership. We then had some conversation as to the course to be pursued and the measures to be introduced, and Mr. Eagar, who was to hold the office of Treasurer, joined us. I intimated my willingness to join in the formation of the Government, and within two hours afterwards the other offices were offered and accepted. The new Government, notwithstanding some apparent inconsistencies in its political composition, was

---

[1] Afterwards Sir James Martin, Chief Justice of the Colony.

destined to render important services to the country. Mr. Martin and I held opposite opinions on several public questions, including questions of taxation and electoral reform ; on others we were in cordial agreement, and our agreement embraced the question of education, the management of destitute children, prison management, and other subjects demanding public attention. We were not long before we embodied our views in measures for the consideration of Parliament.

The Industrial Schools Act, which I hope will long remain on the Statute Book, was entirely the work of Mr. Attorney-General Martin. Its scope in meeting the necessitous circumstances of outcast children is fully explained in the fourth section, which is in these words :—' Every child whose age in the opinion of the person apprehending or ordering the apprehension, as hereinafter mentioned, shall not exceed sixteen years, who shall be found lodging, living, residing, or wandering about in company with reputed thieves or with persons who have no visible lawful means of support, or with common prostitutes, whether such reputed thieves, persons, or prostitutes be the parents or guardians of such child or not, or who shall have no visible lawful means of support, or who shall have no fixed place of abode, or who shall be found begging about any street, highway, court, passage, or other public place, or who shall be found habitually wandering or loitering about the streets, highways, or public places in no ostensible lawful occupation, or who shall be found sleeping in the open air, may be apprehended by any constable or peace officer or by any other person,

and taken before any two Justices of the Peace to be
dealt with as hereinafter is directed.' The Bill provided
for the proper care and instruction of the children
and their due apprenticeship to industrial callings.   Its
provisions were eloquently explained to the Assembly
by its learned author, who never appeared to more
advantage than when speaking on subjects of this
character.   Both Houses took to the Bill very kindly,
and after friendly debate it became law.   Two institutions were soon established under the provisions of this
Act, one on the ship *Vernon*, described in a previous
chapter, and another for girls which has had a more
untoward history.   It is a fact, however painful, that
young girls, who fall within the circumstances of
neglect and destitution contemplated by the law, are
much more difficult to rescue than boys of similar ages.
This arises, strange as it may appear to some persons,
not from the more vicious disposition, but from the
more sensitive and tender nature, of the children.   The
difficulty is twofold, in fixing upon the right system of
treatment and in finding the right person to carry it
out.   Our industrial school for girls, though it has undoubtedly done much good, has not been a pronounced
success.

Side by side with this measure was a Bill, also the
exclusive work of Mr. Martin, ' to establish juvenile Re-
formatories.'   While the Act just referred to stopped
short of the actual criminal class, and aimed at rescuing
the children pushed to the brink of the precipice, the
second measure was designed to meet the case of
juvenile law-breakers actually under the sentence of the

Courts. This Bill was also speedily made law. The
fourth section enacts, 'Whenever any person whose
age shall, in the opinion of the Court or Justices by or
before whom such person shall be convicted as hereinafter mentioned, be under sixteen years shall be convicted of any offence punishable by law either upon
information before a jury or on summary conviction
by imprisonment for the period of fourteen days or any
other longer period, such Court or Justices may in
addition to the sentence which may be then and there
passed as a punishment for such offence direct such
offender to be sent at the expiration of such sentence,
or, instead of passing upon such person the sentence
prescribed by law for such offence, direct such offender
to be sent forthwith to some one of the aforesaid
reformatory schools, to be there detained for a period
of not less than one year and not exceeding five years,
and such offender shall be liable to be detained pur-
suant to such direction. Provided that the Governor
with the advice of the Executive Council may at any
time order any such offender to be discharged from any
such reformatory school.' Not more than one reformatory has been established under this Act, and that one
for young female offenders; and, in perplexing contrast
to the industrial school for girls, it has been a marked
success. The Shaftesbury Reformatory, under the
management of Mrs. Agnes King, is really a credit to
the colony. This seems to prove that success depends
almost wholly upon individual fitness in those placed
in authority over such institutions. No reformatory for
boys has as yet been established; chiefly, I believe,

because the number of boy criminals has not been
considered sufficient to justify the expense of the
separate maintenance of such an institution. But it is
now in contemplation to establish a reformatory for
boys in connection with an experimental farm in one of
the country districts.

While this legislation was being carried through
Parliament, the attention of the Government, and my
attention as Minister especially, was directed to conditions of misery and neglect in some of the public institutions, and of lawlessness and daring crime in
the country which were of a startling character. The
asylums for the sick and for the insane were discovered to be in a state which could not be allowed
to continue without public disgrace, and in some parts
of the country the wild crime of bushranging had put
forth a front of audacity and cruelty which produced a
general feeling of terror. While regularly attending in
my place in Parliament, and bearing my full part in its
proceedings, I was called upon to give my vigilant
attention to the grave problems which had to be solved
in the maintenance of the law and the public security,
and in the general work of administration. These large
subjects will, however, be more properly dealt with in
another chapter. I return to the legislative work of
the Government in the Session of 1866, which fell
more especially to my hands.

On the occasion of my election to the Legislative
Council, in May 1854, I thus stated my opinion in
general terms on the question of education: 'With
regard to the great question of education, I have

already declared myself, as the systems at present stand, in favour of the national system. But so much importance do I attach to the work of mental training as the foundation of every social virtue, that I should be prepared to support any modification or alteration of that system which would more adapt it to the peculiar wants of the remote, thinly populated, and scattered districts of the colony.' As explained, I did not accept office until twelve years after this date, but before the first year of my ministerial life was over I had introduced and succeeded in passing the Public Schools Act of 1866. The Bill provided for the establishment of Public Schools of a non-sectarian character, and for the continuation of support to Denominational schools on certain clearly prescribed conditions, one of which was that they should receive the same class of trained teachers, the same lesson books, and be subject to the same inspection and discipline as the public schools. But one hour a day was to be set apart for denominational teaching by the respective churches. One golden provision of the Bill was that no person, man or woman, should be allowed to enter any school as a teacher who had not been trained for the work of teaching. These were the main features of the new measure, but they constituted a vast change from the previous state of things.

It was proposed to train under the direction of the State all the teachers for all the schools, to render it impossible for any person of influence to advance his dependant to the post of teacher, to put a stop for ever to the interference of the clergy in the school manage-

ment.  The teachers were to be classified according to
their attainments and degrees of aptitude for teaching,
and to receive stipends so regulated and apportioned.
Provision was made to protect the health of the pupils
by allowing a certain measurement of air space for
each child.  The classes of schools extended beyond
public schools and denominational schools, and included
provisional schools where the number of children was
not sufficient to constitute a regular public school, and
in remote places where there might be a group of
only eight or ten children, half-time schools.  In the
case of these last-named schools, the school went to
the children instead of the children going to the school.
The teacher, on horseback or in boat, would travel ten
or twenty miles and teach one small gathering of
children three days, and then on to another cluster of
bush pupils and teach them for three days.

The new system was to be administered by a
Council of Education consisting of five members ap-
pointed by the Governor in Council.  The first Council
consisted of the Hon. James Martin, Premier ; the Hon.
W. M. Arnold, Speaker of the Legislative Assembly ;
Professor Smith, of the University of Sydney ; the Hon.
George Allen, and myself ; and I had the honour to be
elected President.

The introduction of the Bill was the signal for an
ecclesiastical storm.  I was made the central object of
attack, and no limits were set by my reverend and
very reverend assailants to their inventive skill in personal abuse.  My faults were magnified on the darkest
pattern, and where no slender groundwork of fact could

be discovered, there was no scruple in assigning to me all sorts of imaginary crimes. From the first, however, the lay members of the English Church did not warmly sympathise with the heated feelings of their clergy; and in the course of time the clergymen themselves, for the most part, withdrew from the conflict and accepted the new system. But the hierarchy of the Roman Catholic Church were too devoted to the policy of that marvellous organisation to recede from their position, to accept the lessons of experience, or to admit the evidence of truth. The denominational schools, the schools of the Churches, under the provisions of the new law, became greatly improved, and did good work. As will be seen at a later stage, the priesthood would not 'let well alone,' and they were abolished, after an existence of some fifteen years.

In the struggle for the Act of 1866 there were more dangerous enemies than priest or parson—the pretended friends of the cause in Parliament, who had more concern in discrediting the Government than in promoting any form of education. I recollect meeting one influential member behind the Speaker's chair, who abruptly said, 'I shall have to vote against your Bill—I can't stand Denominationalism!' Obviously he had not read the Bill, but with him no good thing could come out of Nazareth. By absences, by ill-concealed sympathy with any kind of opposition, and by other little devices of hindrance, he added his negative quota to delay and the chances of defeat; but I suppose he thought better of his first resolve, for he did not vote against the Bill. Another Liberal member, who vehemently praised the

Bill on the second reading, voted against reducing the minimum number of pupils required for the establishment of a public school in country districts from 'forty' to 'twenty-five,' after he had been conclusively shown in debate that the higher number would prevent schools being established where they were most wanted. The Bill did not go far enough for some ; we went much too far for others. The Bill was read the second time on October 10, 1866, the division showing thirty-six ayes against fourteen noes. The third reading was carried by forty to five. In the Legislative Council the Bill had comparatively a smooth passage, and I know it was with much satisfaction that Sir John Young gave to it the Royal assent on behalf of Her Majesty. The Secretary of State (the Duke of Newcastle) acknowledged the receipt of the Act in a despatch which spoke of it in very complimentary terms.

The Public Schools Act of 1866 was destined to receive the approval of remarkable men in other parts of the world. Mr. W. E. Forster, after successfully conducting his Education Bill through the House of Commons, addressed to me the following letter :

80 Eccleston Square, London, S.W.
October 6, 1870.

Sir,—I beg to thank you for the copy of your Educational Report for 1869, which you have kindly sent me.

I had already received most useful and interesting information with regard to the working of your Act from the able secretary of your Board of Education, Mr. Wilkins. and I must sincerely congratulate you on the good which has been already done by the measure with which, as Colonial Secretary, you were identified.

I wish I may have the same good fortune with regard to the Education Bill which it was my duty to carry through the House of Commons last year, and of which, as finally passed, I must beg your acceptance of a copy.

I have the honour to be, Sir,
Your obedient servant,
W. E. FORSTER.

Henry Parkes, Esq.

Earl Russell, at a later period, cordially concurred in the policy of the law. Other persons of eminence, including my friend Thomas Hughes, conveyed to me at various times their approval. Amongst others, Mr. Carlyle more than once wrote to me approving of the good work done.

For the first four years after the Public Schools Act came into operation, I filled the office of President of the Council of Education, and during that period I often took part in the ceremony of laying the foundation stones or of the opening of new schools. In 1869, having consented to open a new public school at Dundas, a village near Parramatta, I made the occasion serve for an address of some length, expository of the new system and its successful working. This speech was afterwards extensively circulated in pamphlet form. I sent a copy of it to Mr. Carlyle, and received the following letter from him in acknowledgment. The letter has an additional interest, as it also expresses his views on emigration as a question of British policy.

5 Cheyne Row, Chelsea,
September 21, 1870.

Dear Sir,—Your letter came to me in Scotland, and since my return last week I have read carefully your speech on the

Education question.[1] You are very kind to remember me so steadily, and always from time to time to send me some interesting notice of what you are about.

I am greatly pleased with your calm, quiet, lucid and honest speech, and with all the useful and manful labour you have so successfully gone through for one of the most sacred interests in human affairs. The speech, though studiously inoffensive, gives clear indication of the much opposition you have had to confront in achieving such a bit of calm and impartial legislation, surrounded by so many difficulties and contradictions. I well enough understand the clamours of dark sectaries, Protestant and Catholic, especially of your Irish priests, the worst section of that miserable category; but I own myself much surprised that you should have incurred the estrangement of . . . in the adventure. You give no details of that little personal matter. My judgment of . . . and of the Thing you have been advocating and accomplishing, leads me to believe that this little rub will only be temporary. At all events, I can congratulate you on having laid down a plan, judicious, clear, impartial, probably the only sound plan practicable in your colony, which plan is already in vigorous practice there, and will be a blessing to millions on millions of your colonial countrymen, and indeed more or less a benefit to all men long after we are gone. Well done, well done.

There is at present among us a considerable stir about Emigration, a growing desire that the Government would take some charge of co-operating with the colonies in this great interest of ours, which I hope the Government, in spite of its lazy reluctances, will gradually be compelled to do. By a little human arrangement between mother-country and her daughters, you and Sydney, for example, might have as many hardy Englishmen emigrants as you could gradually make room for, to the unspeakable advantage of us and of you. A thousand by the year, or two thousand, if you liked. But there needs co-operation, a mutual stretching out of hands on both sides of the ocean;

---

[1] Speech on the occasion of opening the Public School at Dundas, September 4, 1869.

and, alas, on our side the one thing we are sure of is not a
practical putting forth of hands in any kind of work or government, but a plentiful wagging of tongues in Parliament and
elsewhere. If to you on your side of the water any opportunity
occur, I charge you not to neglect it. The Government is deaf
at this time, and will continue so I know not how long; but
there are various private associations already of magnitude,
and vigorously growing. I specially mention Sir George Grey,
formerly a Governor among you, as the leading man in this
movement here, who might be the properest of all to consult
in the first instance, if you had occasion.

Believe me,

Yours, with many good wishes and regards,

T. CARLYLE.

The Government, during the first year of its existence, not only passed the Public Schools Act, but it
was successful in doing a number of other useful things,
making provision for the Public Service, and pro-
roguing Parliament before Christmas. I was quite a
novice in official business, but I made it a rule to investigate for myself all important matters, to test the
'usages of the office' by common sense and my own
imperfect historical knowledge, and to trust nothing to
others which I could do myself. It was a great advantage to me to be brought into intimate intercourse on
public questions with Governor Sir John Young. He
had held the office of Chief Secretary for Ireland, and
had, I believe, been Whip to Sir Robert Peel; and his
knowledge of Parliamentary life was full and accurate.
He had fine administrative faculties, and had given
much attention to the study of questions in which I
was deeply interested, such as the management of

criminals under sentence, the care of destitute children, and other social reforms.

Up to this period, the Governor exercised the prerogative of pardon in ordinary criminal cases, largely influenced by his own sense of justice and responsibility; it was not until some years afterwards that the responsibility in such cases was almost wholly assumed by the Governor's advisers. If a petition for the remission or mitigation of a criminal's sentence, signed by ' influential ' persons, came before Sir John Young, his first thought was that there was a design to bring pressure to bear upon his judgment rather than to urge the claim for consideration on the merits of the case. In the case of a prisoner well connected in society, he expressed his views in the following letter to me :—

Government House, Sydney,<br>November 8, 1866.

My dear Mr. Parkes,—Please to have the petition in favour of . . . referred to the Judge who tried the case for his observations.

Whatever stress I may be disposed to lay, and you know I do lay the greatest on yours as well as Mr. Martin's opinion, still it is my duty to refer petitions for remission of sentences to the Judges who presided at the trials and to be guided by their reports.

This, you may rely upon, is the only safe course in the interests of the public, however great the temptation to interfere, or however hard it may seem not to exercise leniency in a particular case.

Allowing full weight to what you sent me in a recent note as to various defects in some of the Courts, and the shortcomings which are stated to exist in various directions, still I must consider to what your conclusion leads, viz. to the practice of alter-

ing Judicial sentences at the discretion of the Executive. Now
I have no hesitation in saying that the remedy is infinitely, im-
measurably worse than the disease. The setting aside the
Judge's sentence may in some cases be unavoidable, but it is a
practice fraught with peril—liable to indefinite abuse and
equally indefinite misconstruction. Indeed in every instance
the misconstruction is certain, and so far tends to weaken confidence in the administration of the laws.

The Executive (including the Governor), whatever their
desire to attain an equitable result, have really no accurate
means of sifting the grounds of the opinion, to which they give
effect, if they ignore or contravene that of the Judge. Usually
their interference is invoked, and is rarely ever exercised in any
other instance than that of parties earnest in favour of the convict. The statements made to them are *ex parte*, they are not
tested by cross-examination. Unsworn is taken as against
sworn testimony. The demeanour of witnesses cannot be observed nor one confronted with another, as before the Judge and
Jury. These are grave deficiencies, fatal to an efficient revision
of sentences on the part of the Executive.

In England, and in Ireland where the practice is the same
as in England, and where I had ample experience when I was
Secretary of State, remissions of sentences are not made without
the concurrence of the Judge except in cases of dangerous sick-
ness, of special service in prison, and under regulations of the
kind adopted latterly here. Any deviation from this strict
course is immediately observed upon in Parliament and checked.

Already even in my time (and I have tried to be cautious),
both the Judges in this Colony and the Legislative Assembly
have found occasion to remonstrate against the exercise of this
prerogative.

One case of remission naturally and inevitably leads on to
another, and I know not where we shall stop if we depart from
the example of the mother-country and forget the warning
given by the American States, in a great many of which so
great laxity obtained in conceding remissions, and the evil
proved so intolerable, that the humiliating course for the Gover-

nor and Ministers was resorted to of taking the prerogative out of their hands entirely and vesting it in an independent board. At the same time I see that many of the sentences pronounced in the district Courts seem relatively unequal, and of disproportionate duration. But a remedy might be found for this by conference with or instructions to the D. C. Judges.

Any rule of general application will be safe enough, but the dealing with individual cases is pregnant with mischief, and the dealing with them without reference to the Judge involves a breach of principle which leaves no *locus standi* in any case upon which pressure political, social, or sympathetic, can be brought to bear.

I am sure you will not mistake the animus of these remarks —they are meant rather to guard against possible future dangers than to apply to existing circumstances.

Very truly yours,<br>JOHN YOUNG.

It will be seen by the tenor and suggestive spirit of this letter that the Governor was very sensitive to what he conceived to be the responsibility cast upon himself as the representative of the Queen, while he aimed at holding the scales of justice free from improper influences however previously concealed. The main principle insisted upon by Sir John Young is undoubtedly sound; and in my connection with cases of prisoners in subsequent years I have felt the value of keeping that principle steadily in view. I shall have to examine at greater length the delicate and difficult question of the exercise of the prerogative of pardon when I come to the first Administration formed by myself, and the assumption of the office of Governor by Sir Hercules Robinson.

# CHAPTER IX

AMONG the subjects which engaged my attention on my
first entrance into public life was the care and treatment of the sick and the insane in the Government
asylums. There was at that time but one general
hospital in the city of Sydney; and that was under a
very unsatisfactory system of management, or, speaking
more correctly, it was under no system at all. An influential friend brought under my notice the case of a
young man who had been admitted into the hospital
from one of the ships in harbour, and whom I found,
on visiting the building, in a pitiable state of neglect
and suffering. This circumstance led me to a personal
inspection of all the wards and the condition of the
inmates, and to enquiries as to the staff of attendants
and the general treatment of patients. As the result of
my investigations, I sent a communication to Miss
Florence Nightingale requesting her services in engaging a staff of trained nurses for the colony. That

illustrious lady immediately took up the cause, and in due course a staff of nurses selected by her arrived, under the superintendence of Miss Osburn, a lady admirably qualified for her important office, who endeared herself to all by her amiable character and her many accomplishments. Miss Osburn remained in the service of the colony for a number of years. She had to contend against the usual difficulties which beset persons engaged in any great change from a bad state of things to a better; but she steadily pursued her quiet and unassuming course of usefulness, regardless of the prejudices of old-fashioned doctors, and some slights not always easy to bear. To Miss Nightingale the colony is deeply indebted for the practical interest she has taken, not only in all questions relating to the construction and management of hospitals, but in all matters concerning sanitation and the public health. For many years, after the introduction of the trained nurses, she did me the honour of frequently corresponding with me on these subjects; and one of the honours I have received on which I set a high value is a gift-book from her bearing the following inscription in her handwriting : 'Offered to Henry Parkes with Florence Nightingale's earnest sympathy for all his good work for human welfare. and especially for depauperising work. London, April, 1875.' When I was in England in 1882, I had a long interview with Miss Nightingale in her sick-room, where her afflictions resulting from her noble labours among the sick and wounded soldiers of the Crimea, now kept her a prisoner. Her graciousness and deep Christian goodness were visible in every word and every look; and that sweet refined presence has come to me hundreds of times since then in my struggles and failures. I venture to give the following letter from her hand, selected from many, in illustration of her abiding interest in Australia :—

April 29, 1882.

My dear Sir Henry Parkes,—Your kind note of April 15 was forwarded to me. (I had that very day been obliged to go out of London for a few days' total silence and solitude.)

I will try for the 'documents' you ask for; namely, 'On Hospital Management,' 'On Health Provision for Towns,' and 'Any manual suitable for the guidance of persons in charge of Country Hospitals.' In these latter we are singularly deficient —as also indeed in the first. In the second not so deficient.

How soon do you leave England? As, if you return to Sydney before I can obtain a suitable list, I should like to be able to send the documents after you, seeing that I have been so (unwillingly) impotent in doing as you desire.

I trust that you are not over-fatigued with your having to see and to be seen so much. England has been so glad to bid you welcome.

St. Thomas's Hospital and St. Marylebone Infirmary were particularly honoured by being inspected by you. I hope you found them satisfactory.

I must not trouble you with a long note farther than to give you joy. or rather to give ourselves joy, of your revisiting the old country. I fear I shall not see you again before you leave England for Sydney. May your days be long in the land to which you have secured such blessings. And may her future be a glorious one is the earnest prayer of

Your ever faithful servant,
FLORENCE NIGHTINGALE.

In the introduction of the hospital nurses I acted without the sanction of Parliament, as I regarded delay as unjustifiable in the interests of humanity, but I had the cordial support of my colleagues, and when the expenditure was submitted in the next Session, it was voted without exception being taken to what had been done. Indeed, I may fairly claim that the course I adopted in this instance, nearly a quarter of a century ago, was the first step in establishing the system of trained nursing which now prevails in all the hospitals of the colony, and, I believe, throughout Australia.

85 South Street, Park Lane, London, W.

October 24, 1866.

Sir,—I beg to acknowledge your letter of July 21, relating to the selecting and engaging of four trained and training nurses for the Sydney Infirmary.

Let me, in the first place, assure you that all that I can do shall be done to forward your kind and wise intentions, and that, so far from your application to me requiring any 'apology,' it has, on the contrary, a claim upon me, for Australia has always been a powerful patroness of mine, and I hardly know how to thank you as I could wish for asserting that claim.

You are perhaps not aware that after the Crimean War, a fund was raised, called the 'Nightingale Fund.' Australia interested herself very much in this affair. I applied this Fund exclusively to the training of matrons and nurses for the sick poor, and especially for hospitals. But the demand is always larger than the supply, even for England alone. We are generally engaged years deep in training. We have always more posts to fill than, alas! persons to fill them, and we have never a supply of this valuable article ready on hand. Persons fit to be engaged always *are* engaged. And it is only within the last ten years that means have been taken to ensure a supply at all of trained persons fit to take charge in hospitals.

You see that it is I who have to begin with an 'apology.' I would fain repay part of my heavy debt to Australia, according to my powers, but I shall have to crave your indulgence and time, if we are to supply you with such persons as, after training them, we could recommend.

Your plan is, if I may say so without impertinence, wise, benevolent, and well digested, namely, to begin in the Sydney Infirmary a Training School for Nurses (people so often fancy that hospital nurses can be trained outside a hospital), and gradually to extend it so as to become a training school for nurses for other institutions in the colony.

Of course, upon the receipt of your letter (of July 21) I immediately put myself, and also Captain Mayne, in communication with Mrs. Wardroper, the valued matron (superintendent) of our Training School for *Hospital* Nurses at St. Thomas's Hospital, in order to see how far we could meet your wishes, and how soon, and also carefully to consider Dr. Alfred Roberts's excellent business-like memorandum. I shall venture to ask you to give your consideration to the details which Captain Mayne and Mrs. Wardroper will give concerning what I have submitted to you in general in this letter. We think that it will be necessary to have a matron for the Sydney Infirmary, trained in the same school that the ' four sisters ' asked for are trained in, and we think the staff of assistants proposed rather small.

We venture to lay these things before you, because we always try to obtain for the success of those hospital nursery staffs which we send out, the conditions which in our judgment will alone ensure success.

But I leave Captain Mayne and Mrs. Wardroper to enter into further detail. We shall then trust to receive from you further instructions. and I will now only add, without vain words, that I am deeply touched and pleased at your claiming my poor services, and that

> I am, Sir, with great truth,
> Ever your faithful Servant,
> FLORENCE NIGHTINGALE.

N.B.—I do myself the honour of sending you by this mail the last edition of my ' Notes on Hospitals,' not expecting that you will have time to look into it yourself, but hoping that those who have more immediate business with hospitals will glance over what I have said as to the construction necessary to ensure good nursing and administration. I am sure that it will be a great advantage for our nursing staff, should we be fortunate enough to supply you with one, to work under Dr. Alfred Roberts.

I would also say that I am an invalid, entirely a prisoner to a couch, but, I thank God, still able to work, and that no delay shall proceed from this circumstance. I did not receive yours of July 21 till October 4, but I had already received notice of its advent from Captain Mayne on September 21. Some little delay, but not much, has occurred in our reply from this circumstance.

F. N.

Colonial Secretary's Office, Sydney,
December 24, 1866.

Madam,—I was much gratified to receive your letter of October 24, and to learn from it that notwithstanding the multiplicity of engagements on your hands, and the unfortunate state of your health, you could find time to take an active interest in the subject of my communication to you. Be assured that your pure Christian services in this matter, as in all others, will be appreciated by your countrymen and countrywomen in Australia, who treasure your name as a noble part of their national history.

You are pleased to allude to the movement in Australia in behalf of the ' Nightingale Fund ' some few years ago. Perhaps you will pardon me in saying that, so far from being unaware of what was done on that occasion, it was my hand that wrote the address that was presented to you from this colony. It was my knowledge of your life of great virtue and labour which made me apply to you in the present case with a feeling that I had no right to ask you to undertake an additional burden, and I am happily surprised to find that you so readily devote yourself to this new duty on behalf of suffering human nature in this remote part of the world.

I shall of course be guided by your suggestions in carrying out our plans, and by the outgoing mail I shall cause our Agent in London to be instructed accordingly. Any matter of detail as to the number of ladies which it may be expedient to engage, the time of their departure, or the terms of their individual engagements, is felt to be unimportant in comparison with the complete accomplishment of what we aim at—making the best provision within our power for the efficient management of our hospitals.

The Sydney Infirmary is a large building, but having been erected in the early days of the colony, it is somewhat irregular in its arrangements, but still it is capable of being made a noble institution. It is beautifully situated on an eminence in the very skirt of the city, the back windows overlooking one of the most glorious landscapes in the world. The hospitals in the country towns are comparatively small, as we have only five towns over three thousand inhabitants.

By the mail of January I will forward to you a parcel of public documents that will afford you full information respecting the colony.

I now tender to you the thanks of this Government, and I am sure I might add, of the whole people of New South Wales, for the devoted interest you take in our welfare as a part of the English nation.

> I remain, very respectfully,
> Your faithful Servant,
> HENRY PARKES.

Miss Nightingale.

In a former chapter I made reference to the outrages committed by bushrangers in the years from 1862 to 1867. When I entered upon the duties of office, one whole district in the Southern part of the colony, embracing an area nearly as large as Ireland, was held in a state of terror by a desperate gang of bushrangers, headed by two brothers named Clarke. The district

was full of police, certainly three times the numbers
ordinarily stationed in the several localities, but the
bushrangers eluded all their vigilance and activity.
Their system of 'bush telegraph,' of word of mouth
communication, in which women and girls were often
the most active agents, was organised and kept up with
a completeness and success perfectly surprising. In
this the daring horsemanship of the bush boys and girls
connected with some of the bushrangers was very
striking. A certain class of the small settlers notoriously harboured the offenders. For a time it seemed as
if half the population was in league with crime against
the defenders of law and social security. The police
were outwitted in stratagem and outstripped in speed
in their efforts to arrest the criminals.

As the police force was under my Ministerial control, I felt very keenly my responsibility so long as this
state of things continued. I lost no time in pressing
upon the Inspector-General the necessity for the utmost
effort to cope with the wide-spread lawlessness, and I
required him to report specially from day to day.
Offers to form special parties for the capture of the
Clarkes and their criminal associates were made in
different quarters. One of these offers was made by
John Carroll, formerly an officer of police, and at
this time an officer of Darlinghurst Gaol, a man of very
considerable experience in dealing with criminals. His
conditions were that he should be allowed to select his
companions, should be armed in accordance with his
own choice and discretion, should be placed in a position independent of the regular police, should be secretly

accredited to certain magistrates resident in the district, and should, if successful, receive certain compensation and privileges. After consultation with my colleagues, I agreed on behalf of the Government to these terms. Carroll selected his comrades, three men named Patrick Kennagh, Eneas McDonnell, and John Phegan ; the four men came before me and each individually volunteered to serve in the hazardous enterprise, the three latter agreeing to accept Carroll as their leader. After consultation with the Attorney-General (Mr. Martin), I despatched this volunteer party on their mission on September 22, 1866. The following report from Carroll, dated October 7, will read, in the light of the tragic story soon to be told, as a page from a wild romance.

*Mr. John Carroll to the Colonial Secretary.*

Braidwood, Sunday, October 7, 1866.

Sir,—I have the honour to report, for your information, that, in accordance with an arrangement previously made, I and party pitched our camp within one mile and a half north-east of Clarke's house, ostensibly for the purpose of surveying. We were delayed in Braidwood waiting the return of Mr. Rodd a week, but in the meantime one of our party (Phegan) had been three times to Mrs. Clarke's and her daughters'. At first he was received with a degree of suspicion, which, however, wore away on his second visit. They (the Clarkes) got Phegan to write out a petition for their son, James Clarke, now on Cockatoo Island. Since we were camped as above, Phegan, accompanied by Kennagh. made another visit, and were received kindly. Altogether our plans were progressing most favourably. On last Wednesday morning Tommy and Johnny Clarke passed about 200 yards from our camp, in the direction of their parents' house. They were well mounted, and we were not in a position to pursue; nor could the pieces we had (revolvers) carry that distance with any certainty; so that, on that occasion, we were compelled to let them proceed unmolested. On the same afternoon two of Clarke's girls rode round our camp, and had a good survey of it and ourselves. You will please remember that until this the Clarkes did not know our position, although they understood that Phegan was employed by a survey party. The girls went past us in the direction of a range in our rear, and shouted as if rounding up a mob of horses. We watched them narrowly, and shortly after they returned towards home we saw two of their dogs coming down the range near which the girls had approached. On the following morning, early, we surveyed the range in twos, and came across a bark gunyah, constructed in such a way as not to be noticeable until one would be right on it. The gunyah presented the appearance of being very recently occupied, and we found two empty bottles in it. From the circumstance of the two bushrangers having been seen by us coming from that direction, and of other collateral evidence, we had no doubt of this being one of their rendezvous, and of being able to secure them in it before long; but we had a better plan in view at the time, and we were waiting its accomplishment or failure before trying their capture as before described.

I have now to relate a most providential escape we all had from being shot, and perhaps riddled to death. We had been surveying a flat near our camp, from 9 o'clock on Friday morning till about 4 in the afternoon. At 4 o'clock we went in a body on a neighbouring range, where we could reconnoitre well. We returned to camp about 6, and had just finished our teas and were standing round our fire, which we always allowed to die out, when, all at once (it was very dark) we heard the report of a musket or rifle about 100 yards from us. The ball passed right between us, and entered the tree against which our fire was made, just on a level with our heads. We had our arms out in an instant, but before we could discharge them we were fired upon from two opposite directions. Thank God,

none of us was touched. We each discharged a shot in the
direction of the explosion by the bushrangers, for we had no
other guide in aiming, owing to the night being so very dark,
which was rendered denser by the mizzling rain which had
been falling all day. Our first object, of course, was to get out
of the glare of the fire, which was still burning sufficiently to
afford a good aim at us by the bushrangers. The Clarkes, and
whoever were with them, had evidently lain on the ground,
behind trees. I would suppose there were, at least, four of
them. We kept up random firing for about five minutes,
closing by degrees on the first position taken up by the bushrangers, who always retired on our approach, and in opposite
directions. I cannot speak too highly of the courage displayed
by the party under my charge. They acted most zealously;
indeed, under the circumstances, I thought rashly, in pursuing
under such disadvantages. About 8 o'clock we found that our
ammunition had been inadvertently left in the tent, and to
return to it, from its colour and position, so close to the fire,
which would throw the shadow of anyone passing so clearly as
to afford a good mark for the fire of the bushrangers, appeared
certain death. Kennagh, however (and I cannot speak too
highly of his courage), without a moment's hesitation, made a
rush to the tent, under cover of our fire, and secured the ammunition. The bushrangers now directed their firing to the
tent (which is riddled), but without effect. Kennagh returned
to us unharmed. After this the bushrangers ceased firing, and
as we had no further clue to their position we remained in ambush the whole of the night, expecting every moment to see the
tent attacked, or to be passed by some of the bushrangers. No
further attack was, however, made, and when daylight came no
traces of them could be found, if I except some balls and a flask
half full of powder, which had been dropped by one of them.
How we escaped being at least wounded is a mystery; to God
we must be thankful, for a narrower escape or a more dastardly
attack is not in my recollection.

I am at a loss to know why we should have been so attacked,
for, on the last visit of two of my party to Clarke's house, the

remotest suspicion of who we really were was not entertained. I am inclined to believe that we were observed tracking the bushrangers on the mountain and discovering their shelter. However that may be, it has been found necessary to abandon our first plan.

On Saturday morning we went to see Mr. Stewart, J.P., and took him into our confidence. He was very kind to us, and promised to be able to give us valuable information. I may here mention that our firing was distinctly heard at Mr. Stewart's station, which is about the same distance from our late camp as the Police Station at Wallace's. We were nearly a week camped as described, and with the exception of the Clarke's family, never saw any person. The police ride frequently to and from Braidwood, but we have never met them off the main road; and that the Clarkes should infest that immediate neighbourhood with such impunity and so frequently, without being captured, would require some explanation. I have every hope, that when we have a supply of rifles, to bring in, dead or alive, one or the whole of the gang within a month.

Mr. Rodd, who has been very courteous to us, has already written for the additional pieces and ammunition, which I trust will soon arrive.

I hope shortly to be enabled to report to you our success in the expedition.

I have, &c.

JOHN CARROLL.

For the next three months the doomed men continued their efforts to circumvent the outlaws, moving about as a surveying party, in the wild Tingera district. On January 10, 1867, all four of them were shot dead by the bushrangers, who appeared to have fired from an ambush behind some large trees. For ninety days and nights—since the night skirmish described in Carroll's letter—while the special constables were tracking the marauders, the marauders must have been more closely watching them. What incident or new suspicion, or revelation of lawless spy, determined the savage murder at last, will never be known, for it is morally certain that the lips which might have told the dreadful secret are now sealed for ever. No attempt had been made to rifle the bodies of the dead men; what money or other property they had on their persons was left untouched; and in the case of Carroll, a bank note, not corresponding with those in his possession, was found placed upon his breast, apparently in mockery of his expected reward.

The reign of terror in the unhappy Braidwood district went on under darker distrust and forebodings. Honest men feared to travel the highways by daylight; traders stole forth under cover of night on their business journeys; and insecurity was felt in every home. Increasing the regular police seemed barren of effect. About this time I was invited to visit Mudgee, where I was entertained at two public dinners. On my return journey by the main road (there was no railway in those days) Senior Constable Wright relieved my escort at Keen's Swamp. He accompanied my carriage for many miles; we stayed at a roadside hotel for the night, and his escort continued for several hours the next day. I thus had some opportunities of judging of Wright's character. He was a smart man in personal appearance, and he was singularly alert in observation, noticing the slightest sign of unusual circumstance along the road. I held little chats with him about his experiences in the force, and in the evening I watched his intercourse with the wayfarers at the hotel. The result was that I inwardly formed the purpose to enlist Wright's services to capture Tommy and Johnny Clarke, the Braidwood bushrangers. The next day we met the relief escort in a lone part of the road; I left the carriage, and Wright dismounted; we walked to the edge of the forest, and improvised a sort of bush council of war. I asked the senior constable if he had heard of the depredations of the Clarkes—of course he had; if he knew the Braidwood district—he had never been there. I finally asked him if he would be prepared to go in charge of a picked party of police to attempt the capture of the notorious bushrangers. He promptly replied that he should be glad to be so honoured and trusted. I gave him orders to report himself in Sydney, and resumed my journey. When I reached Sydney I immediately sent for the Inspector-General of Police. I said, 'You have a man named Wright stationed at Keen's Swamp?' 'Yes,' said he; 'one of the smartest men in the force—a capital officer—an invaluable man!' 'Well,' I replied, 'I have made up my mind to send Wright in charge of a select party of police to attempt the capture of the Clarkes.' 'Oh, that will never do!' exclaimed the Inspector-General; 'it would demoralise the whole force; he is, I assure you, quite unfit for it!' I merely remarked that he had just told me that Wright was 'one of the smartest men in the force.' 'So he is,' replied the Inspector-General, 'in his proper place; but he is quite an illiterate man, unfit for command.' 'Very well,' I rejoined, 'we cannot discuss the matter; I represent the Government,

you are an officer of the Government ; Wright is to go
on this service, and you must assist the Government by
assisting him in the undertaking.' Senior Constable
Wright selected his men, and went to the scene of the
long-continued outrages. In the course of time—not a
long time—he tracked the Clarkes to a lonely hut
where they were occasionally harboured. For some
hours shots were exchanged by the small band of
police and the desperadoes in the hut. Wright and his
party closed in upon the hut ; the brother outlaws were
secured, and shortly afterwards they were brought to
Sydney, tried, convicted, and hanged. With other
arrests and convictions the colony was soon freed from
the ravages of the most bloodthirsty gang of bushrangers that ever disgraced it.

Sorely against the wishes of the Inspector-General,
but with the hearty concurrence of my colleagues, I
made Wright a sub-inspector, but he had to bear the
cold shoulder of officialism all his life, which was not a
long one. My experience is that it is often a mistaken
kindness to advance any man in the lower grade of a
departmental service without the approving intervention of those above him.

The visit of His Royal Highness the Duke of Edinburgh to Sydney, in the *Galatea* was unhappily
marked by a tragic occurrence which gave me, in
common with the whole community, much concern.
Prince Alfred, as the people of that day delighted to
call him, received a magnificent welcome ; triumphal
arches of costly and artistic structure, brilliant dis-
plays of fireworks, houses aflame with flags, were only

in harmony with the exuberant loyalty of the people in proclaiming his landing upon our shores as a memorable event. The young sailor was the Queen's son, and that was enough.

On March 12, 1868, a picnic was given at a favourite marine retreat called Clontarf, in support of building a Sailors' Home. His Royal Highness had accepted an invitation to be present. The following description from the 'Sydney Morning Herald' of the chief feature in the preparation for the festivity will show the interest it had evoked :—

About 11 A.M. the R.S.Y. Squadron rendezvoused in Double Bay, and soon after stood out under the command of Commodore Dangar, whose fine yacht, the *Mistral*, led the fleet, followed by the *Xarifa*, *Vivid*, and eleven others, under fore and aft canvas. When off Bradley's they eased off, ran up the harbour, and rounded H.M.S. *Challenger*, saluting Commodore Lambert's pennant as they passed. They then hauled on a wind and worked down the harbour for Clontarf, where their arrival was watched with great interest. The squadron was the largest ever seen in this harbour, and their appearance, when anchored off the spit dressed with flags, was extremely pretty. The yachts of the Prince Alfred Club, ten in number, made the trip to Middle Harbour separately, took their positions abreast of the senior club, and dressed with bunting in a similar style. Seen from the shore the effect was striking ; the twenty-four yachts, decorated with flags of every hue, and numerous other sailing boats anchored about the bight, with the steamers *City of Newcastle* and *Morpeth* moored at the end of each line, produced as pretty a sight as has ever been witnessed in the harbour of Port Jackson. On the ground a large marquee, neatly fitted up, was added to the permanent buildings on the ground as a luncheon saloon. A handsome tent, with suitable appointments, was pitched on the side of the

dell opposite the beach, for the convenience of His Royal
Highness and suite.    From as early an hour as ten o'clock,
when the first steamer departed, it was very evident that the
visitors would be very numerous, and when the last boat landed
its passengers there were between two and three thousand persons
present.

His Royal Highness left the *Galatea* shortly after one
o'clock in the steam yacht *Fairy*, and as she passed, about
two o'clock, between the steamers and yachts which had been
drawn up in two lines near the Clontarf jetty, they saluted by
dipping their flags. He was received by a number of gentlemen,
members of the committee, and escorted to the marquee, where
luncheon had been provided. With His Royal Highness were
his Excellency the Right Hon. the Earl of Belmore, and her
Ladyship the Countess of Belmore, Viscount Newry, the Hon.
Elliott Yorke, Miss Gladstone, Captain Beresford, Mr. Toulmin,
and Lieutenant Haig. Places at a central table were reserved
for them, and here they were joined by, among others, Commodore Lambert and Mrs. Lambert, his Honour Sir Alfred Stephen
and Mrs. Stephen, Mr. Charles Cowper, Captain Lyons, Mons.
Sentis (French Consul), and the Hon. John Hay. Sir William
Manning was in the chair, on his right His Royal Highness
and on his left his Excellency the Governor.

On leaving the luncheon table His Royal Highness
gave Mr. William Manning a donation towards the
erection of the Sailors' Home, and was standing in
conversation on the subject, when a person who had
recently arrived in Sydney, named H. F. O'Farrell,
walked deliberately to within two yards of him, and
fired a shot from a revolver, which struck the un-
suspecting Prince a little to the right of the spine, and
traversed the course of the ribs to the abdomen. The
bullet was eventually extracted, and His Royal Highness
recovered. But the dastardly attack upon the Duke

of Edinburgh's life produced a strange lurid glare in
the political atmosphere, and engendered feelings not
simply acrimonious and bitter, but almost deadly in
the depth and colour of their hatred. Holding the
office of Colonial Secretary, and having in my hands
the administration of the police, I naturally came in for
a little more than my share of the adverse criticisms on
the rumours and transactions which followed the attempted murder. The criminal O'Farrell was seriously
maltreated by the infuriated crowd at Clontarf, and if
he had not been protected by the police and speedily
got away from the scene, it is not improbable that he
might have been *lynched* on the spot. All kinds of
secret conspiracies were conjured into instant existence.
Panic seized the imaginations of sensible and sober-
minded men. Even the Premier (the late Chief Justice,
Sir James Martin), who was by no means a timid man,
went about armed, and had his private residence
guarded at night by armed men. Nothing is easier
than to smile at all this from a comfortable distance of
time or space. But the mingled feelings of indignation,
uneasiness, and alarm were all but universal, and were
contagious to a high degree, and spread widely amongst
those who woke up afterwards to affectedly condemn
the proceedings. In proof of this state of excited
feeling I need only cite the facts that on March 18,
Mr. Martin moved in the Legislative Assembly: 'That
the Standing Orders be suspended with a view to the
passing through all its stages in one day of a Bill
for the better security of the Crown and Government
of the United Kingdom, and for the better suppression

and punishment of seditious practices and attempts.' That this motion was carried by forty-four to two votes; that the Bill was passed through all its stages, sent to the Legislative Council, passed in the same rapid manner by that body, and returned without amendment to the Legislative Assembly before eleven o'clock at night. Even the persons who a few weeks later did their utmost to make political capital out of the occurrences of that disordered time, voted in this precipitate manner for the Treason Felony Act, including Mr. William Macleay. The author of this measure was Sir James Martin, who framed it and conducted it through the Assembly without, as I believe, a single suggestion from any of his colleagues.

I now come to what I think must be regarded by everybody as a painful question—as to whether O'Farrell was insane, or in any degree unaccountable for his actions. After twenty-three years I feel bound to place on record my belief that he was perfectly sane. On the day of the attempted assassination, the police, under the direction of a highly responsible officer, searched the house where O'Farrell had lodged on the previous night, and found in the pocket of an article of dress thrown off by him in his hurried preparation to attend the picnic at Clontarf, a diary, kept in pencil in his handwriting. The genuineness of this diary has been attested on affidavit by the police-officer who found it, and I give the form of attestation in full :—

New South Wales, Sydney to wit.

I, HENRY WAGER, of the city of Sydney, in the colony of New South Wales, the Officer in charge of the Detective Police, in the city of Sydney, in the said colony, do solemnly and sincerely declare as follows :

On the twelfth day of March last, I, by the direction of the Honourable the Colonial Secretary, proceeded, in company with Alexander Baikie, a Sergeant of Police in the Police Force, Sydney, to the Clarendon Hotel, kept by one David J. Powell, and situated in Hunter and George Streets, in the city of Sydney, and from thence to the Currency Lass Hotel, kept by one Daniel Tierney, and situated in Pitt and Hunter Streets, in the said city.

I visited these hotels for the purpose of making search for and taking possession of any books, papers, and other personal effects of Henry James O'Farrell, who had been then recently apprehended, and was in custody upon a charge of wounding His Royal Highness the Duke of Edinburgh.

At the Clarendon Hotel, at which place I was informed the said Henry James O'Farrell was residing. I took possession of certain books, papers, and other personal effects belonging to him ; and amongst the articles so taken possession of by me were the loose leaves of a private journal or diary, in the hand-writing of the said Henry James O'Farrell. The leaves of the said journal were in the pocket of a waistcoat which I was informed and verily believe was the property of the said Henry James O'Farrell.

I have carefully compared the handwriting in the said leaves of the journal with the handwriting of the paper given by the said Henry James O'Farrell, as his dying declaration, as to the commission of the said crime of which he had been found guilty, and have no doubt they were written by the same person.

The Honourable Henry Parkes, then Colonial Secretary, and the Honourable the Minister for Works, were present at the time I made search at the said hotel, and when I took possession of the said books, papers, and personal effects.

I read and examined the leaves of the said journal immediately after I had taken possession of same, and I yesterday carefully examined the said leaves of the said journal;—they are in the same state and condition as when the same were so taken possession of by me as before mentioned. The printed paper, hereto annexed, marked as exhibit 'D,' is a true and exact copy of the said leaves of the said journal.

And I make this solemn declaration, conscientiously believing the same to be true, and by virtue of the provisions of an Act made and passed in the ninth year of the reign of Her present Majesty, intituled '*An Act for the more effectual abolition of Oaths and Affirmations taken and made in various Departments of the Government of New South Wales, and to substitute Declarations in lieu thereof, and for the suppression of voluntary and extra-judicial Oaths and Affidavits.*'

HENRY WAGER.

Declared and subscribed before me, at Sydney, in the colony of New South Wales, this 18th day of September, in the year of our Lord one thousand eight hundred and sixty-eight.
} HOULTON H. VOSS, W.P.M.

I extract from O'Farrell's diary the following remarkable passages. Some words had been expunged from the manuscript before it fell into the hands of the police, and then followed these abrupt sentences :—

How if I should fail, *quod avertat Deus,* I should never forgive myself. Fail! but I cannot; I am alone, and surely I can trust myself. Oh! that the Orangemen would rouse up the apathetic Irish of these parts; one good effect would follow in English capitalists losing heavily by the depreciation of colonial debentures, and the failures consequent on the colonies being in a state of anarchy. If I had had my will, every English ship in these colonial ports should have been destroyed. Shall I

write once more to the dear nine? No: you have written once,
and that is once too often, for the P.O. officials are not over-
scrupulous about opening letters. Be wary, be loyal to them
and to yourself. To think I have not one relation that knows
of my proceedings! What will they say? Threaten to inform
against me, I'll be sworn. *Go in for the Church!* The idea
disgusts me. That is what they would have me do. And yet
I cannot get money unless I lead them to believe I am studying for the Church. I did think of doing so once, and it
plunged me into fever—the having to decide on loyalty to a
Church or to country. What sums I have sent home, and now
to be so pressed for money! Still I have enough, with care
and common prudence. There is no *tedium vitæ* in me, and
yet I am to die in a few days;—let me see ;—in two weeks from
this, and in tolerable company. It will be a fine soul race to
somewhere, or more probably, nowhere, or *nihil*. What non-
sense it is to write like this, and yet I find a grim satisfaction
in thinking of the vengeance. How the nobility of the three
countries will curse me, and the toadying, lickspittle Press hunt
the dictionaries over for terms of abhorrence! But *vengeance
for Ireland* is sweet. Woe to you, England, when the glorious
'nine' carry out their programme. There was a Judas in the
twelve—in our band there was a No. 3 as bad, but his horrible
death will I trust be a warning to traitors. Such another I am
confident is not among the nine. Oh that I were with them!
For, after all, this thing I have to do for vengeance, and to rouse
the Irish here, will cost too dear, as I know I could have done
so much more in England. But it is my duty to the R., and I
will, if able, do it. What is there to prevent me?

After some further wild, irregular writing, giving
vent to his suspicions of persons with whom he had
been in communication, and to his apprehension of
the police, he expressed his sense of horror at the task
assigned to him in the following language :—

That noble nine! Alas, that I should be left behind, and

for such a purpose. Oh, for a gallant cavalry charge, not such
a thing as this! Oh destiny! It must be done! and it must
be done! Fate, fate! A life in irons, in torture, would I
rather have had than that the lot should have fallen on me.
Was Washington criminal for hanging poor Major André?
Was he, seeing he did it in *retaliation?* He did it for his
country, and it checked the cruelty of the English. Three of
us butchered at Manchester! So some hundreds of the '98'
patriots were shot down like dogs in the seething lazar-house.
Woe to thee, England, or rather to your accursed oligarchy!
It is well.

O'Farrell's conduct in prison was uniformly that of
an intelligent, fairly-educated, quietly-behaved man, in
the perfect possession of all his faculties, but suffering
from the remorseful sense of relief from some unlaw-
fully imposed obligation. He spoke freely at all times
of his condition, and the circumstances which led to it.
Some of his conversations were taken down in short-
hand, and they were all of the same tenor and consistency. There was no hesitation or variation in his
statements, nor the least evidence of an attempted
hoax.

Under the law of New South Wales, wounding with
intent to murder is a capital crime. O'Farrell was
tried, convicted, and sentenced to death. Some efforts
were made to obtain a commutation of the sentence ;
but the Executive were firm and unanimous in their
decision to allow the law to take its course. Shortly
before his execution, O'Farrell wrote a brief confession,
the object of which was to unsay—to wipe out as with
a sponge—all which he had so persistently and consis-
tently said since the day of his arrest.

The head of the police at the time was a retired military officer of high character and undoubted ability and vigilance. The following is his report on the whole case :—

Police Department, Inspector-General's Office, Sydney,<br>August 10, 1868.

Sir.—I do myself the honour to transmit herewith the only papers remaining in my possession having reference to the case of the executed convict H. J. O'Farrell, and take the opportunity, in doing so, to express my views respecting the crime for which O'Farrell was convicted, and my reasons for the conclusions I have arrived at.

My opinion, as I have informed the Government from the outset, is that the attempted assassination of His Royal Highness the Duke of Edinburgh was not the unaided act of one individual, but the fruits of the treasonable organisation commonly known as Fenianism ; this opinion has been strengthened by after occurrences and disclosures.

Before the arrival of His Royal Highness the Duke of Edinburgh, the Government were in possession of intelligence, certainly not of a very definite character, that persons ill-disposed towards the English Government would take the opportunity of the visit of His Royal Highness for outrage of some kind ; and you will no doubt remember more than once enquiring the nature of the precautions I proposed to take, and whether it would not be practicable, by the means at the disposal of the Government, to obtain more precise information with regard to any seditious movement on foot.

Various means were employed to obtain information, but the result, though placing it beyond doubt that many disaffected persons, Fenian sympathisers and agents, were in the colony, fell short of evidence definite enough to warrant prosecution.

Corroboration of this, to a great extent, was to be found in many matters noticed by the Press ; some attracted more than passing attention, and the publications of an unconcealed treasonable tendency in the 'Freeman's Journal' were viewed with general disapprobation, participated in by leading members of that party whose organ the newspaper was supposed to be.

The outrages that had taken place elsewhere, avowedly sanctioned by Fenian leaders, and the sympathy such atrocious crimes evoked amongst a certain class, gave rise, no doubt, to many of the surmises that some blow would be struck in the cause during the visit of His Royal Highness to these shores.

Following upon the attempted assassination was the culprit's own statement of the object of the attempt, and the circumstances which led to it. This confession agreed with his private entries in the pocket-book afterwards found by the police, and was also quite in accordance with the plans and organisation of similar plots elsewhere, and having an aspect of truth which in my opinion has not subsequently altered.

Whilst there can be no room for doubt that a large class of persons in New South Wales and the adjacent colonies openly sympathised with the Fenian movement, and had no hesitation in avowing their disaffection, yet there are, in my opinion, no grounds for supposing that O'Farrell had accomplices amongst the residents of New South Wales. There are sufficient grounds for concluding that there were Fenian agents visiting the colonies, and correspondence carried on with centres in Ireland and America; and amongst such persons, I believe, O'Farrell's accomplices would be found.

Many persons were known to be active in the openly expressed object of raising funds in the Fenian cause, under the cloak of applying such contributions for the benefit of the widows of Fenian 'martyrs,' and many were leaving for the States. One man, whose property was searched on the eve of his departure for America, by authority of a search warrant under the Treason Felony Act, openly avowed himself a Fenian, but stated he had taken good care not to bring himself within reach of the law. He had a considerable sum in American gold coin, and was, he stated, an Irishman—naturalised in the United States, to which country he was returning. His papers left no doubt he was a Fenian. The attached extract[1] from the log of the Panama mail steamer *Rakaia*, and communication from the purser, will confirm what I have stated.

The numerous letters threatening assassination, received by gentlemen occupying the highest public stations, shortly following the attempted assassination, must not be forgotten; nor the fact that the threat in one such letter was carried into effect by the attempted assassination of a gentleman whose principles were known to be hostile to those of the extreme Irish party. The other intentions of a similar kind may possibly have been frustrated by the precautionary measures taken.

The last statement made by the convict O'Farrell before his execution is, I think, inconsistent with itself. It has, however, been already the subject of much criticism; and I need only record my belief, founded upon long experience, that dying declarations, made under such circumstances, are seldom to be relied upon.

I have, &c.
JNO. McLERIE,
Inspector-General of Police.

Some months before the meeting of Parliament in October 1868, I visited my constituents at Kiama, and, in the course of a speech which I delivered, I said that I held in my possession, and could produce at any moment, evidence attested by affidavits, which left on my mind the conviction that, not only was the assassination of the Duke of Edinburgh planned, but that some one who had a guilty knowledge of the secret. and whose fidelity was suspected, had been foully murdered. In another part of my speech I expressed the opinion that the same evidence would carry conviction to the mind of any other impartial person. These ex-

---

[1] This extract is not published, as the consent of the purser, who is absent from the colony, cannot be obtained. Note at the time.

pressions were seized upon by certain newspapers that were hostile to the existing Government, and were made the groundwork of the fiercest and most unscrupulous attacks. I had resigned office on a disagreement between myself and colleagues about the dismissal of a public servant. But, having regard to the violent attacks of my opponents, and their noisy demands for fuller explanations, I took all the papers in my possession to the Assembly on the opening of Parliament, on October 13, to meet any question that might be raised. On that day an adverse amendment on the Address was moved by Mr. Robertson, which, although negatived by the casting vote of the Speaker, ultimately led to the resignation of Mr. Martin's Ministry; and, in the debate on Mr. Robertson's motion, several members alluded to my position, but only for the purpose of showing that my retirement had greatly weakened the Government. Not a single word was said respecting the statements which had been made at Kiama. The Assembly met for a short time on several subsequent days in October, and on all those occasions I had the Kiama papers in the House, but no one asked for them.

The new Ministry was formed, and it obtained an adjournment of six weeks for the re-elections; and, before the House re-assembled on December 8, I had been chosen by the Opposition to move a vote of want of confidence. It was then, and not till then, that the storm about the Kiama statements commenced. Questions were asked and motions made which clearly showed that the Colonial Secretary's office had been

thrown open to Mr. Macleay, the principal mover in
the matter, and that this honourable member and the
Ministers were acting in close concert. I met the attack
by offering to lay the papers on the table of the House,
explaining, at the same time, that this could not be
done for a few days (the papers being at my residence
in the country). But on the 15th, Mr. Macleay moved
for a Select Committee, on which he placed, besides
himself, Mr. Robertson, Mr. Forster, Mr. Samuel, Mr.
Hoskins, and Mr. S. C. Brown, all of whom had declared
their personal hostility to me. The other members
were Mr. Martin, Mr. Eagar, Mr. John Stewart, and
myself. In his speech in support of this motion, Mr.
Macleay prejudged the whole case, and indulged in a
strain of violent abuse. I raised no objection to the
proposed committee, nor would I have offered any objection had it been composed entirely of my personal
opponents, as I felt confident that my character could
not suffer from enquiry into my official conduct.

Throughout the subsequent proceedings Mr. Macleay had everything his own way. As he had chosen
his own committee without question, so he decided on
his own plan of enquiry. In good time he framed his
own report (in which worthy work it is believed he had
able assistance out of doors), and he selected his own
plan of operations in the House. The day for the consideration of his report was also fixed by Mr. Macleay
himself, without the slightest regard for the wishes or
convenience of other persons.

In due time Mr. Macleay submitted [my writing at
this time] in the Legislative Assembly a series of reso-

lutions purporting to be based upon the evidence given before his committee, which were intended to blast my public character for life. The following is a copy :—

That this House—having duly considered the Report of, and the Evidence taken before the Select Committee, appointed on the 15th day of December last, ' to enquire into, and report upon, the existence of a Conspiracy for purposes of Treason and Assassination, alleged by a former Colonial Secretary to have subsisted in this country, and to receive all evidence that may be tendered or obtained concerning a murder, alleged by the same person to have been perpetrated by one or more of such conspirators, the victim of which murder is stated to be unknown to the police.'—resolves as follows :

(1) That there is no evidence to warrant the belief that the Government was aware of any plot or intention to assassinate His Royal Highness the Duke of Edinburgh, before his arrival in this country, or at any time previous to the attempt upon his life.

(2) That it does not appear that any extraordinary precautions were taken for the preservation of the life of His Royal Highness, either on the occasion of his landing, or at any period during his stay in this country, up to the moment of his attempted assassination.

(3) That there is no evidence to warrant the belief that the crime of O'Farrell, who attempted to murder the Duke of Edinburgh, was the result of any conspiracy or organisation existing in this country, or, as far as the Government had or have any knowledge, the result of a conspiracy or organisation existing elsewhere.

(4) That there is no evidence whatever of the murder of any supposed confederate in the alleged plot.

(5) That the foregoing Resolutions be embodied in an Address to the Governor, with a request that His Excellency will forward the same to Her Majesty's Secretary of State for the Colonies.

The mover made a long and acrimonious speech in support of his resolutions. I rose immediately upon his sitting down. I did not ask the House to simply negative the motion, but I asked it to omit the resolutions, and substitute others in their place, condemning the report as containing 'numerous statements and inferences not warranted by the evidence ;' and I asked it to expunge the report from the proceedings of the committee. The following are my counter-resolutions :—

1. That all the words after the word ' That ' in the first line be omitted, with the view of substituting the following:— ' The Report of the Select Committee, appointed on December 15, 1868, to enquire into the existence of a conspiracy for purposes of treason and assassination, presented by the chairman on the 3rd instant, contains numerous statements and inferences not warranted by the evidence, and is made an instrument of personal hostility against a member of this House, in disregard of the authorised objects of the enquiry, and manifestly for party purposes. 2. That the evidence shows that several principal officers of the Government—who, from their official position and experience, were best qualified to form a correct judgment of the occurrences, and the state of public feeling during the time of excitement previous and subsequent to the attempt to assassinate the Duke of Edinburgh were and are still of opinion that meetings of seditious were and are held in the colony ; that the criminal O'Farrell was not alone and unaided in his attack upon the life of His Royal Highness ; and that persons openly sympathised with the attempted assassination. 3. That the evidence shows that rumours of intended violence towards His Royal Highness, more or less definite, were in circulation before March 12, 1868 ; and that some of such rumours have proceeded from sources unknown to the Government at the time, and that, therefore, they supply independent evidence in support of the statements of the

official witnesses.   4. That the important results of the enquiry
set forth in the preceding second and third resolutions, and also
other matters of serious moment, which ought to have been
faithfully represented to this House, have been either set aside
altogether or improperly and prejudicially dealt with in the
report.   5. That this House expresses its disapprobation of the
said Report, and directs that it be expunged from the proceedings of the Select Committee.'

I spoke at considerable length, and replied very
unreservedly to the mover's charges, concluding with
the following sentences :—

In conclusion, I shall content myself with nothing less than
what is set forth in my resolutions.   I will not submit to having
a report so dishonest and so scandalous as I have shown this to
be still remaining among the records, to be unfairly quoted at
any moment by persons whose capabilities of unfairness we have
so often witnessed—to be made a handle of in a nefarious way
at the general election, when it is desirable that the verdict of
constituencies shall be honestly taken.   I take my stand upon
this ground, that I am above reproach in this matter—that the
committee, with all its malignity and ingenuity, has failed to
substantiate a charge against me, and that the charges recoil
upon themselves by the unanswerable testimony I have adduced
before the House.   The laws of honourable dealing are against
the authors of this report.   The law of God declares 'Thou shalt
not bear false witness against thy neighbour ;' and I will not
submit to that which would stamp our proceedings with disgrace, and which, if I submit to it, may at some future time fall
upon the head of a worthier man.

My resolutions were substituted for those of Mr.
Macleay, and passed by the Legislative Assembly by
thirty-two to twenty-two votes amidst tumultuous
cheering, the members immediately afterwards rising
to their feet and giving three cheers for the Queen.

Though it was three o'clock in the morning a large crowd waited outside the House for me, and cheered me to the echo. So ended the 'conspiracy' of bitter sectaries and personal calumniators to destroy me in connection with the unhappy O'Farrell case.

In a book like this, whatever I may have wished to do, I could not omit this passage in my life. There were two objects to be served—to vindicate my own reputation, which I now leave with the facts and explanations placed on record, and to give a clear and definite character to the attempted assassination. It seems to me beyond dispute that the attempt upon the Duke of Edinburgh's life emanated from a plot. It is impossible that O'Farrell, a young man in the prime of early manhood, without any known vicious propensities, rational in all his conduct and conversation apart from this criminal act, without any individual motive to commit the crime, not goaded on by cruel or desperate feeling, could have deliberately made up his mind alone, unaided, and unabetted, to shoot the Prince. On the contrary, his own explanations were rational and clear from first to last, if due allowance is made for the state of mind which any man would be in who had taken an oath to abide by the lot, if it fell to him, to commit a murder. As to the existence of such plots at different times the evidence that has existed is overwhelming. To disprove that O'Farrell was the instrument of some such plot the most tortured construction must be put upon evidence, and belief must be refused to explanations for which no other explanations can be substituted. I do not seek to connect his crime with

any party or section of people; his confederates
may have been hare-brained visionaries; but that he
attempted to murder the Duke of Edinburgh in
obedience to an injunction from others, which horrified
his soul, but which he felt must be obeyed, is to my
mind abundantly clear.

As I have said, this lamentable occurrence had a
thoroughly bad influence on the political life of the
country. Crimination and recriminations arising out
of it have not yet lost their effect. In our elections
thousands of votes have been given under the dead
weight of prejudices contracted from the rancorous
animosities of the period. Men who were friends
before were never friends afterwards. The one person
who remained untouched by sinister influence and free
from the ravages of distorted passion was the victim of
the outrage, whose conduct under his suffering was in
the highest sense commendable from first to last.

I copy in this chapter two letters from Mr. Carlyle
which touch upon the chief features of my first months
of Ministerial life, including the Edmonton struggle :—

Chelsea, October 22, 1867.

Dear Sir,—Several weeks ago there arrived from you a
pleasant and very kind letter, testifying in various ways that
you held me in good remembrance, and announcing, especially,
that a colonial gift from your hand was on the road for me.
Last week, after some little delay, due to certain British railway
people, the munificent Sydney box was accurately handed in
here, 'completely safe and correct in every particular' (as I
could now inform the punctual and obliging Mr. Buchanan),
'and *franco* from the Antipodes to this door!' So that all this
is now a thing successful, faithfully achieved; and I am now in

possession of my beautiful ' Possum rug,' which I not a little admire, both as a specimen of useful peltry (probably enough 'one of the *best* rugs' ever made), and on other still more human considerations, for all which kind benefits, and for the *warmth* they are all suited to yield me in their various ways, please to accept my grateful acknowledgments and the best human thanks I have. You owed me nothing for 1862, it is rather I that owe you. There are traits and words about those innocent evenings you spent with us which I shall never forget. Your face is still present to me as if I saw it; and beautiful wise things said of you, by one whom I shall now behold no more!

Of the books &c. I made a cursory examination, and have them lying within reach when time allows of more. I had heard, long since, of your official position; which, I can now flatter myself, is of more stability than usual, and likely, on that and other grounds, to be of far more *utility* perhaps! Everybody seems to believe that whatever lies in you of real service to the colony and its best interests will be strenuously *done*. That is all that can be required of a man; and that is required of every man, in office or not in—tho' so very few even try to perform it!

By the newspapers that came with your letter, I see what babble and bother (about Irish priests, and other *mune* objects) an official man is exposed to; like a rider on express, by village dog's barking; but he ought to ride on, as nearly as possible 'all the same,' with the due flourish of his whip, and (if it must be so) with the due passing salutation or lifting of the hat to said village dog, and, if possible, *arrive* before 'the night' do!

I have been greatly shocked and surprised to hear that there is now—owing to abuses of the *land law*, and to internal intriguings—next to no immigration to your huge colonial continent of late; and that your majority by count of heads don't want any! I could hardly be brought to believe it; but it was from a reporter who had evident facilities for seeing, and who had just returned from a long stay in the country.

Nowhere in all my historical enquiries have I met such an instance of human meanness, short-sighted, barefaced cupidity, and total want of even the pretension to patriotism, on the part of any governing entity, plebeian or princely! King Bomba, the Grand Duke, Great Mogul, and even the King of Dahomey, may hide their diminished heads! I hope always it is not quite so bad as reported.

A week or two ago I sent off to your address a pamphlet that had been worked out of me (for I live quite silent for above a year-and-half gone), which would show what my degree of admiration was of the great things we have been performing here lately, with a view to improve Government! Mr. Duffy had another copy, and I sent no third.

Adieu, dear sir; I wish you all success and prosperity, official and other, and beg a continuance of your regard.

Yours sincerely,<br>T. CARLYLE.

Chelsea, April 27, 1868.

Dear Sir,—Two days ago I received your obliging letter; and am glad to hear that all goes on well with you. By the newspapers you send I sometimes notice what provoking obstruction there is from the Irish Priest species, but rejoice to perceive you can patiently deal with it, and victoriously do some good in spite of *it* and other anarchisms and deliriums! For your two Enactments about Schools, it is certain all men are obliged to you more or less, and above and before all, your own colony in its present posture.

.     .     .     .     .     .     .

Poor England will have to prepare herself for quite other disasters, atrocities, and brute anarchisms at home and abroad . . . !—Did you see in the last *Westminster Review* an amazing and indeed quite unique Article on the Colony of Victoria? If any of your Melbourne &c. Newspapers *can* essentially contradict and extinguish it, by all means let the feat be done! Hardly elsewhere in this universe have I seen, both as regards ourselves and those 'patriotic' Melbourners, a more accursed-

looking thing! But I had better hasten to do the small bit
of service you ask, and shut up the *Pandora's Box* in other
respects.

Here are two Photographs; one of which you are to choose
for yourself; the other by some opportunity you may convey
to Mr. ——

With many kindly regards, and best wishes for your prosperity, official, domestic, and personal,

Yours sincerely,<br>
T. CARLYLE.

One of the early matters that attracted my attention in office was the condition of the asylums for the
insane. Books on the treatment of lunacy, prison discipline, and the care of destitute children, had found a
place in my general reading, and had awakened in my
mind a deep interest in the consideration of such questions. The principal asylum was situated on Turban
Creek, about eight miles from Sydney. I visited this
institution soon after my assumption of office. There
was no sign of garden, or cultivation of any kind in the
grounds surrounding the building; the building itself
presented some features of architectural design, but
the first noticeable evidence of the condition of the
interior was seen in locked doors and barred windows.
I had sat on committees of the Legislature where evidence had been taken as to the management of this
institution; but such enquiries had been almost wholly
confined to trumpery charges of peculation in the
stores, or official favouritism, or negligence in appointments. Inexperienced as I was, it struck me at once
that the root of the evil was much deeper, and that
the management was radically wrong. The prison-

like condition of the whole establishment was to me appalling.

About this time, a gentleman who held the position of surgeon on a ship of war in the harbour applied to me for an order to visit and inspect the asylum. This was the present Inspector-General of the Insane, Dr. Frederick Norton Manning, whose services in the humane cause of the proper care and treatment of the insane have since made his name eminent beyond the colony of New South Wales. In several conversations with Mr. Manning, I became convinced that he was the sort of man which the Government wanted in carrying out a thorough reform in our methods of treatment, and I proposed to him that he should obtain his discharge from the service to which he was then attached, and accept the principal office in our department of lunacy. This he assented to. In the first place, however, Mr. Manning was commissioned to visit Europe and America to enquire into, and report upon, the whole subject of the care and management of the insane as illustrated by the plans of construction, economic arrangements, and systems of treatment, in the best-known asylums. His instructions were full and precise in these respects; and he was accredited to the Imperial Government with a request that he might be officially introduced in foreign countries. Without loss of time Mr. Manning proceeded on his mission, and, having faithfully accomplished it, in due time he returned to the colony. He returned just as I was quitting office, through an unfortunate disagreement with my colleagues about the dismissal of a civil servant where I thought a wrong to an upright officer had been done; but the work so well begun was carried on with a noble purpose and singular aptitude by Mr. Manning. His report has been acknowledged by eminent authorities as an able and a valuable work on the subject.

In 1868, when Mr. Manning took charge, the Government had two asylums, one at Tarban Creek and one at Parramatta, and a private asylum had just been opened under authority. The total number of inmates was 1.230; their unhappy condition has already been indicated.

Dr. Manning, with whose valuable services and successful work we have now to deal, soon discovered a fine taste and a well-informed judgment in treating the natural surroundings of the asylums, as well as great skill and activity in reorganising and systematising matters within. He proved himself to be a man of much culture and refined habits of thought, whose heart was in his work. When he took charge, in 1868, to quote his own words, 'the buildings used for asylums were grim without and comfortless within'; to a large extent they consisted of erections in former times for prison purposes. These have now been wholly abolished, and the new buildings which have taken their place, or occupied new ground, have been erected on the most improved plans, with a view to the healthful care and comfort of the inmates. The dormitories are airy and pleasant; the living rooms are enlivened with pictures and singing birds. All the courtyards contain pet animals and birds. The surrounding grounds have been converted into beautiful gardens, and the outside walls of the buildings are aglow with the bloom of luxuriant creepers. Spacious rooms have been built, where on the Sunday religious services are held, and frequently in the evenings of the week concerts or other entertainments are given to the patients, who are allowed much freedom, many of them engaging in light employments. In their out-of-door life they are permitted and encouraged to take part in innocent games.

On November 30, 1891, the total number of insane persons in the asylums of New South Wales was 3,151 ; but relatively to the increase of population there has been no positive increase, while in England and in other countries during the same period the relative number has increased absolutely. Throughout the period since 1868, the proportion of insane persons to the general population has remained about one to 380. Much has been done, under the supervision of Dr. Manning, in the classification of patients, and in the separation of distinct classes, such as criminals, confirmed idiots, and chronic cases of suffering. In the system established there has been a marked improvement in methods—the patients are more individualised, and the whole treatment adopted is based on hospital rather than on asylum principles. Few things have been more creditable to the colony than the thorough reforms of the last twenty-five years in this province of administration.

During the first period of my official life, it became my duty to give effect to the Industrial Schools Act passed in 1866. I purchased the merchant vessel which for the last twenty-four years has borne an honourable reputation as the Nautical School Ship

*Vernon*, still floating on the waters of Port Jackson, but shortly to be replaced by a finer and more roomy ship. This Institution has been the means of educating and starting in a safe course of industry many hundreds of boys who, it is almost a certainty, would otherwise have perished amidst the haunts of vice and misery. Fortunately, from the first it has been under excellent superintendence; and few visitors ever leave it without a good word for the admirable training which the boys receive. The *Vernon* has sent out into the world 2,348 destitute boys (December 31, 1891), of whom less than 10 per cent. have appeared as the subjects of bad or doubtful reports afterwards. An industrial school for girls has not been so successful, though it has done good work in the rescue of female children from neglect and ruin. Soon after the establishment of this last-named institution, a revolt occurred among the inmates, and I quote here a letter which I directed to be addressed to the superintendent on the occasion as containing my views of the character and objects of the school and the qualities necessary for its conduct and success :—

Colonial Secretary's Office, Sydney, July 22, 1868.

Madam,—I am directed to inform you that the Colonial Secretary has had under his consideration the case of insubordination among the inmates of the Industrial School of which you are Superintendent and the conduct of yourself and the other officers in relation to this occurrence. He has read the documents noted in the margin and has taken much trouble to obtain a correct knowledge of the cause of the late disturbance, in order that the most effectual measures may be adopted to guard against any similar disorders.

Mr. Parkes regrets that the evidence before him leads to

the conclusion that throughout these unfortunate occurrences much blame is justly attributable to yourself as Superintendent. No person who has not fully considered its objects is justified in undertaking the management of an Institution like that which has been committed to your charge ; and the person who accepts so serious a responsibility ought to keep its objects always in view. Representations of the bad behaviour of the inmates cannot be received in apology for the injudicious conduct of the officers. Sufficient self-restraint should be exercised at all times to avoid irritating language or inconsiderate punishment in the treatment of these children. Hurry of the moment, heat of temper, or personal annoyance on the part of the Superintendent is no excuse for ill performance of duty. The school has not been founded for good and obedient children. The Superintendent is not wanted to take charge of children who have been properly instructed and trained. The Legislature wisely sanctions the large expenditure required for its support, to provide a home for the homeless, to establish a moral authority over those who, it may be presumed, have hitherto known little of parental control, to instruct by precept and example a class of helpless young creatures whose only title to be received into such an Institution is that they have been neglected by their natural protectors and allowed to sink into a state of ignorance and vice.

If this is a correct view of the objects and character of the Institution (and the Colonial Secretary does not think that you will take exception to its correctness), much of what you have said in explanation of the late disturbance and of your own conduct must be held to be of little value. It explains nothing to say that the difficulty of management lies in the vicious dispositions of the inmates, for it is in dealing successfully with those vicious dispositions that the Institution has its use.

The Colonial Secretary is not disposed to attach undue weight to the statements of the refractory girls that you on several occasions upbraided them in unbecoming and unseemly language. He has not failed to notice that in the worst expressions complained of, supposing that words of the kind were used, the meaning may have been easily misunderstood or perverted by the class of minds to whom they were addressed; and, knowing the high character you have borne, he cannot bring himself to the belief that you could be provoked into the use of language so unwomanly and gross as is attributed to you in some cases by the testimony of these girls. But the fact that charges of so unseemly a character have been made against you should convince you of the necessity of being at all times circumspect and self-respecting in the language you address to the inmates and in your whole conduct towards them. In a manner unknown to themselves they look to you for an example. If not to you, to whom can the poor creatures look? One of these young girls, in her evidence before the Inspector of Public Charities, expressed herself in touching terms of reproach. 'We thought we came here to be reformed!' So it will ever be, if the thought is suffered to find a resting-place that they are not treated in accordance with the professed anxiety of the State for their moral improvement.

Mr. Parkes is of opinion, however, that the evidence before him shows that your language to the inmates has often been hasty and inconsiderate, and sometimes petulant and unnecessarily harsh. To upbraid these unfortunate girls with their former courses of life or the failings of their parents would be heartless and cruel, and could have but one tendency—to harden them against all amendment and to embitter them against their instructors. Though you deny that you have done this in the direct phrases attributed to you, I am to express regret that there appears to be ground for believing that the feeling must have made itself evident in some form or other in your intercourse with the girls. Mr. Inspector Walker reports that some of the girls made these complaints with unfeigned reluctance and grief; and it cannot be easily believed that girls, however abandoned, would invent charges of this character.

It is observable also from the evidence that there has not been sufficient regularity, order, and decision in the arrangements of the Establishment. The duties of each office should be clearly defined and should be of a character not to interfere with the duties of any other. In no case should you as Superintendent give an order without seeing that it is carried into effect, but you should be very careful not to give an unnecessary or an imprudent order. The whole of the officers should be enjoined to conduct themselves at all times with a due regard for the usefulness of the offices they respectively hold, and without any undue familiarity with the inmates; and to maintain authority and command obedience more by a consistent observance of the rules of kindness and humanity than by resorting to means of coercion and punishment. And it is thought that in so commodious a building the means of classification might be devised by which the elder girls could be separated from the younger ones. Any such arrangement would be salutary in its effects.

.         .         .         .         .         .

Mr. Parkes is glad to observe that the faults in your management are for the most part errors of judgment. No one charges you with inhumanity or neglect of duty. For this reason, and also in consideration of the difficulties inseparable from the organisation of a new Establishment, you will be retained in charge of the Institution. But I am to direct your earnest attention to the suggestions of improvement which have been made with a view to more effective discipline.

I have the honour to be, Madam,

Your obedient servant,

HENRY HALLORAN,

*Under Secretary.*

# CHAPTER X

In the year 1870 I was overtaken by commercial difficulties which rendered it necessary for me to resign my seat in the Legislative Assembly. For some years I had represented Kiama, a beautiful and prosperous district on the Southern coast; the electors had always treated me with generous confidence, and our relations were such as made the position of representative unusually easy and pleasant. But I declined to offer myself again as a candidate, from a keen feeling of humiliation under my misfortunes. My friends, however, determined to nominate me, and, though I was opposed by a resident landholder of large local influence, I was elected by a large majority. The following letter which I addressed to the electors in acknowledgment of the marked honour conferred upon me will show the state of feeling under which I laboured at the time, and the uneasy views I held of the successful issue of the contest.

*To the Electors of Kiama.*

Gentlemen,—In my absence, and without my consent, you have re-elected me to the seat which, by four previous elections, you entrusted to me as your representative in Parliament.

I hope I shall be pardoned if I acknowledge that I should have been glad if your choice at the present time had fallen upon some other person identified with the political interests I have advocated. I believe it would have been better for myself, and perhaps better for all, if I had been left at liberty to take my own course, uninfluenced by any public considerations. Nor can I shut my eyes to the truth that it is not desirable that persons in my situation should be elected to the Legislature.

I feel, nevertheless, I hope with becoming gratitude, that you have conferred upon me a great honour, and that I ought not lightly to disregard your wishes after this manifestation of your continued confidence, which has been marked by a majority of votes in my favour in every part of the constituency. Putting aside the advice of friends, who, I fear, set too high a value on my ability to serve the public, I do not think I should be justified in causing you the trouble and annoyance of another election by declining to accept the duties and responsibilities of your representation.

I am, Gentlemen,<br>Your obedient servant,<br>HENRY PARKES.

Sydney, November 8, 1870.

In due time I took my seat. Strange proceedings had attended the formation of a new Administration which had just been sworn. The chief of the retiring Ministry had been appointed to the high office of Agent-General in England after his defeat in Parliament and before his final relinquishment of office. The leader of the Opposition in the late Ministerial defeat and a leading member of the defeated Ministry had, without any new

circumstance to bridge over their political differences,
coalesced in the new Government.   My first speech was
delivered in condemnation of the appointment of Agent-
General.   The leading journal of the colony next
morning came out with a volley of abuse against me
for my speech; admitting that the appointment was
bad, said the critic, I was not the person to condemn
it.  Incredible as it may appear to strangers, and
Quixotic as it appears to myself at this distance of time,
I thereupon resigned the seat to which I had just been
so handsomely elected.   Without taking time for calm
reflection, I contended that if I could not deal with all
questions with unimpaired privilege and untrammelled
judgment, I ought not to be in the House at all.   After
all the electors had done for me, that was their reward.
Yet the generous people of Kiama to this day, whenever I can spare a day to go amongst them, receive me
with kindness and enthusiasm.

The prospect before me was gloomy enough.   I had
stripped myself of the conventional importance that
attaches to a seat in Parliment.   I was penniless; I was
deserted by many who had profited by my friendship
in former days.   But throughout my life my heart has
always been most buoyant and strenuous in the face of
difficulty, and it did not fail me then.

A gentleman, an old resident of Sydney, who had
made some money at the diamond fields of South
Africa, had lately returned to the colony; and he took
it into his head to start a daily newspaper.   He offered
me employment, which I accepted.   It opened to me a
medium for the expression of my opinions on current

events, and it afforded me the means of subsistence.
For some weeks I worked day and night on this paper.
The following is one of my articles at this time, which
I select because it treats of the state of public matters
to which reference has been made and also deals with
a subject of the highest concern to the friends of constitutional government.

### ' Public Affairs.

'We belong to no party in politics. But there are
questions that transcend all party considerations, and
rise to a magnitude of national importance in the light
of our present interests and our future destiny. It
seems to us that more than one such question rises to
notice from the late Ministerial changes. As Sir James
Martin told the electors of East Sydney, it matters little
to the people what set of men may be receiving the
rewards of office so long as good government is secured
to the country. It may be that a doctrine of political
morality so irrefragable would look better if it were
enforced by some one not directly interested in preserving things as they are. Its soundness cannot be
disputed. It matters very much however by what
means Ministers are brought into existence and sustained in power. Parliamentary government, as it has
been worked out by our countrymen at home. has de-
pended for its unexampled success much more upon a
sense of political honour, upon rules of individual
action clearly recognised although unwritten, and upon
the observance of party obligations. than upon any
principles of government laid down by Locke, Beccaria,

or Jeremy Bentham. And we hold to the belief that unless the same rules of political conduct, the same landmarks of constitutional usage that have guided English statesmen, are adopted by those English colonists who are trying the experiment of governing themselves, Parliamentary government as transplanted among them must be more or less a failure. Though the opposite of absolute despotism, the form of government under which we live is capable of being made something worse than any despotism that is still sustained by high personal qualities, if our public men should cease to follow the guidance of those whose patriotic virtues have created and preserved it in England.

'We shall not concern ourselves just now with the rumours freely circulated of the share which persons unconnected with Parliament are said to have had in the formation of the new Administration. The public may hereafter be better informed on that subject by the discussions in the Assembly, and we are desirous of laying upon ourselves at all times the restraint of correct information. But it has been stated authoritatively, and has not been denied by anyone, that proceedings took place with the concurrence of Sir James Martin, after he was called to the assistance of the Governor, which we venture to say are unprecedented and must be felt as a reproach to our free institutions.

'A meeting of the Opposition in the Assembly, regularly convened by circular, was held to consider the claims of gentlemen to be raised to the position of advisers of the Crown. Of course, the members at such a gathering would meet on equal terms. The youngest

and least experienced would have his voice in the consultation like the oldest and best informed, and every
member of a legislative body soon finds out that there
is something inherent in his relation to the State which
gives his voice a potency. Gentlemen whose sagacity
had never soared above the points in a breed of cattle or
the grazing capabilities of a sheep run, would suddenly
have to decide upon the capacity of their friends for
statesmanship, and few men are disposed to rate themselves incompetent for any task flattering to their
intellect which others assign to them. Modest members
who had often felt the need of advice in giving their
votes on simple questions before the House, would now
be privileged to say who should represent Parliament
in the Executive Council, and be entrusted with ad-
ministering the affairs of the country. Everyone who
was happy enough to form a twenty-ninth or thirtieth
part—whatever may have been the exact proportion of
numerical strength—of Her Majesty's Opposition, was
at liberty to put his spoke into the new wheel of State.
There was no obstacle to his taking his turn at Cabinet-
making except his unavoidable absence.

'Now, it must be obvious that the recognition by
Sir James Martin himself of an assemblage of this
character was a step towards making Government a
delegacy from a mob, a small and privileged mob it
may have been, but nevertheless a mob in all the
essentials of acting without authority or accountability.
Its suggestions and counsels, if acted upon, could lead
to nothing but embarrassment and weakness, and if it
never was intended to act upon them, it was nothing

short of deception to countenance it. No wonder that the result of this meeting gave satisfaction to nobody.

'The notable expedient of balloting for Ministers which arose out of the abortive proceedings at this meeting is worse still; and enough to make all sensible people feel ashamed of our political leaders. A grave gentleman starts the objection that it will be unpleasant to discuss the merits of his friends in their presence, and suggests that each member shall take a list of the Assembly, mark off the six names of his choice, and hand it into the man who holds the fate of all in his hands. This plan, which might have formed part of some design to make government ridiculous, is gravely adopted by the assembled legislators, apparently without any suspicion of the folly of the thing, and it receives the approval of Sir James Martin, with the saving qualification that he should not consider himself bound by the result of the ballot. Could anything be devised more outrageously opposed to the spirit of Responsible Government or more devoid of the sanction of constitutional practice? Who ever heard of an English statesman, holding his Sovereign's commission to form a Government, taking the opinion of his followers in detail, or assenting to a general ballot for his colleagues?

' The scheme of Parliamentary government supposes that a small band of superior men in whose political character and administrative capacity, as a whole, the Legislature has confidence shall govern us so long as they can retain that confidence. The grand security for good government by these men consists in their direct responsibility to a larger body of men, who, in their turn, are responsible to the whole people. But it has never been proposed that these rulers should be elected, directly or indirectly, by the representative body. When a Ministry retires, the practice has been for the Crown to communicate with some member of the Legislature, not less distinguished by his knowledge of the existing political situation and his acquaintance with contemporary political characters, than by his talents and his public services; and he is communicated with because he possesses this knowledge which is supposed to qualify him in a special manner to select the other high servants of the Crown. In the execution of this great commission he is responsible at the same time to the Crown and to the people's representatives. For either to interfere with his execution of this task would be to diminish to the extent of that interference the responsibility which ought to rest upon him alone. The function of the Crown is to see that he is equal to the duty imposed upon him; the function of the Legislature is to see that he honourably performs it.

'We ought not to feel surprised, however much we may regret, that the preliminaries to which we have adverted are speedily followed by negotiations and combinations that shock our sense of political propriety. And herein lies the danger to the people. It is this that makes matters, trifling in themselves, of the highest concern to the well being of the community. Once off the rail, who can answer for the engine which so far has carried the train with speed and security? Those who resort to means that amaze the community

to obtain power are not likely to stop at trifles in
retaining it. But the mischief will not end with their
retirement from office. The next set of Ministers may
commence their deviations from the constitution, not
from the original land-marks, but from the marks left
by their predecessors. We may live to see a Ministry
balloted for in fact, and an Executive Council sworn under
the dictation of some person unknown to the Constitution.'

While I was engaged in this temporary journalistic
work, an American gentleman, Mr. H. H. Hall, who
had established a line of steam vessels between Sydney
and San Francisco, proposed to me that I should accept
the position of his agent in endeavouring to obtain the
support of the several Australian Governments to his
enterprise. No service could have been more congenial
to me, and I accepted the proposal without hesitation.
I believed Mr. Hall to be a man of indomitable energy,
and of large practical knowledge of the business he
had in hand, though I knew him to be crippled in
means, and I had great faith in his ultimate success. As
a member of the Parliament of New South Wales I
had, from the earliest initial steps, given my warmest
support to the Trans-Pacific route for postal and commercial communication, and I entered upon the duties
I now undertook with zeal and perseverance. I visited
all the other colonies, and in all I met with the most
friendly greetings. All the Ministers gave me their
patient attention, with no greater discouragement in
any case than that arising from the closer pressure of
questions of immediate urgency. Especially Sir Arthur

Palmer in Queensland, Sir C. Gavan Duffy in Victoria, Mr. Justice Boucaut in South Australia, and the late T. G. Chapman in Tasmania, extended to me the most marked attention and personal kindness.

All questions relating to the future of the Pacific are full of interest for intelligent men all over the world. Its many groups of fertile lands—the least known the most valuable in view of civilising agencies and the extension of Australian commerce; its comparatively untracked fields for maritime enterprise, these will present to coming generations vast attractions not dreamt of by men of to-day. All relating to the early movement for uniting America and Australia by a chain across the Pacific Ocean must be fraught with abiding interest for enquiring minds. While in Melbourne I addressed the following letter on the subject of my mission to the members of the Victorian Parliament :—

Melbourne, August 22, 1871.

Sir,—I beg permission to address you, as a Member of the Legislature of Victoria, on a matter which I think you will admit to be of public importance. The subject is the expediency of this colony granting support to the Mail Line of Steam Packets established by Mr. H. H. Hall, between Australia and America, in connection with the postal communication now opened across the North American Continent to Europe. In order that I may not be misunderstood, I desire in the first place to explain the position I occupy in asking your attention.

In April last Mr. Hall applied to me in Sydney to visit the other Australian Colonies as his attorney, to represent the claims of his Mail Service to the support of the Australian Governments. Having time at my disposal, at least for a few months, I undertook the mission he proposed, and it is in that

s 2

capacity that I now address you. I may, however, state that I should not have engaged myself in this duty if I had not felt, as an Australian legislator for the last seventeen years, a deep interest in extending our scheme of International intercourse, call it by what postal name you may, to the great English-speaking communities of America ; and it is probable that if this had not been the case no application would have been made to me on the subject.

It will be best to explain also the circumstances in which Mr. Hall seeks the support of Victoria, and that of the other colonies. As the great Trans-Continental Railway which unites the Pacific and Atlantic shores of the United States approached completion, Mr. Hall conceived the idea of establishing regular postal communication with America and Europe, by running a line of Australian steam packets to Honolulu, to which port a line of American steamers was already running from San Francisco. The colonies of New South Wales and New Zealand entered into an agreement to subsidise this pioneer service for twelve months, the amount contributed by New South Wales being 10,000l. As the vessels under this contract had to make the détour of New Zealand, their voyages were open to the objections of unnecessary protraction and of encountering unnecessarily tempestuous weather. During the twelve months Mr. Hall visited America to arrange for the punctual transmission of mails across the Continent, and to effect other improvements of the service ; and on the expiration of his contract, in March last, he reorganised the line by running his packets on the direct route *viâ* Fiji, and through the whole distance to San Francisco, without any change of vessel or unnecessary delay at an intermediate port. I enclose a chart of the mail route as now decided upon, giving the distances of each principal division, and the various steam postal connections with other parts of the world.

The present line consists of the three finest steamships of the Australasian Steam Navigation Company's numerous fleet (which fleet includes upwards of thirty vessels), and the owners are prepared to engage themselves to build other ships to meet the increasing demands of the service. I enclose some particulars of the character of these vessels, and also of the charterer's arrangements for the satisfactory conveyance of mails and passengers.

It is this service, in the hands of the originator of the Pacific route, based upon an experience gained by sixteen complete voyages, and reorganised with the view of affording the greatest amount of advantage to these colonies, which Mr. Hall has brought under the notice of the Government of Victoria, with the hope of receiving a subsidy towards its maintenance. The Parliament of New South Wales has, by a very large majority, granted a subsidy of 15,000l. per annum to the new service. I respectfully submit that this line of mail packets in actual operation is a very different thing from any proposal, let it be made by whomsoever it may, to bring into existence an Ocean Mail Service at some future time, with all the inevitable obstacles and possible casualties which lie in the region of experiment before it. As to the chain of communication thus established, I cannot for a moment conceive that any person whose mind is accustomed to the treatment of large affairs will regard merely from a point of local interest the questions, in a great measure profoundly social and political, which it opens for consideration.

The postal and commercial advantages of the new Mail Line through America to Europe are undeniable and manifold. The direct route across the Pacific pierces, as it were, the Fijian Archipelago, which fertile and beautiful islands already are partly occupied by a numerous British community, and are manifestly destined to become an extensive field for industry and commerce. More distant, it connects Australia with the prosperous little kingdom of the Sandwich Islands, and it terminates at the great commercial city of San Francisco. From this point regular lines of communication branch off to Vancouver's Island and British Columbia; to San Diego, Mazatlan, Manzanillo, Acapulco, and Panama; to Guayaquil, Callao, Cobija, and Valparaiso; to China and Japan. Along the Trans-Continental route the places of importance in the interest

of civilisation and human progress are too numerous to be
touched upon here; but Ogden, Omaha, and Chicago stand
out as marvels of the conquest of nature by the indomitable
forces of our colonising race. The land journey ends in New
York, whence communication is frequent and easy to all parts
of the Dominion of Canada, to the West Indies, to all parts of
the Atlantic coasts of North and South America, and to all
parts of Europe. The finest steamships afloat leave New York
every day for England.

It is impossible to contemplate the immense populations
speaking the English language, numbering from 70,000,000 to
80,000,000 of souls, including the most adventurous and inventive powers of industrial enterprise, the highest forms of
social culture, and the most honoured sources of intelligence
and thought, which this scheme of postal and living intercourse
connects intercommunicably in all the interests of civilisation,
without being impressed with the beneficial influence it must
exercise on the progress of these colonies, so far as reason can
forecast the results that are yet unrevealed in the future. I
venture to think that, as with nations, so with communities
endowed with as many of the attributes of nationhood as these
colonies possess, there are higher objects to be kept in view
than the mere achievement of material prosperity. To be in-
different to the intellectual life, the political tendencies, and
the social manifestations of the great communities in America
which owe their origin to the same national stock as ourselves,
would be to betray an insensibility to our gravest responsibilities
as an undivided Australian people. The sister States of America, and the sister Provinces of Australia, whatever may be
the forms of government in which their free aspirations seek
security and rest, ought to grow up side by side in friendly
intimacy and honourable emulation, warning each other from
internal dangers, instructing each other in national development,
strengthening each other by the example of moral effort, and
supporting each other in the defence of freedom. As time rolls
on, all that is good in the laws and literature of the elder off-
spring should be reflected back in the laws and literature of

the younger. The Pacific Ocean that lies between them—the calmest and most beautiful of oceans—should be the accepted type of the calm and glowing friendship uniting them as the two foremost powers of Christian progress in the next century.

I hope I shall be readily pardoned in speaking to you of these higher political considerations, apart from the value of this Line of Steamships for the delivery of mails and the purposes of commerce. It seems to me that the benefits of the Mail and Passenger Line through America would be extended in a new direction by maintaining the Suez line in conjunction with it. Thus would be formed, so to speak, an open pathway round the world, distinctly marked out, and on which time might be reckoned with something like accuracy, touching upon points of ancient historical interest, and passing through countries rich in the newest marvels of industrial life and activity. In such a world-wide circuit of communication, Australia would be the mid-way resting-place; and it cannot be doubted that, with such means of regular intercourse, a continuous stream of visitors from among the educated and affluent classes of Europe would pass leisurely and observantly through the Australian Colonies; some carrying away with them to other countries a living knowledge of our conditions of life and prospects of advancement, and others settling in our midst with new stores of capital and intelligence. Information respecting the colonies, acquired and disseminated by the instrumentality of influential persons of this class, would be of more value than all the reports, lectures, and books, without the same authority, that could be issued. The postal facilities of such a system would be complete, embracing the Indian Empire and other parts of Asia, with which it is necessary to keep up regular communication.

Being aware that the Cape route to Europe finds favour in a special manner with many intelligent men in Victoria, it is with deference to their opinion, and diffidence in the expression of my own, that I submit for consideration some objections to that route. None of the results of a political and social character which I have endeavoured to indicate can be secured by

it ; and I need not add that postal communication with Fiji,
the Sandwich Islands, and America cannot be so secured. It
would afford us no compensation for closing our communication
with India and China.  Our limited experience of steam navigation by the long sea route is sadly chequered by our recollection of the disasters which have occurred in the cases of the
*Royal Charter*, the *London*, and the *Queen of the Thames*.
But those disasters will be accounted for by circumstances peculiar to each case, and it will be said that they did not in any
way arise from the proper course and destination of the ships.
Leaving out of sight, therefore, the great proportion which the
lost vessels bear to the number of steamships hitherto employed
in the navigation, and confining the question to what is known
as the Cape route, without reference to past accidents, we still
have to reconcile its practicability as a mail route with the un-
alterable laws of nature which array the elements against it for
several months in the year.  Nor is it prudent to ignore our
knowledge that one line of steamers which attempted it some
years ago ruinously failed.  If stormy seas and heavy gales
have to be conquered by increased power of steam, not only
increased cost but increased discomfort and increased liability
to accident must be taken into account.  It can scarcely be
supposed that passengers, travelling for pleasure or for information, will prefer the voyage by way of the Cape, with its unbroken blankness and dreariness, to either of the other routes,
where the monotony of a long journey is relieved and enlivened
by frequent changes of scene and many new objects of interest.
It is only as an immigrant route, and then with powerful
steamers under subsidy, that the Cape route, as it appears to
me, would confer advantages on Victoria, and those advantages,
I still venture to think, would be shared in common with the
other colonies.  The immigrants, once landed in Melbourne,
would disperse themselves, so long as the passage from one
colony to another could be made for twenty shillings, wherever
the remuneration for labour, combined with other circumstances, seemed to present the most attraction.

An Ocean Mail Line connecting Australia with Europe

ought to be, and in its nature is, a federal service. The more widely and generally it extends its operation, the more valuable it is to each community, and to every member of each community, that participates in its benefits. I should consider it a great mistake for New South Wales to relinquish her interest in the Suez Mail Line, though her mail delivery by that route is much later and attended by much less convenience than that of South Australia or Victoria; and I believe the public opinion of the colony accords with this view. Yet New South Wales alone of the Australian colonies has had to bear the expense of opening the American route. For two years she paid at the rate of 55,000l. per annum towards subsidising the Panama Mail Ships, and up to this moment she is the only colony of the Australian group which has supported by a subsidy the Line via San Francisco. It would not be easy to prove that New South Wales has any interest superior to that of Victoria in opening this line of communication. The settlements on the Pacific Route are equally markets for the one colony as for the other; and the intercourse of Victoria with America is greater than that of New South Wales.

In fact, the proposal I have submitted to the Government of Victoria on behalf of Mr. Hall is, that Melbourne shall be the terminus of his line of steamers, asking an additional amount of subsidy to cover the additional cost of such modification of the service. In this case, the ships of the trunk line would depart from and arrive at Melbourne via Sydney, Levuka, and Honolulu, the time for the delivery of the Mails in both directions between this port and San Francisco being thirty-three days, and between this and the port of Liverpool forty-eight days, subject to the usual penalties. It is probable that Queensland will be connected with the main line by a branch steamer running between Moreton Bay and Fiji, and that a branch steamer will also run between Fiji and New Zealand, as marked on the accompanying chart.

I have the honour to be, Sir,

Your most obedient servant,

HENRY PARKES.

Mr. Hall failed at this stage of his enterprise by the
steamers placed under offer to him being withdrawn by
the Company to which they belonged, and my connection with him came to a sudden close.   But he was
a man who knew nothing of any such word as ' defeat ';
and in a short time he managed to get ships built on
the Clyde to his own designs for the service.   By this
time I had returned to political life, and was in office at
the head of my first Administration.   Mr. Hall obtained
a contract from the Government, negotiated by Sir
Saul Samuel, and he successfully established the service.
Eventually he was superseded by his principals on the
ground of the necessity for a more practical man to
direct the management.   Mr. Hall was one of those
' dreamers ' to whom the world owes so much—who do
things while others are considering the best means of
doing them, and who never acknowledge that they have
been outdone.   In some disgust he returned to America,
and a few years afterwards I met him in New York
with a new enterprise upon his hands—nothing less
than an Inter-Oceanic Railway across the isthmus of
Tehuantepec.

The political confusion and the absence of definite
party purpose in New South Wales in 1870 and 1871,
as already glanced at in this chapter, culminated in the
beginning of the following year in the complete dis-
ruption of existing alliances and the exclusion of several
of the Ministers from Parliament.   Early in January,
1872, I was elected for a country constituency, but
within a few days after my return the Legislative
Assembly was dissolved.   I then offered myself as a

candidate for East Sydney, and was duly elected. On account of the strange state of popular discontent into which the colony had been plunged I give my address to the electors :—

*To the Electors of East Sydney.*

Gentlemen,—On five different occasions, extending over a period of eighteen years, you have elected me by large majorities as one of your representatives in the Legislature. On the first of those occasions, in 1854, I expressed opinions on the principal questions of legislation and government which I still hold, with no modification except such as is derived from a fuller knowledge and a maturer judgment. My views, as then explained to you on several subjects of the first importance, have since been embodied in the laws of the country, as, for example, in the Municipalities Act, the Volunteer Act, and the Public Schools Act, which I had the honour to carry successfully through Parliament.

If the present were not an extraordinary emergency, I should, in offering myself again as a candidate for your suffrages, be satisfied to rest my cause on the records of the Legislative Assembly, where I have spent the best years of my life in your service. But the country is in the throes of a crisis such as has never before occurred in our history, and such as all friends of the Constitution must hope will never occur again. At this time, if at any time, the men who have largely shared in the political struggles of the country are entitled to speak boldly, and have a right to be heard.

A little more than a year ago a political combination took place in this country which has no parallel in English history, unless it be indeed the untoward union of Mr. Fox and Lord North, in 1783, which is thus described by Sir Thomas Erskine May :—'The principles of the two parties were irreconcilable ; and their sudden union could not be effected without imputations injurious to the credit of both. Nor could it be disguised that personal ambition dictated this bold stroke for power, in

which principles were made to yield to interest. It was the
alliance of factions, rather than of parties; and on either side it
was a grave political error. Viewed with disfavour by the most
earnest of both parties, it alienated from the two leaders many
of their best followers.' When Sir James Martin and Mr.
Robertson, imitating this bad historical example, agreed to
' bury the tomahawk ' in the spoils of office, it was foreseen that
nothing but disaster to our Parliamentary institutions could
follow that double act of perfidy and betrayal. The pernicious
consequences were not long in developing themselves. While
Sir James Martin openly ridiculed the idea that the people had
any regard for political principle, Mr. Robertson gave early
proof of how well he had attended to the teaching of his new
chief by proposing to double the *ad valorem* duties, which for
two years he had been promising to repeal. Then followed the
grand measure for raising a standing army, for which, as a
beginning, the people are required to pay 20,000*l*. a year to
enable Sir James Martin to keep them in order. To make up
this military expenditure the clerks in the public departments,
the messengers at the office doors, and the mechanics and
labourers in the Government workshops have been compelled to
submit to an arbitrary reduction of pay, with no attempt at an
equitable adjustment of the pressure, even now that Ministers
have had the necessary time upon their hands. An oppressive
Stamp Act, utterly unsuitable to a young community like ours,
has to be added to the first fruits of the Martin-Robertson
compact.

After these and similar transactions, Parliament was prorogued on June 22, and the Ministers immediately re-
warded their supporters in the first session by appointing two
of them Police Magistrates, and by conferring offices and
honours on the relatives and friends of several others. The
Houses were not again called together for the despatch of
business until November 14, making a recess of nearly
five months, and rendering it impossible to make legal provision in the proper constitutional manner for the public service
of 1872. The first measure then submitted to Parliament was

the Land Bill now before the country, which, although it has
since been modified by amendments, to pacify the angry feeling
of the electors, still remains one of the worst Bills ever proposed
in the Australian colonies, framed on no principle and embodying no policy which a community of intelligent men could
recognise and accept. By this measure no advantages are extended to the agricultural settler which would improve his
position, and the best apology which its authors can find for it
is that the 'free selectors' can, if they choose, remain under the
present law; while by its provisions the pastoral tenants of the
Crown will be enabled to secure the most valuable portions of
their runs, up to the extent of 16,000 acres in one block, at an
average of 8s. per acre, with thirteen years for payment, and all
other persons in the country are denied any similar privilege.
To the credit of those members of the late Assembly connected
with the squatting interest, the greater number of them showed
their independence and their contempt for this cunningly-
designed sop by voting against the Government. The crown-
ing transaction, or rather series of transactions, in this down-
ward course of vicious legislation and misgovernment, is that
which has resulted in the collection of the Border Customs
duties, not less in opposition to Sir James Martin's declared
policy of former years than to the latest decision of Parliament.
The Attorney-General has made an elaborate attempt to put
the sister colony in the wrong in this unfortunate dispute,
apparently with a reckless disregard of the difficulties he is
creating in the way of its just settlement. But even if Sir
James Martin's case was not based upon wild assumptions, it is
of no avail for him to rake up the transactions between the
Government of this colony and Victoria for the last nine years.
That part of his case was entirely cut away from him by his
own act, when, on August 9 last, he invited the Victorian
Government to a Conference, 'to avoid, if possible, a renewal of
the inconvenience so seriously felt by the residents in both
colonies from the collection of duties on goods carried across
the Murray.' He thus conceded the principle that it is not
desirable to collect the duties. The real questions that remain

now are—1st. Did he and his colleagues display the necessary capacity and wisdom to ensure success in the negotiations which were opened at his own instance? 2nd. Has he since refused to entertain a just proposal from the sister colony? The only answers that can be given to these questions leave the Government self-condemned.

Throughout these various proceedings, the arbitrary genius, or in other words the inborn Toryism, of the gentlemen at the head of the Government, has for the first time forced its way to the surface, unchecked by any countervailing element in the Administration. The Toryism of Sir James Martin is unlike anything known to modern times; it is the Toryism of the Stuart dynasty, when the will of the obstinate king or the facile minister was sought to be carried out by the corruption of Parliament, by playing off one faction against another, by the employment of secret agents, and by maintaining an unauthorised and irresponsible consultative power within the Cabinet itself. The time is come when the electors must determine whether this noble colony is to be governed, not by the DIVINE RIGHT of James the Second, but by the DIVINE RIGHT of James the Third.

It is to be fervently hoped that this appeal to the people will result in the return of a body of men who will be prepared at all hazards to stem the torrent of chicanery and corruption which has set in upon our free institutions,—who, from an enlightened conviction, and by a firm example, will teach that political triumph does not always accompany the possession of power, but that victory is to be achieved by remaining in Opposition or by retiring from office, so long as the principles of a sound policy are faithfully maintained. What we want—to raise New South Wales to the first place in the Australian group, to which the boundless wealth of her natural resources gives her a fair title—is a public policy suited to the position and capabilities of the country, adopted and carried out in the light of English statesmanship. Our system of education should be extended until it embraces the children of every home. Every form of commerce and industrial enterprise should be

left free to the fullest extent consistent with the needs of the
State. Our lands should be alienated on a freehold basis, with
the largest measure of advantages to those who will turn the
soil to the best account. Our mineral resources should be
developed by a liberal revision of the present law. The benefits
of municipal government should be spread to the utmost practicable limit throughout the colony. Our external defence
should depend upon a Volunteer organisation, numbering within
its ranks the flower of our young men. Above all, we should
encourage in the agricultural, pastoral, and mining pursuits of
the interior the creation of wealth and the formation of society
by the settlement of families and the secure investment of small
capitals. By such means we may raise our country to a condition of prosperity hitherto unknown, and may hope to see our
infant liberties zealously preserved by a brave and an intelligent
people.

I am, Gentlemen,

Your faithful servant,

HENRY PARKES.

Sydney, February 9, 1872.

With this election the march of events was rapid.
The voice of the people could not be mistaken. The
ground was cleared for a new beginning. It is hard to
believe that sensible men could have been guilty of such
perverse courses as have to be explained, but the
facts cannot be changed in their complexion and
significance.

# CHAPTER XI

EARLY in 1872 the Ministry, having sustained defeat in the Legislative Assembly, obtained the power to dis- solve from the Earl of Belmore, who was on the eve of vacating the office of Governor, and who did actually leave the colony a few days afterwards. The first elections told plainly that the advice given by Ministers had been ill-judged, that they had unquestionably lost the confidence of the country; but in the midst of de- feat and condemnation they continued to hold office for three months. I with others took an active part in awakening the country to a sense of the danger from this state of things, where only the convenience or the perverse will of the defeated Ministers appeared to be consulted. I wrote letters in the public press; I sought the opinions of persons admitted to be constitutional authorities; and on my motion the Assembly carried an amendment to the Address in reply by thirty-six to eleven votes in the following words:—

It is a matter of deep regret to us that the circumstances under which the late Assembly was dissolved, and the present Parliament assembled, are of a character to call for the expression of our disapproval.

It has been communicated to us that a monetary arrangement was entered into between your Excellency's Advisers and a private Banking Institution, during the progress of the elections, and the protracted delay in convening Parliament, which, in derogation of the Constitution, interferes with the undoubted and sole power of this House in granting supply to Her Majesty, and seriously impairs its just control over the public expenditure.

We feel constrained to take the earliest opportunity to condemn a course of conduct in the administration of affairs as dangerous to the public interests, and which we are anxious may not be again resorted to.

While these things were going on, several points in the larger question—What is the thing which the term Responsible Government designates in a colony?—presented themselves, with more or less force, to my mind; and my individual views on these special points, fortified by authorities which could not well be impugned or doubted, found expression in my letters. The soundness of the views expressed I submitted to the test of reason by impartial enquiries; and in their publication no desire was felt by me to promote the interest of any particular party, but only to assist in mitigating the abuses of Government, whoever might be in power.

I contended that it could not be a question of light interest to anybody how the country was to be governed. It concerned every person in every rela-

tion of life. No man was above or below the consequences.

I held the opinion that our system of government
might be made a blessing or a curse, according to the
degree of sensibility to the principle of responsibility
entertained by those whose chief business was to govern,
and the degree of subserviency to the views of the executive entertained by those whose chief business was
to represent the country. If Ministers were sufficiently
lax in their notions of their obligations to the Constitution, and the Representatives of the People were sufficiently lax in their notions of the trust reposed in them,
there would be little check upon the abuses of power,
and it would be difficult to fix a limit to the tricks,
devices, evasions, manœuvres, and manipulations, and
the invisible arts of corruption in the practice of these,
by which a worthless administration might be supported. In all times good men had made efficient
government, and systems had failed to convert unstable,
unprincipled, and scheming men into good and efficient
governors. The vitality that was infused into Parliamentary government, in one age by Chatham and in
another by Canning, though the rule of each was brief,
and the paralysis it sustained at the hands of the Cabal
and the Coalition, were pointed to as illustrations of
this historical fact.

Not the least part of the evil flowing from any violation of the true principles of Parliamentary government was the infectious influence which it communi-
cates to the electoral bodies. Where the carrion is, the
crows and kites will congregate. Be the waters pure

and life-giving, or noxious and charged with the seeds of pestilence, the stream flows from its source ever downwards. No greater affliction could befall a free country than the violation of the political sentiments of the people.

I copy two of my letters as they appeared at the time. They express the views which I formed then, and which I still hold, of the unjustifiable character of the transactions of those three months.

## 'LETTER I.

'There seems to be an opinion abroad, apparently received without enquiry, that it is a constitutional practice for a Minister retiring from office to advise the Crown as to his successor. Whether the representative of the Crown in this colony has at any time permitted such practice I do not pretend to say, but it is known that on some occasions no such advice has been given or sought, and it is undeniably the fact that nothing of the kind has ever occurred in modern times between retiring Ministers in England and the Sovereign.

'It will occur to the mind of any person capable of reasoning on the subject, that it would be a logical absurdity for a Minister who has forfeited his position as adviser of the Crown, by the tender of his resignation of office, still to be permitted to advise as to the person who is to be his successor. Having himself failed to obtain the support of Parliament in his Ministerial capacity, how can he be the right person to advise who

is likely to succeed in securing that indispensable support in the government of the country? Having as
Minister passed outside the boundary within which he
can be held responsible to Parliament for his advice
(for by his resignation he has paid the utmost penalty
which Parliament can exact), is he then to advise, without responsibility, on the momentous question of the
formation of another Government?

· For many years after the accession of the House
of Hanover the Whigs sought to establish in their party
a power of nomination to the office of Premier. The
resolute self-will of George the Third broke down this
pretension of the great Whig families. Although the
prerogatives of the Crown, as sought to be exercised
during the long reign from 1760 to 1820, have since
been circumscribed and defined in the interest of the
popular branch of the Legislature, all modern statesmen
are agreed that the right to select the First Minister,
absolute, unrestricted, and uninfluenced, belongs to the
Crown alone, and that the only party in the State entitled
to offer advice in the matter is the Parliament itself.
That principle of Parliamentary government, clear and
distinct, has come out of the constitutional struggles of
two centuries. That principle is stated very concisely,
but very emphatically, by a well-known historian, who
has himself held high office in the Parliament and the
Government of England. I quote from Massey's " History of England during the Reign of George the Third,"
vol. iii. p. 213.

' " If there is one rule better established than another
by the Constitution of this realm, it is this, that the

Sovereign has a right to choose his Minister, *subject only to the approval of Parliament.*"

' So far back as 1812, while the contention for power between the Crown and the Ministers was still going on under the Regency, Mr. Canning, in the House of Commons, delivered himself thus :

' " The Right Hon. Gentleman, and those on his side of the House, seemed to consider that the great families and connections of this country had a kind of right to interfere in the nomination of Ministers. He himself, who was so very humble an individual, who could not boast of any of those high connections, and who, perhaps, though unknown to himself, was influenced by those circumstances of his humble rank, did not certainly believe in the existence of any such right or pretension in the aristocracy. He thought that, in the very best spirit of the Constitution, the Crown had *exclusively* the appointment of Ministers, *subject, of course, to the control or advice of a free Parliament.*"— [*Parliamentary Debates*, vol. xxiii. p. 455.]

· Fifteen years afterwards Mr. Canning asserted this principle in his personal conduct by declining to be a party to carrying out the wish of the King, that he and his colleagues should nominate a peer to the office of Premier in the place of Lord Liverpool. The negotiations resulted in Mr. Canning being authorised by George the Fourth to reconstruct the Ministry ; and though Mr. Peel (afterwards Sir Robert), the Duke of Wellington, Lord Eldon, Lord Bathurst, Lord Westmoreland, Lord Bexley, and others refused to serve under him, and though a protest against his assumption of the premiership, signed by eight dukes, was presented to the King, threatening their organised opposition. Mr. Canning succeeded in forming the first Liberal Ministry of this century, bringing into the Cabinet Lord Lyndhurst, Lord Palmerston, and Mr. Huskisson. So far from any person advising the King to "send for" Mr. Canning, Mr. Canning was "sent for" in spite of the influence of all the great ruling families.

'When, in the early part of 1846, dissensions arose in the Peel Administration on the policy of repealing the Corn Laws, and Lord Stanley determined to retire, Sir Robert Peel tendered his resignation to the Queen, and he explained his conduct in these words to the House of Commons :

'"While I retained the hope of acting with a united Administration, while I thought there was a prospect of bringing this question to a settlement, I determined to retain office and incur its responsibilities. When I was compelled to abandon that hope (my sense of the coming evil remaining the same), I took the earliest opportunity, consistent with a sense of duty and of public honour, of tendering my resignation to the Queen, and leaving Her Majesty the *full opportunity* of consulting other advisers. *I offered no opinion as to the choice of a successor. That is almost the only act which is the personal act of the Sovereign; it is for the Sovereign to determine in whom her confidence shall be placed.*"—[Hans. *Debates*, vol. lxxxiii. p. 1004.]

'In 1852 the first Derby Ministry was defeated on their financial policy, and Lord Derby announced their resignation in the following terms in the House of Lords :

'"Having had a distinct declaration of want of confidence on the part of the House of Commons, and having ascertained that my colleagues unanimously concurred with me as to the only course we ought to pursue, I proceeded to wait upon Her Majesty, and to tender to her, in my own name and that of my colleagues, the humble resignation of our offices. Her Majesty was pleased to accept our resignation; and signified her pleasure, which was acted upon in the same day, to send for and take the advice of two noblemen, members of your Lordships' House, both of them of great experience and considerable ability—of long practice in public life."—[Hans. *Debates*, vol. cxxiii. p. 1701.]

'The two noblemen alluded to by Lord Derby were the Marquis of Lansdowne and the Earl of Aberdeen : but it is clear that the Queen did not ask the retiring Minister for any advice on the expediency or propriety of seeking the counsel of those statesmen. She simply informed him, not as a defeated Minister, but as a peer of the realm and a Privy Councillor of great weight and consideration, of the course she intended to take. It is only in one or other of these latter capacities that English statesmen are ever asked for advice on the selection of the First Minister, because both Peers and members of the Privy Council are responsible to Parliament for the advice they give, whether in office or not. Persons enjoying either rank, and of high standing from personal services and experience in public affairs, have occasionally been asked for such advice, when they neither belonged to the retiring, nor were expected to belong to the incoming, Ministry. This was the case with the Duke of Wellington and the Marquis of Lansdowne in their later years. When Mr. Disraeli resigned in December, 1868, the "Times," on the following morning, stated that there could be no doubt but that the Queen would seek the advice of Earl Russell in the first instance, on account of his long connection with the Liberal Party and his great experience, though it was equally certain that Mr. Gladstone would be entrusted with the formation of the new Government, as the general election had clearly pointed out the latter statesman as the future Premier. ['Times,' December 3, 1868.] But Her Majesty sent direct for Mr. Gladstone, who, at the time, was at Hawarden Castle, more than 200 miles from London; and, though the Cabinet Council, at which Mr. Disraeli and his colleagues determined to resign, was held late in the day on December 2, Mr. Gladstone had an audience of the Queen, at Windsor, at 4 P.M. on the following day. Another of the great daily journals spoke of the Queen's relation to the Ministerial crisis in the following words:

'"The English system of government does not, as is sometimes fancied, go of itself. It is not an automatic contrivance, nor an engine which a child may feed or tend. To discern the real meaning of popular or Parliamentary contests; to act as the interpreter of the national mind; to select its truest representative; and to give effect to its will, are offices involving grave responsibility and calling for more than ordinary intelligence and judgment. To do these things is part of the business of an English monarch. Constitutional Kings and Queens cannot but have, like humbler people, their own political opinions and personal preferences. *The high impartiality and the controlling sense of public duty which, amid the changes of party government, have for a generation kept the private feelings of the Sovereign in abeyance, deserve record and honour.*"—[*Daily News*. December 5, 1868.]

'We know from an unimpeachable source the patriotic view which the reigning Sovereign has always taken of her duty on the occasion of a change of Ministry. The wise and lamented Prince, who was her dearest adviser in life, has told us how scrupulously Queen Victoria guards herself from any personal feeling or any consideration in conflict with the feeling of her Parliament and her people, in selecting her First Minister. Speaking in the House of Lords on the death of the Prince Consort, Earl Russell said :

' " I happen to know from the late Prince himself the view he took of the duty of the Sovereign in such a case. He stated to me, not many months ago, that it was a common opinion that there was only one occasion on which the Sovereign of this country could exercise a decided power, and that was in the choice of the First Minister of the Crown. The Prince went on to say, that in his opinion that was not an occasion on which the Sovereign *could exercise a control or pronounce a decision ;* that when a Minister had retired, from being unable to carry on the Government, there was at all times some other party which was prepared to assume the responsibilities of office, *and was most likely to obtain the confidence of the country.* But, he said, a transfer having been made, whether the Minister was of one party or the other, he thought that the Sovereign ought to communicate with him in the most confidential and unreserved manner with respect to the various measures to be brought forward, the fortunes of the country, and the events that might happen — that whether he belonged to one party or another, the utmost confidence should prevail between the Sovereign and the Minister, who came forward in Parliament as the ostensible possessor of power.'—[Hans. *Debates*, vol. clxv. p. 44.]

'Earl Russell went on to give the weight of his own opinion on the beneficial effect of this unbiassed and scrupulous conduct on the part of Her Majesty in the working of Constitutional government. He continued :

' " I do, my Lords, attribute in great measure to that opinion which the Sovereign held in common with the Prince, the fact that there has been no feeling of bitterness among any party in this country arising from exclusion, and that all parties during these twenty years have united in rendering that homage to the Sovereign which the conduct of Her Majesty has so well deserved, and the country still reaps the benefit of the good counsel which the Prince Consort gave to the Crown."—[Hans. *Debates*, vol. clxv. p. 44.]

' It appears, then, that it is not only the exclusive right, but the duty of the Crown, in view of the public interest, to exercise an independent judgment in selecting the First Minister, and that Her present

Majesty has uniformly disregarded her own feelings and preferences in the performance of this duty. It is equally clear that it is not the practice for retiring Ministers, as such, to offer or to be requested to give advice on such a grave and delicate subject, and that any such practice would be in conflict with the theory of Ministerial responsibility. This part of the case is very lucidly stated by Mr. Todd :—

' " A retiring Minister may, if requested by the Sovereign, suggest that any particular statesman should be empowered to form a new Administration, but such advice should not be obtruded on the Sovereign unasked. *Being debarred by his own resignation, or dismissal from office, from the constitutional right to tender advice to the Crown, he can only do so, if required, in the quality of a Peer or a Privy Councillor;* being still *responsible in that capacity for any advice he may give to the Sovereign."*—[Todd's *Parliamentary Government*, vol. i. p. 222.]

'I have stated the case as I find it elucidated by the most trustworthy records and authorities, and I do not believe a single authenticated instance from modern practice in England can be adduced in opposition to the view I have explained. The Governor, as the representative of the Crown, has few duties to perform which devolve exclusively on his function as Governor, and of these few duties the most important are to decide independently when advice is tendered to dissolve Parliament, and to decide independently on committing the executive power to new hands. In calling a Member of Parliament to the service of the Crown, he is

not—to use the words of the Prince Consort, as quoted
by Earl Russell—" to exercise a control or pronounce a
decision " in determining the special character of the
change, but he is, like Her Majesty, to select the person
who, in his judgment, taking into consideration political
experience, party relations, capacity for public business,
and representative character, is " most likely to obtain
the confidence of the country." '

### ' LETTER II.

' It is said that Lord Belmore's reasons for the late
dissolution will, when they become known, be satisfactory to the public mind. What species of argument
can have been employed to justify that transaction to the
Secretary of State seems at present beyond conjecture.
In view of the whole range of the Governor's intercourse with the Minister, from the date of the acceptance of office until the date of the advice to dissolve,
the Dissolution appears without precedent or justifica-
tion. On the supposition of a case so improbable as
that the Governor had allowed himself to be drawn
into a position which did not leave him entirely free to
exercise his judgment on the state of circumstances
which arose, it may be that the acting on the Minister's
advice could be justified under the qualification of the
embarrassments imposed upon him. But the exigen-
cies of any such case in no way remove, but rather
aggravate, the questionable character of the transaction. The Governor ought to be entirely free and unfettered, " to discern the real meaning of popular or

Parliamentary contests," on all such occasions, and to act on a true interpretation of them. When the late Earl Grey advised the memorable Dissolution on the Reform Bill of 1831, he declared that *nothing but success* would justify the advice he had given, and the same doctrine was held in the House of Lords on a recent occasion. If dissolving the Parliament of the country was a game of haphazard, any person who happened to be Minister could, of course, advise it without blame, and any person who happened to be Governor could assent to the advice without regard to the public interests. But it is the exercise of an extreme power under the Constitution, to be resorted to only in extreme cases, and when there is a rational belief that the views of the Legislature are not in accord with the views of the country. Hence the obligation upon those concerned, both the giver and the receiver of the advice, " to discern the real meaning " of the conflict out of which the advice arises.

' All the features of the late Dissolution are open to criticism and, I think, severe censure. The comparative newness of the late House, the embarrassed state of public business caused by Ministers themselves in not convening Parliament at an earlier date,[1] the general manifestation of an adverse public opinion, the large majorities in the Assembly by which the Administration was defeated,[2] the Supply not granted for the current

---

[1] The public press, with few exceptions, expressed an opinion unfavourable to the Administration, and public meetings had been held in nearly every district in condemnation of the Ministerial Land Bill.

[2] The majorities were 27 to 23, and 38 to 19.

year—all these grave circumstances were against the
Dissolution. Not only the considerations arising out of
this state of things, but the very important circumstance
that the Governor was about to vacate his Government,
and the knowledge of the fact that his successor could
not arrive in the colony for many months, was an additional reason of great weight why the House ought
not to have been dissolved.

'It is a most unusual thing for the Governor of a
colony to dissolve Parliament on the eve of giving up
his Government ; and it seems to me extremely doubtful whether such an exercise of power can be justified
by any reasoning from precedent or analogy in the
Government of England. The examples of the English
system do not, and cannot, apply in all cases to the
systems of Parliamentary government established in the
colonies. The conditions of political existence are in
many respects essentially different. Thus, there exists
no true type of Sovereignty in relation to our Parliament, the Crown being practically held in abeyance in
all intercourse with this branch of the Government, and
its place supplied by an Imperial officer for a fixed term
of years. But the forms of intercourse between the
Sovereign and the British Parliament are preserved and
adapted to our condition as much as possible. It will,
therefore, be admitted, I presume, that where the conditions are not the same, the spirit of the Constitution
ought to exact conformity of action in the closest approach to Imperial practice which our different circumstances will permit. It is not possible to conceive of
the Crown dissolving the Imperial Parliament on the

eve of abdication or of death. On the contrary, every precaution has been taken to render it impossible for such an event to occur at a time when the nation is without a Parliament. Although by common law the Parliament expires with the King, a statute was passed in the reign of Anne which continues it in existence six months after the death of the Sovereign, and requires it immediately to assemble, although it may stand adjourned or prorogued at the time. In the event of a dissolution having been granted previous to the demise of the Crown, the Act 6 Anne, c. 7, revives the defunct Parliament for a like period. Admitting the difference between a change of Governors and a change of Sovereigns, it is a difference inevitable from the nature of things, and not one designed as an improvement upon the Constitution which is our model, nor one that can be held to justify a flagrant disregard of constitutional rule and expediency. If it is considered neither expedient nor safe for the nation to be without a Parliament on the accession of a new Sovereign, it cannot be desirable, to say the least, that this colony should be without a Parliament when it receives a new Governor.

'But the dissolution was altogether unjustified by English precedent or usage. In 1831 Parliament was dissolved on the advice of Earl Grey, who said that " he should not have been justified in recommending it if he had not felt assured that the course he proposed to pursue would be ratified by the decision of the nation." The result proved that Earl Grey had "discerned the real meaning" of the contest. After the passing of the Reform Act, the Parliament elected under the old state of the law was dissolved, December 3, 1832, to make way for the election of the reformed House of Commons. Sir Robert Peel, in 1834, being called upon to form an Administration as the successor to Earl Grey and Lord Melbourne, advised a Dissolution on the broad intelligible ground that he proposed an entirely new policy. The next Dissolution was on the accession of Her present Majesty, in 1837, and had no political significance. In 1841, Lord Melbourne, being defeated on a motion of want of confidence, by Sir Robert Peel, by a majority of *one* (312 to 311) in a full House, advised Her Majesty to dissolve, which advice was accepted. The appeal to the country was made on the policy of lightening the burdens on trade and commerce. Sir Robert Peel's second Administration remained in office till 1846, when, after carrying the repeal of Corn Laws, he was defeated by a combination of Whigs, Radicals, and Protectionists. That great Minister was then at the height of his popularity, and the Parliament was five years old; he did not, however, advise a Dissolution, but retired from office. In 1847 Parliament, under the first Administration of Lord John Russell, was dissolved by effluxion of time. In 1852, Lord Derby, coming into power, announced the policy of returning to modified protective duties, and on that policy he obtained a Dissolution. In 1857 Mr. Cobden moved a vote of censure on the Chinese War under Lord Palmerston's first Administration, which was carried by a majority of sixteen. On the advice of Lord Palmerston Parliament was thereupon dissolved. So well had the veteran Premier " discerned the real

meaning" of the contest, that he came back to the
House of Commons with a clear majority of eighty-five,
while Mr. Cobden himself lost his seat.  The second
Derby Administration was, in 1859, defeated on their
Reform Bill, and obtained a Dissolution.  Under Lord
Palmerston's second Administration, Parliament was
dissolved, in 1865, without political significance, having
lasted more than six years.  Lord Palmerston died
before the assembling of the new Parliament, and Earl
Russell became Premier, Mr. Gladstone assuming the
lead of the House of Commons.  This Administration
was defeated on June 18, 1866, by Lord Dunkellin's
amendment on their Reform Bill, and they resigned
office, though it was generally understood that the
Queen would have granted them a Dissolution.  The
last Dissolution was in 1868, when Mr. Disraeli ap-
pealed to the new constituencies under his own Reform Act, on Mr. Gladstone's proposal to disestablish
the Irish Church.  On finding the electoral returns
against them, Mr. Disraeli and his colleagues resigned
before all the elections were concluded—namely, on
December 2, the writs being returnable on the 10th.
The following is a copy of the Prime Minister's circular
to his supporters :—

' "If Parliament were sitting I should not have
adopted this course ; but as the public acts of a
Ministry should not be misunderstood, and as there
are no other means of explaining their motives, I have
taken the liberty of thus addressing the Conservative
members in both Houses of Parliament.

' " When Her Majesty's Government, in the spring of

this year, were placed in a minority in the House of
Commons on the question of Disestablishing the Church
in Ireland, they had to consider that the policy proposed had never been submitted to the country, and
they believed that the country would not sanction it.

' " They therefore felt it their duty to advise Her
Majesty to dissolve Parliament ; but to make an appeal
to the obsolete constituency would have been an absurdity, and the candid opinion of the country coin-
cided with that of Parliament, that no course could be
satisfactory unless the voices of the enlarged electoral
body were ascertained. All means were, therefore,
taken by the Ministry to expedite that appeal, and a
special statute was passed for the purpose.

' " Although the General Election has elicited, in the
decision of numerous and vast constituencies, an expression of feeling which, in a remarkable degree, has
justified their anticipations, and which, in dealing with
the question in controversy, no wise statesman would
disregard, it is now clear that the present Administration cannot expect to command the confidence of the
newly elected House of Commons.

' " Under these circumstances, Her Majesty's Ministers
have felt it due to their own honour, and to the policy
they support, not to retain office unnecessarily for a
single day. They hold it to be more consistent with
the attitude they have assumed, and with the convenience of public business at this season, as well as more
conducive to the just influence of the Conservative
party, at once to tender the resignation of their offices
to Her Majesty, rather than to wait for the assembling

of a Parliament in which, in the present aspect of affairs, they are sensible that they must be in a minority.

'"In thus acting, Her Majesty's Government have seen no cause to modify those opinions upon which they deemed it their duty to found their counsel to the Sovereign on the question of the Disestablishment and Disendowment of the Church. They remain convinced that the proposition of Mr. Gladstone is wrong in principle, probably impracticable in conduct, and, if practicable, would be disastrous in its effects.

'" While ready at all times to give a fair consideration and willing aid to any plan for the improvement of the Church in Ireland, to the policy which they opposed last Session, rife, as they believe it to be, with many calamities to society and the State, they will continue, in whatever position they occupy, to offer an uncompromising resistance.

'" B. DISRAELI.

'" Downing-street, December 2, 1868."

'Here are all the Dissolutions of the Reformed Parliament from 1831 to 1868, and where will anything be found giving a colour of sanction to the Dissolution of the Assembly in February last?

'Parliamentary Reform, the Financial Policy of the Country, the justice of a Foreign War, the Disestablishment of the Church, were the broad questions submitted to the electors. But what is more deserving of notice is the hesitation and forbearance with which English statesmen, especially those at the head of the Liberal party, approach the prerogative of Dissolution. With the single exception of the appeal made by Lord Melbourne, their advice has always been justified by the result. They have on all occasions "discerned the real meaning" of the contest, and been successful.

'Nothing can be more unwarranted by reason and precedent than the notion, loosely entertained by some few politicians, that a Ministry is entitled to a Dissolution when they encounter defeat in Parliament because the House was elected under the Administration of their predecessors. That would be reducing a principle of the Constitution to a mere rule of child's play—"It was your turn last, it is my turn now!" The circumstances under which the existing Legislature was elected may be fairly considered, with many other circumstances, when the whole question of the expediency of dissolving it is under review; but not because other persons filled the offices of Government when the election took place. Those circumstances would form matter for consideration as part of the case for the decision of the Crown, just to the extent that the questions of policy formerly submitted to the electors may be held to affect the questions again to be submitted, but only in reference to the public interest, and not in deference to the supposed claim of a defeated Ministry.

'In the arrangements for the elections and the assembling of the new Parliament, our Administration is equally at fault. In England the new House of Commons must be called together by law within *thirty-five* days from the issue of the writs. On the

30th instant, Sir James Martin will have continued himself in office *eighty-nine* days, without a Parliament, since he caused the late Assembly to be dissolved. The English writs are issued with the least possible delay ; here they were delayed several days to suit the electioneering plans of the Ministers. The election for East Sydney was then hurried through within five days, and that for West Sydney within seven days, notwithstanding the long delay which has since taken place in convening the new Parliament, the principal Ministers themselves being candidates for those electorates. No time ought to be lost in restraining by legislation the power of Ministers to trifle—not to say tamper—with the Constitution, and to impair the public value of their own appeal to the people, by making the arrangements for a General Election subservient to their own official interests.'

On the constitutional questions involved in these lamentable proceedings, I wrote to Professor Hearn, the author of the ' Government of England,' and I give our correspondence on the subject here :

Sydney, April 24, 1872.

Sir,—I take the liberty of sending to you two numbers of the ' Sydney Morning Herald' which contain letters of mine under the signature of a 'Constitutionalist' on questions of Parliamentary government, which appear to me to be pressing for consideration by these Australian Communities.

With your permission, I will state the case of this colony at the present moment.

Sir James Martin accepted office as First Minister on December 16, 1870. Parliament had then been in Session several months, and little business had been done, chiefly owing to the weakness of the previous Government. The new Ministry, on this account, very properly received much consideration from the Assembly during the latter part of that Session, although much dissatisfaction was felt at the manner in which the new Administration had been formed. As the financial year of New South Wales terminates on December 31, that Session properly belonged to 1870. On prorogation (June 22, 1871), Sir James Martin took a recess of 144 days, not calling Parliament together for the Session proper to 1871 until November 14, when it was quite impossible to consider the estimates and transact the necessary business within the year. During the recess the First Minister and two of his colleagues had attended a conference at Melbourne, which, in the general opinion here, resulted through their incompetency to the discredit of this colony. The proceedings of the Administration at the conference, and other causes, led to their early defeat by decisive majorities, on which Sir James Martin obtained the power of Dissolution. Supply had been voted for the month of January only when Parliament was dissolved on February 1. Four out of the six Ministers with seats in the Assembly were defeated by their former constituencies, and only Sir James Martin himself succeeded in obtaining election elsewhere, though all of them stood a second, and one of them stood a third electoral contest. The new Parliament is convened for the 30th instant, eighty-nine days after the Dissolution. In the meantime the Bank of New South Wales, under some arrangement not explained to the people, pays the salaries of the civil servants, on the heads of the departments, as I understand, making over their interest in them in anticipation of an Appropriation Act.

It is in this state of things that my letters have been written, and I should highly esteem the favour if you could give me your views on the questions raised.

Your obedient Servant,

HENRY PARKES.

University of Melbourne, April 30, 1872.

Sir,—I have to acknowledge the receipt of your letter of the 24th instant, and of two 'Sydney Morning Heralds' containing the letters to which your letter to me refers. The third paper has not yet arrived.

I do not think that it would be proper in me to volunteer an opinion upon the course which in the particular circumstances of the case the late Governor of New South Wales, or his adviser, thought fit to pursue. With reference, however, to the general questions of constitutional law, on which only, I presume, that you wish for my views, I have no difficulty in expressing my opinions.

As to the propriety of a retiring Minister advising the Crown in the choice of his successor, I concur in the views you express in your letter to the 'Herald,' and I have nothing material to add to the authorities therein cited. In the Victorian Constitution Act, and I presume in that of New South Wales also, the distinction is clearly marked between the political officers whom the Governor alone appoints, and all other officers whom he appoints with the advice of his Executive Council. I fancy that the popular notion has arisen from the exaggerative doctrine that the Crown can do no act without some responsible adviser. Under colonial constitutions such as ours, the choice of a Ministry, or at least of a Premier, seems to me to be a duty cast upon the Governor of the same nature as his duty in superintending the issue of the public revenue. With respect to the prerogative of Dissolution, I have said all that I have to say in the 'Government of England,' pp. 154-499. It seems to me that the limited duration of our Parliaments makes the exercise of this prerogative a matter of much greater delicacy than it is in England. So far as I have been able to judge, it appears the great stumbling-block to Australian Governors. There appears to me to be one plain practical rule in the matter, viz. that a Dissolution ought never to be tried until every other means of carrying on the Government has been exhausted.

Your own research on these subjects has rendered any citation of authorities on my part superfluous. Perhaps you will permit me to call your attention to the English Reform Act of 1867 or 1868, which gets rid of the old rule as to the dissolution of Parliament on the demise of the Crown. I observe that you only refer to the Act of Anne. Probably we shall have an awkward question some day as to the effect of demise of the Crown upon our Legislative bodies.

I remain, &c.

W. E. HEARN.

Returning to the proceedings of the new Parliament, an effort was made to obtain a new government without having recourse to me, though I had been marked out by the course of events as the proper person, as the failure of the member selected will show. Mr. William Forster was entrusted with the task by His Excellency the Administrator (Sir Alfred Stephen), but after endeavours extending over several days, he returned his commission. I was then sent for on May 9, and on the 14th the formation of the new Ministry was announced to Parliament. This, the first ministry formed by me, existed until February 8, 1875.

Sir Hercules Robinson arrived on Sunday, June 2, and assumed the office of Governor on the following day. Though his appointments hitherto had been confined to Crown colonies, Sir Hercules Robinson was well acquainted with the principles and the working of Parliamentary government, having obviously acquired his knowledge from a close study of the English Constitution in all its later developments. He was a man of much personal dignity, who walked and rode like a king; though capable of stern action, he was gracious

and kindly in his bearing; his mind was singularly
acute in argumentative examination; and his methods
of enquiry were lucid and searching. As he was passionately addicted to sport, evinced on all fitting occasions a high public spirit, and carried about with him
an air of superiority, it is not surprising that the new
Governor became popular with all classes. It was my
happy fortune to be on the most friendly relations
with His Excellency during the whole period of his
administration. I was in office when he arrived, and
I was in office when he left the colony, nearly seven
years afterwards. In his high place he was an able
man, fond of work and not afraid of conflict.

This Ministry had to encounter strong opposition
in Parliament. Sir James Martin and Sir John Robertson sat directly in front of us, with several able men
beside and behind them, but the popular feeling very
generally was with us. There was a wide field of work
to exhaust our energies. One or two bold steps were
taken in recasting the departmental machinery of
government. Hitherto, in imitation of the English law
appointments, we had clumsily yoked in the weak
Ministerial team (at this time confined to seven offices)
an Attorney-General and a Solicitor-General, without
reference either to the non-cabinet standing of those
officials in England or to the vast difference in the
population and circumstances of the two countries.
The office of Solicitor-General was abolished, and a
large administrative department, presided over by a
Minister of Justice, was created in its place. With the
exception of the lawyers, I believe all classes approved

of the change. To this Minister, who may be a lay-man, is assigned the administration of the prisons, the courts of justice, and minor divisions of the public service in close relation to the execution of the laws. The Attorney-General remains, though a member of the Executive Council, for the most part limited to his duties as legal adviser of the Crown, and as public prosecutor. A Department of Mines, presided over by a Minister, was created by Act of Parliament, and fore-seeing what must soon come, tentative steps were adopted towards bringing into existence a Department of Public Instruction.

In the last preceding administration a spirit of quasi-militarism had been suffered to display itself in somewhat extravagant forms. I had myself at all times been in favour of fostering the sentiment among the permanent residents, especially the young men born of the soil, of military enrolment for the defence of the country. The Ministry proposed, and Parliament assented to, a reduction of the permanent force lately enlisted, with a view to giving encouragement to the Volunteer principle.

In one thing I hope I may lay claim to the approval of friends and opponents alike—in the efforts I have uniformly made to fill the highest offices of the State by the best men. In filling the office of Chief Justice in 1873, Sir James Martin, after much consideration, was finally selected, in disregard of all other considera-tions except his legal attainments and standing at the Bar. I was never forgiven in some quarters for that appointment, but it met with the general approval of the public and of the profession. Sir James was respected as a great judge. Time after time, in the appointment of other judges of the Supreme Court, the like considerations alone have been allowed to have weight. The same may, I think, be said (and has been indeed often said) of other important appointments, where example in official conduct not less than personal competency or merit in past service, is of the utmost value to the public. In July 1873 it devolved upon Ministers to recommend the high appointment of President of the Legislative Council. I selected Sir John Hay (who for the next eighteen years so worthily filled the chair), and my colleagues all concurred in the selection, which, on submission to the Governor, received His Excellency's warm approval.[1] The following correspondence is now published in vindication of the correctness of the views of all parties to that appointment, and as serving to illustrate the considerations which I can safely say have at all times influenced me in performing this class of a Minister's duties.

Rose Bay, July 18, 1873.

Dear Mr. Parkes,—As Colonial Secretary you have already received my acknowledgment of the honour conferred upon me by my appointment as President; but I feel that something more is due from me on the occasion.

When I waited on His Excellency, at his request, on Friday last, he informed me that on the matter being first mooted he and you had been quite agreed in the opinion that the office should be tendered to me in the first instance, and in desiring that I would accept it. I had then the opportunity of thanking

---

[1] Sir John Hay died January 20, 1882.

Sir H. Robinson personally, and I trust that you will now accept my assurance that I am very much gratified by the compliment itself, and still more by the manner in which it has been paid to me. Its value is greatly enhanced by the fact that you must have acted on the principle that an appointment of which the honour is more to be considered than the emolument should be the result not of canvass but of selection.

I have also learned that the members of the Executive Council were unanimous in their approval, and I hope you will do me the favour of conveying to your colleagues individually my thanks for this expression of their good opinion.

I remain, yours truly,<br>
JOHN HAY.

Sydney, July 14, 1873.

My dear Mr. Hay,—I thank you for your note of the 10th, which is very gratifying to me, as affording a further proof, if such were wanted, that the high appointment conferred upon you will secure to the country an appreciative discharge of duties attached to it.

If I have one wish more fervent than another in the great position I am permitted to occupy, it is that, whenever I am called upon to retire from it, I shall not be justly open to the reproach of having done anything to lower the tone of our public life or to debase the character of our young institutions. It was in this spirit that, after the fullest consideration, you were thought of as President of the Legislative Council.

I cannot pay you a higher compliment than by frankly assuring you that you were appointed because I and my colleagues considered that in view of what was due to the Legislative Council itself, and what was equally due to the meritorious and dignified course pursued by you in both Houses of Parliament, it was the best appointment that we could make—the one most calculated to raise the Council in public respect, and to encourage others to a praiseworthy course of conduct by the recognition of a worthy example.

It is gratifying to us that His Excellency the Governor

cordially concurred in these views. Accept my sincere congratulations upon your assumption of your new duties.

Faithfully yours,

HENRY PARKES.

Among the measures of legislation submitted by the Government was the Electoral Bill of 1873, which recast many of the electorates, where by the increase of population great inequalities had grown up, and extended the number of members of the Legislative Assembly, and carried out other much-needed changes to improve the representation of the people. The Bill was read the second time in the Assembly by thirty-four to five votes, and, after lengthy consideration in committee, read the third time by twenty-nine to thirteen, and duly sent to the Legislative Council. That body read the Bill the second time by ten to three, but so materially altered its provisions in committee, imposing additional charges on the people, that when it was returned to the Assembly it had to be laid aside on the ruling of the Speaker. It is worth while to note the course pursued by the nominee Council in dealing with this Bill, which was confined to reforming the representation of the people in the Assembly, and to place in contrast with it the course of treatment dealt out by the same body in the same year to a Bill sent up by the Assembly to reform its own constitution. 'A Bill to amend the Constitution Act and to provide for the representation of the people in the Legislative Council,'—in plain English, to abolish the nominee principle and make the Upper Chamber elective— was introduced by me in the Assembly early in 1873.

It was read the second time on February 27 by a majority of thirty-three to twelve; it passed through its further stages, and was sent to the Council, when that House, in a spirit of insolence which could only be generated by the vicious principle of nomineeism, refused to receive it on the following resolution :—

That this Council declines to take into consideration any Bill repealing those sections of the Constitution Act which provide for the Constitution of the Legislative Council, unless such Bill shall be originated in this Chamber.

If the hereditary principle in the House of Lords is fundamentally objectionable on theoretical and equitable grounds, the principle of nomination in Colonial Councils is ten times more objectionable on grounds of common sense and simple justice between man and man. The sense of security for the natural term of life, and the absence of all accountability to any power or authority whatever, act upon the half-educated and vulgar minds found in all these Colonial Councils with a stupefying force quite pestilential to their own moral nature, and often very hurtful to the public interests. Even upon the better class of minds the effect is visibly pernicious; and it grows upon the victims stealthily, without their being conscious of the gradual change from manliness to superciliousness, from natural self-respect to upstartism. I only just touch upon the evil in this place, as it will be my duty to speak at some length in another chapter on this radical defect in the Constitution of New South Wales.

Owing to fortuitous circumstances, the question of

electoral reform was put off from time to time—chiefly through changes of Ministries developing nothing but feebleness. But it fell to my lot eventually to legislate on the subject, and my Bill of 1873, with some modifications, though passed long afterwards, is now the law.

For my part I seized the first opportunity to render it legally impossible for any reckless or self-serving Minister of the future to profit by Sir James Martin's example. In the new Electoral Act I inserted the following clause: ' The day to be fixed for the meeting of Parliament after the return of the writs for General Elections shall not be later than the seventh clear day after the date on which such writs shall have been made returnable.' Such is the present law, and I do not think it is likely to be repealed.

I have dwelt at some length on this disagreeable episode in our political history on account of its exceptional importance in working out the law of the Constitution.

# CHAPTER XII

AMONG the many differences of procedure and custom in carrying out Responsible Government in the colonies may be mentioned the course adopted in regard to individual Ministers on a change of Government. In 1856 it was decided in England that persons sworn of the Executive Council in one of the colonies should be designated 'The Honourable' while they remained members of that body. For some years in New South Wales the practice was that when a Ministry resigned as a body the Ministers individually resigned their seats in the Council. But in the adjoining colony of Victoria the retiring Ministers have never resigned their seats in the Executive Council, and there exists there a body of Executive Councillors not holding office. I believe the practice is similar in other of the colonies. This anomaly in practice led me to submit the matter to Sir Arthur Helps, the late accomplished Clerk of the Privy Council, and I give here the interesting letter which I received in reply. Though the letter is marked 'confidential,' I cannot conceive of any reason why it should be longer withheld from the public, after the lapse of nineteen years and the death of most of the persons named in it, and especially considering the value it must possess for Australian statesmen.

[Private and Confidential]
Kew, Surrey,
August 21, 1873.

Sir,—I have received your letter of June 11.

As I know but little of the state of Colonial Government, or of Colonial Society, it is with real diffidence that I venture to give any opinion upon the points submitted for my consideration.

It would be churlish, however, to refuse to give any answer to a letter so kindly worded as yours. I therefore attempt to make some reply, and I can assure you that I have given as much thought as I could to the questions which you have proposed to me.

I must premise that the answer seems to me to depend mainly upon the nature of your Executive Council, as to whether it has most resemblance to our Cabinet or to our Privy Council.

It appears to me, from your account of it, that it most resembles our Cabinet, except that it is presided over by your Governor, as the representative of the Sovereign. Moreover, the small number of its members, and the fact that almost every person in it holds some office, makes it still more resemble that Committee of the Privy Council in Great Britain, which we call a 'Cabinet,' but which has, properly, no official designation and no official existence.

Such being the case, that your Executive Council resembles our Cabinet, I am decidedly of opinion that in the absence of the Governor, the Prime Minister should act as President of the Executive Council. With regard to your second question, I am again influenced by the fact (as I assume it to be) of the resem-

blance of your Executive Council to a Cabinet rather than to a
Privy Council, and I doubt whether it would be judicious to
arrange that members of the Executive Council on retiring
from their political offices, should retain their seats as Executive Councillors.  This question appears to me to be a much
more difficult one than the first, and to depend upon circumstances respecting which I have very little knowledge.  I
mean, for instance, the habits of political thought and conduct
which prevail in the colony.

Here, at home, the system of retaining as Privy Councillors
those persons who have once held such office as makes them
eligible has acted admirably.  Those Privy Councillors who are
not in immediate connection with the Administration of the day,
never, by any chance, seek to interfere with that Administration.  They, however, are often very useful—most useful—
members of the Privy Council.  The Ministry of the day can
call upon them, and often *does* call upon them, to sit upon
Committees of Council which are called together to decide upon
questions which are not, or ought not to be, of a party character.
And, moreover, the Ministry of the day can summon to its aid
members of the Privy Council who have special knowledge upon
some particular subject.

For instance, the late Lord Kingsdown and the late Dr.
Lushington were great authorities on any matters relating to
international law.  Whatever Government was in, these emi-
nent men were summoned to a Council whenever such matters
were at issue.  To show you how men of different politics
have sat at these Councils, I may mention that I have served
as Clerk of a Committee of Council consisting of the Lord
Chancellor (Lord Campbell), Sir James Graham, the Lord
President (Lord Granville), Sir Edward Ryan, Lord Justice
Knight Bruce, Mr. Walpole, the Chancellor of the Exchequer
(Mr. Gladstone), and Mr. Lowe, Her Majesty's Attorney-
General and Solicitor-General as Assessors to the Committee,
and the Lord-Advocate for Scotland.  Now the question arises
in my mind whether (and this I say confidentially to you)
political feeling and political action are with you in the same

comparatively placid state as with us—whether, if you were to make your ex-Executive Councillors continue to be Councillors, you could reasonably conclude that they would never endeavour to embarrass the Government of the day, and would be ready to be called upon, as our Privy Councillors are, to assist the Government in any matter relating to party. If I felt sure of that, I should say, notwithstanding the resemblance of your Executive Council to a Cabinet, and notwithstanding the smallness of its numbers (for that latter drawback would soon be removed), by all means let the Executive Councillors, when they are out of office, retain their seats on the Executive Council.

I am sorry that my reply to your second question should not be of a decisive kind; but I think you will admit that in the absence of full knowledge upon the important points I have raised, it would be presumptuous in me to give a decisive opinion.

I have the honour to be, Sir,

Your obedient servant,

ARTHUR HELPS.

The Honourable Henry Parkes,
Colonial Secretary's Office, Sydney.

It was decided by the Imperial authorities that a person holding office as Prime Minister, and of course being a member of the Executive Council for one year, and others standing in the same relation to the State for three years, should be permitted to retain the title of 'Honourable' on making personal application for such distinction after retiring from office. But during the thirty-six years of Parliamentary government there have not been more than five or six applicants in New South Wales for this distinction, and these, with one exception, have not been among the leading men who have held office. Of late years retiring Ministers do not appear to have resigned their seats in the Council, and I suppose the rule may be considered as obsolete.

Perhaps we ought not to look for the same delicate appreciation of political relations in a colonial leader as is found in men of high education and long experience in the Imperial Parliament. At all events, in our actual Parliamentary life, we have some droll instances of political etiquette and decorum; such, for example, as a member rushing in from a caucus meeting and announcing to the House that he had just been elected 'Leader of the Opposition,' and from day to day speaking of himself as such 'leader' or as 'Leader of the party behind him,' or on occasion addressing the Chair about his 'followers.' Of course we all know how leadership has grown, and how it has asserted itself, in the annals of the House of Commons. History has told us with apt illustration, with what watchful restraint, what careful examination of its traditions, what clear insight into the springs of inner life, and what consummate patience, Peel at one time, and Gladstone at another, rose to the leadership of the House of Commons. Neither ever went through the process of election. The title of both was admitted almost as a matter of course by general expectation and acceptance. So I suppose it will be in Australia as time goes on. Another amusing weakness among members is the free use of the term 'my honourable friend.' I have heard one loquacious member, in replying to the speech of another member, apply to him the words 'my honourable friend' twenty times in fifteen minutes, and the two gentlemen were known to be anything but friends after all. A practice is permitted—and is almost grown into a habit with some—of members walking about the

Chamber, exchanging a word with one here and with another there, then settling down into a seat for a few minutes, and then repeating the exercise. An anecdote is told of William Cobbett, that he persistently took the seat on the Treasury bench which was usually occupied by Sir Robert Peel, then Prime Minister, and that he defended his conduct by reasoning that he was as much entitled to the seat as any other member. Cobbett was, however, laughed and chaffed out of his vagary, and no other member cared to imitate him. In the Assembly of New South Wales a dozen members in an evening's sitting may be seen competing for the Treasury seats during the temporary absence of Ministers. These may possibly seem small matters, but they largely tend to impair the dignity of a deliberative assembly, and they would not be tolerated in a church nor in a public meeting. Like the proverbial continuous dropping of the rain-drops, these things, persisted in day by day, probably have a more abiding effect in vitiating the character of the House than would be produced by occasional outbreaks of worse conduct arising from over-heated passion or strong provocation.

In the conduct of administration the Australians have also brought into existence some anomalies which would perplex the lover of strict constitutional consistency in form and usage. While the Government of England has been steadily settling through the latest generations into something like a recognised harmonious organisation, a Colonial Government during its one generation of existence has often spasmodically drifted

into the most incongruous forms of departmental action. I have pointed out in an early chapter with what
a dead weight of official lawyers the Government of
New South Wales was launched into existence by Mr.
Wentworth's Constitution. At the present time (1892),
in three of the colonies, the Attorney-General, instead of
confining himself to his legitimate sphere as law officer
of the Crown, is acknowledged as the political chief of
the Administration, while two of the actual Premiers
are wandering about in distant parts of the world.

Arising out of these loose notions of ministerial connection and relevancy we have the self-contradictory
term of 'Acting Premier' lightly bandied about, and
quietly repeated day after day by pretentious newspapers, as if there ever was in the Government of England an acting Prime Minister, or as if the thing were
conceivable. Under the British Constitution (and that
is what we all claim to possess in Australia) the Crown,
either directly or by deputation, as in the colonies,
commissions the person who is deemed to be best fitted,
by political standing, knowledge of affairs, general
capacity, weight of public character, and the degree in
which he commands confidence, to form an Administration. No stipulation is made as to who are to be his
associates. He receives his commission direct from
the Crown or from the Crown's representative, as the
sole responsible former of the Ministry. He consults
no one, and ought not to consult anyone—because no
secret or irresponsible advice or assistance ought to
come into play—in selecting his colleages. He is
nominated by the Crown itself; they are nominated by

him for the Crown's approval.  He thus becomes First
Minister, not by any empty ceremony or rule, nor as a
matter of form, but by the acceptance and creative
exercise of primal authority.  In this first exercise of
authority he is directly responsible to Parliament, and
his wisdom will be found in his ability to justify his
conduct.  Henceforward, at every step of the Administration over which he presides he is responsible for the
whole of its conduct.  How, then, can there be an
Acting Prime Minister? and how can the person who
has accepted that great position delegate to another his
indefinable powers which often take form and are called
into activity by unanticipated and unforeseen emergen-
cies?  In England no men of the rank of Cabinet
Ministers would consent to serve under one of themselves nominated by their accepted chief as ' Acting
Premier'; but then no man could be found to propose
any such arrangement.

Some time ago I had occasion to write to a distinguished person on the relations between the Crown
and Ministers, more especially in respect to the acceptance of any office of profit, and I then expressed my
views in the following propositions :

1. That the Prime Minister, the constructor and
    leader of the Ministry, cannot resign without
    his resignation including the whole Ministry
    [of course the Crown on its own judgment
    can send for any eligible person among the
    late Ministers to reconstruct].
2. That on tender of resignation the function of

Adviser ceases and only such opinion may be offered on any subject as is invited.

3. That in the case of any Minister, most of all in that of the Chief, the moment the intention is entertained to accept employment *under Government*, ineligibility for the performance of the executive and administrative duties of Government has begun, and resignation should at once follow.

4. That no Minister can be a party to appointing himself to a permanent civil office without his conduct being justly regarded as derogatory to the character and honour of Government.

5. That in the case of a contemplated reconstruction of Government, no person can be designated for that duty by the retiring Minister, except on the invitation of the Representative of the Crown.

Parliamentary government in Australia has proved itself upon the whole a remarkable success; but this is not saying that it has been free from serious mistakes and some lamentable blots. Any contrast, though made from imperfect data, between the Australia of 1855 and the Australia of 1892 would convincingly show the vast progress which has marked the Parliamentary interval of thirty-seven years. Making all fair allowance for the beneficial working of those moral and commercial agencies which would have come into increasingly active operation under any form of political institutions, still the results which are directly attributable to the legislative and administrative discernment, wisdom, and

vigour of the new Constitution are immense. They are
to be seen in the extension of railways and the greatly
improved means of communication in all directions, in
the scores upon scores of substantial bridges which span
rivers and creeks where dangerous crossings served the
purposes of travel in the last generation, in the wider
spread of settlement and the better class of rural home-
steads, in the gradual sweep of cultivation over the
wild land, in the beauty-spots of orchard and flower
garden round poor men's homes; above all, in the
beneficent provision, reaching everywhere, for the
instruction of the happy children, in the popular
demand for municipal institutions, in the multiplica-
tion of books accessible to the many, in the more
systematic ordering of towns and villages, in the
higher efficiency introduced into the departments of
justice and police—in a word, in every feature of
society. Yet there is an unreasoning desire to push
on, a rude impatience of all restraint, which attacks
any difficulty or delay in Parliament as in all other
provinces of colonial life. If an inconvenient precedent is cited which the Chair decides is a bar to
further progress in that direction or at that time, it is
forthwith pronounced a musty relic of a barbarous age
—a cobweb to be swept away. A like feeling arrays
itself against forms of procedure which are the embodiment of the wisdom of generations. And occasionally
when anything goes wrong the constitution of the Legislature is to be forthwith amended to provide a remedy.
Party action in Parliament is to give way to perfect
harmony, where the best men on all sides are to unite
in doing the best work.

There is not much difference in the Constitutions of the several Australian colonies, and all of them are imperfect instruments. But each of these Constitutions is sufficiently definitive, and at the same time sufficiently elastic, to admit of a sound and healthy system of free government. The constitution of a free people depends, as eminently in the case of the Constitution of the United States, upon the wisdom, the loyal attachment, the liberal interpretation, and the just conceptions of the men who work it. The evils of Party government, of which we hear much in the colonies as elsewhere, may be admitted, and they cannot be denied; but then every good thing is susceptible of abuse. What the people of Australia have to do is to follow faithfully in the footsteps of the founders of Parliamentary government, to scrupulously guard the ballot-box from corruption, and to reason out all questions of public policy by opposing sides acting from clear and honest beliefs. The greatest questions in relation to the public welfare admit of no compromise, nor yet of settlement or accommodation, except by the voice of the majority. What ground for agreement or accommodation can be discovered between freedom of commercial intercourse and restriction of commercial intercourse, or between denominational and non-sectarian education? If it be impossible to reconcile opposing principles, how otherwise, if not by conflict of thought and argument, and the final preponderance of votes, is the question to be determined? It is not Party in any true sense, but Party so-called, brought together by other means than attachment to and promulgation of openly avowed principles, which works the mischief at the ballot-box or in the Parliamentary arena. Australian patriotism should set aloft as its noblest aims in all its struggles, purity, honest conviction, and unbending courage. Instead of the abolition of Party, we want an intelligent and a conscientious adherence to Party lines, the strongest cast of which is quite consistent with personal respect and courtesy in political intercourse.

One of the measures of this—my first Administration—was a Bill to repeal the *ad valorem* Customs duties which had been imposed by the previous Government. The Treasurer, Mr. George Alfred Lloyd, conducted the Bill through the Assembly and dealt with the policy of Free Trade, as proposed by the measure, with much ability and intelligence. In this course of legislation we had the warm sympathy of Sir Hercules Robinson. who, we found, was a strong free-trader from economic enquiry and conviction. On the subject of our fiscal policy and on the important question of introducing the elective principle in the constitution of the Upper Chamber, I had a lengthy correspondence with Earl Grey, two of whose letters I introduce here, on account of the permanent interest which must attach to his Lordship's opinions :—

Howick, Lesbury, Northumberland,<br>February 4. 1874.

Sir,—I have to thank you for your letter of December 1, which reached me a few days ago, and also for that of November 3, which I received a month earlier. I sincerely congratulate you upon having been able to accomplish a very important reform in the financial and commercial policy of New South Wales, and I feel no doubt that its good effect on the industry

and trade of the colony will soon be apparent.  I hope that this
result of your measures may before long lead the other Australian colonies to follow your good example, and abandon the unwise policy of protection.

But though the new tariff of New South Wales is a great
improvement on the old one, and as great an advance towards
the adoption of a sound system as could reasonably be looked
for at once, it would be a mistake to regard it as giving full
effect to the principle of Free Trade.  If I am not mistaken,
the new tariff provides for the imposition of duties upon various
articles which are also produced in the colony and come into its
market without being subject to similar taxation.  Now, in all
these cases, the true principle of Free Trade is departed from,
since an artificial stimulus is given to the home production of
all articles which the home producer is allowed to sell without
paying the duties charged upon them when imported, and the
consumers are taxed to give this stimulus without benefit to the
revenue.  For this reason, since the adoption of the policy of
Free Trade, it has been a rule, strictly observed in this country,
to allow no article, subject to a duty when imported from abroad,
to be raised at home for sale, unless it pays a similar duty.
Thus, as you are aware, the growth of tobacco in the United
Kingdom is prohibited, except in very small quantities, for the
use of the grower, and beet-root sugar made here pays the same
duty as imported sugar.  In so far as it is at variance with this
rule, the new tariff of New South Wales departs from the principles of Free Trade, and to the same extent must tend to
impoverish the colony, or at least to check its advance in wealth
by diverting labour and capital from their natural, and therefore most productive employments, into others of which the
profit depends on the artificial encouragement they receive.

I may take this opportunity of apologising for not having
answered your letter of August 8, which I received in October.
I did not do so because I had little to add in reply to it to what
I had already written in my former letter, if I remember it cor-
rectly.  In most of what you say against a nominated Upper
Chamber I concur, but the question is whether there are not

objections scarcely less strong against any form of an elected
Upper Chamber which has yet been suggested, whether it is
advisable to have any such Chamber at all, and whether, instead
of attempting to alter the constitution of the Council, it would
not be wiser to abolish it altogether, making at the same time
some improvements in the constitution of the Assembly? I do
not find any reasons urged in your letter against the conclusion
I came to on this question, except that any such change as I
suggested would be impracticable. No doubt it would be so in
the present state of opinion in Australia, but have the reasons
for the view I have taken of the subject ever been brought
under the consideration of the colonial public? If not, I should
have been glad if you had submitted them to the judgment of
the people of New South Wales, by publishing my letter to you,
or extracts from it, in the newspapers.

As you say you had not been able to find a copy of my essay
on Parliamentary Government in the colony, I presume it is not
in the library of the Legislature. I have not a spare copy by
me, or I would have sent it to you to be placed there. Perhaps
when I am in London I may find one and do so.

I am, faithfully yours,

GREY.

The Honourable H. Parkes.

Sydney, April 10, 1874.

My Lord.—I am duly in receipt of your letter of February 4.
Your remarks respecting the tariff of this colony as left by the
legislation of the present Administration are perfectly just; but
we have not imposed any of the existing taxes—our efforts have
been confined to the work of remission, stopping short of remit-
ting all. It is probable that the tariff will be reduced to a
purely Free Trade basis at an early date.

I am deeply sensible of the value of your views on the
Legislative Council question, or rather on the question of the
best form of legislature for the colonies, and I feel much indebted
to you for the trouble you have taken in explaining those views
to me. I understand your present letter as authorising me to

publish your letter of May 27 last year, either whole or in part. Without this distinct intimation from yourself, I should not have considered myself at liberty to give publicity to your arguments and opinions. I shall now take occasion to place your letters, so far as they relate to this subject, before the public of this colony.

I send by present mail public documents on the question:

1. Report of the Legislative Council on the Legislative Council Bill.

2. Minutes of the Proceedings of the Legislative Council, Nos. 40 to 43.

As I informed you in my letter of August 8, 1873, would probably be the case, the Bill of the present Ministry was introduced in the Council this Session, having been passed in the Assembly by large majorities during last Session. An amendment was made on the motion to read the Bill the second time, to the effect that it be referred for the consideration of a Select Committee. This amendment was carried, and the report and evidence now sent form the result. By reference to pages 144 and 145 of Minutes of Proceedings, you will see the ultimate decision of the Council after the committee had reported, which was in favour of the nominations being removed from the influence of the responsible Ministers, and of a maximum limit to the nomination of members. I need not point out that these recommendations, if carried into effect, would make the Council independent of even the indirect force of public opinion and place it in direct hostility to the representative principle. A Colonial Upper Chamber, appointed in this arbitrary manner, without reference to the responsible advisers of the Crown, and to which, after a defined limit, no further nominations could be made, would be, as compared with the House of Lords, a legislative oligarchy, while it would necessarily be composed of incomparably inferior persons as to legislative fitness. This, then, is the state in which the Council itself has left the question to be put before the constituencies at the approaching General Election.

After the further consideration which I have been able to

bestow upon the subject, I cannot modify my views in favour of two Houses. A colony like New South Wales cannot possess a class of statesmen or political thinkers who have been born and nurtured amidst the best political influences, and who pass through life in constant communication with men of culture and elevated station. But, as compared with that of an old nation, the population of a colony contains a much larger proportion of enterprising, spirited, and self-reliant men. The mere fact of removal from one side of the world to the other may be accepted as implying some decision of character, and when that step is taken as the result of acquired information and with a definite purpose of self-advancement by industrious effort, it affords, I think, evidence of no small amount of practical intelligence. Such, to a large extent, is the character of the immigrant part of the population. In New South Wales we have now much of the stability of long-settled family life, and a numerous body of native-born men and women, very many of whom have been reared in circumstances of comfort, fairly educated, and accustomed to think and act for themselves with a keen sense of their personal freedom and independence. In the present Assembly there are at least thirty out of the seventy-two members who are native Australians. Then, there is a much larger proportion of the population here than in England who are possessors of property and leisure.

I have said thus much generally on behalf of the raw material in the colony for legislative purposes. It may be rougher, but it is not less sound, I hope, than that of the mother-country, and it is, comparatively speaking, more plentiful. Your Lordship's strongest argument against a Second Chamber is, I think, that it is likely to absorb the better men, and by doing so impoverish the Assembly. But will that really be the case? Will it not be the case here, as it is elsewhere, that men of capacity who have for years taken part in the heated conflicts of the Assembly, will still find a sphere of usefulness by removing to the calmer atmosphere and the less severe labours of the Council, who otherwise would retire with their trained talent and refined experience into private life? And as time advances will not this class of public men more and more increase? Even in our short trial of Parliamentary government, several of the more valuable members of the Council have been men of this stamp, removed from, but who in any case would not probably have remained members of, the Assembly. If it is admitted, as is admitted by your arguments and suggestions, that there must be some check upon legislative action—some counterpoise to the impulsive exercise of legislative power—it still appears to me that the machinery of Government will work more smoothly and successfully by having this controlling force lodged in a Second Chamber rather than in a second class of legislators in a single Chamber. A single Legislative Chamber, composed of different classes of members, would be distracted by inherent antagonisms peculiar to its formation, and the work of its hands would, I fear, be often more perverse and ill-considered than would be that of a single Chamber on a level elective basis.

The radical misconception in the efforts to construct a Second Chamber in the colonies has, it seems to me, been in the supposition that we could create any kind of Chamber like the British House of Lords. That is simply impossible, and the idea must be given up before a healthy conception of the work can be formed. The title to legislative authority in a country like this must be derived from the people themselves, and the only principle by which strength can be given and confidence secured is that of election. If the choice lies between the laws being made by a single voice and the making of them being only possible by two distinct voices, I cannot resist the conclusion that it is wiser and safer to accept the two. The problem to be solved appears to me to consist in giving to both voices an equal authority, and yet imparting to one a tone as free as possible from caprice and passion.

It is with a sincere feeling of respect for your Lordship's character that I venture thus imperfectly to express my inability to concur in your views in favour of a single Chamber.

I have the honour to be, my Lord,

Your most obedient servant,

HENRY PARKES.

The Right Honourable the Earl Grey.

13 Carlton House Terrace,
May 4, 1874.

Sir,—On hearing from you some months ago that you had
not been able to obtain in New South Wales a copy of my
essay on Parliamentary Government, I informed you that if on
my arrival in London I found that I had one to spare I would
send it to you. Accordingly I beg now to forward to you the
accompanying volume, and I have to request that when you
have looked at it (if you can find time to do so) you will be good
enough to present it in my name to the library of the Legislature. Though it is ten years since this essay was published,
and great changes have in that time taken place in the colonies,
I venture to think that it contains some observations which
may still be found not altogether unworthy of your attention,
and of that of the members of the Legislature, with reference to
the question as to the expediency of altering the constitution of
the Legislative Council which has led to so much debate in the
colony, and which as I understand still remains unsettled.

This question is one of great importance, and it seems to
have been discussed with much ability both by the advocates
and the opponents of the proposed change; but as an impartial
observer from a distance I must doubt whether either party has
sufficiently considered the objections to the arrangement for
which it contends, and whether in the heat of the controversy
both have not fallen into serious errors.—So far as regards the
reasons which have been urged against allowing the present
nominee Council to continue, I must express my concurrence
with the supporters of the rejected Bill; but I am not equally
satisfied that to make the Council an elective body in the manner
proposed would be likely to ensure such a judicious exercise of the
power of legislation as is required for the welfare of the colony.
The elective Council, I fear, would either be without power
enough to exercise any substantial power over legislation,
or else it would be liable to bring the whole machine of government to a standstill by differences with the Assembly.
All experience shows that differences would be likely to arise

between the two branches of the Legislature, and I do not perceive that under the plan proposed there would have been any sufficient provision for averting the difficulties which would thus be occasioned. The creation of an elective Council would also either have the effect of weakening the Assembly by withdrawing from it able and useful members, or else must fail to obtain the authority and command of the public respect which it could only derive from being composed of men of high character and capacity. It is not reasonable to suppose that out of its present limited population, New South Wales could command the services of enough men of this stamp to form two really efficient legislative bodies, sufficiently numerous for the due performance of their functions. For it must be borne in mind that it is of great importance for the efficiency of a legislative body that it should be tolerably numerous. This is more particularly true where the system of ' responsible,' or in other words of party government, has been adopted, since under this system of government the popular branch of the Legislature is so powerful that if it consists of only a small number of members, individual votes become of so much value as to give a great temptation to abuse.

These considerations have led me to the conclusion that instead of attempting to improve the Legislative Council by rendering it elective, it would be advisable to abolish it. I am aware that this conclusion is quite opposed to the generally received opinion that the division of a Legislature into two houses is indispensable in order to check hasty and injudicious legislation. Whether this commonly received opinion is correct, even as regards large nations, may admit of some doubt, nor would it be easy to show that in any country where no Upper House has been found existing and deriving authority from long prescription, the problem of creating such a body, and getting it to work well with the popular branch of the Legislature, has been satisfactorily solved. But passing by this question, it is sufficient to observe that in young communities like the British colonies, experience appears to me to be clearly unfavourable to the division of the Legislature into two distinct bodies. At the same time I am not prepared to deny that mistakes very injurious to the colony would probably be committed by the Legislative Assembly of New South Wales as now constituted, if no provision were made to secure greater deliberation and judgment in the work of legislation than could be looked for were the Council to be simply abolished. I fully recognise the necessity for imposing some check upon the hasty and unwise measures a purely democratic body like the Assembly might adopt, but I believe that this check might be much more usefully applied within than without its walls.

In the volume I now send you, I have expressed my opinion that in this respect the constitution given to New South Wales in 1842, under which the Legislature consisted of a single chamber, one third of the members being nominees, was better than that which was substituted for it a few years later. I adhere to that opinion, and I still believe, for the reasons fully explained in my essay, that the change which was made was a mistake, and that the system of responsible government would have worked far better in New South Wales if the old constitution of the Legislature had been retained. To restore it, however, would be impossible, and I only refer to it in order to point out that it deserves to be considered whether the principle on which it was founded might not be adopted to the extent of dispensing with any second branch of the Legislature, and of introducing into the Assembly a limited number of members who should not owe their seats to popular election, without being as formerly nominees. What I would venture to suggest is that in abolishing the Council, a limited number of seats in the Assembly (say eight or ten) should be given to members chosen by the Assembly itself, and holding their seats for life, or till they resigned them. The first life members might be named in the Act for altering the constitution, and it might be provided that vacancies should be filled up only when not less than three had occurred, when the Assembly should elect by cumulative vote the persons to succeed to them.

By this arrangement we might fairly expect that the ablest and most experienced men of different political parties would

Y 2

obtain seats in the Assembly, and that holding these seats for
life they would be able to act with independence on their own
judgment. The advice of such men would be of the highest
value to the Assembly in determining the questions that come
before it, and a useful check on rash legislation. You will find
that in the essay I have sent you I have contended that the want
of such an element as would thus be supplied in the composition
of the Assembly, has been greatly felt in the House of Commons
since the passing of the Reform Act of 1832. Before that Act
was passed, the rotten boroughs (as they were called) practically
provided, though in a faulty manner, for securing the presence
in the House of Commons, in an independent position, of the
most eminent men of all parties. Since the passing of the first
Reform Act, the loss of this advantage has been very seriously
felt, and it is likely to be still more so in the time to come, in
consequence of the new Reform Act of 1867. This fact strongly
supports my opinion that the introduction of a few life members,
appointed in the manner I have described, would be an important improvement in the composition of the Assembly of
New South Wales. It would also, I am convinced, prove a far
more effective security against rash legislation by a purely
democratic Assembly, than could be afforded by the creation of
any Council that could be devised, whether on the principle of
election or of nomination. Any such Council could only stop
unwise measures on the part of the Assembly at the risk of
bringing both legislation and the whole machine of Government
to a stand. But by introducing within the Assembly itself a
limited number of able and independent men, their restraining
influence upon the members representing the popular feeling of
the moment would act with far more effect, and all risk of the
extreme inconvenience arising from differences between two independent houses would be averted. I am persuaded that the
passing of such a measure as I have now suggested would afford
the best and safest mode of terminating the controversy as to
the Legislative Council, which has been raised in the colony,
and I would add that the passing of such a measure might be
rendered easier by providing that the present members of the

Council should be the first life-members of the Assembly.   Probably this would bring into that body more life members than would be desirable, but this need not be more than a temporary inconvenience, as it might be provided that no new life members should be chosen till they had fallen below any smaller number which might be fixed upon as that to be permanently maintained.   Even the inconvenience of a temporary excess in the number of life members might be avoided, if those who have now seats in the Council should be able to agree among themselves as to which of them should forego the privilege of being brought into the Assembly.

I have only, in conclusion, to apologise for the length of this letter, which I have been led to write by the deep interest I feel in the welfare of the thriving colony of New South Wales.

I have the honour to be, Sir,

Your obedient Servant,

GREY.

The Honourable H. Parkes.

About this time I first communicated with Mr. Gladstone.   I had been an admirer of that statesman for many years, and I was beginning to think in a new light of the relations between the colonies and the parent country, and of the bonds which might eventually be devised to unite all the Australian colonies under one federal constitution.   The subject, which I submitted in general terms to Mr. Gladstone, may be gathered from the following extract from my letter: ' Any new national importance that could be given to these young States would tend to bind them more firmly to Great Britain, and would tend more and more to develope their resources by inducing men who have made fortunes to remain permanently amongst us.   A Federal Government, including uniformity in Customs laws, would come more speedily from a higher political status. I should feel deeply indebted to you if you could examine the question which I have merely suggested.'

Hawarden Castle, Chester,<br>July 30, 1874.

Dear Sir,—I beg to acknowledge your interesting letter of June 5, and to express the pleasure with which I learn that, while we are locally separated by so vast a distance, we are nevertheless united by sympathy as attached subjects of the British Crown.

The subject which you mention to me is very large and comprehensive. It is also one by no means new to my thoughts. I think you may rest assured that the people of England have no wish to limit in any respect by pressure upon the colonies their powers of self-government. The less there is of such pressure, the greater probably will be the desire to maintain the Imperial connection. All that can be fairly asked, and that must in justice be desired, is that the responsibility of England shall be relaxed or contracted in proportion to the limitation of her power. In their present mood, and with the prosperity that prevails among the classes possessed of influence, it is not unlikely to happen that England may be too remiss in providing for the reciprocal character of any measures that may be adopted. At any rate, I am sure you may be confident that no restrictive views will prevail to the prejudice of colonial freedom.

Wishing you all comfort and good success in the discharge of your important duties.

I remain, dear Sir,<br>Your very faithful servant,<br>W. E. GLADSTONE.

Honourable H. Parkes.

Colonial Secretary's Office, Sydney,<br>September 26, 1874.

Sir,—I thank you for your letter of July 30, and for the frank expression of your views on the relations of England to the colonies. There can be no ground for apprehension that the loyalty of the colonies to the parent Nation or Imperial rule will diminish under the influences of self-government, and I unreservedly subscribe to the maxim, as stated by you, that England should be relieved of responsibility in proportion as her power is withdrawn from these outlying parts of the Empire. So far back as 1858, I made a motion in the Legislative Assembly to the effect that this colony should provide for its own military defence.

The grievance under which we sometimes fret, but more frequently laugh, is that England, as represented by her eminent men, and by her literature, forms no adequate conception of our importance. I enclose a table prepared here recently with much care, showing the aggregate and relative importance of these colonies. If at any moment of leisure you will compare the account given in the latest Gazetteer, you will see how we are popularly underrated.

I take the liberty of sending this table because I fear that in my letter of June 5 (having referred to a memorandum I made of it), I mechanically wrote 200,000 instead of 2,000,000 as the Australian population.

With great respect,<br>I remain, Sir,<br>Your faithful servant,<br>HENRY PARKES.

The Right Honourable<br>
W. E. Gladstone, M.P., &c., &c.

During this administration an agreement was entered into by the Governments of Victoria, South Australia, and New South Wales for suspending the collection of Border Customs duties, practically estab-

lishing overland free trade between the three colonies
for three years; but the treaty was abrogated by Victoria before the expiration of that term, and no similar
measure has since been attempted.

The electric telegraph uniting the colonies with
England was also established, and important steps were
taken towards improving the ocean mail services, including the opening of the new route between Australia
and America.

These various questions of high concern to the
colonies, led to much controversy; but the Government
carried their measures in Parliament by large majorities.    Indeed the Ministry was in the end only defeated
on a question of the exercise of the prerogative of pardon in criminal cases, which was tortured by heated
passions and false representation into a charge of mal-
administration.   As this discloses some of the worst
features of Australian public life, while it was the cause
of widening the recognised sphere of ministerial responsibility, the circumstances of the case are explained at
some length.

While I was in England as Emigration Commissioner, in 1862, the crime of bushranging broke out
with much violence in New South Wales, and in particular the name of Frank Gardiner became notorious
as that of the reputed leader of a gang who stopped
and robbed the gold escort at Eugowra.   Several young
men, arrested on the charge of being engaged in the
escort robbery, were tried before Sir Alfred Stephen,
Chief Justice, and capitally convicted of the crime, one
of them suffering death.   Gardiner, however, was not

apprehended until February 1864, when he was discovered keeping a store at Apis Creek in Queensland,
under the name of Christie. He was brought up for
trial before Sir Alfred Stephen in July following, not
for the escort robbery, but on two charges not capital,
of which he was convicted, receiving three cumulative
sentences amounting to thirty-two years' imprisonment,
the first two years in irons. The late Sir James Martin,
then Attorney-General, and afterwards Chief Justice,
made a minute on Gardiner's complicity in the Eugowra
outrage in these words :—'The only capital case
against Gardiner appears to be the case of the escort
robbery, and as to that it seems to me that a conviction could not be reasonably expected,' adding his
reasons for this opinion.

In 1871—a little more than seven years after
Gardiner's conviction—two sisters of the prisoner got
up a petition for his release; and they succeeded in
obtaining in support of their petition the signatures of
many respectable persons, including some who had
held high offices in the colony. Mr. William Bede
Dalley, who had held high office as Solicitor-General,
and who was afterwards Attorney-General of the
colony, signed his name to the following recommendation :—'We the undersigned beg most respectfully to
recommend the foregoing petition to your Excellency's
merciful consideration, the more especially from the
desire to reform evidenced by the prisoner before capture, and his conduct since his incarceration ; and trust
that your Excellency may be pleased, under all the
circumstances of the case, *to deem the period of the*

*sentence already expired sufficient for the ends of justice.'*
Attached to the recommendation of the petition were
the names of several members of Parliament, and those
of a number of magistrates and well-known merchants
and traders. Mr. William Forster, M.P., who had
filled the office of Colonial Secretary at the time of
Gardiner's conviction, was specially referred to in the
body of the petition. It stated that, on the occasion
of an outbreak of prisoners in the gaol, Gardiner's
conduct was 'so noticed by the Inspector-General of
Police that he assured the prisoner that he would see
the Colonial Secretary (Mr. Forster), and have a record
of it made for the future benefit of the prisoner.' The
petition, with this special reference to himself, was
taken to Mr. Forster (now out of office) for his signature; and, with his attention thus challenged, he wrote,
and subscribed his name under, the following words:
'Having been referred to in a petition for the mitigation of the sentence of Francis Christie, as holding the
office of Colonial Secretary when an outbreak occurred
in Darlinghurst Gaol, I have much pleasure in testifying to the fact of Christie's good conduct on that occasion, as well as to his general conduct during the
entire period of his incarceration, so far as it came
under my notice in either case. I am glad to record
this opinion, so that it may operate as it ought in the
prisoner's favour. And, so far as these and other circumstances mentioned in the petition entitle his case
to the favourable consideration of the Government, I
am willing to add my testimony and recommendation.'
The 'recommendation' of Mr. Forster was dated

December 29, 1871—about seven years and six months after Gardiner's conviction—and it was written immediately below Mr. Dalley's 'recommendation,' which expressed the hope that the Governor would be pleased, 'under all the circumstances of the case, *to deem the period of the sentence already expired sufficient for the ends of justice.*' About the same time the petition was brought to me for my signature, but I refused to sign it.

I entered upon the duties of the Colonial Secretary's Office on May 14, 1872, and the petition for the mitigation of Gardiner's sentence came to me in due course to be dealt with. As the prayer for the mitigation principally rested on the ground of Gardiner's good conduct in prison, I sent the petition in the first instance to the Inspector of Prisons for his report. As reports from this officer are not called for in all cases, my calling for a report from him in Gardiner's case was subsequently attempted to be tortured into evidence that I had some design to favour the prisoner. But it must be obvious to every intelligent and unprejudiced mind that, in a case of so much importance, where the question was one mainly of the prisoner's good conduct, if I had not obtained the report of the only officer whose business it was to be well acquainted with his prison life, I should have greatly failed in my duty, and laid myself open to well-merited blame. With this report, and reports from the officers of the gaol, and all other papers connected with the case, the petition was sent for the report of the Chief Justice, who had tried and sentenced Gardiner. So far from seeing any impropriety in the report from the Inspector of

Prisons, the Chief Justice in his own report characterised that officer's remarks as ' very judicious.'

Having thus brought together all the facts of the
case, the opinions and testimony of the principal officers
who had had charge of the prisoner, and the views of
the judge by whom he had been tried, I submitted the
petition to the Governor with a written minute of my
own explaining the standing of the principal persons
whose names were appended to it. This I did more
fully in conversation with His Excellency about the
same time, but I certainly had no desire, and never intended at any time, to do more than fairly explain both
sides of the case. I took this course of explanation
because His Excellency, having but recently arrived in
the colony, could not be supposed to know either the
special features of the prisoner's case or the positions
of the persons who were using their influence in his
favour, two of whom were ex-members of the Executive Council. Up to this time I had regarded the
prerogative of pardon as vested absolutely in the Representative of the Crown, and I was aware, of my own
knowledge, that two Governors at least—Sir John Young
and the Earl of Belmore—had exercised it, as a rule,
without the advice of Ministers.

On receiving this petition, in December, 1872, what
did the Governor himself do? He did not grant the
prayer of the petitioners. He did not concur in the
recommendation of Mr. Attorney-General Dalley in
December 1871—that the ends of justice would be
answered by the seven years and six months of his sentence which the prisoner had then suffered, and that he

might be released instantly unconditionally. He did not yield to the specious 'recommendation' of Mr. Forster, who had recorded his opinion in December 1871 also, 'that it might operate as it ought in the prisoner's favour.' Sir Hercules Robinson judged the case on its merits, possibly attaching some weight to the opinions of the two ex-members of the Executive Council, but really mastering for himself the perplexities which surround the abnormal condition of our prison population. He knew that good-conduct prisoners were immured for unlimited years within the four dead walls of the same gaol in few Christian countries. His decision, I believe, while merciful to the prisoner, was just to society, and thoroughly sound in the interests of criminal treatment. He decided that, if the prisoner's conduct continued good for the term of ten years, he might then be allowed to exile himself. In arriving at this decision Sir Hercules Robinson took care to state that he 'did not concur with the petitioners that the sentence which the prisoner had undergone was sufficient for the ends of justice.'

Several months after this decision in favour of Gardiner's exile—namely, in the early part of 1874—another petition was got up by one of the prisoner's sisters, praying that he might be released in the colony; and the name of Mr. Attorney-General Dalley was appended to this second petition. The case was again referred to the Inspector of Prisons for his report, and was then submitted to the Governor with the following words covered by my initials:—'The Sheriff strongly deprecates a compliance with the prayer of the petition.' The Governor minuted the petition simply ' Refused.'

This case, as favoured by the powerful influence of Mr. Forster in 1871, as dealt with ministerially by me, and as decided by Her Majesty's representative in 1872, was in 1874 made the subject of noisy agitations, inflamed by political passion and distracted by misrepresentations, in order to overthrow the Government whose measures and policy were generally approved by the country. Mr. Forster himself, amongst others, vigilantly assisted in the manœuvre.

Two considerations seem to justify this rather lengthy reference to the Gardiner case. It led to an entire change in the treatment of prisoners' appeals for a merciful exercise of the prerogative, and it was made the discreditable means of overthrowing the Government.

The case of Gardiner became the subject of frequent questioning and reference in the House, and Mr. Edward Combes, then member for Bathurst, gave notice of a condemnatory motion, which, as the case had been considered in connection with twenty-three others, finally took the following form : ' That this House disapproves of the release of the long-sentenced prisoners whose names are set forth in the returns laid upon the table of this House by the Honourable the Colonial Secretary on May 22, 1874, including the name of the notorious prisoner Gardiner.' Mr. Combes made his motion on June 3, as an amendment on going into Supply, and the debate was continued over several nights, closing on June 11 with a division of 26 to 26.

The motion was negatived by the Speaker's casting vote.

In the meantime Ministers had addressed themselves to the consideration of the position in which the prerogative of pardon was actually exercised, and what ought to be our responsibility in relation to its exercise. It appeared to me, and I believe to my colleagues also, that the questions we had to consider were perplexed rather than cleared of perplexities by recent despatches from the Imperial Government on the subject. The result of our deliberations was embodied in the following paper :

'MINUTE FOR HIS EXCELLENCY THE GOVERNOR.

I have given much consideration to the expediency of changing the system of treatment in the cases of petitions presented for the absolute or conditional pardon of convicted offenders, and have carefully read the correspondence on the subject, commencing with Lord Belmore's despatch of July 14, 1869, and closing with Lord Kimberley's despatch of February 17, 1873.

The minute of Mr. Robertson, which gave rise to this correspondence, does not appear to me to deal with the real question which the despatches of the Secretary of State present for determination in the colony. That question, in any view, is the extent to which the Minister is to have an active voice in the decision of these cases ; but in my view it is much more—it is whether the Minister is virtually to decide in every case upon his own direct responsibility, subject of course to the refusal of the Crown to accept his advice, which refusal at any time should be held to be, as in all other cases, tantamount to dispensing with his services. The seventh paragraph of the minute alone touches the question of the Minister's relation to the Crown, and it seems to prescribe a position for the

Minister in which, on submitting petitions to the Governor, he is to express an opinion on each case, to be 'viewed as embodying no more than a recommendation,' after which he is to have no further concern in the matter. I cannot subscribe to this principle of Ministerial conduct, if this be what was intended by Mr. Robertson.

There can be no question, I believe, that from the beginning of the present reign the Home Secretary in England decides absolutely in all matters of this kind in the name of the Crown, and that the Crown does not in practice interfere. At no former time when the Crown took an active part in such decisions could the Crown, in the nature of things, be subject to a superior or an instructing authority. The wide difference between the position of the Minister and his relations to the Crown and to Parliament in the colony and in England is at once apparent on reading the despatches from the Secretary of State. The Governor is invested with the prerogative of the Crown to grant pardons, and, by the letter of the instructions conveyed to him by Lord Kimberley's circular of November 1, 1871, he 'is bound to examine personally each case in which he is called upon to exercise the power entrusted to him.' By the instructions previously conveyed to the Governor of this colony by Lord Granville, in reply to Lord Belmore's despatch of July 14, 1869, he is told that 'the responsibility of deciding upon such applications rests with the Governor,' and, in reference obviously to advice that may be tendered, it is expressly added that the Governor 'has undoubtedly a right to act upon his own independent judgment.' And, finally, after the question has been re-opened by Sir Alfred Stephen, it is repeated by Lord Kimberley's despatch of February 17, 1873, that 'in granting pardons' the Governor 'has strictly a right to exercise an independent judgment.'

'It seems to be clear that the 'portion of the Queen's prerogative' entrusted to the Governor of a colony, unlike the prerogative in England, is intended to be a reality in its exercise. It is undeniably the case that the representative of the Crown in a colony, unlike the Crown itself, is subject to a superior or instructing authority. What, then, is the position of the Minister, and what is intended to be the nature of the advice he may be called upon to give, and under what circumstances is that advice to be given?

In no sense of responsibility in this respect has the Minister in this colony hitherto been in the same position as the Home Secretary in England. He has neither exercised the function of pardon, nor as a rule been asked for advice. Except in rare cases, and then only in a limited degree, when special features or new facts have presented themselves, he has never actively interfered. What would be his position if he entered upon a system of partial advice, and accepted in matters of the gravest moment a secondary or limited authority, irreconcilable with the nature of his duties and responsibilities as a Minister under Parliamentary government?

Lord Granville says, ' The Governor would be bound to allow great weight to the recommendation of his Ministry.' The circular of November 1, 1871, says, ' He will of course pay due regard to the advice of his Ministers.' Lord Kimberley, in his despatch of February 17, 1873, repeats the words of Lord Granville.

It cannot be doubted that the advice here intended is wholly distinct in its nature from the advice given in the general conduct of affairs. In the general case the advice is uniformly accepted, as the first condition of the adviser continuing to hold office. In all his acts the Minister's responsibility to Parliament is simple, undivided, and direct. But in pardoning convicted offenders, the Governor, although he is to ' pay due regard to the advice of his Ministers,' is at the same time informed by the Secretary of State that he ' is bound to examine personally each case in which he is called upon to exercise the power entrusted to him,' and that with him rests the responsibility. The exceptional advice implied seems to be of the nature of opinions or suggestions to which weight may be attached as coming from persons ' responsible to the colony for the proper administration of justice and the prevention of crime,' but which in any case, or in every case, may be partially or wholly disregarded.

It does not appear to be clear that the Governor is required by the Secretary of State to seek even this secondary class of advice in all cases. It would rather seem that the instruction does not necessarily extend beyond cases in which pardons are proposed to be granted, in which cases the Minister would simply have to concur in a decision already formed, or be placed in the somewhat invidious position of objecting to the extension of mercy. This view would shut out from the Minister's limited power of advice the numerous cases in which much concern is frequently felt by portions of the public, where a merciful consideration is prayed for and is refused.

I entertain grave doubts whether any change at present from the system which has hitherto prevailed will be beneficial to the colony. In a community so small as ours the distinctions between classes are very slight. The persons entrusted with authority and the relatives and friends of prisoners move closely together. The means of political pressure are easily accessible. A larger share by the Minister in the exercise of the prerogative of pardon would not, in my judgment, be more satisfactory to the public. But if a change is to take place, and the cases of prisoners are to be decided on the advice of Ministers, I can see no sufficient reason for making a distinction between this class of business and the ordinary business of Government. The Minister ought to enquire into and examine each case, and each case ought to be decided on his advice. The refusal of the Governor to accept his advice in any case of this kind ought to have the same significance and effect as a similar refusal in any other case. In no other way can the Minister be fairly responsible to Parliament for what is done. Either ' the responsibility of deciding upon such applications ' must still ' rest with the Governor,' as Lord Granville expresses it, or it must rest with the Minister in the only way in which it would be just to hold him responsible.

HENRY PARKES.

Colonial Secretary's Office, Sydney,
May 30, 1874.

The change proposed—namely, that the prerogative

of pardon should in future be exercised on the advice
of Ministers—met with the approval of the Governor,
who signified his concurrence, with a full explanation
of his own views, in the minute which is here sub-
joined :—

### Minute by the Governor for the Executive Council.

I have read the minute of the Honourable the Colonial
Secretary upon the subject of pardons, and it has occurred to me
that the difficulty of dividing the responsibility in this matter,
in the manner suggested by the late Secretary of State, can
perhaps best be illustrated by showing how such a system would
work in the practical transaction of business.

Hitherto the practice here has been for all applications for
mitigation of sentences to be submitted to the Governor for his
independent decision thereon. Some are sent to him direct
through the post by the petitioners, others are presented personally by influential persons interested, whilst the remainder
reach him through the Colonial Secretary's office, without any
expression of opinion from the Minister. Taken altogether
these applications are numerous. I have not kept any count of
them, but I should think that a weekly average of twelve would
certainly be below the number. All are carefully perused by
the Governor. Some—in which the grounds stated, even if
proved, would be insufficient to justify remission—are summarily
rejected; others, upon which enquiry may seem desirable, are
referred for the report of the Sheriff and the sentencing official,
and sometimes the opinion of the Crown Law Officer is asked
for. Previous petitions and papers in each case (if any) are
carefully perused, and eventually the Governor gives his decision
according to his own independent judgment. The papers are
then sent to the Colonial Secretary's office, where the necessary
official steps are taken to carry the decision into effect, without,
I believe, in ordinary cases, the matter being even brought
under the notice of the Minister.

z 2

If a change such as has been suggested were to be carried out, the first question to be decided would be by whom should all petitions and applications for mitigation of sentences be considered in the first instance—by the Governor or by the Minister?

If, as at present, by the Governor, what would be the consequence under the instructions contained in the Secretary of State's circular despatch of November 1, 1871? The words of that despatch are as follows:

'The Governor, as invested with a portion of the Queen's prerogative, is bound to examine personally each case in which he is called upon to exercise the power entrusted to him, although, in a colony under Responsible Government, he will of course pay due regard to the advice of his Ministers, who are responsible to the colony for the proper administration of justice and prevention of crime, *and will not grant and pardon without receiving their advice thereupon.*'

The last few words which I have underlined are not quoted by the Colonial Secretary in his minute, but they are important as showing the precise view taken by the Secretary of State. The Governor apparently may, after personally examining any petition for mitigation, and after giving due weight to the advice of his Ministers, exercise an independent judgment, and reject the application. He may say ' No ' on his own authority, but he can only say ' Yes ' on the advice of a Minister. The idea would seem to be to make the Governor and the Ministers mutually act as checks on each other. Either can negative a prayer for pardon, but both must concur before any such application can be granted. If, therefore, the petitions were considered in the first instance by the Governor, all cases rejected by him would at once be withdrawn from the cognisance or control of the Minister—a proceeding of which the latter might justly complain if any responsibility at all were to be imposed on him in this matter. In all cases in which the Governor proposed to mitigate the sentence, his decision would have to be approved and confirmed by the Minister, who might, if he saw fit, veto the merciful intentions of the Governor. It appears to me the Governor and the Minister would occupy somewhat anomalous positions in such cases. Under a constitutional form of Government the Crown is supposed to accept or reject the advice of responsible Ministers: in this matter the Minister would adopt or reject as he pleased the advice of the Representative of the Crown!

But suppose, on the other hand, that all petitions were considered and reported on in the first instance by the Minister, what would then be the result? Why, all cases rejected by the Minister need never be sent on at all to the Governor, to whom they would be addressed. For, as the Governor could not pardon without the advice of the Minister, there would be no object in troubling him with applications which he could not comply with. In cases in which the Minister advised a mitigation, the Governor could of course, if he saw proper, in the exercise of his 'undoubted right,' reject such advice—upon being prepared to accept the consequences. But practically he would never do so, except in cases which in his view involved such a gross abuse of the prerogative that both the Secretary of State and local public opinion would be likely to support him in the adoption of extreme measures. In all ordinary cases, in which neither Imperial interests nor policy were involved, the Governor, whatever his own private opinion might be, · would be bound to allow great weight to the recommendation of his Ministry, who are responsible to the colony for the proper administration of justice and prevention of crime.' Practically under such a system the prerogative of mercy would be transferred from the Governor to the Minister charged with such duties.

It was perhaps the recognition of some such difficulties which led to the suggestion of a compromise between these two systems, thrown out in Lord Kimberley's last despatch on the subject. In effect, his Lordship appears to suggest that the Governor might continue, as at present, to examine into and deal with all petitions for pardon; but that he should, before granting a mitigation of sentence in any case, ascertain by means of informal consultation that the Minister concurred in

such a step. I fear that such a plan would not work well, and
that its effect would simply be to fritter away any real or clearly-
defined responsibility in such matters. In the first place, who
would be responsible for the appeals rejected upon which charges
of sectarian partiality or official corruption might possibly be
based ? Is the Governor to remain responsible for refusals, and
the Minister to become responsible for pardons ? Again, if the
Minister is to be responsible for pardons, he would have, unless
his concurrence were a mere matter of form, to go through all
the reports and papers in each case in which a pardon was proposed by the Governor; and, as I have before shown, he would
have to place upon the papers in writing his final acceptance or
rejection of the Governor's advice. If such grave matters were
disposed of in informal conversations, such a loose mode of transacting business would inevitably result in mistakes and mis-
apprehensions. The Governor might decide a case under the
full impression that the Minister concurred in his view, and yet
he might find subsequently that there was some misunderstand-
ing, and that his decision was repudiated and condemned.

For these reasons I entirely concur in the conclusion arrived
at by the Honourable the Colonial Secretary in his minute—
that the responsibility for the exercise here of the Queen's prerogative of pardon must either, as heretofore, rest solely with
the Governor, or it must be transferred to a Minister who will
be subject in this as in the discharge of other administrative
functions only to those checks which the Constitution imposes
on every servant of the Crown who is at the same time responsible to Parliament. The real question at issue is thus brought
within narrow limits.

The Colonial Secretary expresses 'grave doubts whether
any change at present from the system which has hitherto prevailed here will be beneficial to the colony,' and he thinks
that under the circumstances existing here the prerogative of
pardon will be better exercised by the Governor than by the
Minister. If the validity of such an argument were once admitted, it might perhaps be held to extend to other branches of
administrative business. But the very essence of the Constitu-

tion is responsibility to Parliament for the administration of local affairs ; and possessing, as the system does within itself, a prompt and effectual means of correcting any abuse of power, there can be little doubt that political training and official experience will soon impose restraints upon those impulses which sometimes mar the earlier attempts at self-government.

I have felt ever since my first arrival in the colony that the practice which has hitherto prevailed here, of entrusting an important branch of local administration solely to an officer who is not responsible to Parliament, is highly objectionable ; and as I fail to see that any plan of divided responsibility in such a matter can be devised, I can only repeat here what I have on several occasions since the receipt of Lord Kimberley's last despatch stated to the Colonial Secretary in conversation—namely, that I am quite prepared to adopt a change of system ; and I think for the future all applications for mitigation of sentences should be submitted to me through the intervention of a responsible Minister, whose opinion and advice as regards each case should be specified in writing upon the papers.

HERCULES ROBINSON.

Government House, June 1, 1874.

The Executive Council, on June 2, approved of the change, which was at once acted upon in all new cases. This step was not taken by me without serious misgivings, which I still feel, as to the entire wisdom of the change. But it seemed that the Ministers of the day had forced upon them by an unscrupulous party movement the choice between responsibility without authority and the authority of an active judgment coupled with a just responsibility. The new practice has now been substantially approved by the Secretary of State.[1]

Having regard to the exceptional state of the pre-

---

[1] See Lord Carnarvon's despatch of October 7, 1874, No. 54.

rogative question up to that time, Ministers did not
look upon Mr. Combes' motion as one entitled to
political significance; and, as we were then over-
burdened with public business, we paid no attention
to it.

The next Session opened on November 3. The
Governor had sent down to the House on June 25
previous a minute explaining his reasons for the
course he had taken in the Gardiner case. The Opposition (led by the late Sir John Robertson) did not
fail to attack the Government the moment the House
met, but the Governor's minute on the Gardiner case
did not form one of his grounds of attack. He submitted an amendment on the address, censuring the
Government for not calling Parliament together at an
earlier date, for its conduct in the matter of the Pacific
Mail Service, and for other matters; but his motion
contained no word of censure on the Governor's minute.
On this motion of censure Mr. Robertson was beaten
by 37 to 13, showing with sufficient clearness the feeling of the Assembly on the general policy of the
Government. On November 25 Mr. Combes brought
forward a resolution condemning the Governor's minute,
on which the House divided, with 28 to 28, the motion
being again negatived by the Speaker's casting vote.
Ministers could not regard this decision by the vote of
the Speaker as they regarded the decision of June 11.
The terms of the motion, and the course of action
virtually marked by disapproval, were wholly different,
and assumed more distinctly a political complexion.
We could not hope after this vote to conduct business

in the Assembly with satisfaction, and we therefore advised the Crown to dissolve the House, which in any case was approaching, under the new Triennial Act, the end of its existence.

The general election that followed resulted in the return of a large majority of members who either openly approved, or abstained from expressing disapproval of, the general policy of the Government. The new Parliament met on January 27, 1875, and Mr. Robertson (afterwards Sir John), having learned a lesson from Mr. Combes, abstained from attacking the Government on general grounds, but moved an amendment on the address in the following words :

We would desire, with reference to the important matter which led to the dissolution of the late Parliament, most respectfully to express our regret that your Excellency's responsible Ministers should have advised you to communicate to the Legislative Assembly your minute to the Executive Council, dated June 23 last, with reference to the release of the prisoner Gardiner, because it is indefensible in certain of its allegations, and because, if it is considered to be an answer to the respectful and earnest petitions of the people, it is highly undesirable to convert the records of this House into a means of conveying censure or reproof to our constituents ; and if it refer to the discussions in this Chamber, then it is in spirit and effect a breach of the constitutional privileges of Parliament.

Thus, the Governor's minute, which had been entirely overlooked by Mr. Robertson in the beginning of November, was in January made Mr. Robertson's battleground. The division was taken before midnight on the 28th, and in a House of 62 members the Government was defeated by a majority of four.

The defeated Ministers did not wait for any further expression of the feeling of Parliament, but on the next day our resignations were tendered to the Governor, who, however, declined for several days to accept them. His Excellency very naturally felt aggrieved by the words in the amendment which declared that his minute was 'indefensible in certain of its allegations.' The address as amended was presented by the Speaker, no motion having been made for its presentation by the House. Thus ended my first Administration, which retired on February 8, 1875, having held office within a few days of two years and nine months.

# CHAPTER XIII

IN OPPOSITION—AN UNAPPROPRIATED SURPLUS A PUBLIC EVIL—MY
SECOND ADMINISTRATION—SIR HERCULES ROBINSON AND CON
DITIONAL DISSOLUTIONS—THE TRIAL OF 'NEW BLOOD '—MY WITH-
DRAWAL FROM POLITICAL ACTIVITY—WEAK GOVERNMENTS—UNION
OF THE OPPOSITION—AGAIN 'SENT FOR '—MY THIRD ADMINIS-
TRATION.

My place for the next two years was in Opposition.
I regularly attended the House and took my full share
in the debates. Mr. Forster, the new Treasurer, made
his budget speech on April 1, and estimated his surplus
at the end of the year at 857,305*l*. 12*s*. 8*d*., which
proved to be an under-estimate. Holding the opinion
that large surpluses loosely held in the Treasury may
become the source of pernicious public transactions, I
moved on May 16, the following resolutions, which
were carried without division :

(1)  That the experience of the last three years has established the fact that the revenue derived from all sources is
largely in excess of the necessary expenditure of the Government.

(2)  That the existence of a large cash surplus at the
credit of the Government is unsound in principle and policy,
and ought not to be continued.

(3)  That the existing surplus ought to be expended without unnecessary delay, not less than 150,000*l*. per annum, in

promoting immigration from Great Britain and Ireland, and the balance in carrying out works of public improvement.

(1) That a measure ought to be passed into law for regulating the introduction of immigrants, and that the proposals and plans for all public works to be carried out by the expenditure of the said surplus ought to be submitted for the approval of this House.

The Government sustained repeated defeats during its rather uneasy existence, and on March 6, 1877, I moved :—

That the retention of office by Ministers after having suffered, within nine sitting 'days, four general defeats on motions expressive of condemnation and want of confidence, is subversive of the principles of the Constitution.

This resolution was carried by 31 to 28 votes. When the House next met the Premier announced that Ministers had advised a dissolution which, as no Appropriation Act covered the period necessary for a General Election, Sir Hercules Robinson had granted, on the condition that the requisite Supply should be first obtained. It has always struck me as almost unaccountable that a man of such clear insight as Sir Hercules Robinson did not see that he was inviting an Assembly, flushed with victory over the Government, to refuse Supply. No Assembly would refuse Supply to a Government with the power of dissolution in its hands, for fear of the use that would be made of it as evidence of obstructing an appeal to the electors, from which members would know they could not escape. But to make it an open condition that members should grant Supply for the express purpose of terminating their parliamentary existence, is simply leaving it to them to say whether they will be dissolved or not dissolved. In this instance, the House very soon said 'No'! When the Treasurer moved that the House go into Committee of Supply, Mr. Pidding-ton, the Treasurer of the late Administration, moved as an amendment :—

That whilst this House is anxious to proceed with the public business on the formation of an Administration entitled to the confidence of Parliament, it declines to grant supplies to a defeated Government under circumstances which would in all probability result in two general elections within a short period of time.

Mr. Piddington's amendment was passed by thirty-three to twenty-seven votes. Of course there was no dissolution; and, giving the Governor credit for the highest motives, it seems to me quite clear that it would have been far better if the advice of the retiring Ministers had been unconditionally accepted. The Assembly had become demoralised and distempered, and amidst criminations and recriminations the minds of many well-meaning members had become befogged, and a dissolution was needed to clear the political atmosphere.

I was commissioned to form a new Administration, and the new Ministers entered upon office on March 22. It was the only short-lived Ministry with which I have been connected. It lasted until August 16, or four months and twenty-five days. We had as smooth a time as the toad under the harrow of which we are often told. Leading members of the Opposition would talk for hours on an item of fifty pounds in the Estimates, and insist upon every explanation we offered being more fully explained; and these were the Estimates which our predecessors should have passed long before we accepted office. We did little and had little satisfaction in what we attempted to do. Eventually the management of the Assembly was taken out of our hands by moving and carrying the adjournment against us. Thereupon, I too advised a dissolution, and received from Sir Hercules Robinson the reply that he could only deal with us as he had dealt with our predecessors—accept our advice on the condition that we obtained the necessary Supply. My immediate answer was that I must press His Excellency to accept our resignations. So we made way again for Sir John Robertson.

It was during this short Administration that I received through the Governor from the Secretary of State (Lord Carnarvon), the offer of the dignity of a K.C.M.G. I had previously received the offer of the C.M.G., which I had declined, not that I undervalued the distinction, and I was fully aware that educated Englishmen would accept the C.M.G. who would not consent to be made a Knight Bachelor; but, though I count myself a loyal and dutiful subject of Her Majesty, I honestly had no desire to be decorated. When the new offer was made I consulted friends and one or two members of my own family, and the result was that I accepted the honour so graciously bestowed, with the flattering sense that I had won it honourably. The same may be said of my acceptance of the Grand Cross which was conferred upon me by Her Majesty ten years afterwards. I never took any step which could be construed into seeking any mark of my Sovereign's favour, but I hold that residence in a distant colony in no sense impairs the status of the subject, and that he is entitled equally with his fellows at the seat of Empire to any dignity or elevation which the Sovereign may be pleased to extend to him.

A Ministry formed by Sir John Robertson was sworn on August 17 ; but on September 19, on attempting to suspend the Standing Orders to enable a Consolidated Revenue Bill to pass through all its stages in one day, the Government was defeated by twenty-eight to twenty-seven votes. So again, in little more than a month, advice was tendered for the dissolution of Parliament, and was again met by the Governor with the condition that Supply must be first obtained. The Ministers on this occasion informed His Excellency that they could not accept a dissolution with any condition annexed to it, and tendered their resignations, thirty-four days after their assumption of office. Mr. Alexander Stuart first, and then Mr. S. C. Brown, was asked to form another Ministry, but, both failing, Sir John Robertson was desired to withdraw his resignation, and an unconditional dissolution was granted.

The elections did not prove favourable to Ministers, and on the opening of the new House on November 28, the following amendment to the Address, moved by Mr. J. S. Farnell, was carried by thirty-three to thirty-one votes :—

We feel bound to express our grave doubts as to the satisfactory conduct of public business until your Excellency can secure the advice of members of this House entitled to its confidence.

Resignation of course followed, and I was requested by Sir Hercules Robinson to form a new Ministry. But there was a feeling among many members of the Assembly in favour of 'new blood,' and, failing to obtain the co-operation of gentlemen whom I considered best qualified to conduct the affairs of the country, I returned my commission. A Ministry was then formed by Mr. Farnell, which entered upon its official life on December 18, and continued to hold office without much interference until December 6 following, when it was defeated by forty-one to twenty-two votes on the second reading of a 'Bill to regulate the Alienation, Occupation, and Administration of the Crown Lands.'

Sir John Robertson was now sent for to form a Ministry, and succeeded so far as to submit his list of names for approval, but, for reasons never fully explained, he suddenly abandoned his task; and at the same time resigned his seat in the Legislative Assembly.

During Mr. Farnell's tenure of office the Opposition consisted virtually of two wings, one led by Sir John Robertson, and one whose political sympathies were with me. But in reality I took but little part in the proceedings of Parliament, and devoted myself more closely than at any other period of my public life to my personal affairs. I had been so sobered by the waste of public time, and the disasters that must ever arise from weak and distracted governments, that I was fairly weaned from the political ambition which had stirred me in previous years. It would have been a

happy thing for me if I had continued to ' turn a deaf
ear to the charmer.' But the Opposition held a meeting and united the two sections, electing me in my
absence as their leader. Mr. James Watson (Treasurer
in the next Government) was deputed to inform me of
the result. I attended the meeting (which was waiting
for my answer) with a feeling of reluctance, and after
some discussion accepted the position assigned to me.
When the House met the same day I gave notice of
the following resolution :—

> That an Address be presented to the Governor, respectfully
> informing His Excellency that this House declines to proceed
> with public business while the present Ministers are allowed to
> retain office.

My resolution was carried by 30 to 21 votes. The
Farnell Ministry at once resigned, and I received His
Excellency's commission to form a Government, which
was completed the same day, and continued in office
from December 21, 1878, until January 4, 1883,
and proved to be the longest-lived Ministry of New
South Wales.

This Government did a large amount of work both
in Parliament and in its executive capacity. My first
step, on receiving my commission, was to put myself
in communication with Sir John Robertson, and I took
this step without consultation with anyone. There was
much political agreement between him and me, and
we had been separated chiefly by the acerbity of personal feeling and that disposition to attribute wrong
motives which grows from men not frankly meeting

each other. As his friends in Parliament had joined in nominating me, I felt it would be nothing more than a graceful act to offer him a place in the Administration. As he had retired from the Assembly, I proposed to recommend his appointment to the Upper Chamber, and submitted for his acceptance the position of Vice-President of the Executive Council without ministerial office. He fell in with this arrangement in an equally cordial spirit, and the following names were submitted to his Excellency the Governor :—

| | |
|---|---|
| Sir Henry Parkes . | Colonial Secretary. |
| Sir John Robertson . | Vice-President of the Executive Council ; Representative of Government in the Legislative Council. |
| James Watson . . | Colonial Treasurer. |
| Francis Bathurst Suttor . | Minister of Justice and Public Instruction. |
| William Charles Windeyer | Attorney-General. |
| James Hoskins . | Secretary for Lands. |
| John Lackey . . . | Secretary for Public Works. |
| Saul Samuel . . . | Postmaster-General. |
| Ezekiel Alexander Baker . | Secretary for Mines. |

The Parliamentary achievements of the last four years had been very slender and unsatisfactory. There had been four changes of Ministry and two dissolutions. Perhaps the most serious consequence of frequent political changes is the displacement of experienced and the introduction of inexperienced men. In such commonplace commotions, so distasteful to men of culture and strength, the material for feeble and short-sighted Ministers rises to the surface, and, what is worse, a feeling of disgust restrains able men whose time is of value from offering their services to the country. This directly leads to frivolous discussion and foolish attempts to strain the forms of Parliamentary usage, often for no better object than to enable members to indulge in some petty personal spite. If majorities give the boon of life to a Ministry, it is impossible for the Ministry at such times not to absorb some of the impurities from a source so disturbed or distempered. These remarks are intended to apply to Parliamentary government in old countries; but the evil is of aggravated form in new communities, where nearly all men come to the business of legislation and government from occupations not at all calculated to fit them for the performance of the grave duties to which they have been elected. Of all public afflictions to which a free people may be subjected, a weak Government is by no means the most endurable. It is so occupied day by day in trying to find and retain props as a substitution for inherent stability, and its steps are so beclouded by uncertainty of vision, that it has no clear-sighted strength for the proper work of Government. Precedent tyrannically controls its flabby energies, and when it is brought face to face with difficulty it is barren of all resource. It was after a protracted season of political misfortune that my third Administration began its existence.

END OF THE FIRST VOLUME.

PRINTED BY
SPOTTISWOODE AND CO., NEW-STREET SQUARE
LONDON

OF WORKS IN
# GENERAL LITERATURE
PUBLISHED BY
## LONGMANS, GREEN, & CO.
39 PATERNOSTER ROW, LONDON, E.C.

5 EAST 16TH STREET, NEW YORK, AND 82 HORNBY ROAD, BOMBAY.

## INDEX OF AUTHORS.

# CONTENTS.

## History, Politics, Polity, Political Memoirs, &c.

**Abbott.**—*A HISTORY OF GREECE.*
By EVELYN ABBOTT, M.A., LL.D.
Part I.—From the Earliest Times to the
Ionian Revolt. Crown 8vo., 10s. 6d.
Part II.—500-445 B.C. Crown 8vo., 10s. 6d.

**Acland and Ransome.**—*A HAND-
BOOK IN OUTLINE OF THE POLITICAL HIS-
TORY OF ENGLAND TO 1894.* Chronologically
Arranged. By A. H. DYKE ACLAND, M.P.,
and CYRIL RANSOME, M.A. Crown 8vo., 6s.

*ANNUAL REGISTER (THE).* A
Review of Public Events at Home and
Abroad, for the year 1894. 8vo., 18s.
Volumes of the *ANNUAL REGISTER* for the
years 1863-1893 can still be had. 18s. each.

**Armstrong.**—*ELIZABETH FARNESE;*
The Termagant of Spain. By EDWARD ARM-
STRONG, M.A. 8vo., 16s.

**Arnold** (THOMAS, D.D.), formerly
Head Master of Rugby School.
*INTRODUCTORY LECTURES ON MOD-
ERN HISTORY.* 8vo., 7s. 6d.
*MISCELLANEOUS WORKS.* 8vo., 7s. 6d.

**Bagwell.**—*IRELAND UNDER THE
TUDORS.* By RICHARD BAGWELL, LL.D.
(3 vols.) Vols. I. and II. From the first
invasion of the Northmen to the year 1578.
8vo., 32s. Vol. III. 1578-1603. 8vo. 18s.

**Ball.**—*HISTORICAL REVIEW OF THE
LEGISLATIVE SYSTEMS OPERATIVE IN IRE-
LAND,* from the Invasion of Henry the Second
to the Union (1172-1800). By the Rt. Hon.
J. T. BALL. 8vo., 6s.

**Besant.**—*THE HISTORY OF LONDON.*
By WALTER BESANT. With 74 Illustrations.
Crown 8vo., 1s. 9d   Or bound as a School
Prize Book, 2s. 6d.

**Brassey** (LORD).—PAPERS AND AD-
DRESSES.
*NAVAL AND MARITIME.* 1872-1893.
2 vols. Crown 8vo., 10s.

**Brassey** (LORD).—PAPERS AND AD-
DRESSES—*Continued.*
*MERCANTILE MARINE AND NAVIGA-
TION,* from 1871-1894. Crown 8vo., 5s.
*IMPERIAL FEDERATION AND COLON-
ISATION FROM 1880 to 1894.* Cr. 8vo., 5s.
*POLITICAL AND MISCELLANEOUS,*
1861-1894. Crown 8vo 5s.

**Bright.**—*A HISTORY OF ENGLAND.*
By the Rev. J. FRANCK BRIGHT, D.D.
Period I. *MEDIÆVAL MONARCHY:* A.D.
449 to 1485. Crown 8vo., 4s. 6d.
Period II. *PERSONAL MONARCHY.* 1485 to
to 1688. Crown 8vo., 5s.
Period III. *CONSTITUTIONAL MONARCHY.*
1689 to 1837. Crown 8vo., 7s. 6d.
Period IV. *THE GROWTH OF DEMOCRACY.*
1837 to 1880  Crown 8vo., 6s.

**Buckle.**—*HISTORY OF CIVILISATION
IN ENGLAND AND FRANCE, SPAIN AND
SCOTLAND.* By HENRY THOMAS BUCKLE.
3 vols. Crown 8vo., 24s.

**Burke.**—*A HISTORY OF SPAIN* from
the Earliest Times to the Death of Ferdinand
the Catholic. By ULICK RALPH BURKE,
M.A. 2 vols. 8vo., 32s.

**Chesney.**—*INDIAN POLITY:* a View of
the System of Administration in India. By
General Sir GEORGE CHESNEY, K.C.B.,
With Map showing all the Administrative
Divisions of British India. 8vo., 21s.

**Creighton.**—*HISTORY OF THE PAPACY
DURING THE REFORMATION.* By MANDELL
CREIGHTON, D.D., LL.D., Vols. I. and II.,
1378-1464, 32s. Vols. III. and IV., 1464-
1518, 24s. Vol. V., 1517-1527, 8vo., 15s.

**Curzon.**—*PERSIA AND THE PERSIAN
QUESTION.* By the Hon. GEORGE N.
CURZON, M.P. With 9 Maps, 96 Illustrations, Appendices, and an Index. 2 vols.
8vo., 42s.

# History, Politics, Polity, Political Memoirs, &c.—*continued.*

**De Tocqueville.**—*DEMOCRACY IN AMERICA.* By ALEXIS DE TOCQUEVILLE. 2 vols. Crown 8vo., 16s.

**Dickinson.**—*THE DEVELOPMENT OF PARLIAMENT DURING THE NINETEENTH CENTURY.* By G. LOWES DICKINSON, M.A. 8vo, 7s. 6d.

**Ewald.**—*THE HISTORY OF ISRAEL.* By HEINRICH EWALD. 8 vols., 8vo., Vols. I. and II., 24s. Vols. III. and IV., 21s. Vol. V., 18s. Vol. VI., 16s. Vol. VII., 21s. Vol. VIII., 18s.

**Fitzpatrick.** — *SECRET SERVICE UNDER PITT.* By W. J. FITZPATRICK. 8vo., 7s. 6d.

**Froude** (JAMES A.).

*THE HISTORY OF ENGLAND,* from the Fall of Wolsey to the Defeat of the Spanish Armada.

> *Popular Edition.* 12 vols. Cr. 8vo. 3s. 6d. each.
> *Silver Library Edition.* 12 vols. Cr. 8vo. 3s. 6d. each.

*THE DIVORCE OF CATHERINE OF ARAGON.* Crown 8vo., 6s.

*THE SPANISH STORY OF THE ARMADA,* and other Essays. Silver Library Edition, Cr. 8vo., 3s. 6d.

*THE ENGLISH IN IRELAND IN THE EIGHTEENTH CENTURY.* Cabinet Edition. 3 vols. Cr. 8vo., 18s. Silver Library Ed. 3 vols. Cr. 8vo., 10s.6d.

*ENGLISH SEAMEN IN THE SIXTEENTH CENTURY.* Cr. 8vo., 6s.

*SHORT STUDIES ON GREAT SUBJECTS.* 4 vols. Cr. 8vo., 3s. 6d. each.

*CÆSAR: a Sketch.* Cr. 8vo, 3s. 6d.

**Gardiner** (SAMUEL RAWSON, D.C.L., LL.D.).

*HISTORY OF ENGLAND,* from the Accession of James I. to the Outbreak of the Civil War, 1603-1642. 10 vols. Crown 8vo., 6s. each.

*A HISTORY OF THE GREAT CIVIL WAR,* 1642-1649. 4 vols. Cr. 8vo., 6s. ea.

*A HISTORY OF THE COMMONWEALTH AND THE PROTECTORATE.* 1649-1660. Vol. I. 1649-1651. With 14 Maps. 8vo., 21s.

*THE STUDENT'S HISTORY OF ENGLAND.* With 378 Illust. Cr. 8vo., 12s. Also in Three Volumes, price 4s. each. Vol. I. B.C. 55 —A.D. 1509. 173 Illus. Vol. II. 1509-1689. 96 Illustrations. Vol. III. 1689-1885. 109 Illustrations.

**Greville.**—*A JOURNAL OF THE REIGNS OF KING GEORGE IV., KING WILLIAM IV., AND QUEEN VICTORIA.* By CHARLES C. F. GREVILLE, formerly Clerk of the Council. 8 vols. Crown 8vo., 6s. each.

**Hearn.**—*THE GOVERNMENT OF ENGLAND:* its Structure and its Development. By W. EDWARD HEARN. 8vo., 16s.

**Herbert.**—*THE DEFENCE OF PLEVNA,* 1877. Written by One who took Part in it. By WILLIAM V. HERBERT. With Maps. 8vo., 18s.

**Historic Towns.**—Edited by E. A. FREEMAN, D.C.L., and Rev. WILLIAM HUNT, M.A. With Maps and Plans. Crown 8vo., 3s. 6d. each.

| | |
|---|---|
| Bristol. By Rev. W. Hunt. | Oxford. By Rev. C. W. |
| Carlisle. By Mandell | Boase. |
| Creighton, D.D., Bishop of Peterborough. | Winchester. By G. W. Kitchin, D.D. |
| Cinque Ports. By Montague Burrows. | York. By Rev. James Raine. |
| Colchester. By Rev. E. L. Cutts. | New York. By Theodore Roosevelt. |
| Exeter. By E. A. Freeman. | Boston (U.S.) By Henry Cabot Lodge. |
| London. By Rev. W. J. Loftie. | |

**Joyce.**—*A SHORT HISTORY OF IRELAND,* from the Earliest Times to 1608. By P. W. JOYCE, LL.D. Crown 8vo., 10s. 6d.

**Lang.**—*ST. ANDREWS.* By ANDREW LANG. With 8 Plates and 24 Illustrations in the Text by T. HODGE. 8vo., 15s. net.

**Lecky** (WILLIAM EDWARD HARTPOLE, M.P.).

*HISTORY OF ENGLAND IN THE EIGHTEENTH CENTURY.* Library Edition. 8 vols. 8vo., £7 4s. Cabinet Edition. ENGLAND. 7 vols. Crown 8vo., 6s. each. IRELAND. 5 vols. Crown 8vo., 6s. each.

*HISTORY OF EUROPEAN MORALS FROM AUGUSTUS TO CHARLEMAGNE.* 2 vols. Crown 8vo., 16s.

*HISTORY OF THE RISE AND INFLUENCE OF THE SPIRIT OF RATIONALISM IN EUROPE.* 2 vols. Crown 8vo., 16s.

*THE EMPIRE:* its value and its Growth. An Inaugural Address delivered at the Imperial Institute, November 20, 1893. Cr. 8vo., 1s. 6d.

# History, Politics, Polity, Political Memoirs, &c.—*continued.*

## Macaulay (LORD).

*COMPLETE WORKS.*

Cabinet Edition.  16 vols.  Post 8vo.,
£4 16s.
Library Edition.  8 vols.  8vo., £5 5s.

*HISTORY OF ENGLAND FROM THE*
*ACCESSION OF JAMES THE SECOND.*

Popular Edition.  2 vols.  Cr. 8vo., 5s.
Student's Edition.  2 vols.  Cr. 8vo., 12s.
People's Edition.  4 vols.  Cr. 8vo., 16s.
Cabinet Edition.  8 vols.  Post 8vo., 48s.
Library Edition.  5 vols.  8vo., £4.

*CRITICAL AND HISTORICAL ESSAYS,*
*WITH LAYS OF ANCIENT ROME,* in 1
volume.

Popular Edition.  Crown 8vo., 2s. 6d.
Authorised Edition.  Crown 8vo., 2s. 6d.,
or 3s. 6d., gilt edges.
Silver Library Edition.  Cr. 8vo., 3s. 6d.

*CRITICAL AND HISTORICAL ESSAYS.*

Student's Edition.  1 vol.  Cr. 8vo., 6s.
People's Edition.  2 vols.  Cr. 8vo., 8s.
Trevelyan Edition.  2 vols.  Cr. 8vo., 9s.
Cabinet Edition.  4 vols.  Post 8vo., 24s.
Library Edition.  3 vols.  8vo., 36s.

*ESSAYS* which may be had separately
price 6d. each sewed, 1s. each cloth.

| | |
|---|---|
| Addison and Walpole. | Frederick the Great. |
| Croker's Boswell's Johnson. | Ranke and Gladstone. |
| Hallam's    Constitutional | Milton and Machiavelli. |
| History. | Lord Byron. |
| Warren   Hastings.    3d. | Lord Clive. |
| sewed. 6d. cloth. | Lord Byron, and The |
| The Earl of Chatham (Two | Comic   Dramatists of |
| Essays). | the Restoration. |

*MISCELLANEOUS WRITINGS*

People's Edition.  1 vol.  Cr. 8vo., 4s. 6d.
Library Edition.  2 vols.  8vo., 21s.

*MISCELLANEOUS    WRITINGS    AND*
*SPEECHES.*

Popular Edition.  Crown 8vo., 2s. 6d.
Cabinet Edition.  Including Indian Penal
Code, Lays of Ancient Rome, and Miscel-
laneous Poems.  4 vols.  Post 8vo., 24s.

*SELECTIONS FROM THE WRITINGS OF*
*LORD MACAULAY.* Edited, with Occa-
sional Notes, by the Right Hon. Sir G. O.
Trevelyan, Bart.  Crown 8vo.,6s.

## May.—*THE CONSTITUTIONAL HIS-*
*TORY OF ENGLAND* since the Accession
of George III.  1760-1870.  By Sir THOMAS
ERSKINE MAY, K.C.B. (Lord Farnborough).
vols.  Cr. 8vo., 18s.

## Merivale (THE LATE DEAN).

*HISTORY OF THE ROMANS UNDER*
*THE EMPIRE.*
Cabinet Edition.  8 vols.  Cr. 8vo., 48s.
Silver Library Edition.  8 vols.  Crown
8vo., 3s. 6d. each.

*THE FALL OF THE ROMAN REPUBLIC:*
a Short History of the Last Century of the
Commonwealth.  12mo., 7s. 6d.

## Montague. — *THE    ELEMENTS    OF*
*ENGLISH CONSTITUTIONAL HISTORY.* By
F. C. MONTAGUE, M.A.  Crown 8vo.,
3s. 6d.

## Moore. —*THE AMERICAN CONGRESS :*
a History of National Legislation and
Political Events, 1774-1895.  By JOSEPH
WEST MOORE.  8vo., 15s. net.

## O'Brien.—*IRISH IDEAS.  REPRINTED*
*ADDRESSES.* By WILLIAM O'BRIEN.  Cr.
8vo. 2s. 6d.

## Richman.—*APPENZELL : PURE DE-*
*MOCRACY AND PASTORAL LIFE IN INNER-*
*RHODEN.* A Swiss Study.  By IRVING B.
RICHMAN, Consul-General of the United
States to Switzerland.  With Maps.  Crown
8vo., 5s.

## Seebohm (FREDERIC).

*THE ENGLISH VILLAGE COMMUNITY*
Examined in its Relations to the Manorial
and Tribal Systems, &c.  With 13 Maps
and Plates.  8vo., 16s.

*THE TRIBAL SYSTEM IN WALES:*
Being Part of an Inquiry into the Struc-
ture and Methods of Tribal Society.
With 3 Maps.  8vo., 12s.

## Sharpe.—*LONDON AND THE KINGDOM:*
a History derived mainly from the Archives
at Guildhall in the custody of the Corpora-
tion of the City of London.  By REGINALD
R. SHARPE, D.C.L., Records Clerk in the
Office of the Town Clerk of the City ot
London.  3 vols.  8vo.  10s. 6d. each.

## Sheppard. — *MEMORIALS    OF    ST.*
*JAMES'S PALACE.* By the Rev. EDGAR
SHEPPARD, M.A.,    Sub-Dean of H.M.
Chapels Royal.  With 41 Full-page Plates (8
Photo-Intaglio) and 32 Illustrations in the
Text.  2 vols.  8vo., 36s. net.

## Smith.—*CARTHAGE AND THE CARTH-*
*AGINIANS.* By R. BOSWORTH SMITH, M.A.,
With Maps, Plans, &c.  Cr. 8vo., 3s. 6d.

# History, Politics, Polity, Political Memoirs, &c.—*continued.*

**Stephens.**—*A History of the French Revolution.* By H. Morse Stephens. 3 vols. 8vo. Vols. I. and II. 18s. each.

**Stubbs.**—*History of the University of Dublin,* from its Foundation to the End of the Eighteenth Century. By J. W. Stubbs. 8vo., 12s. 6d.

**Sutherland.**—*The History of Australia and New Zealand,* from 1606 to 1890. By Alexander Sutherland, M.A., and George Sutherland, M.A. Crown 8vo., 2s. 6d.

**Taylor.**—*A Student's Manual of the History of India.* By Colonel Meadows Taylor, C.S.I., &c. Cr. 8vo., 7s. 6d.

**Todd.**—*Parliamentary Government in the British Colonies.* By Alpheus Todd, LL.D. 8vo., 30s. net.

**Wakeman and Hassall.**—*Essays Introductory to the Study of English Constitutional History.* By Resident Members of the University of Oxford. Edited by Henry Offley Wakeman, M.A., and Arthur Hassall, M.A. Crown 8vo., 6s.

**Walpole** (Spencer).

*History of England from the Conclusion of the Great War in 1815 to 1858.* 6 vols. Crown 8vo., 6s. each.

*The Land of Home Rule :* being an Account of the History and Institutions of the Isle of Man. Crown 8vo., 6s.

**Wolff.**—*Odd Bits of History:* being Short Chapters intended to Fill Some Blanks. By Henry W. Wolff. 8vo., 8s. 6d.

**Wood-Martin.**—*Pagan Ireland: an Archæological Sketch.* A Handbook of Irish Pre-Christian Antiquities. By W. G. Wood-Martin, M.R.I.A. With 512 Illustrations. Crown 8vo., 15s.

**Wylie.**—*History of England under Henry IV.* By James Hamilton Wylie, M.A., one of H. M. Inspectors of Schools. 3 vols. Crown 8vo. Vol. I., 1399-1404, 10s. 6d. Vol. II., 15s. Vol. III., 15s. Vol. IV.    [*In the press.*

## Biography, Personal Memoirs, &c.

**Armstrong.**—*The Life and Letters of Edmund J. Armstrong.* Edited by G. F. Armstrong. Fcp. 8vo., 7s. 6d.

**Bacon.**—*The Letters and Life of Francis Bacon, including all his Occasional Works.* Edited by James Spedding. 7 vols. 8vo., £4 4s.

**Bagehot.**—*Biographical Studies.* By Walter Bagehot. Crown 8vo., 3s. 6d.

**Blackwell.**—*Pioneer Work in Opening the Medical Profession to Women:* Autobiographical Sketches. By Dr. Elizabeth Blackwell. Cr. 8vo., 6s.

**Boyd** (A. K. H., D.D., LL.D., Author of 'Recreations of a Country Parson,' &c.).

*Twenty-Five Years of St. Andrews.* 1865-1890. 2 vols. 8vo. Vol. I. 12s. Vol. II. 15s.

*St. Andrews and Elsewhere:* Glimpses of Some Gone and of Things Left. 8vo., 15s.

**Buss.**—*Frances Mary Buss and her Work for Education.* By Annie E. Ridley. With 5 Portraits and 4 Illustrations. Crown 8vo, 7s. 6d.

**Carlyle.**—*Thomas Carlyle :* A History of his Life. By James Anthony Froude.
1795-1835. 2 vols. Crown 8vo., 7s.
1834-1881. 2 vols. Crown 8vo., 7s.

**Erasmus.**—*Life and Letters of Erasmus.* By James Anthony Froude. Crown 8vo., 6s.

**Fox.**—*The Early History of Charles James Fox.* By the Right Hon. Sir G. O. Trevelyan, Bart.
Library Edition. 8vo., 18s.
Cabinet Edition. Crown 8vo., 6s.

**Halford.**—*The Life of Sir Henry Halford, Bart., G.C.H., M.D., F.R.S.,* President of the Royal College of Physicians, Physician to George III., George IV., William IV., and to Her Majesty, Queen Victoria. By William Munk, M.D., F.S.A. 8vo., 12s. 6d.

**Hamilton.**—*Life of Sir William Hamilton.* By R. P. Graves. 3 vols. 15s. each. Addendum. 8vo., 6d. sewed.

**Havelock.**—*Memoirs of Sir Henry Havelock,* K.C.B. By John Clark Marshman. Crown 8vo., 3s. 6d.

**Luther.**—*Life of Luther.* By Julius Köstlin. With Illustrations from Authentic Sources. Translated from the German. Crown 8vo., 7s. 6d.

## Biography, Personal Memoirs, &c.—*continued.*

**Macaulay.**—*THE LIFE AND LETTERS OF LORD MACAULAY.* By the Right Hon. Sir G. O. TREVELYAN, Bart., M.P.
*Popular Edition.* 1 vol. Cr. 8vo., 2s. 6d.
*Student's Edition* 1 vol. Cr. 8vo., 6s.
*Cabinet Edition.* 2 vols. Post 8vo., 12s.
*Library Edition.* 2 vols. 8vo., 36s.

**Marbot.** — *THE MEMOIRS OF THE BARON DE MARBOT.* Translated from the French. Crown 8vo., 7s. 6d.

**Seebohm.** - *THE OXFORD REFORMERS —JOHN COLET, ERASMUS AND THOMAS MORE :* a History of their Fellow-Work. By FREDERIC SEEBOHM. 8vo., 14s.

**Shakespeare.** - *OUTLINES OF THE LIFE OF SHAKESPEARE.* By J. O. HALLI-WELL-PHILLIPPS. With Illustrations and Fac-similes. 2 vols. Royal 8vo., £1 1s.

**Shakespeare's** *TRUE LIFE.* By JAMES WALTER. With 500 Illustrations by GERALD E. MOIRA. Imp. 8vo., 21s.

**Stephen.**—*ESSAYS IN ECCLESIASTI-CAL BIOGRAPHY.* By Sir JAMES STEPHEN. Crown 8vo., 7s. 6d.

**Turgot.**—*THE LIFE AND WRITINGS OF TURGOT,* Comptroller-General of France, 1774-1776. Edited for English Readers by W. WALKER STEPHENS. 8vo., 12s. 6d.

**Verney.** —*MEMOIRS OF THE VERNEY FAMILY.*
Vols. I. & II., *DURING THE CIVIL WAR.* By FRANCES PARTHENOPE VERNEY. With 38 Portraits, Woodcuts and Fac-simile. Royal 8vo., 42s.
Vol. III., *DURING THE COMMONWEALTH.* 1650-1660. By MARGARET M. VERNEY. With 10 Portraits. &c. Royal 8vo., 21s.

**Walford.** — *TWELVE ENGLISH AUTHORESSES.* By L. B. WALFORD. Crown 8vo., 4s. 6d.

**Wellington.**—*LIFE OF THE DUKE OF WELLINGTON.* By the Rev. G. R. GLEIG, M.A. Crown 8vo., 3s. 6d.

**Wolf.**—*THE LIFE OF JOSEPH WOLF, ANIMAL PAINTER.* By A. H. PALMER. With 53 Plates and 14 Illustrations in the Text. 8vo., 21s.

## Travel and Adventure, the Colonies, &c.

**Arnold** (SIR EDWIN, K.C.I.E.).
*SEAS AND LANDS.* With 71 Illustrations. Cr. 8vo., 3s. 6d.
*WANDERING WORDS.* With 45 Illustrations. 8vo., 18s.
*AUSTRALIA AS IT IS,* or Facts and Features, Sketches, and Incidents of Australia and Australian Life with Notices of New Zealand. Crown 8vo., 5s.

**Baker** (SIR S. W.).
*EIGHT YEARS IN CEYLON.* With 6 Illustrations. Crown 8vo., 3s. 6d.
*THE RIFLE AND THE HOUND IN CEYLON.* With 6 Illus. Cr. 8vo., 3s. 6d.

**Bent** (J. THEODORE, F.S.A., F.R.G.S.).
*THE RUINED CITIES OF MASHONA-LAND :* being a Record of Excavation and Exploration in 1891. With Map, 13 Plates, and 104 Illustrations in the Text. Crown 8vo., 3s. 6d.
*THE SACRED CITY OF THE ETHIO-PIANS :* being a Record of Travel and Research in Abyssinia in 1893. With 8 Plates and 65 Illustrations in the Text. 8vo., 18s.

**Bicknell.**—*TRAVEL AND ADVENTURE IN NORTHERN QUEENSLAND.* By ARTHUR C. BICKNELL. With 24 Plates and 22 Illustrations in the Text. 8vo, 15s.

**Brassey** (THE LATE LADY).
*THE LAST VOYAGE TO INDIA AND AUSTRALIA IN THE 'SUNBEAM'.* With Charts and Maps, and 240 Illus. 8vo., 21s.
*A VOYAGE IN THE 'SUNBEAM;' OUR HOME ON THE OCEAN FOR ELEVEN MONTHS.*
*Library Edition.* With 8 Maps and Charts, and 118 Illustrations. 8vo. 21s.
*Cabinet Edition.* With Map and 66 Illustrations. Crown 8vo., 7s. 6d.
*Silver Library Edition.* With 66 Illustrations. Crown 8vo., 3s. 6d.
*Popular Edition.* With 60 Illustrations. 4to., 6d. sewed, 1s. cloth.
*School Edition.* With 37 Illustrations. Fcp., 2s. cloth, or 3s. white parchment.
*SUNSHINE AND STORM IN THE EAST.*
*Library Edition.* With 2 Maps and 141 Illustrations. 8vo., 21s.
*Cabinet Edition.* With 2 Maps and 114 Illustrations. Crown 8vo., 7s. 6d.
*Popular Edition.* With 103 Illustrations. 4to., 6d. sewed, 1s. cloth.
*IN THE TRADES, THE TROPICS, AND THE 'ROARING FORTIES.'*
*Cabinet Edition.* With Map and 220 Illustrations. Crown 8vo., 7s. 6d.
*Popular Edition.* With 183 Illustrations. 4to., 6d. sewed, 1s. cloth.
*THREE VOYAGES IN THE 'SUNBEAM'.* Popular Edition. With 346 Illustrations. 4to., 2s. 6d.

# Travel and Adventure, the Colonies, &c.—*continued.*

**Brassey.**—*VOYAGES AND TRAVELS OF LORD BRASSEY, K.C.B., D.C.L.*, 1862-1894. Arranged and Edited by Captain S. EARDLEY-WILMOT. 2 vols. Cr. 8vo., 10s.

**Froude** (JAMES A.).

*OCEANA: or England and her Colonies.* With 9 Illustrations. Crown 8vo., 2s. boards, 2s. 6d. cloth.

*THE ENGLISH IN THE WEST INDIES:* or, the Bow of Ulysses. With 9 Illustrations. Crown 8vo., 2s. boards, 2s. 6d. cloth.

**Howitt.**—*VISITS TO REMARKABLE PLACES.* Old Halls, Battle-Fields, Scenes, illustrative of Striking Passages in English History and Poetry. By WILLIAM HOWITT. With 80 Illustrations. Crown 8vo., 3s. 6d.

**Knight** (E. F.).

*THE CRUISE OF THE 'ALERTE':* the Narrative of a Search for Treasure on the Desert Island of Trinidad. With 2 Maps and 23 Illustrations. Crown 8vo., 3s. 6d.

*WHERE THREE EMPIRES MEET:* a Narrative of Recent Travel in Kashmir, Western Tibet, Baltistan, Ladak, Gilgit, and the adjoining Countries. With a Map and 54 Illustrations. Cr. 8vo., 3s. 6d.

**Lees and Clutterbuck.** -B.C. 1887: *A RAMBLE IN BRITISH COLUMBIA.* By J. A. LEES and W. J. CLUTTERBUCK. With Map and 75 Illustrations. Crown 8vo., 3s. 6d.

**Murdoch.**—*FROM EDINBURGH TO THE ANTARCTIC:* an Artist's Notes and Sketches during the Dundee Antarctic Expedition of 1892-93. By W. G. BURN-MURDOCH. With 2 Maps and numerous Illustrations. 8vo., 18s.

**Nansen** (FRIDTJOF).

*THE FIRST CROSSING OF GREENLAND.* With numerous Illustrations and a Map. Crown 8vo., 3s. 6d.

*ESKIMO LIFE.* With 31 Illustrations. 8vo., 16s.

**Peary.** — *MY ARCTIC JOURNAL:* a year among Ice-Fields and Eskimos. By JOSEPHINE DIEBITSCH-PEARY. With 19 Plates, 3 Sketch Maps, and 44 Illustrations in the Text. 8vo., 12s.

**Quillinan.**—*JOURNAL OF A FEW MONTHS' RESIDENCE IN PORTUGAL,* and Glimpses of the South of Spain. By Mrs. QUILLINAN (Dora Wordsworth). New Edition. Edited, with Memoir, by EDMUND LEE, Author of " Dorothy Wordsworth," &c. Crown 8vo, 6s.

**Smith.**—*CLIMBING IN THE BRITISH ISLES.* By W. P. HASKETT SMITH. With Illustrations by ELLIS CARR, and Numerous Plans.

Part I. *ENGLAND.* 16mo., 3s. 6d.

Part II. *WALES AND IRELAND.* 16mo., 3s. 6d.

Part III. *SCOTLAND.* [*In preparation.*

**Stephen.** — *THE PLAY-GROUND OF EUROPE.* By LESLIE STEPHEN. New Edition, with Additions and 4 Illustrations. Crown 8vo., 6s. net.

*THREE IN NORWAY.* By Two of Them. With a Map and 59 Illustrations. Crown 8vo., 2s. boards, 2s. 6d. cloth.

**Whishaw** (FRED. J.).

*OUT OF DOORS IN TSARLAND:* a Record of the Seeings and Doings of a Wanderer in Russia. Crown 8vo, 7s. 6d.

*THE ROMANCE OF THE WOODS:* Reprinted Articles and Sketches. Crown 8vo., 6s.

# Veterinary Medicine, &c.

**Steel** (JOHN HENRY).

*A TREATISE ON THE DISEASES OF THE DOG.* With 88 Illustrations. 8vo., 10s. 6d.

*A TREATISE ON THE DISEASES OF THE OX.* With 119 Illustrations. 8vo., 15s.

*A TREATISE ON THE DISEASES OF THE SHEEP.* With 100 Illustrations. 8vo., 12s.

*OUTLINES OF EQUINE ANATOMY:* a Manual for the use of Veterinary Students in the Dissecting Room. Cr. 8vo., 7s. 6d.

**Fitzwygram.** - *HORSES AND STABLES.* By Major-General Sir F. FITZWYGRAM, Bart. With 56 pages of Illustrations. 8vo., 2s. 6d. net.

**"Stonehenge."** — *THE DOG IN HEALTH AND DISEASE.* By "STONEHENGE". With 78 Wood Engravings. 8vo., 7s. 6d.

**Youatt** (WILLIAM).

*THE HORSE.* Revised and Enlarged by W. WATSON, M.R.C.V.S. With 5 Wood Engravings. 8vo., 7s. 6d.

*THE DOG.* Revised and Enlarged. With 33 Wood Engravings. 8vo., 6s.

# Sport and Pastime.

## THE BADMINTON LIBRARY.

Edited by the DUKE of BEAUFORT, K.G., assisted by ALFRED E. T. WATSON.

Crown 8vo., price 10s. 6d. each Volume.

*ARCHERY.* By C. J. LONGMAN, Col. H. WALROND, Miss LEGH and Viscount DILLON. With 195 Illustrations.

*ATHLETICS AND FOOTBALL.* By MONTAGUE SHEARMAN. With 51 Illus.

*BIG GAME SHOOTING.* By C. PHILLIPPS-WOLLEY, Sir SAMUEL W. BAKER, W. C. OSWELL, F. C. SELOUS, &c.
Vol. I. Africa and America. With 77 Illustrations.
Vol. II. Europe, Asia, and the Arctic Regions. With 73 Illustrations.

*BILLIARDS.* By Major W. BROAD-FOOT, R.E. With Illustrations, and Diagrams. [*In the Press.*

*BOATING.* By W. B. WOODGATE. With 49 Illustrations and 4 Maps.

*COURSING AND FALCONRY.* By HARDING COX and the Hon. GERALD LASCELLES. With 76 Illustrations.

*CRICKET.* By A. G. STEEL, the Hon. R. H. LYTTELTON, ANDREW LANG, R. A. H. MITCHELL, W. G. GRACE, and F. GALE. With 64 Illustrations.

*CYCLING.* By the EARL OF ALBEMARLE and G. LACY HILLIER. With 63 Illustrations.

*DANCING.* By Mrs. LILLY GROVE, F.R.G.S., &c. With 131 Illustrations.

*DRIVING.* By the DUKE OF BEAUFORT. With 65 Illustrations.

*FENCING, BOXING, AND WRESTLING.* By WALTER H. POLLOCK, F. C. GROVE, C. PREVOST, E. B. MITCHELL, and WALTER ARMSTRONG. With 42 Illustrations.

*FISHING.* By H. CHOLMONDELEY-PENNELL, the MARQUIS OF EXETER, HENRY R. FRANCIS, G. CHRISTOPHER DAVIES, R. B. MARSTON, &c.
Vol. I. Salmon, Trout, and Grayling. With 158 Illustrations.
Vol. II. Pike and other Coarse Fish. With 133 Illustrations.

*GOLF.* By HORACE G. HUTCHINSON, the Rt. Hon. A. J. BALFOUR, M.P., Sir W. G. SIMPSON, Bart., LORD WELLWOOD, H. S. C. EVERARD, ANDREW LANG, and other Writers. With 89 Illustrations.

*HUNTING.* By the DUKE OF BEAUFORT, K.G., MOWBRAY MORRIS, the EARL OF SUFFOLK AND BERKSHIRE, Rev. E. W. L. DAVIES, DIGBY COLLINS, GEORGE H. LONGMAN, &c. With 53 Illustrations.

*MOUNTAINEERING.* By C. T. DENT, Sir F. POLLOCK, Bart., W. M. CONWAY, DOUGLAS FRESHFIELD, C. E. MATHEWS, &c. With 108 Illustrations.

*RACING AND STEEPLE-CHASING.* By the EARL OF SUFFOLK AND BERKSHIRE, W. G. CRAVEN, ARTHUR COVENTRY, and A. E. T. WATSON. With 58 Illustrations.

*RIDING AND POLO.* By Captain ROBERT WEIR, J. MORAY BROWN, the DUKE OF BEAUFORT, K.G., &c. With 59 Illustrations.

*SEA FISHING.* By JOHN BICKERDYKE, W. SENIOR, A. C. HARMSWORTH, and Sir H. W. GORE-BOOTH, Bart. With 197 Illustrations.

*SHOOTING.* By LORD WALSINGHAM, Sir RALPH PAYNE-GALLWEY, Bart., LORD LOVAT, LORD C. LENNOX KERR, the Hon. G. LASCELLES, and A. J. STUART-WORTLEY.
Vol. I. Field and Covert. With 105 Illustrations.
Vol. II. Moor and Marsh. With 65 Illustrations.

*SKATING, CURLING, TOBOGGANING, ICE-SAILING, AND BANDY.* By J. M. HEATHCOTE, C. G. TEBBUTT, T. MAXWELL WITHAM, the Rev. JOHN KERR. With 284 Illustrations.

*SWIMMING.* By ARCHIBALD SINCLAIR and WILLIAM HENRY. With 119 Illustrations.

*TENNIS, LAWN TENNIS, RACKETS AND FIVES.* By J. M. and C. G. HEATHCOTE, E. O. PLEYDELL-BOUVERIE, A. C. AINGER, &c. With 79 Illustrations.

*YACHTING.*
Vol. I. Cruising, Construction, Racing Rules. Fitting-Out, &c. By Sir EDWARD SULLIVAN, Bart., LORD BRASSEY, K.C.B., C. E. SETH-SMITH, C.B., &c. With 114 Illustrations.
Vol. II. Yacht Clubs, Yachting in America and the Colonies, Yacht Racing, &c. By R. T. PRITCHETT, the EARL OF ONSLOW, G.C.M.G., &c. With 195 Illustrations.

## Sport and Pastime—*continued.*
### FUR AND FEATHER SERIES.
Edited by A. E. T. WATSON.
Crown 8vo., price 5s. each Volume.

*THE PARTRIDGE.* Natural History by the Rev. H. A. MACPHERSON; Shooting, by A. J. STUART-WORTLEY; Cookery, by GEORGE SAINTSBURY. With 11 Illustrations and various Diagrams in the Text.

*THE GROUSE.* Natural History by the Rev. H. A. MACPHERSON; Shooting, by A. J. STUART-WORTLEY; Cookery, by GEORGE SAINTSBURY. With 13 Illustrations and various Diagrams. in the Text.

*THE HARE AND THE RABBIT.* By the Hon. GERALD LASCELLES, &c.
[*In preparation.*

*THE PHEASANT.* Natural History by the Rev. H. A. MACPHERSON; Shooting, by A. J. STUART-WORTLEY; Cookery, by ALEXANDER INNES SHAND. With 10 Illustrations and various Diagrams.

*WILD FOWL.* By the Hon. JOHN SCOTT-MONTAGU, M.P., &c.
[*In preparation.*

*THE RED DEER.* By CAMERON OF LOCHIEL, LORD EBRINGTON, &c.
[*In preparation.*

**Bickerdyke.**—*DAYS OF MY LIFE ON WATERS FRESH AND SALT*; and other Papers. By JOHN BICKERDYKE. With Photo-Etched Frontispiece and 8 Full-page Illustrations. Crown 8vo., 6s.

**Campbell-Walker.**—*THE CORRECT CARD :* or, How to Play at Whist; a Whist Catechism. By Major A. CAMPBELL-WALKER, F.R.G.S. Fcp. 8vo., 2s. 6d.

*DEAD SHOT (THE):* or, Sportsman's Complete Guide. Being a Treatise on the Use of the Gun, with Rudimentary and Finishing Lessons on the Art of Shooting Game of all kinds. By MARKSMAN. Crown 8vo., 10s. 6d.

**Ellis.**—*CHESS SPARKS :* or, Short and Bright Games of Chess. Collected and Arranged by J. H. ELLIS, M.A. 8vo., 4s. 6d.

**Falkener.**—*GAMES, ANCIENT AND ORIENTAL, AND HOW TO PLAY THEM.* By EDWARD FALKENER. With numerous Photographs, Diagrams, &c. 8vo., 21s.

**Ford.**—*THE THEORY AND PRACTICE OF ARCHERY.* By HORACE FORD. New Edition, thoroughly Revised and Re-written by W. BUTT, M.A. With a Preface by C. J. LONGMAN, M.A. 8vo., 14s.

**Francis.**—*A BOOK ON ANGLING :* or, Treatise on the Art of Fishing in every Branch ; including full Illustrated List of Salmon Flies. By FRANCIS FRANCIS. With Portrait and Coloured Plates. Crown 8vo., 15s.

**Gibson.**—*TOBOGGANING ON CROOKED RUNS.* By the Hon. HARRY GIBSON. With Contributions by F. DE B. STRICKLAND and 'LADY-TOBOGANNER'. With 40 Illustrations. Crown 8vo., 6s.

**Hawker.**—*THE DIARY OF COLONEL PETER HAWKER,* Author of ' Instructions to Young Sportsmen.' 2 vols. 8vo., 32s.

**Lang.**—*ANGLING SKETCHES.* By ANDREW LANG. With 20 Illustrations. Cr. 8vo., 3s. 6d.

**Longman.**—*CHESS OPENINGS.* By FREDERICK W. LONGMAN. Fcp. 8vo., 2s. 6d.

**Maskelyne.**—*SHARPS AND FLATS :* a Complete Revelation of the Secrets of Cheating at Games of Chance and Skill. By JOHN NEVIL MASKELYNE, of the Egyptian Hall. With 62 Illustrations. Crown 8vo., 6s.

**Payne-Gallwey** (SIR RALPH, Bart.).
*LETTERS TO YOUNG SHOOTERS* (First Series). On the Choice and use of a Gun. With 41 Illustrations. Crown 8vo., 7s. 6d.
*LETTERS TO YOUNG SHOOTERS* (Second Series). On the Production, Preservation, and Killing of Game. With Directions in Shooting Wood-Pigeons and Breaking-in Retrievers. With Portrait and 103 Illustrations. Crown 8vo., 12s. 6d.

**Pole** (W., F.R.S.).
*THE THEORY OF THE MODERN SCIENTIFIC GAME OF WHIST.* Fcp. 8vo., 2s. 6d.
*THE EVOLUTION OF WHIST:* a Study of the Progressive Changes which the Game has undergone. Cr. 8vo., 6s.

**Proctor** (RICHARD A.).
*HOW TO PLAY WHIST: WITH THE LAWS AND ETIQUETTE OF WHIST.* Cr 8vo., 3s. 6d.
*HOME WHIST:* An Easy Guide to Correct Play. 16mo., 1s.

**Ronalds.**—*THE FLY-FISHER'S ENTOMOLOGY.* By ALFRED RONALDS. With 20 coloured Plates. 8vo., 14s.

**Wilcocks.**—*THE SEA FISHERMAN:* Comprising the Chief Methods of Hook and Line Fishing in the British and other Seas and Remarks on Nets, Boats, and Boating By J. C. WILCOCKS. Illustrated. Cr. 8vo., 6s

# Mental, Moral, and Political Philosophy.

### LOGIC, RHETORIC, PSYCHOLOGY, ETC.

**Abbott.**—*THE ELEMENTS OF LOGIC.* By T. K. ABBOTT, B.D. 12mo., 3s.

**Aristotle.**

*THE POLITICS:* G. Bekker's Greek Text of Books I., III., IV. (VII.), with an English Translation by W. E. BOLLAND, M.A.; and short Introductory Essays by A. LANG, M.A. Crown 8vo., 7s. 6d.

*THE POLITICS:* Introductory Essays. By ANDREW LANG (from Bolland and Lang's ' Politics '). Crown 8vo , 2s. 6d.

*THE ETHICS:* Greek Text, Illustrated with Essay and Notes. By Sir ALEXANDER GRANT, Bart. 2 vols. 8vo., 32s.

*THE NICOMACHEAN ETHICS:* Newly Translated into English. By ROBERT WILLIAMS. Crown 8vo., 7s. 6d.

*AN INTRODUCTION TO ARISTOTLE'S ETHICS.* Books I.-IV. (Book X. c. vi.-ix. in an Appendix). With a continuous Analysis and Notes. By the Rev. EDW. MOORE, D.D., Cr. 8vo. 10s. 6d.

**Bacon** (FRANCIS).

*COMPLETE WORKS.* Edited by R. L. ELLIS, JAMES SPEDDING and D. D. HEATH. 7 vols. 8vo., £3 13s. 6d.

*LETTERS AND LIFE,* including all his occasional Works. Edited by JAMES SPEDDING. 7 vols. 8vo., £4 4s.

*THE ESSAYS:* with Annotations. By RICHARD WHATELY, D.D. 8vo., 10s. 6d.

*THE ESSAYS.* Edited, with Notes, by F. STORR and C. H. GIBSON. Crown 8vo, 3s. 6d.

*THE ESSAYS:* with Introduction, Notes, and Index. By E. A. ABBOTT, D.D. 2 Vols. Fcp. 8vo., 6s. The Text and Index only, without Introduction and Notes, in One Volume. Fcp. 8vo., 2s. 6d.

**Bain** (ALEXANDER, LL.D.).

*MENTAL SCIENCE.* Cr. 8vo., 6s. 6d.

*MORAL SCIENCE.* Cr. 8vo., 4s. 6d.

*The two works as above can be had in one volume, price 10s. 6d.*

*SENSES AND THE INTELLECT.* 8vo., 15s.

*EMOTIONS AND THE WILL.* 8vo., 15s.

*LOGIC, DEDUCTIVE AND INDUCTIVE.* Part I. 4s. Part II. 6s. 6d.

*PRACTICAL ESSAYS.* Cr. 8vo., 3s.

**Bray** (CHARLES).

*THE PHILOSOPHY OF NECESSITY:* or, Law in Mind as in Matter. Cr. 8vo,, 5s.

*THE EDUCATION OF THE FEELINGS:* a Moral System for Schools. Cr. 8vo., 2s. 6d.

**Bray.**—*ELEMENTS OF MORALITY,* in Easy Lessons for Home and School Teaching. By Mrs. CHARLES BRAY. Crown 8vo., 1s. 6d.

**Davidson.**—*THE LOGIC OF DEFINITION,* Explained and Applied. By WILLIAM L. DAVIDSON, M.A. Crown 8vo., 6s.

**Green** (THOMAS HILL).—*THE WORKS* OF. Edited by R. L. NETTLESHIP.

Vols. I. and II. Philosophical Works. 8vo., 16s. each.

Vol. III. Miscellanies. With Index to the three Volumes, and Memoir. 8vo., 21s.

*LECTURES ON THE PRINCIPLES OF POLITICAL OBLIGATION.* With Preface by BERNARD BOSANQUET. 8vo., 5s.

**Hodgson** (SHADWORTH H.).

*TIME AND SPACE:* A Metaphysical Essay. 8vo., 16s.

*THE THEORY OF PRACTICE:* an Ethical Inquiry. 2 vols. 8vo., 24s.

*THE PHILOSOPHY OF REFLECTION.* 2 vols. 8vo., 21s.

**Hume.**—*THE PHILOSOPHICAL WORKS* OF DAVID HUME. Edited by T. H. GREEN and T. H. GROSE. 4 vols. 8vo., 56s. Or separately, Essays. 2 vols. 28s. Treatise of Human Nature. 2 vols. 28s.

**Justinian.**—*THE INSTITUTES OF JUSTINIAN:* Latin Text, chiefly that of Huschke, with English Introduction, Translation, Notes, and Summary. By THOMAS C. SANDARS, M.A. 8vo., 18s.

**Kant** (IMMANUEL).

*CRITIQUE OF PRACTICAL REASON, AND OTHER WORKS ON THE THEORY OF ETHICS.* Translated by T. K. ABBOTT, B.D. With Memoir. 8vo., 12s. 6d.

*FUNDAMENTAL PRINCIPLES OF THE METAPHYSIC OF ETHICS.* Translated by T. K. ABBOTT, B.D. (Extracted from ' Kant's Critique of Practical Reason and other Works on the Theory of Ethics.') Crown 8vo, 3s.

*INTRODUCTION TO LOGIC, AND HIS ESSAY ON THE MISTAKEN SUBTILTY OF THE FOUR FIGURES.* Translated by T. K. ABBOTT. 8vo., 6s.

**Killick.**—*HANDBOOK TO MILL'S SYSTEM OF LOGIC.* By Rev. A. H. KILLICK, M.A. Crown 8vo., 3s. 6d.

# Mental, Moral and Political Philosophy—*continued.*

**Ladd** (GEORGE TRUMBULL).

*PHILOSOPHY OF MIND :* An Essay on the Metaphysics of Psychology. 8vo., 16s.

*ELEMENTS OF PHYSIOLOGICAL PSYCHOLOGY.* 8vo., 21s.

*OUTLINES OF PHYSIOLOGICAL PSYCHOLOGY.* A Text-book of Mental Science for Academies and Colleges. 8vo., 12s.

*PSYCHOLOGY, DESCRIPTIVE AND EXPLANATORY :* a Treatise of the Phenomena, Laws, and Development of Human Mental Life. 8vo., 21s.

*PRIMER OF PSYCHOLOGY.* Cr. 8vo., 5s. 6d.

**Lewes.**—*THE HISTORY OF PHILOSOPHY,* from Thales to Comte. By GEORGE HENRY LEWES. 2 vols. 8vo., 32s.

**Max Müller** (F.).

*THE SCIENCE OF THOUGHT.* 8vo., 21s.

*THREE INTRODUCTORY LECTURES ON* THE SCIENCE OF THOUGHT. 8vo., 2s. 6d.

**Mill.**—*ANALYSIS OF THE PHENOMENA* OF THE HUMAN MIND. By JAMES MILL. 2 vols. 8vo., 28s.

**Mill** (JOHN STUART).

*A SYSTEM OF LOGIC.* Cr. 8vo., 3s. 6d.

*ON LIBERTY.* Crown 8vo., 1s. 4d.

*ON REPRESENTATIVE GOVERNMENT.* Crown 8vo., 2s.

*UTILITARIANISM.* 8vo., 2s. 6d.

*EXAMINATION OF SIR WILLIAM HAMILTON'S PHILOSOPHY.* 8vo., 16s.

*NATURE, THE UTILITY OF RELIGION, AND THEISM.* Three Essays. 8vo., 5s.

**Romanes.**—*MIND AND MOTION AND MONISM.* By the late GEORGE JOHN ROMANES, LL.D., F.R.S. Cr. 8vo., 4s. 6d.

**Stock.**—*DEDUCTIVE LOGIC.* By ST. GEORGE STOCK. Fcp. 8vo., 3s. 6d.

**Sully** (JAMES).

*THE HUMAN MIND :* a Text-book of Psychology. 2 vols. 8vo., 21s.

*OUTLINES OF PSYCHOLOGY.* 8vo., 9s.

*THE TEACHER'S HANDBOOK OF PSYCHOLOGY.* Crown 8vo., 5s.

*STUDIES OF CHILDHOOD.* 8vo, 12s. 6d.

**Swinburne.**—*PICTURE LOGIC :* an Attempt to Popularise the Science of Reasoning. By ALFRED JAMES SWINBURNE, M.A. With 23 Woodcuts. Crown 8vo., 5s.

**Thomson.**—*OUTLINES OF THE NECESSARY LAWS OF THOUGHT :* a Treatise on Pure and Applied Logic. By WILLIAM THOMSON, D.D., formerly Lord Archbishop of York. Crown 8vo., 6s.

**Whately** (ARCHBISHOP).

*BACON'S ESSAYS.* With Annotations. 8vo., 10s. 6d.

*ELEMENTS OF LOGIC.* Cr. 8vo., 4s. 6d.

*ELEMENTS OF RHETORIC.* Cr. 8vo., 4s. 6d.

*LESSONS ON REASONING.* Fcp. 8vo., 1s. 6d.

**Zeller** (Dr. EDWARD, Professor in the University of Berlin).

*THE STOICS, EPICUREANS, AND SCEPTICS.* Translated by the Rev. O. J. REICHEL, M.A. Crown 8vo., 15s.

*OUTLINES OF THE HISTORY OF GREEK PHILOSOPHY.* Translated by SARAH F. ALLEYNE and EVELYN ABBOTT. Crown 8vo., 10s. 6d.

*PLATO AND THE OLDER ACADEMY.* Translated by SARAH F. ALLEYNE and ALFRED GOODWIN, B.A. Crown 8vo. 18s.

*SOCRATES AND THE SOCRATIC SCHOOLS.* Translated by the Rev. O. J. REICHEL, M.A. Crown 8vo., 10s. 6d

---

## MANUALS OF CATHOLIC PHILOSOPHY.

*(Stonyhurst Series).*

*A MANUAL OF POLITICAL ECONOMY.* By C. S. DEVAS, M.A. Crown 8vo., 6s. 6d.

*FIRST PRINCIPLES OF KNOWLEDGE.* By JOHN RICKABY, S.J. Crown 8vo., 5s.

*GENERAL METAPHYSICS.* By JOHN RICKABY, S.J. Crown 8vo., 5s.

*LOGIC.* By RICHARD F. CLARKE, S.J. Crown 8vo., 5s.

*MORAL PHILOSOPHY (ETHICS AND NATURAL LAW).* By JOSEPH RICKABY, S.J. Crown 8vo., 5s.

*NATURAL THEOLOGY.* By BERNARD BOEDDER, S.J. Crown 8vo., 6s. 6d.

*PSYCHOLOGY.* By MICHAEL MAHER, S.J. Crown 8vo., 6s. 6d.

# History and Science of Language, &c.

**Davidson.**—*LEADING AND IMPORTANT ENGLISH WORDS:* Explained and Exemplified. By WILLIAM L. DAVIDSON, M.A. Fcp. 8vo., 3s. 6d.

**Farrar.**—*LANGUAGE AND LANGUAGES:* By F. W. FARRAR, D.D., F.R.S. Crown 8vo., 6s.

**Graham.**—*ENGLISH SYNONYMS,* Classified and Explained : with Practical Exercises. By G. F. GRAHAM. Fcp. 8vo., 6s.

**Max Muller (F.).**

*THE SCIENCE OF LANGUAGE.*—Founded on Lectures delivered at the Royal Institution in 1861 and 1863. 2 vols. Crown 8vo., 21s.

*BIOGRAPHIES OF WORDS, AND THE HOME OF THE ARYAS.* Crown 8vo., 7s. 6d.

**Max Müller (F.)**—*continued.*

*THREE LECTURES ON THE SCIENCE OF LANGUAGE, AND ITS PLACE IN GENERAL EDUCATION,* delivered at Oxford, 1889. Crown 8vo., 3s.

**Roget.**—*THESAURUS OF ENGLISH WORDS AND PHRASES.* Classified and Arranged so as to Facilitate the Expression of Ideas and assist in Literary Composition. By PETER MARK ROGET, M.D., F.R.S. Recomposed throughout, enlarged and improved, partly from the Author's Notes, and with a full Index, by the Author's Son, JOHN LEWIS ROGET. Crown 8vo, 10s. 6d.

**Whately.**—*ENGLISH SYNONYMS.* By E. JANE WHATELY. Fcp. 8vo., 3s.

# Political Economy and Economics.

**Ashley.**—*ENGLISH ECONOMIC HISTORY AND THEORY.* By W. J. ASHLEY, M.A. Crown 8vo., Part I., 5s. Part II. 10s. 6d.

**Bagehot.**—*ECONOMIC STUDIES.* By WALTER BAGEHOT. Crown 8vo., 3s. 6d.

**Barnett.**—*PRACTICABLE SOCIALISM.* Essays on Social Reform. By the Rev. S. A. and Mrs. BARNETT. Crown 8vo., 6s.

**Brassey.**—*PAPERS AND ADDRESSES ON WORK AND WAGES.* By Lord BRASSEY. Edited by J. POTTER, and with Introduction by GEORGE HOWELL, M.P. Crown 8vo., 5s.

**Devas.**—*A MANUAL OF POLITICAL ECONOMY.* By C. S. DEVAS, M.A. Cr. 8vo., 6s. 6d. (*Manuals of Catholic Philosophy.*)

**Dowell.**—*A HISTORY OF TAXATION AND TAXES IN ENGLAND,* from the Earliest Times to the Year 1885. By STEPHEN DOWELL, (4 vols. 8vo.) Vols. I. and II. The History of Taxation, 21s. Vols. III. and IV. The History of Taxes, 21s.

**Macleod** (HENRY DUNNING).

*BIMETALISM.* 8vo., 5s. net.

*THE ELEMENTS OF BANKING.* Cr. 8vo., 3s. 6d.

*THE THEORY AND PRACTICE OF BANKING.* Vol. I. 8vo., 12s. Vol. II. 14s.

**Macleod** (HENRY DUNNING)—*continued.*

*THE THEORY OF CREDIT.* 8vo. Vol. I., 10s. net. Vol. II., Part I., 10s. net. Vol. II., Part II., 10s. 6d.

*A DIGEST OF THE LAW OF BILLS OF EXCHANGE, BANK-NOTES,* &c.                                 [*In the press.*

**Mill.**—*POLITICAL ECONOMY.* By JOHN STUART MILL.

*Popular Edition.* Crown 8vo., 3s. 6d.

*Library Edition.* 2 vols. 8vo., 30s.

**Symes.**—*POLITICAL ECONOMY:* a Short Text-book of Political Economy. With Problems for Solution, and Hints for Supplementary Reading. By Professor J. E. SYMES, M.A., of University College, Nottingham. Crown 8vo., 2s. 6d.

**Toynbee.**—*LECTURES ON THE INDUSTRIAL REVOLUTION OF THE 18TH CENTURY IN ENGLAND:* Popular Addresses, Notes and other Fragments. By ARNOLD TOYNBEE. With a Memoir of the Author by BENJAMIN JOWETT, D.D. 8vo., 10s. 6d.

**Webb.**—*THE HISTORY OF TRADE UNIONISM.* By SIDNEY and BEATRICE WEBB. With Map and full Bibliography of the Subject. 8vo., 18s.

# Evolution, Anthropology, &c.

**Babington.** — *FALLACIES OF RACE THEORIES AS APPLIED TO NATIONAL CHARACTERISTICS.* Essays by WILLIAM DALTON BABINGTON, M.A. Crown 8vo., 6s.

**Clodd** (EDWARD).

*THE STORY OF CREATION:* a Plain Account of Evolution. With 77 Illustrations. Crown 8vo., 3s. 6d.

*A PRIMER OF EVOLUTION:* being a Popular Abridged Edition of 'The Story of Creation'. With Illustrations. Fcp. 8vo., 1s. 6d.

**Lang.** — *CUSTOM AND MYTH:* Studies of Early Usage and Belief. By ANDREW LANG. With 15 Illustrations. Crown 8vo., 3s. 6d.

**Lubbock.** — *THE ORIGIN OF CIVILISATION,* and the Primitive Condition of Man. By Sir J. LUBBOCK, Bart., M.P. With 5 Plates and 20 Illustrations in the Text. 8vo., 18s.

**Romanes** (GEORGE JOHN, LL.D., F.R.S.).

*DARWIN, AND AFTER DARWIN:* an Exposition of the Darwinian Theory, and a Discussion on Post-Darwinian Questions. Part I. THE DARWINIAN THEORY. With Portrait of Darwin and 125 Illustrations. Crown 8vo., 10s. 6d.

Part II. POST-DARWINIAN QUESTIONS: Heredity and Utility. With Portrait of the Author and 5 Illus. Cr. 8vo., 10s. 6d.

*AN EXAMINATION OF WEISMANNISM.* Crown 8vo., 6s.

---

# Classical Literature, Translations, &c.

**Abbott.** — *HELLENICA.* A Collection of Essays on Greek Poetry, Philosophy, History, and Religion. Edited by EVELYN ABBOTT, M.A., LL.D. 8vo., 16s.

**Æschylus.** — *EUMENIDES OF ÆSCHYLUS.* With Metrical English Translation. By J. F. DAVIES. 8vo., 7s.

**Aristophanes.** — *THE ACHARNIANS OF ARISTOPHANES,* translated into English Verse. By R. Y. TYRRELL. Crown 8vo., 1s.

**Becker** (PROFESSOR).

*GALLUS:* or, Roman Scenes in the Time of Augustus. Illustrated. Post 8vo., 3s. 6d.

*CHARICLES:* or, Illustrations of the Private Life of the Ancient Greeks. Illustrated. Post 8vo., 3s. 6d.

**Cicero.** — *CICERO'S CORRESPONDENCE.* By R. Y. TYRRELL. Vols. I., II., III., 8vo., each 12s. Vol. IV., 15s.

**Farnell.** — *GREEK LYRIC POETRY:* a Complete Collection of the Surviving Passages from the Greek Song-Writing. Arranged with Prefatory Articles, Introductory Matter and Commentary. By GEORGE S. FARNELL, M.A. With 5 Plates. 8vo., 16s.

**Lang.** — *HOMER AND THE EPIC.* By ANDREW LANG. Crown 8vo., 9s. net.

**Mackail.** — *SELECT EPIGRAMS FROM THE GREEK ANTHOLOGY.* By J. W. MACKAIL, Fellow of Balliol College, Oxford. Edited with a Revised Text, Introduction, Translation, and Notes. 8vo., 16s.

**Rich.** — *A DICTIONARY OF ROMAN AND GREEK ANTIQUITIES.* By A. RICH, B.A. With 2000 Woodcuts. Crown 8vo., 7s. 6d.

**Sophocles.** — Translated into English Verse. By ROBERT WHITELAW, M.A., Assistant Master in Rugby School; late Fellow of Trinity College, Cambridge. Crown 8vo., 8s. 6d.

**Tyrrell.** — *TRANSLATIONS INTO GREEK AND LATIN VERSE.* Edited by R. Y. TYRRELL. 8vo., 6s.

**Virgil.**

*THE ÆNEID OF VIRGIL.* Translated into English Verse by JOHN CONINGTON. Crown 8vo., 6s.

*THE POEMS OF VIRGIL.* Translated into English Prose by JOHN CONINGTON. Crown 8vo., 6s.

*THE ÆNEID OF VIRGIL,* freely translated into English Blank Verse. By W. J. THORNHILL. Crown 8vo., 7s. 6d.

*THE ÆNEID OF VIRGIL.* Books I. to VI. Translated into English Verse by JAMES RHOADES. Crown 8vo., 5s.

**Wilkins.** — *THE GROWTH OF THE HOMERIC POEMS.* By G. WILKINS. 8vo., 6s.

# Poetry and the Drama.

**Acworth.**—*BALLADS OF THE MARA-THAS.* Rendered into English Verse from the Marathi Originals. By HARRY ARBUTHNOT ACWORTH. 8vo., 5s.

**Allingham** (WILLIAM).

*IRISH SONGS AND POEMS.* With Frontispiece of the Waterfall of Asaroe. Fcp. 8vo., 6s.

*LAWRENCE BLOOMFIELD.* With Portrait of the Author. Fcp. 8vo., 3s. 6d.

*FLOWER PIECES: DAY AND NIGHT SONGS: BALLADS.* With 2 Designs by D. G. ROSSETTI. Fcp. 8vo., 6s. large paper edition, 12s.

*LIFE AND PHANTASY:* with Frontispiece by Sir J. E. MILLAIS, Bart., and Design by ARTHUR HUGHES. Fcp. 8vo., 6s.; large paper edition, 12s.

*THOUGHT AND WORD, AND ASHBY MANOR:* a Play. Fcp. 8vo., 6s.; large paper edition, 12s.

*BLACKBERRIES.* Imperial 16mo., 6s.

*Sets of the above 6 vols. may be had in uniform Half-parchment binding, price 30s.*

**Armstrong** (G. F. SAVAGE).

*POEMS:* Lyrical and Dramatic. Fcp. 8vo., 6s.

*KING SAUL.* (The Tragedy of Israel, Part I.) Fcp. 8vo., 5s.

*KING DAVID.* (The Tragedy of Israel, Part II.) Fcp. 8vo., 6s.

*KING SOLOMON.* (The Tragedy of Israel, Part III.) Fcp. 8vo., 6s.

*UGONE:* a Tragedy. Fcp. 8vo., 6s.

*A GARLAND FROM GREECE:* Poems. Fcp. 8vo., 7s. 6d.

*STORIES OF WICKLOW:* Poems. Fcp. 8vo., 7s. 6d.

*MEPHISTOPHELES IN BROADCLOTH:* a Satire. Fcp. 8vo., 4s.

*ONE IN THE INFINITE:* a Poem. Crown 8vo., 7s. 6d.

**Armstrong.**—*THE POETICAL WORKS OF EDMUND J. ARMSTRONG* Fcp. 8vo., 5s.

**Arnold** (Sir EDWIN, K.C.I.E.).

*THE LIGHT OF THE WORLD:* or the Great Consummation. Cr. 8vo., 7s. 6d. net.

*POTIPHAR'S WIFE,* and other Poems. Crown 8vo., 5s. net.

*ADZUMA:* or the Japanese Wife. A Play. Crown 8vo., 6s. 6d. net.

*THE TENTH MUSE,* and other Poems. Crown 8vo., 5s. net.

**Beesly.** — *BALLADS AND OTHER VERSE.* By A. H. BEESLY. Fcp. 8vo., 5s.

**Bell.**—*CHAMBER COMEDIES:* a Collection of Plays and Monologues for the Drawing Room. By Mrs. HUGH BELL. Cr. 8vo., 6s.

**Cochrane.**—*THE KESTREL'S NEST,* and other Verses. By ALFRED COCHRANE. Fcp. 8vo., 3s. 6d.

**Goethe.**

*FAUST,* Part I., the German Text, with Introduction and Notes. By ALBERT M. SELSS, Ph.D., M.A. Crown 8vo., 5s.

*FAUST.* Translated, with Notes. By T. E. WEBB. 8vo., 12s. 6d.

**Ingelow** (JEAN).

*POETICAL WORKS.* 2 vols. Fcp. 8vo., 12s.

*LYRICAL AND OTHER POEMS.* Selected from the Writings of JEAN INGELOW. Fcp. 8vo., 2s. 6d. cloth plain, 3s. cl. gilt.

**Kendall.**—*SONGS FROM DREAMLAND.* By MAY KENDALL. Fcp. 8vo., 5s. net.

**Lang** (ANDREW).

*BAN AND ARRIÈRE BAN:* a Rally of Fugitive Rhymes. Fcp. 8vo., 5s. net.

*GRASS OF PARNASSUS.* Fcp. 8vo., 2s. 6d. net.

*BALLADS OF BOOKS.* Edited by ANDREW LANG. Fcp. 8vo., 6s.

*THE BLUE POETRY BOOK.* Edited by ANDREW LANG. With 100 Illustrations. Crown 8vo., 6s.

*Special Edition, printed on India paper. With Notes, but without Illustrations.* Crown 8vo., 7s. 6d.

**Lecky.**—*POEMS.* By W. E. H. LECKY, M.P. Fcp. 8vo., 5s.

**Lytton** (THE EARL OF), (OWEN MEREDITH).

*MARAH.* Fcp. 8vo., 6s. 6d.

*KING POPPY:* a Fantasia. With 1 Plate and Design on Title-Page by ED. BURNE-JONES, A.R.A. Cr. 8vo., 10s. 6d.

*THE WANDERER.* Cr. 8vo., 10s. 6d.

*LUCILE.* Crown 8vo., 10s. 6d.

*SELECTED POEMS.* Cr. 8vo., 10s. 6d.

**Macaulay.**—*LAYS OF ANCIENT ROME, &c.* By Lord MACAULAY.

Illustrated by G. SCHARF. Fcp. 4to., 10s. 6d.

——————— Bijou Edition. 18mo., 2s. 6d. gilt top.

——————— Popular Edition. Fcp. 4to., 6d. sewed, 1s. cloth.

Illustrated by J. R. WEGUELIN. Crown 8vo., 3s. 6d.

Annotated Edition. Fcp. 8vo., 1s. sewed, 1s. 6d. cloth.

## Poetry and the Drama—*continued.*

**Murray** (ROBERT F.).—Author of 'The Scarlet Gown'. His Poems, with a Memoir by ANDREW LANG. Fcp. 8vo., 5s. net.

**Nesbit.**—*LAYS AND LEGENDS.* By E. NESBIT (Mrs. HUBERT BLAND). First Series. Crown 8vo., 3s. 6d. Second Series. With Portrait. Crown 8vo., 5s.

**Peek** (HEDLEY) (FRANK LEYTON).

*SKELETON LEAVES:* Poems. With a Dedicatory Poem to the late Hon. Roden Noel. Fcp. 8vo., 2s. 6d. net.

*THE SHADOWS OF THE LAKE,* and other Poems. Fcp. 8vo., 2s .6d. net.

**Piatt** (SARAH).

*AN ENCHANTED CASTLE,* AND OTHER POEMS: Pictures, Portraits, and People in Ireland. Crown 8vo., 3s. 6d.

*POEMS:* With Portrait of the Author. 2 vols. Crown 8vo., 10s.

**Piatt** (JOHN JAMES).

*IDYLS AND LYRICS OF THE OHIO VALLEY.* Crown 8vo., 5s.

*LITTLE NEW WORLD IDYLS.* Cr. 8vo., 5s.

**Rhoades.**—*TERESA AND OTHER POEMS.* By JAMES RHOADES. Crown 8vo., 3s. 6d.

**Riley** (JAMES WHITCOMB).

*OLD FASHIONED ROSES:* Poems. 12mo., 5s.

*POEMS:* Here at Home. Fcp. 8vo., 6s. net.

**Shakespeare.**—*BOWDLER'S FAMILY SHAKESPEARE.* With 36 Woodcuts. 1 vol. 8vo., 14s. Or in 6 vols. Fcp. 8vo., 21s.

*THE SHAKESPEARE BIRTHDAY BOOK.* By MARY F. DUNBAR. 32mo., 1s. 6d.

**Sturgis.**—*A BOOK OF SONG.* By JULIAN STURGIS. 16mo. 5s.

## Works of Fiction, Humour, &c.

**Anstey** (F., Author of 'Vice Versâ').

*THE BLACK POODLE,* and other Stories. Crown 8vo., 2s. boards, 2s. 6d. cloth.

*VOCES POPULI.* Reprinted from 'Punch'. First Series. With 20 Illustrations by J. BERNARD PARTRIDGE. Crown 8vo., 3s. 6d.

*THE TRAVELLING COMPANIONS.* Reprinted from 'Punch'. With 25 Illust. by J. BERNARD PARTRIDGE. Post 4to., 5s.

*THE MAN FROM BLANKLEY'S:* a Story in Scenes, and other Sketches. With 24 Illustrations by J. BERNARD PARTRIDGE. Fcp. 4to., 6s.

**Arnold.**—*THE STORY OF ULLA,* and other Tales. By EDWIN LESTER ARNOLD. Crown 8vo., 6s.

**Astor.**—*A JOURNEY IN OTHER WORLDS:* a Romance of the Future. By JOHN JACOB ASTOR. With 10 Illustrations. Cr. 8vo., 6s.

**Baker.**—*BY THE WESTERN SEA.* By JAMES BAKER, Author of 'John Westacott'. Crown 8vo., 3s. 6d.

**Beaconsfield** (THE EARL OF).

*NOVELS AND TALES.* Cheap Edition. Complete in 11 vols. Cr. 8vo., 1s. 6d. each.

| | |
|---|---|
| Vivian Grey. | Henrietta Temple. |
| The Young Duke, &c. | Venetia. Tancred. |
| Alroy, Ixion, &c. | Coningsby. Sybil. |
| Contarini Fleming,&c. | Lothair. Endymion. |

*NOVELS AND TALES* The Hughenden Edition. With 2 Portraits and 11 Vignettes. 11 vols. Crown 8vo., 42s.

**Boulton.** *JOSEPHINE CREWE.* By HELEN M. BOULTON. Crown 8vo., 6s.

**Carmichael.**—*POEMS.* By JENNINGS CARMICHAEL (Mrs. FRANCIS MULLIS). Crown 8vo. 6s. net.

**Clegg.**—*DAVID'S LOOM:* a Story of Rochdale life in the early years of the Nineteenth Century. By JOHN TRAFFORD CLEGG. Cr. 8vo., 2s. 6d.

**Deland.** *PHILIP AND HIS WIFE.* By MARGARET DELAND, Author of 'John Ward'. Crown 8vo., 6s.

**Dougall** (L.).

*BEGGARS ALL.* Cr. 8vo., 3s. 6d.

*WHAT NECESSITY KNOWS.* Crown 8vo., 6s.

## Works of Fiction, Humour, &c.—*continued.*

**Doyle** (A. CONAN).

*MICAH CLARKE:* A Tale of Monmouth's Rebellion. With 10 Illustrations. Cr. 8vo., 3s. 6d.

*THE CAPTAIN OF THE POLESTAR,* and other Tales. Cr. 8vo., 3s. 6d.

*THE REFUGEES:* A Tale of Two Continents. With 25 Illus. Cr. 8vo., 3s. 6d.

*THE STARK MUNRO LETTERS.* Cr. 8vo. 6s.

**Farrar** (F. W., DEAN OF CANTERBURY).

*DARKNESS AND DAWN:* or, Scenes in the Days of Nero. An Historic Tale. Cr. 8vo., 7s. 6d.

*GATHERING CLOUDS:* a Tale of the Days of St. Chrysostom. 2 vols., 8vo., 28s.

**Fowler.**—*THE YOUNG PRETENDERS.* A Story of Child Life. By EDITH H. FOWLER. With 12 Illustrations by PHILIP BURNE-JONES. Crown 8vo., 6s.

**Froude.**—*THE TWO CHIEFS OF DUNBOY:* an Irish Romance of the Last Century. By JAMES A. FROUDE. Cr. 8vo., 3s. 6d.

**Gerard.**—*AN ARRANGED MARRIAGE.* By DOROTHEA GERARD. Crown 8vo., 6s.

**Gilkes.**—*THE THING THAT HATH BEEN:* or, a Young Man's Mistakes. By A. H. GILKES, M.A. Crown 8vo., 6s.

**Haggard** (H. RIDER).

*JOAN HASTE.* With 20 Illustrations. Crown 8vo., 6s.

*THE PEOPLE OF THE MIST.* With 16 Illustrations. Crown 8vo., 6s.

*MONTEZUMA'S DAUGHTER.* With 24 Illustrations. Crown 8vo., 6s.

*SHE.* With 32 Illustrations. Crown 8vo., 3s. 6d.

*ALLAN QUATERMAIN.* With 31 Illustrations. Crown 8vo., 3s. 6d.

*MAIWA'S REVENGE:* Crown 8vo., 1s. boards, 1s. 6d. cloth.

*COLONEL QUARITCH, V.C.* Cr. 8vo. 3s. 6d.

*CLEOPATRA.* With 29 Illustrations. Crown 8vo., 3s. 6d.

*BEATRICE.* Cr. 8vo., 3s. 6d.

*ERIC BRIGHTEYES.* With 51 Illustrations. Crown 8vo., 3s. 6d.

*NADA THE LILY.* With 23 Illustrations. Crown 8vo., 3s. 6d.

*ALLAN'S WIFE.* With 34 Illustrations. Crown 8vo., 3s. 6d.

*THE WITCH'S HEAD.* With 16 Illustrations. Crown 8vo., 3s. 6d.

**Haggard** (H. RIDER).—*continued.*

*MR. MEESON'S WILL.* With 16 Illustrations. Crown 8vo., 3s. 6d.

*DAWN.* With 16 Illustrations. Cr. 8vo., 3s. 6d.

**Haggard and Lang.**—*THE WORLD'S DESIRE.* By H. RIDER HAGGARD and ANDREW LANG. With 27 Illustrations. Crown 8vo., 3s. 6d.

**Harte.**—*IN THE CARQUINEZ WOODS* and other stories. By BRET HARTE. Cr. 8vo., 3s. 6d.

**Hornung.**—*THE UNBIDDEN GUEST.* By E. W. HORNUNG. Crown 8vo., 3s. 6d.

**Lemon.**—*MATTHEW FURTH.* By IDA LEMON. Crown 8vo., 6s.

**Lyall** (EDNA).

*THE AUTOBIOGRAPHY OF A SLANDER.* Fcp. 8vo., 1s. sewed.

Presentation Edition. With 20 Illustrations by LANCELOT SPEED. Crown 8vo., 2s. 6d. net.

*DOREEN.* The Story of a Singer. Crown 8vo., 6s.

**Matthews.**—*HIS FATHER'S SON:* a Novel of the New York Stock Exchange. By BRANDER MATTHEWS. With 13 Illustrations. Cr. 8vo. 6s.

**Melville** (G. J. WHYTE). WORKS BY

| | |
|---|---|
| The Gladiators. | Holmby House. |
| The Interpreter. | Kate Coventry. |
| Good for Nothing. | Digby Grand. |
| The Queen's Maries. | General Bounce. |

Crown 8vo., 1s. 6d. each.

**Oliphant** (MRS).

*MADAM.* Cr. 8vo., 1s. 6d.

*IN TRUST.* Cr. 8vo., 1s. 6d.

**Prince.**—*THE STORY OF CHRISTINE ROCHEFORT.* By HELEN CHOATE PRINCE. Crown 8vo., 6s.

**Payn** (JAMES).

*THE LUCK OF THE DARRELLS.* Cr. 8vo., 1s. 6d.

*THICKER THAN WATER.* Cr. 8vo., 1s. 6d.

**Phillipps-Wolley.**—*SNAP:* a Legend of the Lone Mountain. By C. PHILLIPPS-WOLLEY. With 13 Illustrations. Crown 8vo., 3s. 6d.

**Quintana.**—*THE CID CAMPEADOR:* an Historical Romance. By D. ANTONIO DE TRUEBA Y LA QUINTANA. Translated from the Spanish by HENRY J. GILL, M.A., T.C.D. Crown 8vo, 6s.

**Rhoscomyl.**—*THE JEWEL OF YNYS GALON:* being a hitherto unprinted Chapter in the History of the Sea Rovers. By OWEN RHOSCOMYL. Cr. 8vo., 6s.

# Works of Fiction, Humour, &c.—*continued.*

**Robertson.**—*NUGGETS IN THE DEVIL'S PUNCH BOWL*, and other Australian Tales. By ANDREW ROBERTSON. Cr. 8vo., 3s. 6d.

**Sewell** (ELIZABETH M.).

A Glimpse of the World. | Amy Herbert.
Laneton Parsonage. | Cleve Hall.
Margaret Percival. | Gertrude.
Katharine Ashton. | Home Life.
The Earl's Daughter. | After Life.
The Experience of Life. | Ursula. Ivors.

Cr. 8vo., 1s. 6d. each cloth plain. 2s. 6d. each cloth extra, gilt edges.

**Stevenson** (ROBERT LOUIS).

*STRANGE CASE OF DR. JEKYLL AND MR. HYDE.* Fcp. 8vo., 1s. sewed. 1s. 6d. cloth.

*MORE NEW ARABIAN NIGHTS—THE DYNAMITER.* Crown 8vo., 3s. 6d.

**Stevenson and Osbourne.** *THE WRONG BOX.* By ROBERT LOUIS STEVENSON and LLOYD OSBOURNE. Cr. 8vo., 3s. 6d.

**Suttner.**—*LAY DOWN YOUR ARMS* (*Die Waffen Nieder*): The Autobiography of Martha Tilling. By BERTHA VON SUTTNER. Translated by T. HOLMES. Cr. 8vo., 1s. 6d.

**Trollope** (ANTHONY).

*THE WARDEN.* Cr. 8vo., 1s. 6d.

*BARCHESTER TOWERS.* Cr. 8vo., 1s. 6d.

*TRUE (A) RELATION OF THE TRAVELS AND PERILOUS ADVENTURES OF MATHEW DUDGEON, GENTLEMAN: Wherein is truly set 'down the Manner of his Taking, the Long Time of his Slavery in Algiers, and Means of his Delivery. Written by Himself, and now for the first time printed. Cr. 8vo., 5s.

**Walford** (L. B.).

*MR. SMITH:* a Part of his Life. Crown 8vo., 2s. 6d.

*THE BABY'S GRANDMOTHER.* Cr. 8vo., 2s. 6d.

*COUSINS.* Crown 8vo., 2s. 6d.

*TROUBLESOME DAUGHTERS.* Cr. 8vo., 2s. 6d.

*PAULINE.* Crown. 8vo., 2s. 6d.

*DICK NETHERBY.* Cr. 8vo., 2s. 6d.

*THE HISTORY OF A WEEK.* Cr. 8vo. 2s. 6d.

*A STIFF-NECKED GENERATION.* Cr. 8vo. 2s. 6d.

*NAN, and other Stories. Cr. 8vo., 2s. 6d.

*THE MISCHIEF OF MONICA.* Cr. 8vo., 2s. 6d.

*THE ONE GOOD GUEST.* Cr. 8vo. 2s. 6d.

'*PLOUGHED,*' and other Stories. Crown 8vo., 6s.

*THE MATCHMAKER.* Cr. 8vo., 6s.

**West** (B. B.).

*HALF-HOURS WITH THE MILLIONAIRES: Showing how much harder it is to spend a million than to make it. Cr. 8vo., 6s.

*SIR SIMON VANDERPETTER, and MINDING HIS ANCESTORS. Cr. 8vo., 5s.

*A FINANCIAL ATONEMENT. Cr. 8vo.

**Weyman** (STANLEY).

*THE HOUSE OF THE WOLF.* Cr. 8vo., 3s. 6d.

*A GENTLEMAN OF FRANCE.* Cr. 8vo., 6s.

*THE RED COCKADE.* Cr. 8vo., 6s.

## Popular Science (Natural History, &c.).

**Butler.**—*OUR HOUSEHOLD INSECTS.* An Account of the Insect-Pests found in Dwelling-Houses. By EDWARD A. BUTLER, B.A., B.Sc. (Lond.). With 113 Illustrations. Crown 8vo., 6s.

**Furneaux** (W.).

*THE OUTDOOR WORLD:* or The Young Collector's Handbook. With 18 Plates 16 of which are coloured, and 549 Illustrations in the Text. Crown 8vo., 7s. 6d.

*BUTTERFLIES AND MOTHS* (British). With 12 coloured Plates and 241 Illustrations in the Text. Crown 8vo., 12s. 6d.

**Graham.**—*COUNTRY PASTIMES FOR BOYS.* By P. ANDERSON GRAHAM. With 252 Illustrations from Drawings and Photographs. Crown 8vo. 6s.

**Hartwig** (DR. GEORGE).

*THE SEA AND ITS LIVING WONDERS.* With 12 Plates and 303 Woodcuts. 8vo., 7s. net.

*THE TROPICAL WORLD.* With 8 Plates and 172 Woodcuts. 8vo., 7s. net.

*THE POLAR WORLD.* With 3 Maps, 8 Plates and 85 Woodcuts. 8vo., 7s. net.

*THE SUBTERRANEAN WORLD.* With 3 Maps and 80 Woodcuts. 8vo., 7s. net.

## Popular Science (Natural History, &c.)—*continued.*

**Hartwig** (DR. GEORGE).—*continued.*

*THE AERIAL WORLD.* With Map, 8 Plates and 60 Woodcuts. 8vo., 7s. net.

*HEROES OF THE POLAR WORLD.* 19 Illustrations. Cr. 8vo., 2s.

*WONDERS OF THE TROPICAL FORESTS.* 40 Illustrations. Cr. 8vo., 2s.

*WORKERS UNDER THE GROUND.* 29 Illustrations. Cr. 8vo., 2s.

*MARVELS OVER OUR HEADS.* 29 Illustrations. Cr. 8vo., 2s.

*SEA MONSTERS AND SEA BIRDS.* 75 Illustrations. Cr. 8vo., 2s. 6d.

*DENIZENS OF THE DEEP.* 117 Illustrations. Cr. 8vo., 2s. 6d.

*VOLCANOES AND EARTHQUAKES.* 30 Illustrations. Cr. 8vo., 2s. 6d.

*WILD ANIMALS OF THE TROPICS.* 66 Illustrations. Cr. 8vo., 3s. 6d.

**Hayward.**—*BIRD NOTES.* By the late JANE MARY HAYWARD. Edited by EMMA HUBBARD. With Frontispiece and 15 Illustrations by G. E. LODGE. Cr. 8vo., 6s.

**Helmholtz.**—*POPULAR LECTURES ON SCIENTIFIC SUBJECTS.* By HERMANN VON HELMHOLTZ. With 68 Woodcuts. 2 vols. Cr. 8vo., 3s. 6d. each.

**Hudson.** —*BRITISH BIRDS.* By W. H. HUDSON, C.M.Z.S. With a Chapter on Structure and Classification by FRANK E, BEDDARD, F.R.S. With 16 Plates (8 of which are Coloured), and over 100 Illustrations in the Text. Crown 8vo., 12s. 6d.

**Proctor** (RICHARD A.).

*LIGHT SCIENCE FOR LEISURE HOURS.* Familiar Essays on Scientific Subjects. 3 vols. Cr. 8vo., 5s. each.

*CHANCE AND LUCK:* a Discussion of the Laws of Luck, Coincidence, Wagers, Lotteries and the Fallacies of Gambling, &c. Cr. 8vo., 2s. boards. 2s. 6d. cloth.

*ROUGH WAYS MADE SMOOTH.* Familiar Essays on Scientific Subjects. Silver Library Edition. Cr. 8vo., 3s. 6d.

*PLEASANT WAYS IN SCIENCE.* Cr. 8vo., 5s. Silver Library Edition. Cr. 8vo., 3s. 6d.

*THE GREAT PYRAMID, OBSERVATORY, TOMB AND TEMPLE.* With Illustrations. Cr. 8vo., 5s.

*NATURE STUDIES.* By R. A. PROCTOR, GRANT ALLEN, A. WILSON, T. FOSTER and E. CLODD. Cr. 8vo., 5s. Silver Library Edition. Crown 8vo.,3s. 6d.

**Proctor** (RICHARD A.).—*continued.*

*LEISURE READINGS.* By R. A. PROCTOR, E. CLODD, A. WILSON, T. FOSTER and A. C. RANYARD. Cr. 8vo., 5s.

**Stanley.** — *A FAMILIAR HISTORY OF BIRDS.* By E. STANLEY, D.D., formerly Bishop of Norwich. With Illustrations. Cr. 8vo., 3s. 6d.

**Wood** (REV. J. G.).

*HOMES WITHOUT HANDS:* A Description of the Habitation of Animals, classed according to the Principle of Construction. With 140 Illustrations. 8vo., 7s., net.

*INSECTS AT HOME:* A Popular Account of British Insects, their Structure, Habits and Transformations. With 700 Illustrations. 8vo., 7s. net.

*INSECTS ABROAD:* a Popular Account of Foreign Insects, their Structure, Habits and Transformations. With 600 Illustrations. 8vo., 7s. net.

*BIBLE ANIMALS:* a Description of every Living Creature mentioned in the Scriptures. With 112 Illustrations. 8vo., 7s. net.

*PETLAND REVISITED.* With 33 Illustrations. Cr. 8vo., 3s. 6d.

*OUT OF DOORS;* a Selection of Original Articles on Practical Natural History. With 11 Illustrations. Cr. 8vo., 3s. 6d.

*STRANGE DWELLINGS:* a Description of the Habitations of Animals, abridged from 'Homes without Hands'. With 60 Illustrations. Cr. 8vo., 3s. 6d.

*BIRD LIFE OF THE BIBLE.* 32 Illustrations. Cr. 8vo., 3s. 6d.

*WONDERFUL NESTS.* 30 Illustrations. Cr. 8vo., 3s. 6d.

*HOMES UNDER THE GROUND.* 28 Illustrations. Cr. 8vo., 3s. 6d.

*WILD ANIMALS OF THE BIBLE.* 29 Illustrations. Cr. 8vo., 3s. 6d.

*DOMESTIC ANIMALS OF THE BIBLE.* 23 Illustrations. Cr. 8vo., 3s. 6d.

*THE BRANCH BUILDERS.* 28 Illustrations. Cr. 8vo., 2s. 6d.

*SOCIAL HABITATIONS AND PARASITIC NESTS.* 18 Illustrations. Cr. 8vo., 2s.

# Works of Reference.

**Longmans'** *GAZETTEER OF THE WORLD.* Edited by GEORGE G. CHISHOLM, M.A., B.Sc. Imp. 8vo., £2 2s. cloth, £2 12s. 6d. half-morocco.

## Maunder's (Samuel) Treasuries.

*BIOGRAPHICAL TREASURY.* With Supplement brought down to 1889. By Rev. JAMES WOOD. Fcp. 8vo., 6s.

*TREASURY OF NATURAL HISTORY:* or, Popular Dictionary of Zoology. With 900 Woodcuts. Fcp. 8vo., 6s.

*TREASURY OF GEOGRAPHY*, Physical, Historical, Descriptive, and Political. With 7 Maps and 16 Plates. Fcp. 8vo., 6s.

*THE TREASURY OF BIBLE KNOWLEDGE.* By the Rev. J. AYRE, M.A. With 5 Maps, 15 Plates, and 300 Woodcuts. Fcp. 8vo., 6s.

*TREASURY OF KNOWLEDGE AND LIBRARY OF REFERENCE.* Fcp. 8vo., 6s.

**Maunder's (Samuel) Treasuries—** *continued.*

*HISTORICAL TREASURY.* Fcp. 8vo., 6s.

*SCIENTIFIC AND LITERARY TREASURY.* Fcp. 8vo., 6s.

*THE TREASURY OF BOTANY.* Edited by J. LINDLEY, F.R.S., and T. MOORE, F.L.S. With 274 Woodcuts and 20 Steel Plates. 2 vols. Fcp. 8vo., 12s.

**Roget.** -- *THESAURUS OF ENGLISH WORDS AND PHRASES.* Classified and Arranged so as to Facilitate the Expression of Ideas and assist in Literary Composition. By PETER MARK ROGET, M.D., F.R.S. Crown 8vo., 10s. 6d.

**Willich.** --*POPULAR TABLES* for giving information for ascertaining the value of Lifehold, Leasehold, and Church Property, the Public Funds, &c. By CHARLES M. WILLICH. Edited by H. BENCE JONES. Crown 8vo., 10s. 6d.

# Children's Books.

**Crake** (REV. A. D.).

*EDWY THE FAIR;* or, The First Chronicle of Æscendune. Cr. 8vo., 2s. 6d.

*ALFGAR THE DANE;* or, The Second Chronicle of Æscendune. Cr. 8vo. 2s. 6d.

*THE RIVAL HEIRS:* being the Third and Last Chronicle of Æscendune. Cr. 8vo., 2s. 6d.

*THE HOUSE OF WALDERNE.* A Tale of the Cloister and the Forest in the Days of the Barons' Wars. Crown 8vo., 2s. 6d.

*BRIAN FITZ-COUNT.* A Story of Wallingford Castle and Dorchester Abbey. Cr. 8vo., 2s. 6d.

**Lang** (ANDREW).--EDITED BY.

*THE BLUE FAIRY BOOK.* With 138 Illustrations. Crown 8vo., 6s.

*THE RED FAIRY BOOK.* With 100 Illustrations. Crown 8vo., 6s.

*THE GREEN FAIRY BOOK.* With 99 Illustrations. Crown 8vo., 6s.

*THE YELLOW FAIRY BOOK.* With 104 Illustrations. Cr. 8vo., 6s.

*THE BLUE POETRY BOOK.* With 100 Illustrations. Cr. 8vo., 6s.

*THE BLUE POETRY BOOK.* School Edition, without Illustrations. Fcp. 8vo., 2s. 6d.

**Lang** (ANDREW).—EDITED BY—*cont.*

*THE TRUE STORY BOOK.* With 66 Illustrations. Cr. 8vo., 6s.

*THE RED TRUE STORY BOOK.* With 100 Illustrations. Crown 8vo., 6s.

**Meade** (L. T.).

*DADDY'S BOY.* With Illustrations. Crown 8vo., 3s. 6d.

*DEB AND THE DUCHESS.* With Illustrations. Cr. 8vo., 3s. 6d.

*THE BERESFORD PRIZE.* Cr. 8vo., 3s. 6d.

**Molesworth—***SILVERTHORNS.* By Mrs. MOLESWORTH. With Illustrations. Cr. 8vo., 5s.

**Stevenson.—***A CHILD'S GARDEN OF VERSES.* By ROBERT LOUIS STEVENSON. Fcp. 8vo., 5s.

**Upton.** -- *THE ADVENTURES OF TWO DUTCH DOLLS AND A 'GOLLIWOGG'.* Illustrated by FLORENCE K. UPTON, with Words by BERTHA UPTON. With 31 Coloured Plates and numerous Illustrations in the Text. Oblong 4to., 6s.

**Wordsworth.—***THE SNOW GARDEN, AND OTHER FAIRY TALES FOR CHILDREN.* By ELIZABETH WORDSWORTH. With 10 Illustrations by TREVOR HADDON. Crown 8vo., 5s.

## Longmans' Series of Books for Girls.

Price 2s. 6d. each.

*ATELIER (THE) DU LYS*: or, an Art Student in the Reign of Terror. By the same Author.

*MADEMOISELLE MORI*: a Tale of Modern Rome.

*IN THE OLDEN TIME*: a Tale of the Peasant War in Germany.

*THE YOUNGER SISTER.*

*ATHERSTONE PRIORY.* By L. N. Comyn.

*THE STORY OF A SPRING MORNING*, etc. By Mrs. Molesworth. Illustrated.

*THE PALACE IN THE GARDEN.* By Mrs. Molesworth. With Illustrations. Crown 8vo., 2s. 6d.

*THAT CHILD.*

*UNDER A CLOUD.*

*HESTER'S VENTURE.*

*THE FIDDLER OF LUGAU.*

*A CHILD OF THE REVOLUTION.*

*NEIGHBOURS.* By Mrs. Molesworth.

*THE THIRD MISS ST. QUENTIN.* By Mrs. Molesworth.

*VERY YOUNG; AND QUITE ANOTHER STORY.* Two Stories. By Jean Ingelow.

*CAN THIS BE LOVE?* By Louisa Parr.

*KEITH DERAMORE.* By the Author of ' Miss Molly '.

*SIDNEY.* By Margaret Deland.

*LAST WORDS TO GIRLS ON LIFE AT SCHOOL AND AFTER SCHOOL.* By Mrs. W. Grey.

*STRAY THOUGHTS FOR GIRLS.* By Lucy H. M. Soulsby, Head Mistress of Oxford High School. 16mo., 1s. 6d. net.

## The Silver Library.

CROWN 8vo. 3s. 6d. EACH VOLUME.

**Arnold's (Sir Edwin) Seas and Lands.** With 71 Illustrations. 3s. 6d.

**Bagehot's (W.) Biographical Studies.** 3s. 6d.

**Bagehot's (W.) Economic Studies.** 3s. 6d.

**Bagehot's (W.) Literary Studies.** With Portrait. 3 vols. 3s. 6d. each.

**Baker's (Sir S. W.) Eight Years in Ceylon.** With 6 Illustrations. 3s. 6d.

**Baker's (Sir S. W.) Rifle and Hound in Ceylon.** With 6 Illustrations. 3s. 6d.

**Baring-Gould's (Rev. S.) Curious Myths of the Middle Ages.** 3s. 6d.

**Baring-Gould's (Rev. S.) Origin and Development of Religious Belief.** 2 vols. 3s. 6d. each.

**Becker's (Prof.) Gallus**: or, Roman Scenes in the Time of Augustus. Illustrated. 3s. 6d.

**Becker's (Prof.) Charicles**: or, Illustrations of the Private Life of the Ancient Greeks. Illustrated. 3s. 6d.

**Bent's (J. T.) The Ruined Cities of Mashonaland.** With 117 Illustrations. 3s. 6d.

**Brassey's (Lady) A Voyage in the ' Sunbeam '.** With 66 Illustrations. 3s. 6d.

**Clodd's (E.) Story of Creation**: a Plain Account of Evolution. With 77 Illustrations. 3s. 6d.

**Conybeare (Rev. W. J.) and Howson's (Very Rev. J. S.) Life and Epistles of St. Paul.** 46 Illustrations. 3s. 6d.

**Dougall's (L.) Beggars All**: a Novel. 3s. 6d.

**Doyle's (A. Conan) Micah Clarke.** A Tale of Monmouth's Rebellion. 10 Illustrations. 3s. 6d.

**Doyle's (A. Conan) The Captain of the Polestar,** and other Tales. 3s. 6d.

**Doyle's (A. Conan) The Refugees**: A Tale of Two Continents. With 25 Illustrations. 3s. 6d.

**Froude's (J. A.) Short Studies on Great Subjects.** 4 vols. 3s. 6d. each.

**Froude's (J. A.) Thomas Carlyle**: a History of his Life.
1795-1835. 2 vols. 7s.
1834-1881. 2 vols. 7s.

**Froude's (J. A.) Cæsar**: a Sketch. 3s. 6d.

**Froude's (J. A.) The Spanish Story of the Armada,** and other Essays. 3s. 6d.

**Froude's (J. A.) The Two Chiefs of Dunboy**: an Irish Romance of the Last Century. 3s. 6d.

**Froude's (J. A.) The History of England,** from the Fall of Wolsey to the Defeat of the Spanish Armada. 12 vols. 3s. 6d. each.

**Froude's (J. A.) The English in Ireland.** 3 vols. 10s. 6d.

**Gleig's (Rev. G. R.) Life of the Duke of Wellington.** With Portrait. 3s. 6d.

**Haggard's (H. R.) She**: A History of Adventure. 32 Illustrations. 3s. 6d.

**Haggard's (H. R.) Allan Quatermain.** With 20 Illustrations. 3s. 6d.

**Haggard's (H. R.) Colonel Quaritch, V.C.**: a Tale of Country Life. 3s. 6d.

**Haggard's (H. R.) Cleopatra.** With 29 Full-page Illustrations. 3s. 6d.

**Haggard's (H. R.) Eric Brighteyes.** With 51 Illustrations. 3s. 6d.

**Haggard's (H. R.) Beatrice.** 3s. 6d.

**Haggard's (H. R.) Allan's Wife.** With 34 Illustrations. 3s. 6d.

**Haggard's (H. R.) The Witch's Head.** With 16 Illustrations. 3s. 6d.

**Haggard's (H. R.) Mr. Meeson's Will.** With 16 Illustrations. 3s. 6d.

**Haggard's (H. R.) Nada the Lily.** With 23 Illustrations. 3s. 6d.

**Haggard's (H. R.) Dawn.** With 16 Illusts. 3s. 6d.

**Haggard's (H. R.) and Lang's (A.) The World's Desire.** With 27 Illustrations. 3s. 6d.

**Harte's (Bret) In the Carquinez Woods and other Stories.** 3s. 6d.

**Helmholtz's (Hermann von) Popular Lectures on Scientific Subjects.** With 68 Illustrations. 2 vols. 3s. 6d. each.

**Hornung's (E. W.) The Unbidden Guest.** 3s. 6d.

**Howitt's (W.) Visits to Remarkable Places.** 80 Illustrations. 3s. 6d.

## The Silver Library — *continued.*

**Jefferies' (R.) The Story of My Heart:** My Autobiography. With Portrait. 3s. 6d.

**Jefferies' (R.) Field and Hedgerow.** With Portrait. 3s. 6d.

**Jefferies' (R.) Red Deer.** 17 Illustrations. 3s. 6d.

**Jefferies' (R.) Wood Magic:** a Fable. With Frontispiece and Vignette by E. V. B. 3s. 6d.

**Jefferies (R.) The Toilers of the Field.** With Portrait from the Bust in Salisbury Cathedral. 3s. 6d.

**Knight's (E. F.) The Cruise of the 'Alerte':** the Narrative of a Search for Treasure on the Desert Island of Trinidad. With 2 Maps and 23 Illustrations. 3s. 6d.

**Knight's (E. F.) Where Three Empires Meet:** a Narrative of Recent Travel in Kashmir, Western Tibet, Baltistan, Gilgit. With a Map and 54 Illustrations. 3s. 6d.

**Lang's (A.) Angling Sketches.** 20 Illustrations. 3s. 6d.

**Lang's (A.) Custom and Myth:** Studies of Early Usage and Belief. 3s. 6d.

**Lees (J. A.) and Clutterbuck's (W. J.) B. C. 1887, A Ramble in British Columbia.** With Maps and 75 Illustrations. 3s. 6d.

**Macaulay's (Lord) Essays and Lays of Ancient Rome.** With Portrait and Illustration. 3s. 6d.

**Macleod's (H. D.) Elements of Banking.** 3s. 6d.

**Marshman's (J. C.) Memoirs of Sir Henry Havelock.** 3s. 6d.

**Max Müller's (F.) India, what can It teach us?** 3s. 6d.

**Max Müller's (F.) Introduction to the Science of Religion.** 3s. 6d.

**Merivale's (Dean) History of the Romans under the Empire.** 8 vols. 3s. 6d. each.

**Mill's (J. S.) Political Economy.** 3s. 6d.

**Mill's (J. S.) System of Logic.** 3s. 6d.

**Milner's (Geo.) Country Pleasures:** the Chronicle of a Year chiefly in a Garden. 3s. 6d.

**Nansen's (F.) The First Crossing of Greenland.** With Illustrations and a Map. 3s. 6d.

**Phillipps-Wolley's (C.) Snap:** a Legend of the Lone Mountain. 13 Illustrations. 3s. 6d.

**Proctor's (R. A.) The Orbs Around Us.** 3s. 6d.

**Proctor's (R. A.) The Expanse of Heaven.** 3s. 6d.

**Proctor's (R. A.) Other Worlds than Ours.** 3s.6d.

**Proctor's (R. A.) Rough Ways made Smooth.** 3s. 6d.

**Proctor's (R. A.) Pleasant Ways In Science.** 3s. 6d.

**Proctor's (R. A.) Myths and Marvels of Astronomy.** 3s. 6d.

**Proctor's (R. A.) Nature Studies.** 3s. 6d.

**Rossetti's (Maria F.) A Shadow of Dante.** 3s. 6d.

**Smith's (R. Bosworth) Carthage and the Carthaginians.** With Maps, Plans, &c. 3s. 6d.

**Stanley's (Bishop) Familiar History of Birds.** 160 Illustrations. 3s. 6d.

**Stevenson (R. L.) and Osbourne's (Ll.) The Wrong Box.** 3s. 6d.

**Stevenson (Robert Louis) and Stevenson's (Fanny van de Grift) More New Arabian Nights.—The Dynamiter.** 3s. 6d.

**Weyman's (Stanley J.) The House of the Wolf:** a Romance. 3s. 6d.

**Wood's (Rev. J. G.) Petland Revisited.** With 33 Illustrations. 3s. 6d.

**Wood's (Rev. J. G.) Strange Dwellings.** With 60 Illustrations. 3s. 6d.

**Wood's (Rev. J. G.) Out of Doors.** 11 Illustrations. 3s. 6d.

# Cookery, Domestic Management, Gardening, etc.

**Acton.** — *MODERN COOKERY.* By Eliza Acton. With 150 Woodcuts. Fcp. 8vo., 4s. 6d.

**Bull (Thomas, M.D.).**

*HINTS TO MOTHERS ON THE MANAGEMENT OF THEIR HEALTH DURING THE PERIOD OF PREGNANCY.* Fcp. 8vo., 1s. 6d.

*THE MATERNAL MANAGEMENT OF CHILDREN IN HEALTH AND DISEASE.* Fcp. 8vo., 1s. 6d.

**De Salis (Mrs.).**

*CAKES AND CONFECTIONS À LA MODE.* Fcp. 8vo., 1s. 6d.

*DOGS:* A Manual for Amateurs. Fcp. 8vo., 1s. 6d.

*DRESSED GAME AND POULTRY À LA MODE.* Fcp. 8vo., 1s. 6d.

*DRESSED VEGETABLES À LA MODE.* Fcp. 8vo., 1s. 6d.

*DRINKS À LA MODE.* Fcp. 8vo., 1s.6d.

*ENTRÉES À LA MODE.* Fcp. 8vo., 1s. 6d.

**De Salis (Mrs.).—WORKS BY—**continued.

*FLORAL DECORATIONS.* Fcp. 8vo., 1s. 6d.

*GARDENING À LA MODE.* Fcp. 8vo. Part I., Vegetables, 1s. 6d. Part II., Fruits, 1s. 6d.

*NATIONAL VIANDS À LA MODE.* Fcp. 8vo., 1s. 6d.

*NEW-LAID EGGS.* Fcp. 8vo., 1s. 6d.

*OYSTERS À LA MODE.* Fcp. 8vo., 1s. 6d.

*PUDDINGS AND PASTRY À LA MODE.* Fcp. 8vo., 1s. 6d.

*SAVOURIES À LA MODE.* Fcp. 8vo., 1s.6d.

*SOUPS AND DRESSED FISH À LA MODE.* Fcp. 8vo., 1s. 6d.

*SWEETS AND SUPPER DISHES À LA MODE.* Fcp. 8vo., 1s. 6d.

*TEMPTING DISHES FOR SMALL INCOMES.* Fcp. 8vo., 1s. 6d.

*WRINKLES AND NOTIONS FOR EVERY HOUSEHOLD.* Crown 8vo., 1s. 6d.

## Cookery, Domestic Management, &c.—*continued*.

**Lear.** —*MAIGRE COOKERY.* By H. L. SIDNEY LEAR. 16mo,, 2s.

**Poole.** *COOKERY FOR THE DIABETIC.* By W. H. and Mrs. POOLE. With Preface by Dr. PAVY. Fcp. 8vo., 2s. 6d.

**Walker.** —*A BOOK FOR EVERY WO-MAN.* Part I., The Management of Children in Health and out of Health. By JANE H. WALKER, L.R.C.P.I., L.R.C.S., M.D. (Brux). Crown 8vo., 2s. 6d.

**Walker.** *A HANDBOOK FOR MO-THERS:* being Simple Hints to Women on the Management of their Health during Pregnancy and Confinement, together with Plain Directions as to the Care of Infants. By JANE H. WALKER, L.R.C.P.I., L.R.C.S., and M.D. (Brux). Crown 8vo., 2s. 6d.

## Miscellaneous and Critical Works.

**Allingham.** —*VARIETIES IN PROSE.* By WILLIAM ALLINGHAM. 3 vols. Cr. 8vo., 18s. (Vols. 1 and 2, Rambles, by PATRICIUS WALKER. Vol. 3, Irish Sketches, etc.)

**Armstrong.** —*ESSAYS AND SKETCHES.* By EDMUND J. ARMSTRONG. Fcp. 8vo., 5s.

**Bagehot.** —*LITERARY STUDIES.* By WALTER BAGEHOT. With Portrait. 3 vols. Crown 8vo., 3s. 6d. each.

**Baring-Gould.** —*CURIOUS MYTHS OF THE MIDDLE AGES.* By Rev. S. BARING-GOULD. Crown 8vo., 3s. 6d.

**Battye.** —*PICTURES IN PROSE OF NATURE, WILD SPORT, AND HUMBLE LIFE.* By AUBYN TREVOR BATTYE, F.L.S., F.Z.S. Crown 8vo., 6s.

**Baynes.** —*SHAKESPEARE STUDIES,* and other Essays. By the late THOMAS SPENCER BAYNES, LL.B., LL.D. With a Biographical Preface by Professor LEWIS CAMPBELL. Crown 8vo., 7s. 6d.

**Boyd** (A. K. H.) ('**A.K.H.B.**'). And see Miscellaneous Theological Works, p. 24.

*AUTUMN HOLIDAYS OF A COUNTRY PARSON.* Crown 8vo., 3s. 6d.

*COMMONPLACE PHILOSOPHER.* Cr. 8vo., 3s. 6d.

*CRITICAL ESSAYS OF A COUNTRY PARSON.* Crown 8vo., 3s. 6d.

*EAST COAST DAYS AND MEMORIES.* Crown 8vo., 3s. 6d.

*LANDSCAPES, CHURCHES, AND MORA-LITIES.* Crown 8vo., 3s. 6d.

*LEISURE HOURS IN TOWN.* Crown 8vo., 3s. 6d.

*LESSONS OF MIDDLE AGE.* Crown 8vo., 3s. 6d.

*OUR LITTLE LIFE.* Two Series. Crown 8vo., 3s. 6d. each.

**Boyd** (A. K. H.) ('**A.K.H.B.**').— *continued*.

*OUR HOMELY COMEDY: AND TRA-GEDY.* Crown 8vo., 3s. 6d.

*RECREATIONS OF A COUNTRY PARSON.* Three Series. Crown 8vo., 3s. 6d. each. Also First Series. Popular Edition. 8vo., 6d.

**Butler** (SAMUEL).

*EREWHON.* Crown 8vo., 5s.

*THE FAIR HAVEN.* A Work in De-fence of the Miraculous Element in our Lord's Ministry. Cr. 8vo., 7s. 6d.

*LIFE AND HABIT.* An Essay after a Completer View of Evolution. Cr. 8vo., 7s. 6d.

*EVOLUTION, OLD AND NEW.* Cr. 8vo., 10s. 6d.

*ALPS AND SANCTUARIES OF PIED-MONT AND CANTON TICINO.* Illustrated. Pott 4to., 10s. 6d.

*LUCK, OR CUNNING, AS THE MAIN MEANS OF ORGANIC MODIFICATION?* Cr. 8vo., 7s. 6d.

*EX VOTO.* An Account of the Sacro Monte or New Jerusalem at Varallo-Sesia. Crown 8vo., 10s. 6d.

**Gwilt.** —*AN ENCYCLOPÆDIA OF AR-CHITECTURE.* By JOSEPH GWILT, F.S.A. Illustrated with more than 1100 Engravings on Wood. Revised (1888), with Alterations and Considerable Additions by WYATT PAPWORTH. 8vo., £2 12s. 6d.

**James.** —*MINING ROYALTIES:* their Practical Operation and Effect. By CHARLES ASHWORTH JAMES, of Lincoln's Inn, Barrister-at-Law. Fcp. 4to., 5s.

# Miscellaneous and Critical Works - *continued.*

**Jefferies.**—(RICHARD).

*FIELD AND HEDGEROW:* last Essays. With Portrait. Crown 8vo., 3s. 6d.

*THE STORY OF MY HEART:* my Autobiography. With Portrait and New Preface by C. J. LONGMAN. Crown 8vo., 3s. 6d.

*RED DEER.* With 17 Illustrations by J. CHARLTON and H. TUNALY. Crown 8vo., 3s. 6d.

*THE TOILERS OF THE FIELD.* With Portrait from the Bust in Salisbury Cathedral. Crown 8vo., 3s. 6d.

*WOOD MAGIC:* a Fable. With Frontispiece and Vignette by E. V. B. Crown 8vo., 3s. 6d.

*THOUGHTS FROM THE WRITINGS OF RICHARD JEFFERIES.* Selected by H. S. HOOLE WAYLEN. 16mo., 3s. 6d.

**Johnson.**—*THE PATENTEE'S MANUAL:* a Treatise on the Law and Practice of Letters Patent. By J. & J. H. JOHNSON, Patent Agents, &c. 8vo., 10s. 6d.

**Lang** (ANDREW).

*LETTERS TO DEAD AUTHORS.* Fcp. 8vo., 2s. 6d. net.

*BOOKS AND BOOKMEN.* With 2 Coloured Plates and 17 Illustrations. Fcp. 8vo., 2s. 6d. net.

*OLD FRIENDS.* Fcp. 8vo., 2s. 6d. net.

*LETTERS ON LITERATURE.* Fcp. 8vo., 2s. 6d. net.

*COCK LANE AND COMMON SENSE.* Fcp. 8vo., 6s. 6d. net.

**Laurie.** — *HISTORICAL SURVEY OF PRE-CHRISTIAN EDUCATION.* By S. S. LAURIE, A.M., LL.D. Crown 8vo., 12s.

**Leonard.**—*THE CAMEL:* Its Uses and Management. By Major ARTHUR GLYN LEONARD, late 2nd East Lancashire Regiment. Royal 8vo., 21s. net.

**Max Müller** (F).

*INDIA: WHAT CAN IT TEACH US?* Crown 8vo., 3s. 6d.

*CHIPS FROM A GERMAN WORKSHOP.*

Vol. I. Recent Essays and Addresses. Crown 8vo., 6s. 6d. net.

Vol. II. Biographical Essays. Crown 8vo., 6s. 6d. net.

Vol. III. Essays on Language and Literature. Crown 8vo., 6s. 6d. net.

Vol. IV. Essays on Mythology and Folk Lore. Crown 8vo., 8s. 6d. net.

**Macfarren.** — *LECTURES ON HARMONY.* By Sir GEORGE A. MACFARREN. 8vo., 12s.

**Milner** (GEORGE).

*COUNTRY PLEASURES:* the Chronicle of a Year chiefly in a Garden. Cr. 8vo., 3s. 6d.

*STUDIES OF NATURE ON THE COAST OF ARRAN.* With 10 Full-page Copperplates and 12 Illustrations in the Text by W. NOEL JOHNSON. Cr. 8vo., 6s. 6d. net.

**Poore.**—*ESSAYS ON RURAL HYGIENE.* By GEORGE VIVIAN POORE, M.D., F.R.C.P. With 13 Illustrations. Crown 8vo., 6s. 6d.

**Proctor** (RICHARD A.).

*STRENGTH AND HAPPINESS.* With 9 Illustrations. Crown 8vo., 5s.

*STRENGTH:* How to get Strong and keep Strong, with Chapters on Rowing and Swimming, Fat, Age, and the Waist. With 9 Illustrations. Crown 8vo., 2s.

**Richardson.** - *NATIONAL HEALTH.* A Review of the Works of Sir Edwin Chadwick, K.C.B. By Sir B. W. RICHARDSON, M.D. Crown 8vo., 4s. 6d.

**Rossetti.** *A SHADOW OF DANTE:* being an Essay towards studying Himself, his World and his Pilgrimage. By MARIA FRANCESCA ROSSETTI. With Frontispiece by DANTE GABRIEL ROSSETTI. Cr. 8vo., 10s. 6d. Cheap Edition, 3s. 6d.

**Solovyoff.**- *A MODERN PRIESTESS OF ISIS (MADAME BLAVATSKY).* Abridged and Translated on Behalf of the Society for Psychical Research from the Russian of VSEVOLOD SERGYEEVICH SOLOVYOFF. By WALTER LEAF, Litt.D. With Appendices. Crown 8vo., 6s.

**Stevens.**- *ON THE STOWAGE OF SHIPS AND THEIR CARGOES.* With Information regarding Freights, Charter-Parties, &c. By ROBERT WHITE STEVENS, Associate-Member of the Institute of Naval Architects. 8vo., 21s.

**Van Dyke.**—*A TEXT-BOOK OF THE HISTORY OF PAINTING.* By JOHN C. VAN DYKE, of Rutgers College, U.S. With Frontispiece and 109 Illustrations in the Text. Crown 8vo., 6s.

**West.**—*WILLS, AND HOW NOT TO MAKE THEM.* With a Selection of Leading Cases. By B. B. WEST, Author of "Half-Hours with the Millionaires". Fcp. 8vo., 2s. 6d.

## Miscellaneous Theological Works.

**\*.\*** *For Church of England and Roman Catholic Works see* MESSRS. LONGMANS & CO.'S
*Special Catalogues.*

**Balfour.** — *THE FOUNDATIONS OF
BELIEF:* being Notes Introductory to the
Study of Theology. By the Right Hon.
ARTHUR J. BALFOUR, M.P. 8vo., 12s. 6d.

**Boyd** (A. K. H.).
*OCCASIONAL AND IMMEMORIAL DAYS:*
Discourses. Crown 8vo., 7s. 6d.

*COUNSEL AND COMFORT FROM A
CITY PULPIT.* Crown 8vo., 3s. 6d.

*SUNDAY AFTERNOONS IN THE PARISH
CHURCH OF A SCOTTISH UNIVERSITY
CITY.* Crown 8vo., 3s. 6d.

*CHANGED ASPECTS OF UNCHANGED
TRUTHS.* Crown 8vo., 3s. 6d.

*GRAVER THOUGHTS OF A COUNTRY
PARSON.* Three Series. Crown 8vo.,
3s. 6d. each.

*PRESENT DAY THOUGHTS.* Crown
8vo., 3s. 6d.

*SEASIDE MUSINGS.* Cr. 8vo., 3s. 6d.

*' To MEET THE DAY'* through the
Christian Year : being a Text of Scripture,
with an Original Meditation and a Short
Selection in Verse for Every Day. Crown
8vo., 4s. 6d.

**De la Saussaye.** — *A MANUAL OF
THE SCIENCE OF RELIGION.* By Professor
CHANTEPIE DE LA SAUSSAYE. Translated
by Mrs. COLYER FERGUSSON (née MAX
MULLER). Crown 8vo., 12s. 6d.

**Kalisch** (M. M., Ph.D.).
*BIBLE STUDIES.* Part I. Pro-
phecies of Balaam. 8vo., 10s. 6d. Part
II. The Book of Jonah. 8vo., 10s. 6d.

*COMMENTARY ON THE OLD TESTA-
MENT:* with a New Translation. Vol. I.
Genesis. 8vo., 18s. Or adapted for the
General Reader. 12s. Vol. II. Exodus.
15s. Or adapted for the General Reader.
12s. Vol. III. Leviticus, Part I. 15s.
Or adapted for the General Reader. 8s.
Vol. IV. Leviticus, Part II. 15s. Or
adapted for the General Reader. 8s.

**Macdonald** (GEORGE, LL.D.).
*UNSPOKEN SERMONS.* Three Series.
Crown 8vo., 3s. 6d. each.

*THE MIRACLES OF OUR LORD.*
Crown 8vo., 3s. 6d.

*A BOOK OF STRIFE, IN THE FORM
OF THE DIARY OF AN OLD SOUL:* Poems.
18mo., 6s.

10,000/12/95.

**Martineau** (JAMES, D.D., LL.D.).
*HOURS OF THOUGHT ON SACRED
THINGS:* Sermons, 2 vols. Crown 8vo.,
7s. 6d. each.

*ENDEAVOURS AFTER THE CHRISTIAN
LIFE.* Discourses. Crown 8vo., 7s. 6d.

*THE SEAT OF AUTHORITY IN RE-
LIGION.* 8vo., 14s.

*ESSAYS, REVIEWS, AND ADDRESSES.*
4 Vols. Crown 8vo., 7s. 6d. each.
I. Personal; Political. II. Ecclesiastical; Historical.
III. Theological; Philosophical. IV. Academical;
Religious.

*HOME PRAYERS,* with *TWO SERVICES*
for Public Worship. Crown 8vo., 3s. 6d.

**Max Müller** (F.).
*HIBBERT LECTURES ON THE ORIGIN
AND GROWTH OF RELIGION,* as illustrated
by the Religions of India. Cr. 8vo., 7s. 6d.

*INTRODUCTION TO THE SCIENCE OF
RELIGION:* Four Lectures delivered at the
Royal Institution. Crown 8vo., 3s. 6d.

*NATURAL RELIGION.* The Gifford
Lectures, delivered before the University
of Glasgow in 1888. Crown 8vo., 10s. 6d.

*PHYSICAL RELIGION.* The Gifford
Lectures, delivered before the University
of Glasgow in 1890. Crown 8vo., 10s. 6d.

*ANTHROPOLOGICAL RELIGION.* The
Gifford Lectures, delivered before the University of Glasgow in 1891. Cr. 8vo., 10s. 6d.

*THEOSOPHY, OR PSYCHOLOGICAL RE-
LIGION.* The Gifford Lectures, delivered
before the University of Glasgow in 1892.
Crown 8vo., 10s. 6d.

*THREE LECTURES ON THE VEDÂNTA
PHILOSOPHY,* delivered at the Royal
Institution in March, 1894. 8vo., 5s.

**Phillips.** — *THE TEACHING OF THE
VEDAS.* What Light does it Throw on the
Origin and Development of Religion? By
MAURICE PHILLIPS, London Mission,
Madras. Crown 8vo., 6s.

**Romanes.** — *THOUGHTS ON RELIGION.*
By GEORGE J. ROMANES, LL.D., F.R.S.
Crown 8vo., 4s. 6d.

**SUPERNATURAL RELIGION :**
an Inquiry into the Reality of Divine Revelation. 3 vols. 8vo., 36s.

*REPLY (A) TO DR. LIGHTFOOT'S
ESSAYS.* By the Author of ' Supernatural
Religion '. 8vo., 6s.

*THE GOSPEL ACCORDING TO ST.
PETER:* a Study. By the Author of
' Supernatural Religion '. 8vo., 6s.

**Thom.** — *A SPIRITUAL FAITH.* Sermons. By JOHN HAMILTON THOM. With
a Memorial Preface by JAMES MARTINEAU,
D.D. With Portrait. Crown 8vo., 5s.